FOREWORD.

Few individuals have made more meaningful contributions to the American sporting ethic and conservational awareness than George Bird Grinnell. Indeed, the scope and diversity of his efforts in this regard may well be unmatched, although those of others, such as his close friend Theodore Roosevelt, are better known. Grinnell was a key figure in the founding of the Boone and Crockett Club, he worked wonders in making the hunting public aware of the need to protect game animals and habitat through his writings and as long-time editor of *Forest and Stream* magazine, and today's Audubon Society is a lineal descendant of a small organization he founded in 1886. He was a staunch advocate of a system of national parks, the key figure in founding the American Game Association, and, of special note in connection with the present work, a tireless spokesman on behalf of waterfowl conservation.

Grinnell was born on September 20, 1849, in Brooklyn, New York. Both his parents, George Blake Grinnell and Helen Lansing Grinnell, came from patrician New England stock. When young George was only seven years old the family moved to Audubon Park, where the widow of the famed naturalist and artist still lived. Mrs. Audubon gave the young boy his first formal schooling, and from this early exposure to natural history came the abiding passion for the outdoors that would be the central feature of Grinnell's life.

Following those formative years with Mrs. Audubon, Grinnell studied at Churchill's Military School at Ossining, New York, before entering Yale. He received his B.A. from that prestigious Ivy League institution in 1870 and was subsequently awarded a Ph.D. in 1880. In the interim between taking these two degrees, Grinnell enjoyed a number of experiences afield that would markedly influence the course of his later career. He was part of a group that travelled throughout the American West collecting fossils, and in two successive summers he served as naturalist for expeditions to the Black Hills and the headwaters of the Yellowstone River. From these experiences he developed a great love for the West and Indians, important topics during his later literary career.

His devotion to nature and sport soon had so captivated the young man that he abandoned all pretense of making the family business in banking and finance his life's work. The economic disaster known as the Panic of 1873 merely added to his resolve. Thus it was that in 1876 he accepted the post of natural history editor at *Forest and Stream*. Four years later, when it looked as if financial troubles might lead to the magazine's demise, he became its principal owner and editor in chief. For the next three decades, until the sale of *Forest and Stream* in 1911, the publication held a solid, perhaps unrivalled, place among popular American periodicals devoted to the outdoors.

AMERICAN DUCK SHOOTING

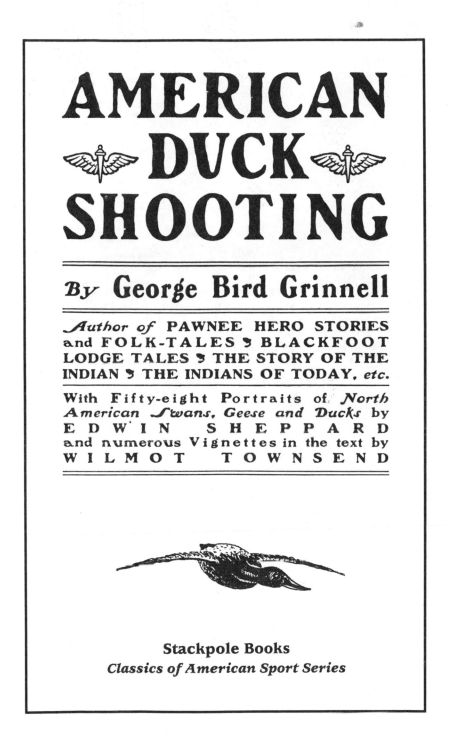

By **George Bird Grinnell**

Author of **PAWNEE HERO STORIES** and **FOLK-TALES** ❧ **BLACKFOOT LODGE TALES** ❧ **THE STORY OF THE INDIAN** ❧ **THE INDIANS OF TODAY,** *etc.*

With Fifty-eight Portraits of *North American Swans, Geese and Ducks* by E D W I N   S H E P P A R D and numerous Vignettes in the text by W I L M O T   T O W N S E N D

Stackpole Books
Classics of American Sport Series

AMERICAN DUCK SHOOTING: Copyright © 1901 by Field and Stream Publishing Company

Foreword copyright © 1991 by Stackpole Books

Published by
STACKPOLE BOOKS
Cameron and Kelker Streets
P.O. Box 1831
Harrisburg, PA 17105

Cover design by Tracy Patterson

Printed in the United States of America

10 9 8 7 6 5 4 3

Library of Congress Cataloging-in-Publication Data

Grinnell, George Bird, 1849–1938.
    American duck shooting / George Bird Grinnell.
        p.   cm. – (Classics of American sport series)
    Reprint, with new introd. Originally published: New York : Forest and Stream Pub. Co., 1901.
    Includes index.
    ISBN 0-8117-2427-1
    1. Duck shooting–United States.   2. Ducks–United States.
3. Waterfowl shooting–United States.   4. Anatidae–United States.
I. Title.   II. Series: Classics of American sport.
SK333.D8G8   1991
799.2′4841–dc20   91-8789
                                                                                      CIP

As an editor Grinnell was a committed, concerned conservationist, and he regularly took up the literary cudgel against game hogs, market hunters, and others of that ilk whom he considered a disgrace to the hunting world. He also sounded an early alarm against waterfowling prodigality, bemoaned the bison's abysmal decline, and fought the good fight on various related fronts. Some indication of how forthright he could be in print, although he was the quintessence of a quiet gentleman in person, is given by the circumstances that brought him and Theodore Roosevelt together. He accorded TR's *Hunting Trips of a Ranchman* a rather mixed review, praising the author's intellect but pointing out a number of mistakes as an indication of inexperience as a hunter. In his forthright manner TR stormed the offices of *Forest and Stream*, demanding an explanation, and to the future president's amazement Grinnell stuck by his guns while presenting his views in a most persuasive fashion.

Out of this potentially explosive confrontation evolved a warm friendship from which the American public reaped enormous dividends. These benefits took many forms—the creation of national parks and forests, appreciation of the importance of properly managing natural resources, and the genesis of a true conservation ethic in the United States. There is little doubt that the pair stimulated one another's literary efforts, and they worked together on a number of projects. Especially noteworthy in this regard was their collaboration as co-editors of the early volumes in the Boone and Crockett Club's publications series, *American Big-Game Hunting, Hunting in Many Lands,* and *Trail and Camp-fire.*

Even as he worked closely with Roosevelt and continued in his self-ordained role as a spokesman for nature through the pages of *Forest and Stream*, Grinnell was involved in a myriad of other activities. A consummate sportsman, he loved to hunt and was particularly eloquent in capturing the elusive qualities that constitute the emotional and philosophical appeal of sport. Late in the 1880s he published the first of what would become a series of popular books on Indians and the High Plains (he would later serve two presidents as an adviser on and representative to Indian tribes), and his many books for young readers on the outdoor adventures of a protagonist named Jack were set in the West. The present work, which initially appeared in 1901, was his first book devoted exclusively to sport.

American Duck Shooting is today quite rare, and seldom does one see it make an appearance in the catalogs of out-of-print booksellers. That consideration alone might justify its reprinting, but its pages carry a timeless message that far transcends matters such as scarcity or collectibility. Grinnell noted and commented with telling effect on the decline of waterfowl long before the issue caught the public's eye. He decried overhunting and the shameful neglect of authorities when it came to regulating duck hunting and other shooting sports, and his was a clarion call that sadly would go largely unheeded until waterfowl numbers became dangerously low. Still, his message was an important one, and somehow it is heartening to know that there were voices such as his crying in the wilderness long before the first federal duck stamp made its appearance.

Of course, there is more, much more, to *American Duck Shooting* than its conservation message. All who are stirred by the music of whistling wings at dawn, all who thrill to the gabbling chorus of ducks gathering at dusk, will know that here is an author who shared their love. Better still, he possessed a rare ability to convey the wonder that is waterfowling to his readers. For all these reasons the book is an enduring one, and in re-reading it while contemplating the thrust of Grinnell's life, I could not help but be struck by the manner in which the man and his milieu afford an object lesson that today's so-called "animal activists" would find singularly instructive should they care to heed it.

American Duck Shooting was penned at the height of Grinnell's career, and in many ways it is his most important book on hunting. *American Game Bird Shooting* (1911), which might be considered a companion volume, is also of considerable note, as are his *Hunting at High Altitudes* (1913) and *Hunting and Conservation* (1925). As the considerable time span of these volumes suggest, Grinnell was active as a writer over much of his life, even though he gave up his editorship of *Forest and Stream* in 1911.

Having married fairly late in life (to Elisa Williams in 1902), Grinnell had no children. Instead, he devoted his middle and later years as a crusader for some of the same causes that had occupied so much of his attention as an editor. His tireless efforts as a proponent of a national parks system ultimately led to his election as president of the National Parks Association in 1925. That same year saw him honored, and justly so, by the Roosevelt Memorial Association, and a few years earlier his alma mater had awarded him an honorary Doctorate of Laws.

The gold medal he received from the Roosevelt Memorial Association was simply inscribed "for distinguished service in the promotion of outdoor life." Doubtless those words pleased Grinnell immensely, and certainly they were appropriate. After all, his entire life (he died on April 11, 1938 in New York) was in effect an ongoing crusade for the preservation of the "outdoor life," which he viewed as being an integral part of the American experience.

As we ponder the dedication that led to this recognition, it should also be remembered that as his brain children, both the Boone and Crockett Club and the Audubon Society are lasting symbols of the natural world Grinnell cherished. His articles and books on the outdoors are a legacy this reprint helps to perpetuate. Thanks to these and countless other endeavors, George Bird Grinnell ranks well in the forefront of the founding fathers of American conservation. Most of all though, as today we struggle to perpetuate that which Grinnell helped preserve, this book serves as a poignant reminder that the fight, while unending, is well and truly worth the effort it entails.

Jim Casada

THE CANVAS-BACK.
Reduced from Audubon's Plate.

PREFACE.

HIS VOLUME DEALS WITH
duck shooting, *past as well as
present, and with the different
ways in which the sport has been
and is practiced.   It tells of an
abundance of fowl in the land,*
not to be seen to-day, nor perhaps ever again.   It
contains accounts of shooting, often by unwise
methods, often to unnecessary excess; of shooting
which has reduced the multitudes of our fowl from what
they were to what they are.   Such accounts may well
serve as warnings to us, teaching us now the exercise of
a moderation we were too thoughtless to deem necessary
in the old days.

Since the several methods of duck shooting necessarily
grade into one another, there will often be in one account repetition of what has been said in another.   This
seems inevitable, however, if a clear idea is to be given
of each variety of the sport.

3

In the accuracy of the descriptions of the different species of wildfowl every confidence is felt, for they have passed under the eye of Mr. Robert Ridgway, the former President of the American Ornithologists Union, whose eminence in his chosen field of life work is so well known. I owe him cordial thanks for his kindness in this matter, as well as for various suggestions, looking toward making more complete the technical portion of the book.

The book covers—as it should—a wide range of territory; for a volume on wildfowl shooting, if limited to the experiences of a single individual, would furnish but an inadequate presentation of the subject for the whole continent. In the endeavor to make the volume justify its title, assistance has been asked from gunners whose experience has been longer than mine, or has extended over shooting grounds with which I am not familiar.

My friends, Messrs. Wm. Trotter and C. R. Purdy, both duck shooters of long experience, have kindly aided me on different points, and my acknowledgments are due to them.

The portraits of wildfowl by Mr. Edwin Sheppard,

so well known as the illustrator of Baird, Brewer &
Ridgway's great work and of Mr. Elliot's trilogy of
game bird volumes, speak for themselves.

The pen sketches drawn by Mr. Wilmot Townsend
hardly need be commented on. Mr. Townsend is an en-
thusiastic gunner and has devoted much time to study-
ing wildfowl in their homes. The drawings which he
has made will call up to every gunner of experience
memories of a happy past.

Mr. William Brewster has kindly permitted me to
use the photographs illustrating the nesting of the
Golden Eye, which accompanied his interesting paper on
the subject in the Auk.

The very useful chart of the duck, in the back of the
book, is taken by the kind permission of the author from
Mr. Charles B. Cory's Birds of Eastern North America
—Water Birds. *G. B. G.*

October, 1901.

CONTENTS.

——— ———

PAGE

PREFACE.   3

PART I.

———

THE DUCK FAMILY.

SWANS.   33

    AMERICAN SWAN   34
    TRUMPETER SWAN.   36

GEESE AND BRANT.   39

    BLUE GOOSE.   43
    LESSER SNOW GOOSE.   46
    GREATER SNOW GOOSE.   48
    ROSS'S GOOSE.   51
    WHITE-FRONTED GOOSE.   53
    CANADA GOOSE.   56
    HUTCHINS'S GOOSE.   58
    WESTERN GOOSE.   58
    CACKLING GOOSE.   59
    BARNACLE GOOSE.   65
    BRANT.   67
    BLACK BRANT.   69
    EMPEROR GOOSE.   72

	PAGE
TREE DUCKS	75
Black-bellied Tree Duck	76
Fulvous-bellied Tree Duck	79

THE TRUE DUCKS.

NON-DIVING DUCKS	85
Mallard	87
Black Duck or Dusky Duck	93
Florida Dusky Duck	95
Mottled Duck	97
Gadwall	103
European Widgeon	107
American Widgeon, Bald-pate	110
European Teal	116
Green-winged Teal	118
Blue-winged Teal	122
Cinnamon Teal	126
Shoveller	131
Pintail	134
Wood Duck	139
DIVING DUCKS	143
Rufous-crested Duck	145
Canvas-back Duck	147
Redhead Duck	160
Broad-bill	164
Little Black-head	167
Ring-necked Duck	170
Golden-eye, Whistler	173
Barrow's Golden-eye	178
Buffle-head Duck	181
Old-squaw, Long-tailed Duck	185
Harlequin Duck	189
Labrador Duck	192

PAGE

STELLER'S DUCK. 195
SPECTACLED EIDER. 197
COMMON EIDER. 200
AMERICAN EIDER. 202
PACIFIC EIDER. 205
KING EIDER. 208
AMERICAN SCOTER. 211
AMERICAN VELVET SCOTER.......................... 213
VELVET SCOTER. 216
SURF SCOTER, SKUNK-HEAD.......................... 217
RUDDY DUCK. 220
MASKED DUCK. 223

FISH DUCKS. 225
AMERICAN MERGANSER. 226
RED-BREASTED MERGANSER, SHELDRAKE................. 230
HOODED MERGANSER. 234

PART II.

WILDFOWL SHOOTING.

SWAN SHOOTING. 244
GOOSE SHOOTING. 250
ON THE STUBBLES................................... 251
ON THE SAND-BARS................................. 254
WITH LIVE DECOYS................................. 260
DRIVING. 274

BRANT SHOOTING. 279
FROM A BATTERY................................... 279
BAR SHOOTING. 294

PAGE

DUCK SHOOTING. 317

    PASS SHOOTING. 317
    SHOOTING IN THE OVERFLOW............................. 333
    RIVER SHOOTING. 335
    IN THE WILD RICE FIELDS............................. 351
    CORNFIELD SHOOTING IN THE MIDDLE WEST.............. 371
    POINT SHOOTING. 377
    SEA SHOOTING ON THE ATLANTIC....................... 418
    WADING THE MARSHES................................. 430
    BATTERY SHOOTING. 433
    SHOOTING FROM A HOUSE-BOAT........................ 440
    ICE HOLE SHOOTING................................... 447
    WINTER DUCK SHOOTING ON LAKE ONTARIO............. 453
    SHOOTING IN THE ICE................................. 455
    SAILING. 460
    STUBBLE SHOOTING. 461
    CALIFORNIA MARSH SHOOTING......................... 464
    CHESAPEAKE BAY DUCK SHOOTING..................... 472

PART III.

THE ART OF DUCK SHOOTING.

GUNS AND LOADING................................ 493

    HOW TO HOLD.. 502
    WHEN TO SHOOT...................................... 506
    FLIGHT OF DUCKS.................................... 508
    ETIQUETTE OF THE BLIND............................. 510

CHESAPEAKE BAY DOG............................. 515

DECOYS. 522

    WOODEN DECOYS. 522
    LIVE DECOYS. 526
    BREEDING WILDFOWL. 532

PAGE

BLINDS, BATTERIES AND BOATS.................... 546

HOW BLINDS ARE MADE............................. 546
THE BATTERY. 549
SKIFFS AND SNEAK BOATS.......................... 557
OTHER CRAFT. 573
ICE WORK. 572

THE DECREASE OF WILDFOWL.

CAUSES. 582

SPRING SHOOTING. 589
CONTRACTION OF FEEDING GROUNDS.................... 593
SIZE OF BAGS...................................... 594
NATURAL ENEMIES. 596
LEAD POISONING. 598
SELF-DENIAL NEEDED. 603
BATTERIES AND BUSH BLINDS........................ 605
NIGHT SHOOTING................................... 607
WHAT SHALL BE DONE?.............................. 608

LIST OF ILLUSTRATIONS.

FULL-PAGE PLATES.

PAGE

THE CANVAS-BACK.   1
From Audubon's "Birds of America."

THE BLACK DUCK.   18
From Audubon's "Birds of America."

THE SHOVELLER.   237
From Audubon's "Birds of America."

A GOLDEN-EYE NESTING PLACE.   240
Photographed by Wm. Brewster.

THE REDHEAD.   490
From Audubon's "Birds of America."

"A BIRD IN THE HAND".   492
Photographed by Wm. Brewster.

A PRAIRIE SHOOTING WAGON.   578

INDIANS GATHERING DUCK EGGS IN ALASKA.   .   .   579

PORTRAITS OF SPECIES.

	PAGE
AMERICAN SWAN.	34
TRUMPETER SWAN.	36
BLUE GOOSE.	43
LESSER SNOW GOOSE.	46
GREATER SNOW GOOSE.	48
ROSS'S GOOSE.	51
WHITE-FRONTED GOOSE.	53
CANADA GOOSE.	56
HUTCHINS'S GOOSE.	57
WHITE-CHEEKED GOOSE.	57
CACKLING GOOSE.	59
BARNACLE GOOSE.	65
BRANT.	67
BLACK BRANT.	69
EMPEROR GOOSE.	72
BLACK-BELLIED TREE DUCK.	76
FULVOUS-BELLIED TREE DUCK.	79
MALLARD.	87
BLACK DUCK OR DUSKY DUCK.	92
FLORIDA DUSKY DUCK.	95
MOTTLED DUCK.	97
GADWALL.	103
EUROPEAN WIDGEON.	107
AMERICAN WIDGEON, BALD-PATE.	110
EUROPEAN TEAL.	116
GREEN-WINGED TEAL.	118
BLUE-WINGED TEAL.	122
CINNAMON TEAL.	126
SHOVELLER.	131
PINTAIL.	134
WOOD DUCK.	139
RUFOUS-CRESTED DUCK.	145
CANVAS-BACK DUCK.	137
REDHEAD DUCK.	160
BROAD-BILL.	164
LITTLE BLACK-HEAD.	167

  PAGE

Ring-necked Duck. 170
Golden-eye, Whistler. 173
Barrow's Golden-eye. 178
Buffle-head Duck. 181
Old-squaw, Long-tailed Duck.......................... 185
Harlequin Duck. 189
Labrador Duck. 192
Steller's Duck. 195
Spectacled Eider. 197
Common Eider. 200
American Eider. 202
Pacific Eider. 205
King Eider. 208
American Scoter. 211
American Velvet Scoter................................ 213
Velvet Scoter. 216
Surf Scoter, Skunk-head.............................. 217
Ruddy Duck. 220
Masked Duck. 223
American Merganser. 226
Red-breasted Merganser, Sheldrake.................... 230
Hooded Merganser. 234

GENERAL ILLUSTRATIONS.

Goose Decoys on a Bar................................. 281
The Battery Rigged, Facing page...................... 434
Swivel Guns from Spesutia Island, Facing page........ 435
Plan of Single Battery............................... 551
Plan of Double Battery............................... 553
Sneak Boat. 558
Nee-pe-nauk Boat. 560
Loyd Boat. 561
Sassafras Dug-out. 562
Mexican Cypress Pirogue.............................. 563

	PAGE
WOLF RIVER CANOE	563
BOB STANLEY BOAT	564
SENACHWINE IRON SKIFF	565
HENNEPIN DUCK BOAT	566
MONITOR MARSH BOAT	567
DE PERE RED CEDAR BOAT	567
MISSISSIPPI SCULL BOAT	568
KOSHKONONG FLAT BOAT	569
KOSHKONONG MONITOR	569
TOLLESTON BOAT	570
NORTH CANOE	571

Fifty Vignettes in Text.

Chart of Duck Bound in with Back Cover.

PART I.

THE DUCK FAMILY.

THE BLACK DUCK.
Reduced from Audubon's Plate.

THE DUCK FAMILY.

No group of birds is more important to man than that known as the duck family. They are called the *Anatidæ,* from the Latin word *Anas,* a duck; and belong to the Order *Anseres,* or Lamellirostral Swimmers,—birds whose bills are provided with lamellæ, by which are meant the little transverse ridges found on the margins of the bills of most ducks. Sometimes the lamellæ appear like a row of white blunt teeth; in the shoveller, they constitute a fine comb-like structure, which acts as a strainer, while in the case of the mergansers they have the appearance of being real teeth, which, however, they are not, since teeth are always implanted in sockets in the bone of the jaw; and this is true of no known birds, except some Cretaceous forms of Western America and the Jurassic *Archæopteryx.*

The bill is variously shaped in the members of the duck family. Usually it is broad and depressed, as in the domestic duck; or it may be high at the base and approach the conical, as in some geese; broadly spread, or spoon-shaped, as in the shoveller duck, or almost cylindrical and hooked at the tip, as in the mergansers. Whatever its shape, the bill is almost wholly covered

with a soft, sensitive membrane or skin, and ends at
the tip in a horny process which is termed the nail.
From this fact the family is sometimes called *Ungui-*
rostres, or nail-beaked.

The body is short and stout, the neck usually long;
the feet and legs are short. The wings are moderately
long and stout, giving power of rapid and long-continued flight. There are various anatomical characteristics, most of which need not be considered here.

One of these, however, is common to so many species, and is so frequently inquired about by sportsmen,
that it may be briefly mentioned. In the male of most
ducks the windpipe just above the bronchial tubes on
the left side is expanded to form a bony, bulb-
ous enlargement, called the labyrinth. Except in one
or two species the female does not possess this enlargement, and there are some of the sea ducks (*Fuli-*
gulinæ) in which it is not found. The labyrinth
varies greatly in different species. In some it is round
and comparatively simple, in others large and instead of being more or less cylindrical in shape it has
the form of a long three-cornered box. The labyrinth
has been stated to have relation to the voice of the bird,
but what this relation is has yet to be proved.

In addition to the labyrinth, some species of ducks
have an enlargement of the windpipe near the throat,
and the swans have the windpipe curiously coiled within the breast bone.

The plumage of these birds is well adapted for protection against wet and cold. All possess large oil

glands, and the overlying feathers, which are constantly kept oiled, protect the down beneath them from moisture and form a covering whose warmth enables the
birds to endure an Arctic temperature. There is a great
variety in the coloring of the plumage. The sexes in
the swans and most geese are alike, but in the ducks the
male is usually more highly colored than the female.
The males of some species are among our most beautiful birds, as the mallard, harlequin, wood duck and the
odd little mandarin duck of Eastern Asia, while in
others the colors are duller, and in the female and
young are often extremely modest and subdued. Most
of the fresh water ducks possess a patch of brilliant
iridescent color on the secondary feathers of the wing
which is usually either green or violet. This is called
the speculum. A less brilliant speculum is seen in some
of the sea ducks.

The males of certain species possess peculiar developments of plumage or of bill, such as the curled tail
feathers of the mallard, the long pointed scapulars and
long tail feathers of the old squaw and the sprig-tail,
the peculiar wing feathers of the mandarin duck, the
stiff feathers on the face in some sea ducks, the crests of
many species, and the singular processes and swellings
on the bills of certain sea ducks.

The Duck family is divided into three sections—the
Swans, the Geese and the Ducks proper. These last
again are subdivided into shoal water or river ducks,
and sea or diving ducks.

The swans are characterized by their large size and

extremely long necks, and are usually white in color, although the Australian black swan forms a notable exception. The naked skin of the bill extends back to the eyes. Only two species—with a European form attributed to Greenland—are found in North America. One of these, the common swan, covers the whole country, while the slightly larger trumpeter swan is found chiefly in the West. The swans constitute a sub-family of the *Anatidæ,* and are known to ornithologists as the *Cygninæ.*

Less in size than the swans and in form intermediate between them and the ducks are the geese. They have necks much longer than the ducks, yet not so long as the swans. Like the swans, they feed by stretching down their necks through the water and tearing up vegetable food from the bottom. Geese and swans do not dive, except to escape the pursuit of enemies. Most species are found within the limits of the United States only in autumn or winter, and breed far to the north, although up to the time of the settlement of the western country the Canada goose commonly nested on the prairies and along the Missouri River, sometimes building its nest in trees; that is to say, on the tops of broken cottonwood stubs, standing thirty or forty feet above the ground. The settling up of the country has, for the most part, deprived these birds of their summer home, and it may be questioned whether they now breed regularly anywhere within the United States, except in the Yellowstone Park, where protection is afforded them.

With the geese are to be included the tree ducks, a group connecting the sub-families of the geese and the ducks, and known by naturalists as *Dendrocygna.* They are found only on the southern borders of the United States, and thus will but seldom come under the notice of North American sportsmen. They are really duck-like, tree-inhabiting geese. There are several species, occurring chiefly in the tropics.

The true ducks are divided into three groups, known as *Anatinæ,* or shoal-water ducks, *Fuligulinæ,* or sea ducks, and *Merginæ,* fish ducks, or mergansers. These three groups are natural ones, although the birds belonging to them are constantly associated together during the migrations, and often live similar lives. No one of the three is confined either to sea coast or interior, but all are spread out over the whole breadth of the continent. In summer the great majority of the birds of each group migrate to the farther north, there to raise their young, while others still breed sparingly within the United States, where formerly they did so in great numbers.

As is indicated by one of their English names, the fresh water ducks prefer fresh and shallow water, and must have this last because they do not dive for their food, but feed on what they can pick up from the bottoms and margins of the rivers and pools which they frequent. The sea ducks, on the other hand, are expert divers, many of them feeding in water from fifteen to thirty feet deep. The food of the mergansers is assumed to consist largely of small fish, which they capture by pursuing them under the water. They are expert divers.

The food of the fresh water ducks is chiefly vegetable, consisting of seeds, grasses and roots, which they gather from the water. That of the sea ducks is largely animal, and often consists exclusively of shell-fish, which they bring up from the bottom. Yet with regard to the food of the two groups there is no invariable rule, and many of the sea ducks live largely on vegetable matter, while the fresh water ducks do not disdain any animal matter which may come in their way. Both groups, with some possible exceptions, are fond of grain, which they eat greedily when it is accessible. The far-famed canvas-back derives its delicious flavor from the vegetable food which it finds in the deep, fresh or brackish waters of lakes, slow flowing streams and estuaries, while the widgeon, which is one of the typical fresh water ducks and is equally toothsome, feeds only in shoal water.

The flavor of any duck's flesh depends entirely on its food, and a bird of whatever kind which is killed after living for a month or two in a region where proper vegetable food is to be found will prove delicious eating, whether it be canvas-back, redhead, widgeon, black duck or broad-bill. On the other hand, a black duck, redhead, broad-bill or canvas-back, which has spent a month or two in the salt water, where its food has been chiefly shell-fish, will be found to have a strong flavor of fish. Thus the fine feathers of a canvas-back are not necessarily a guarantee that the bird wearing them possesses the table qualities that have made the species famous.

Hybrids between different species of the fresh water ducks occur quite frequently, and many perfectly authentic examples of this have been examined by competent authority, although in many instances a supposed hybrid is nothing more than some species with which the gunner is unfamiliar. In his great work, "The Birds of North America," Audubon figured a hybrid under the name Brewer's duck. Hybrids between the mallard and the muscovy, the black duck and the pintail are not uncommon. One of the latter, which I still possess, I killed in Wyoming, and I have killed several black duck–mallard hybrids in North Carolina. Besides these, ducks have been killed which appear to indicate a cross between mallard and gadwall, between teal and pintail, and even between wood duck and redhead. On the other hand, some years ago, when my gunner picked up a male English widgeon which I had killed, he suggested that it was a hybrid between a redhead and a widgeon.

It is to be noted that the hybrids supposed to be a cross between the black duck and mallard, while possessing the general appearance of the black duck, appear to exceed either parent in size, and the males often possess the curved tail feathers of the male mallard.

Ducks and geese are to a great extent nocturnal in their habits. Many, if not all of them, migrate by night, and in localities where they are greatly disturbed on their feeding grounds they are likely to pass the hours

of day in the open water far from the shore and not
to visit their feeding grounds until evening or even
dark night.   In many places along the New England
coast it is the practice during cloudy nights, when the
moon is large, to visit the hills in the line of flight to
shoot at the ducks and geese which fly over from their
daily resting place on the salt water to their nightly
feeding ground in ponds, rivers and shallow bays, or
before daylight in the morning, to resort to the same
places, in the hope of getting a shot at the birds as they
fly back toward the sea.

During moonlight nights the birds frequently feed
at intervals all night long, and in many places advantage is taken of this habit to shoot them either by
moonlight or by fire lighting.

Ducks are found all over the world, and appear
equally at home in the tropics and on the borders of the
Arctic ice.   There are about two hundred known
species, of which not far from sixty are found in North
America.   Their economic importance is due not
merely to the fact that they occur in such numbers as
to furnish a great deal of food for man, but also because of the feathers and down which they produce.
To the inhabitants of many regions they furnish clothing, in part, as well as food.   In some parts of the
world, whole communities are largely dependent for
their living on the products of these birds, subsisting
for portions of the year entirely on their flesh and eggs,
and deriving a large part of their revenue from the
sale of feathers and down.   Many examples might be

cited of places in northern latitudes where the gathering of eggs, birds or feathers forms at certain seasons of the year the principal industry of the people.

A familiar species, whose economic importance to dwellers in high latitudes can hardly be overestimated, is the well-known eider duck. This bird is occasionally shot on the Long Island coast in winter, and is then a common visitor to northern New England. Its slightly differing forms breed on the sea-coasts of the northern parts of the world, and are very abundant in the Arctic regions.

In Greenland, Iceland and Norway the breeding grounds of the eider duck are protected by laws which have the universal support of the inhabitants. Indeed, these breeding grounds are handed down from father to son as property of great value. Every effort is made to foster and encourage the birds. Sometimes cattle are removed from islands where they have been ranging in order that the ducks may breed there undisturbed, and a careful watch is kept against depredations by dogs and foxes. According to Dr. Stejneger: "The inhabitants [of parts of Norway] take great care of the breeding birds, which often enter their houses to find suitable nesting places, and cases are authenticated in which the poor fisherman vacated his bed in order not to disturb the female eider which had selected it as a quiet corner wherein to raise her young. In another instance the cooking of a family had to be done in a temporary kitchen, as a fanciful bird had taken up her abode on the fireplace."

On many of the breeding grounds in Iceland and
Norway the birds are so tame as to pay little attention
to the approach of strangers. Often the nests occur in
such numbers that it is difficult to walk among them
without stepping on them. On the little island of
Vidoe, near Reikjavik, almost all the hollows among
the rocks with which the ground is strewn are occupied
by nests of the birds. Here, too, they occupy burrows
especially prepared for them, as with the sheldrakes in
Sylt.

In Baird, Brewer and Ridgway's "North American
Birds," Dr. T. M. Brewer quotes Mr. C. W. Shepard,
who, in a sketch of his travels in northern Iceland,
gives the following account of the tameness and breeding there of the eider:

"The islands of Vigr and Oedey are their headquarters in the northwest of Iceland. In these they live in
undisturbed tranquillity. They have become almost domesticated, and are found in vast multitudes, as the
young remain and breed in the place of their birth.
As the island (Vigr) was approached we could see
flocks upon flocks of the sacred birds, and could hear
their cooing at a great distance. We landed on a
rocky, wave-worn shore. It was the most wonderful
ornithological sight conceivable. The ducks and their
nests were everywhere. Great brown ducks sat upon
their nests in masses, and at every step started from
under our feet. It was with difficulty that we avoided
treading on some of the nests. On the coast of the
opposite shore was a wall built of large stones, just

above the high-water level, about three feet in height
and of considerable thickness. At the bottom, on both
sides of it, alternate stones had been left out, so as to
form a series of square compartments for the ducks to
nest in. Almost every compartment was occupied, and
as we walked along the shore a long line of ducks flew
out, one after the other. The surface of the water also
was perfectly white with drakes, who welcomed their
brown wives with loud and clamorous cooing. The
house itself was a marvel. The earthen walls that
surrounded it and the window embrasures were occupied by ducks. On the ground the house was
fringed with ducks. On the turf slopes of its roof we
could see ducks, and a duck sat on the door-scraper.
The grassy banks had been cut into square patches,
about eighteen inches having been removed, and each
hollow had been filled with ducks. A windmill was in-
fested, and so were all the outhouses, mounds, rocks and
crevices. The ducks were everywhere. Many were so
tame that we could stroke them on their nests; and
the good lady told us that there was scarcely a duck on
the island that would not allow her to take its eggs
without flight or fear. Our hostess told us that when
she first became possessor of the island the produce of
down from the ducks was not more than fifteen pounds
in a year; but that under her careful nurture of twenty
years it had risen to nearly one hundred pounds annually. Most of the eggs are taken and pickled for
winter consumption, one or two only being left in each
nest to hatch."

Although breeding in great numbers on the coast of Labrador and in other Canadian waters, the eider duck is practically not protected there, and indeed is scarcely made use of commercially in America. We have not yet advanced sufficiently to take advantage of our opportunities.

Dr. Leonhard Stejneger, in the "Standard Natural History," writing of the European sheldrake (*Tadorna*)—which must not be confounded with any of the birds (*Mergus*) which we of the United States call sheldrakes—almost parallels Mr. Shepard's account, but on a smaller scale. He says: "The inhabitants on several of the small sandy islands off the western coast of Jutland—notably, the Island of Sylt—have made the whole colony of sheldrakes breeding there a source of considerable income by judiciously taxing the birds for eggs and down, supplying them in return with burrows of easy access and protecting them against all kinds of injury. The construction of such a duck burrow is described by Johann Friedrich Naumann, who says that all the digging, with the exception of the entrance tunnel, is made from above. On top of small rounded hills, covered with grass, the breeding chambers are first dug out to a uniform depth of two or three feet. These are then connected by horizontal tunnels and finally with the common entrance. Each breeding chamber is closed above with a tightly fitting piece of sod, which can be lifted up like a lid when the nest is to be examined and plundered. Such a complex burrow may contain from ten to twenty nest chambers, but in the latter case there are usually two entrances. The birds, which, on account of the protection extended to them through ages, are quite tame, take very eagerly to the burrows. As soon as the female has laid six eggs the egging commences, and every one above that number is taken away, a single bird often laying twenty or thirty eggs in a season. The birds are so tame that, when the lid is opened, the female still sits on the nest, not walking off into the next room until touched by the egg-gatherer's hand. When no more fresh eggs are found in the nest, the down composing the latter is also collected, being in quality nearly equal to eider down."

The importance of the wildfowl to the natives of northern climes has been indicated, and it is well known that in the United States the killing of these birds on their migrations and during their winter residence is a matter of some commercial moment, giving employment to many men and requiring the investment of not a little capital. Years ago, when the birds were far more numerous than now, isolated posts of the Hudson's Bay Co. in Canada depended for support during a part of the year on the geese that they killed during the migrations and dried or smoked. Gunning for the market occupies many men during the winter, and the occasional great rewards received for a day's work in the blind or the battery lead many to make a serious business of it, though it is quite certain that, taking the season through, the work will not pay ordinary day's wages to the man who guns. Nevertheless, we knew

of a gunner who in January, 1900, killed $130 worth
of birds in a day, and of another who in February,
1899, killed $206 worth in one day. It must be remem-
bered that this gunning is going on during the whole
winter all over the South every day except Sunday.
The number of birds killed must be very great and must
far exceed those hatched and reared each year.

SWANS.

The swans are the largest of our water fowl, and the American species measure nearly or quite five feet in length. The naked skin of the bill runs back to the eye, covering the lores; the bill is high at the base, but broad and flattened toward the tip; the tarsus is reticulate, and shorter than the middle toe. In our species the feathers do not come down to the tibio-tarsal joint. The two American species are white in the adult plumage, the immature birds being gray.

Both species belong to the restricted genus *Olor*, which is distinguished from the true *Cygnus* by not having a tubercle at the base of the bill. Thus in the ornithologies, and in the American Ornithologists' Union Check List, the generic name is given as *Olor*, but the term *Cygnus* will answer the purposes of this volume.

Although the two swans are much alike, they may readily be distinguished by the characters to be hereafter given; that is to say, the number of the tail feathers and the position of the nostril opening in the bill.

Edwin Sheppard

AMERICAN SWAN.

Cygnus columbianus (ORD).

The common swan is slightly smaller than the trumpeter, but is colored like it, except that on the naked lores, just before the eye, there is a spot of yellow. This, however, is not invariably present, and is usually lacking in the young birds. The tail feathers are 20 instead of 24, and this with the fact that the nostrils open half way down the bill (instead of being in the basal half, as in the trumpeter swan), will always serve to distinguish the two.

The young are gray, with a pink bill, which later turns white, and finally black. As the young grow older, the body becomes white, then the neck, and last of all the head.

During the autumn, winter and spring this swan occurs in greater or less abundance all over the United States, occasionally being found as far south as Florida. It is rarely seen, however, off the New England coast. Its breeding grounds are in Alaska, and Dr. Dall reported it common all along the Yukon, and says that it arrives with the geese about May 1st, but appears coming down the Yukon instead of up the stream. It breeds in the great marshes, near the mouth of that river.

This species is said to be much more common on the Pacific than on the Atlantic coast, in winter resorting in great numbers to lakes in Washington, Oregon and portions of California, where it is often found mingled with the trumpeter swan. It is common in winter on the South Atlantic coast, being usually abundant in the Chesapeake Bay and in Currituck Sound and to the southward. Congregating in great flocks, its snowy plumage and musical call notes are pleasing features of this wide water. Few swans are killed, and the old-time gunners declare that swans are as numerous as they ever were, or are even increasing.

The whooping swan of Europe (*Cygnus cygnus*) is supposed to occur in Greenland, and is therefore given in the ornithologies as a bird of America. It has not been taken on this continent. It is white in color, and has the bill black at the tip, with the lores and basal portion of the bill yellow.

Edwin Sheppard.

TRUMPETER SWAN.

Cygnus buccinator (RICH.).

The plumage of the trumpeter swan is white throughout; the naked black skin of the bill extends back to the eyes, covering what is called the lores, and the bill and feet are wholly black. The tail feathers are twenty-four in number, and this character will distinguish it from our only other swan, the species just mentioned. The bill is longer than the head, and the bird measures about five feet in total length. The spread of wings is great, sometimes ten feet. Audubon records a specimen which weighed 38 pounds.

The young are gray, the head often washed with

rusty, but grow whiter as they advance in years. The gray of the head and neck is the last to disappear. In the young the bill is flesh color at the base, dusky at tip; feet gray.

The trumpeter swan is a western species, and is scarcely found east of the Mississippi River. Formerly it bred over much of the western country, though undoubtedly most of the birds repaired to the far North to rear their young. Many years ago I found it breeding on a little lake in Nebraska, and I have seen it in summer on the Yellowstone Lake, in Wyoming. The nest is built on the ground, and the eggs are white or cream color.

In agreement with what is known of the trumpeter swan in the United States, its breeding grounds in the North appear to be inland. Explorers give the Hudson's Bay as one of its resorts, where it is said to be one of the earliest migratory birds to arrive. It breeds on the islands and in the marshes, and on the shores of the fresh water lakes, and is said to lay from five to seven eggs. It is stated also that it is monogamous, and that the mating is for life. During the period of the molt, when the swans are unable to fly, they are eagerly pursued by the Indians, not always successfully, since they are able to swim and to flap over the water as fast as a canoe can be paddled. The swan breeds also in the barren grounds on the head of the Fraser River, and at various points on the Mackenzie River; it has been reported also from Norton Sound.

The note of the trumpeter, from which it takes its

name, is loud and resonant, and so closely resembles
that of the sandhill crane that it is not always easy to
distinguish the two apart.   Authors connect the great
power and volume of the trumpeter's voice with the
curiously convoluted windpipe of the species.   The
young birds are very good eating, while the older ones,
as a·rule, are very tough and hardly edible.

GEESE AND BRANT.

SUB-FAMILY *Anserinæ*.

The geese stand midway between the swans and the ducks in size and general appearance, though their actual affinities are not these, the swans and ducks being more nearly related structurally than is either group to the geese. From the swans the geese may be distinguished by their smaller size and shorter neck, by having the lores, or space between the eye and bill, feathered instead of naked, and the bill proportionately shorter, deeper and much less broad, in some forms approaching a conical shape. They differ from the ducks in their greater size, longer necks and legs, and usually in the shape of the bill, which is relatively stouter and less broad than in most ducks. An important difference is seen also in the tarsus, or naked portion of the leg, between the joint just where the feathers end and that below, where the toes spread out. In the geese this tarsus is covered with a naked skin, marked with small divisions like the meshes of a net, while in the ducks the front of the tarsus is covered by overlapping plates which are termed scales or scutellæ. Thus in the geese the tarsus is said to be reticulate; in the ducks it is scutellate.

In all our species the sexes are alike, but they are very

different in some South American and Old World species.

In the sub-family are included the dozen species and sub-species of geese found in North America. They are divided into four genera, two of which contain a single species each, the others several each. One genus is almost confined to Alaska, while another has a general distribution in the Northern Hemisphere. The snow goose and its forms and the blue goose have a wide range, while little is known about that of Ross's goose. The dark-colored or gray geese, included in the genus *Branta,* are very abundant along both coasts of the continent, yet are by no means lacking in the interior. They include the common Canada goose, with its forms, and the barnacle and brant geese. The brant and its Western relative, the black brant, are chiefly maritime in habit, and are seldom found in the interior. On the other hand, the snow goose, and some of its forms, are regular visitants to certain points on the Atlantic coast. A few years ago a flock of these birds was always to be found in winter in the mouth of the Delaware River. Stray birds are sometimes seen on the New England coast and on Long Island. On the beach which lies outside of Currituck Sound a flock of five hundred or a thousand of these birds is found each winter.

The gray geese, so called, all have the bills, feet, head and neck black. There are patches or touches of white about the cheeks or throat, whence they have been called cravat geese; the upper parts of the body are dark gray and the belly and tail coverts white. The white-fronted goose, genus *Anser,* is much paler gray, has the bill and feet pink, and has no black except spots on breast and belly. In the genus *Chen* three forms are pure white, except for the quill feathers of the wings, which are black. All have the head white in adult plumage. *Philacte,* the Alaska type, is grayish or bluish in color, variously marked with white.

The North American geese are birds of powerful flight, non-divers, well adapted for progression on the land, usually breeders in high latitude, but wintering in open waters. Some are large birds, while others are smaller than some of the ducks, the weight in different species varying from 15 to 3 pounds.

They feed almost altogether on vegetable matter, largely grass and aquatic plants; and sometimes, after feeding for a time on the roots of certain sedges and other water plants, their flesh becomes very unpalatable from the strong flavor given it by this food.

Geese are noisy birds, the voice of the smaller ones being shrill and cackling, while the cry of others, like the common Canada goose, is sonorous and resonant.

Many years ago the geese, during the spring and autumn migration, were so enormously abundant in portions of Minnesota and in California that they did a vast amount of damage by eating the young wheat just appearing above the ground. In those days it was possible to approach quite close to them on horseback, and the rider, having gotten as near to them as practicable, would charge upon the feeding flock, get among them

before they could rise out of reach, and knock down
several with a short club which he carried in his hand.
It may be questioned whether this method of killing
geese has been employed for a long time.   In more recent years it is said to have been necessary for the California ranchers during the migrations to employ armed
men, whose business it was to ride about, shooting with
rifles at the feeding flocks and endeavoring to keep
them constantly on the wing.

BLUE GOOSE.

Chen cærulescens (LINN.).

In the adult the head and upper part of the neck are white; the rest of the neck, breast, back and rump bluish, or brownish-blue, many of the feathers with paler edges; wing light bluish gray; secondaries blackish, edged with white; primaries black, fading to gray at the base; tail brown, white margined; under parts brownish gray and white, sometimes mostly white, and upper and under tail coverts white, or nearly so. The bill is pale pink, with white nail and a black line along the margin of each mandible. The legs and feet are pink or reddish.

The young resemble the adult, but have the head and neck grayish brown. The length of this goose is about 28 inches; the wing measures 16.

Like many others of our inland water fowl, this goose often has the plumage of head, neck, breast and belly stained with rusty orange, as if soiled by iron rust.

The blue goose is an inhabitant of the interior, ranging from the Hudson's Bay district south along the Mississippi Valley to the Gulf of Mexico. It is not found on either the Atlantic or Pacific coast, except that in a few cases it has been taken on the extreme northern coast of Maine. Little or nothing is known about its breeding habits, though the Eskimo and Indians are authority for the statement that it breeds in the interior of Labrador; and the occurrence of the species in Maine would seem to lend color to this story. Moreover, Mr. G. Barnston, in his paper on the Geese of Hudson's Bay, states that in the migration, the blue goose crosses James Bay, coming from the eastern coast, while at the same time the snow goose makes its appearance coming from the north.

This species was long thought to be the young of the snow goose, and was so figured by Audubon, appearing on the same plate with that species. Occasionally specimens are found which have considerably more white on them than is given in the description above, but on the whole, it seems to be very well established that the species is a valid one. The color of the head and upper neck varies somewhat with age, the white of these parts growing purer and less intermingled with dark feathers as the bird grows older.

This is one of the so-called brant of the Mississippi Valley, and is known by a number of names, among which are blue brant, bald-headed goose, white-headed goose, *oie bleu* and bald brant. Being confined to the inland districts of the country, it is shot chiefly on the stubbles or the sand bars or in corn fields.

LESSER SNOW GOOSE.

Chen hyperborea (PALL.).

The adult is entirely white, except the primaries, or quill feathers of the first joint of the wing, which are black, changing to ash gray at the base. The bill is dark red, with black line along the margin of mandibles; the nail white; the legs and feet red; length, about 25 inches; wing, 15 1-2. In the young the head, neck and upper parts are pale grayish, with the wing coverts and tertiary feathers brown, edged with white. The primaries are black, and the rest of the upper parts white. The bill and feet are dark.

The true snow goose is a bird of Western distribution, reaching from the Mississippi Valley westward to

46

the coast, and as far south as Texas and Southern California. It, nevertheless, occurs sometimes on the Atlantic coast, and I have known of its being killed on Long Island. It is perhaps the most abundant goose found in California, and occurs in large numbers all over the country from the valley of the Mississippi west to the Rocky Mountains, where it is often associated with the larger snow goose, to be described later. On the plains of Montana, near the foot-hills of the Rocky Mountains, they are abundant, and when they first arrive are quite gentle, so that I have often ridden on horseback within easy shooting distance of them, although a man on foot would not have been permitted to approach so near.

In the Hudson's Bay district both forms of snow goose are abundant, and in old times used to form an important article of subsistence for the Hudson's Bay posts. Of late years, however, they have become so scarce that this source of food supply can no longer be depended upon.

While the flesh of both the snow geese is highly esteemed by some people, I have never considered it desirable. Usually it has a strong taste of sedge, so pronounced as to be, to some palates, very disagreeable.

GREATER SNOW GOOSE.

Chen hyperborea nivalis (FORST.).

Precisely similar in all respects to the preceding, but larger. While the length of *C. hyperborea* is about 25 inches, with a wing 15 1-2 inches, that of the present sub-species is 34 inches, with a wing over 17 inches. The two forms are often found associated together, and it is frequently difficult to determine to which one a bird belongs.

The snow geese differ from many of their fellows in feeding largely on the land. They walk about much as do the domestic geese, nipping the grass and such other herbs as please their taste, and resort to the water chiefly for resting.

The nest of the greater snow goose, as described by Mr. Macfarlane, consists merely of a hollow or depression in the soil, lined with down and feathers. The eggs are large and are yellowish-white.

All these interior geese, such as the blue goose and all the white geese, are known among the Indians and Hudson's Bay people of the north as wavies, the blue goose being called the blue wavy, the snow goose the large wavy, and Ross's goose the small wavy. The larger snow goose is common in Alaska. They do not breed in the neighborhood of the Yukon, but proceed further north to rear their young. The fall migration takes place in September, and by the end of that month all the snow geese are gone. In summer they proceed as far south as Texas and Cuba, where they are reported as abundant.

As already remarked, snow geese are seen every winter in the mouth of the Delaware, and also on the coast of North Carolina, about Currituck Sound.

The spectacle of a flock of these white geese flying is a very beautiful one. Sometimes they perform remarkable evolutions on the wing, and if seen at a distance look like so many snowflakes being whirled hither and thither by the wind. Scarcely less beautiful is the sight which may often be seen in the Rocky Mountain region during the migration. As one rides along under the warm October sun he may have his attention attracted by sweet, faint, distant sounds, interrupted at first, and then gradually coming nearer and clearer, yet still only a murmur; the rider hears it from above, before, behind and all around, faintly sweet and musically discordant, always softened by distance, like the sound of far-off harps, of sweet bells jangled, of the distant baying of mellow-voiced hounds. Looking up into the sky above him he sees the serene blue far on high, flecked with tiny white moving shapes, which seem like snowflakes drifting lazily across the azure sky; and down to earth, falling, falling, falling, come the musical cries of the little wavies that are journeying toward the south land. They pass, and slowly the sounds grow faint and fainter, and the listener thinks involuntarily of the well-known lines:

> Oh, hark, oh, hear! how thin and clear,
>   And thinner, clearer, farther going!
> Oh, sweet and far from cliff and scar
>   The horns of Elfland faintly blowing!

These birds and Ross's geese often stop to rest and feed on the Montana plains during their migration. I have more than once killed them with a rifle at St. Mary's Lake in the late autumn, and have started them from the little prairie pools, where they were feeding on a small farinaceous tuber, which is the root of some water plant.

ROSS'S GOOSE.

Chen rossii (CASSIN).

In color the plumage of the little Ross's goose is precisely similar both in adult and young to that of the larger snow geese; that is, pure white, except for the primaries, which are black, becoming ash color at the base. The bill and feet are red; the nail white. The base of the bill is usually covered with wart-like excrescences, or is wrinkled and roughened. There is great difference in the bills, no two being just alike. The young are white, tinged with gray, the centre of the feathers often being dark colored.

Ross's goose is the smallest of our geese, being about

the size of the mallard duck, and weighing from two and a half to three pounds. At a distance it is hard to distinguish it from the snow goose, but the voice is shriller, and the birds rise on the wing more readily than most of the geese, springing into the air and going upward more like mallards or black ducks than like geese. The range of this goose is given in the books as Arctic America in summer, and the Pacific coast to Southern California in winter; but, as a matter of fact, not very much is known about it. It has been taken quite frequently in California in winter, but is nowhere abundant.

In Northwestern Montana it is a common fall migrant, coming rather later than the snow goose, and being abundant on the heads of Milk River, Cutbank and Two Medicine Lodge creeks through October and the first half of November. A few years ago Mr. Jos. Kipp captured there and partially domesticated no less than nine of these birds, but unfortunately, before the winter was over, all of them were killed by dogs. Dr. J. C. Merrill tells us that this goose is not uncommon in the vicinity of Fort Missoula, and Captain Bendire has taken it in Eastern Oregon in the spring. It is not a bird that is likely to be met with by sportsmen except in the localities referred to, and there it is usually shot by being approached under cover.

I have seen it there in flocks of from seventy-five to one hundred, and have known of sixteen birds falling to the two discharges of a double-barreled gun. The flesh of those that I have eaten was delicious.

WHITE-FRONTED GOOSE.

Anser albifrons (GMEL.).

In the genus *Anser* the bill is much less stout than in *Chen,* and the nail, which terminates it, is thinner and less strong. The present species is generally grayish-brown in color, the feathers immediately about the bill being in adults white, bordered behind by dark brown. The head and neck are grayish-brown, darkest on crown of head and back of neck. The body is grayish, many of the feathers being tipped with white. The primaries are black, the rump slate-brown, the upper and under tail coverts white, and the tail grayish-brown margined with white. The under parts are grayish, variously, often heavily, blotched with blackish-brown;

53

bill, legs and feet, pinkish; the nail of the bill white; length, 28 inches; wing, over 15. The young closely resembles the adult, but lacks the white about the bill, this part being dark brown; it has no black blotches on the lower parts. The nail of the bill is blackish.

The white-fronted goose is found in the northern parts of both the Old and the New World, though the two forms are separated by many ornithologists and made different races. The American bird is slightly larger than that of Europe, but the difference is small, and size is the only distinction. At all events, for the purposes of the gunner, they may be considered a single species. The white-fronted goose is generally distributed throughout this country from the far north to our southern border, but is rare on the Atlantic coast. A specimen was taken recently in Currituck Sound. N. C., but none of the local gunners, knew what it was. The species occurs in Cuba as well as in Greenland.

In all the Mississippi Valley region it is abundant during the migrations, where it is known as laughing goose, speckled belly, harlequin brant, pied brant, prairie brant, and often simply as brant. It is abundant also in California, and occurs in large numbers as far south as Southern California. In summer the white-fronted goose is found in Alaska, where some breed, and in great numbers on the islands of the Arctic Ocean. All northern explorers report it as abundant on the Mackenzie and throughout the country bordering the Barren Lands. In America it appears to be generally a bird of western distribution.

The white-fronted goose feeds largely on grass, and in former times did much damage to the young crops of wheat on the western coast during its migrations. It is said to feed also on berries, and to be seldom seen on the water except at night or when molting. The southward migration is undertaken late in September, and the flocks of white-fronted geese usually make their appearance on the western prairies early in October, when they are often associated with snow geese, in company with which they feed and journey to and from their feeding grounds.

The flesh of the white-fronted goose is highly esteemed, and is spoken of as being more delicate than that of any other goose, except possibly the young of the salt water brant.

The nest of the white-fronted goose is usually built on the low ground, near fresh water ponds or marshes, and the six or eight yellowish-white eggs are commonly covered with down when the mother leaves them.

CANADA GOOSE.

Branta canadensis (Linn.).

Of all the so-called gray geese, the most common and best known is the Canada goose. Of this there are four different forms—the Canada goose, *Branta canadensis;* Hutchins's goose, *Branta canadensis hutchinsii;* white-cheeked goose, *Branta canadensis occidentalis;* and cackling goose, *Branta canadensis minima.* Of these the common wild goose and Hutchins's goose are distributed over the whole United States, the latter being chiefly western in its distribution, while the white-cheeked or western goose and the cackling goose are exclusively western, although the last named occasionally occurs in the Mississippi Valley.

HUTCHINS'S GOOSE.

WHITE-CHEEKED GOOSE.

The Canada goose has a triangular white patch on each cheek, the two meeting under the throat, though rarely they are separated by a black line. The head, neck, wing quills, rump and tail are black; the lower belly, upper and under tail coverts white; the upper parts are dark grayish-brown, the feathers with paler tips, and the lower parts are gray, fading gradually into the white of the belly. The tail feathers number from eighteen to twenty. The bird's length is from 36 to 40 inches, wing 18. The young are similar to the adult, but the white cheek patches are sometimes marked with black, and the black of the neck fades gradually into the grayish of the breast.

Branta canadensis hutchinsii (RICH.).

Hutchins's goose exactly resembles the Canada goose in color, but is smaller, and has fourteen or sixteen tail feathers. The length of Hutchins's goose is about 30 inches, wing 16 inches or over.

Branta canadensis occidentalis (BAIRD).

The western goose closely resembles the Canada goose, although it is slightly smaller. At the base of the black neck there is a distinct white collar running around the neck, and separating the black from the gray and brown of the body. "This white collar," Mr.

CACKLING GOOSE.

Ridgway writes me, "is a seasonal character, and may occur in all the sub-species. It fades out in summer and reappears with the fresh molt in autumn. Of this fact I had proof in a domesticated Hutchins's goose which my father had for some eight or ten years." The back and wings are slightly paler than in the Canada goose, while the feathers of the breast are perhaps a little darker. The tail feathers are 18 to 20, as in the Canada goose; the bird's length is from 33 to 36 inches, wing 18 inches or less. This sub-species is also called the white-cheeked goose.

Branta canadensis minima RIDGW.

The cackling goose bears the same relation to the western goose that Hutchins's does to the Canada goose, except that the difference in size is much greater.

The tail feathers are 14 to 16; the length of the bird is about 24 inches; wing about 14 inches. The coloring is almost exactly that of the western goose.

Of these four forms, the Canada goose is the only one of general distribution throughout North America. It is found from the Arctic Ocean to the Gulf of Mexico, and from the Atlantic to the Pacific; and during the migrations is abundant in New England, as well as over the more sparsely settled parts of the country. On the Pacific coast it is less common than the western goose, but inland it is found in numbers.

The common wild goose is an early migrant, and often passes North while the waters are still sealed in their icy fetters. Soon after its arrival in the North, however, the water becomes open, and the birds mate and separate to select their summer homes. The six or eight eggs are laid in nests, sometimes in the marshes, sometimes on higher land, not far from water, and again on the broken-off stubs of trees, or even in a nest among the branches, high above the ground. The eggs are ivory white, and are carefully brooded by the mother bird. Early in June the young are hatched and taken to the water. Usually they are accompanied by both parents, and at this time, if danger approaches, they follow the mother in a long line, imitating her movements, sinking lower and lower in the water as she sinks in her attempt to hide, and finally diving and scattering under the water when she dives. Soon after the young birds appear the old ones begin to molt, and this is a period of danger for them, many being killed at this time by the Eskimo and the Indians.

All along the Missouri River and its tributaries, and by lakes scattered over the great plains, the Canada goose formerly bred in considerable numbers, and twenty years ago broods of these birds were commonly seen during the summer along these rivers and upon the prairies near these little lakes. The settlement of the western country, however, has made such breeding places no longer available, and the geese are therefore obliged to journey further to the North before rearing their young.

The wild goose is readily domesticated, and this fact is taken advantage of by gunners, who capture crippled birds, keep them until cured, and subsequently use them as decoys to draw the passing flocks within gun-shot of their places of concealment. Not infrequently the geese breed in confinement, though it is probable this does not take place until the females are three years old. Sometimes such domesticated geese, when tethered out as decoys, escape and swim off to join flocks of wild geese, but as the tame ones commonly cannot fly, they are left behind by the flocks when these move away, and frequently turn about and make their way back to the place where their fellow captives are confined. A case of this sort came under my notice in Currituck Sound in the winter of 1900, when an old gander belonging to the Narrows Island Club, that had slipped his loops and gotten away, made his way back, after three weeks of freedom, nearly to the goose pen where the rest of the stand were kept. The superintendent of the club had heard the goose calling for several days and recognized his voice, and after considerable search found him in one of the little leads in the island.

The flight of the wild goose is firm, swift and steady. The birds commonly fly in a V or triangle, though sometimes they spread out into a great crescent whose convexity is directed forward.

The alertness and wariness of this bird have become proverbial, and when at rest, either on the land or water, it is particularly watchful and difficult of approach. Geese are exceedingly gregarious, and where a flock is resting on the water all birds passing near them are likely to lower their flight, and after making one or two circles in the air, to join the resting birds. For this reason, when flying alone or in companies of two or three, the goose may often be called up to wooden decoys by an imitation of its cry. Where geese are abundant it is exceedingly common for the gunners to call such single birds to within gunshot.

In windy weather the geese, when their flight obliges them to face the gale, fly low, and often barely top the reeds of the marshes among which they are wintering. In foggy weather, or when snow is falling, they also fly low, keeping close to the water, apparently looking for a place in which to alight. At such times they come to decoys with especial readiness. Sometimes in foggy weather, when flying over the land, they seem to become confused and fly about in circles, as if they had quite lost their way.

Hutchins's goose, though so like the Canada goose in coloring, differs from it in habits. Its breeding place is further to the North, and is on the coast near the salt water. There their nests are usually constructed in marshes near the sea, but Audubon quotes Captain Ross as stating that they sometimes breed on ledges of the cliffs. In winter this species is found in California and in Texas; and on the Pacific coast great numbers are killed from blinds, and also from behind domestic animals, trained to approach them gradually, as if feeding. Hutchins's goose is common in Alaska, and is reported there by all the explorers. Mr. Macfarlane found them also breeding on the shores and islands of the Arctic Sea.

Whether Hutchins's goose is found at all on the North Atlantic coast appears to be an unsettled question. The books and the gunners alike state that it used to be found there, but if it occurs at present it is very unusual.

Like the Canada goose, Hutchins's goose sometimes has its nest in trees. A case of this kind is cited by Dr. Brewer, who states that in one instance four eggs of this species were found in the deserted nest of a crow or hawk, built on the fork of a pine tree and at a height of nine feet. The parent bird was shot on the nest.

Besides the ordinary book names applied to this species, Mr. Gurdon Trumbull, in his admirable "Names and Portraits of Birds," quotes Eskimo goose, mud goose, goose brant, marsh goose and prairie goose, as well as the general term, brant, which is commonly applied to all the smaller geese. Mr. Elliot says that among the Aleutians this bird is called the tundrina goose.

The habits of the cackling goose do not appear to differ at all from those of the Canada goose, but its range is a very narrow one, being restricted during the summer to the Bering seacoast of Alaska, its principal breeding place being the shores of Norton Sound. It does not occur during the breeding season anywhere south of the Alaska Peninsula, the breeding birds from Cook's Inlet southward being the white-cheeked goose. During migration it extends along the Pacific coast as far as California, but the birds seen in summer along the inlets of the British Columbia and Alaska coast are not this species, but the white-cheeked goose. It reaches California in its southward migration about the middle of October, and departs again for the North in April.

BARNACLE GOOSE.

Branta leucopsis (Bechst.).

Another species of this group is the barnacle goose (*Branta leucopsis*), which is entitled to mention here only to complete the list of our wildfowl. It is a straggler from Europe, where it is very common. No doubt it regularly occurs in Greenland. A specimen has been taken near Rupert House, at the southern end of Hudson's Bay, and others in Nova Scotia, on Long Island and in Currituck Sound, in North Carolina. It is not a bird likely to be met with by the sportsmen, and yet, if met with it should at once be reported, since every instance of its capture is of interest. It is a small bird, only a little larger than a brant, and may be known by

its having almost the whole head white. The lores—
that is to say, the space between the eye and the bill—
the back of head, neck and breast, are black; the wings
and back are gray, the feathers being tipped by a black
bar and margined with white. The under parts are
pale grayish; the bill, feet and legs black. The young
have the white cheek patches dotted with black, and
the feathers of the back tipped with reddish-brown.

It seems noteworthy that the few specimens of this
bird taken in America differ from specimens from Europe, in being somewhat paler.

The barnacle goose breeds in great numbers in Siberia and Spitzbergen, and it is found in winter in great
numbers on the west coast of Great Britain and the
north coast of Ireland. In some places in England the
barnacle goose has been to some extent domesticated,
and has bred in captivity.

BRANT.

Branta bernicla (LINN.).

Two species of brant, known as the brant or brant goose (*Branta bernicla*), and the black brant (*Branta nigricans*), occupy respectively the Atlantic and Pacific coasts of America. Both are salt water birds, and, as a rule, do not venture inland. They are found almost exclusively on tide waters, although stragglers have occasionally been taken in the Mississippi Valley. The common brant of the Atlantic coast is common to the Old and the New World. Both these species are small geese, but little larger than Ross's goose, which, as already stated, is about the size of a mallard duck.

The common brant has the head, neck, breast and fore back black, with narrow touches of white on either side of the neck, just below the head. The upper parts are brownish-gray, much as in the Canada goose, but each feather is narrowly margined with grayish. The under parts are grayish-white, fading into pure white on the belly, the upper and under tail coverts being also white. The middle of the rump and the quill feathers of the wing are blackish. The tail is black, as are the bill, legs and feet. The young is not noticeably different, except that the white touches on the neck are likely to be absent, and white bars cross the wing, formed by the white tips of the secondary feathers.

BLACK BRANT.

Branta nigricans (Lawr).

The black brant is like its eastern relative, but instead of having the faint white neck touches, it has a broad white collar about its neck, which, however, does not quite meet behind. The general color of this bird is much darker than that of its eastern relative. The upper parts, wings and under parts are dark brown, in sharp contrast to the white belly and upper and under tail coverts. The length is about 25 inches, and the wing 12 1-2 inches.

The brant goes to the far North to breed, and its nest was long unknown. Captain Fielden found the nest and eggs in latitude 82 degrees 33 minutes north, and subsequently many others in the same neighborhood. These nests were on the beach, near the water. In Greenland Dr. Walker, who found this species near Godthaab, as well as in the mouth of Bellot's Straits, saw nests built in the cliffs which formed the sides of the strait. On the European side of the water the bird has been found breeding in great numbers at Spitzbergen, where the ground was sometimes covered with its nests.

During its migrations the brant appears on the New England coast in October or November, and is found from there south along the Atlantic as far as South Carolina. Its favorite wintering grounds seem to be the coasts of Virginia and North and South Carolina, where it remains in great flocks all winter, unless driven further southward by extremely severe weather. It is a gentle, unsuspicious bird, and is readily decoyed. On the Massachusetts coast it is killed chiefly in spring on the sand bars, to which it resorts for the purpose of sanding. In its more southern haunts it is commonly shot from a battery or a bush blind.

Brant do not dive for their food, but feed in the same way as do geese, ducks and other shoal water wildfowl, by stretching the long neck down to the bottom and pulling up the grass that grows there. It is thus evident that they can only feed at certain stages of the tide.

Brant are not uncommon in captivity, and are used in New England as decoys on the sand bars. The flocks of migrating birds rarely come up to the land or to points of marsh where there is any opportunity for concealment, and thus few are shot from the shore, except on the bars.

The range of the black brant has already been given. Two or three specimens have been taken on the Atlantic coast, but these were merely stragglers. On the Pacific coast in winter it is found on salt water bays and estuaries, from the straits of Fuca south to San Diego. They make their appearance in October, and leave again in April.

Black brant appear to be very little shot, notwithstanding their great numbers. On their northward migration they usually proceed in small flocks of from twenty to fifty, but at times collect in such immense numbers that great quantities of them are killed. This is especially true if the birds have to wait near the edge of the ice for the northern waters, which they are seeking, to become open.

The black brant breeds near the Arctic Ocean. Mr. Macfarlane found their nests on little islands in fresh water ponds or in rivers, and saw many others on the shores or on islands in Franklin Bay. The number of eggs in a nest was usually five.

In its migration this species follows the Alaskan coast, over the Bering Sea, passing outside of St. Michael's Island, proceeding to Stewart's Island, and thence northward across the open sea to Golofin Sound. They are found in Norton Sound by the middle of May, and breed in this neighborhood in great numbers.

EMPEROR GOOSE.

Philacte canagica (Sevast.).

The emperor is one of the handsomest of the American geese. It is a bird of very limited distribution, being confined to the Bering Sea and its vicinity, though very rarely specimens straggle southward in winter along the Pacific coast of the United States as far as California. The emperor goose may be known from all the other North American geese by the remarkable form of its bill; this is extremely short, with a very broad and thick nail, which occupies almost one-third of the length. The tarsus, or naked portion of the leg, between the toes and the joint above, is very short in proportion to the toes.

In the adult emperor goose the head and back of the neck are white; the front and sides of the throat and neck are brownish-black, slightly spotted with white; the tail is slate-color at the base and white at the end; the rest of the plumage is bluish, each feather having at its end a narrow bar of white, bordered by a crescent-shaped black marking. The secondary feathers of the wing are slaty-black, margined with white; the long quills black. The bill is bluish or purplish; the nail white, darker at the edges, and the legs and feet bright yellow.

The young are similar to the adult, but have the head and neck lead color, sometimes sprinkled with white.

All the explorers of Alaska have found this species more or less abundant in that territory. It also occurs on some of the islands of the Bering Sea, as well as on the Commander Islands, on the Siberian coast. Mr. H. W. Elliot tells us that flocks sometimes land on the Pribilof Islands in an exhausted condition, so that the natives run them down on the grass, the birds being unable to fly. Mr. Dall speaks of the exceedingly strong odor of garlic proceeding from the raw flesh and skin, and says that this odor makes the work of skinning the birds very disagreeable. With cooking, the smell disappears.

The emperor geese breed on the flat, marshy islands of the Alaskan coast, the nest sometimes being placed amid the driftwood, even below high-water mark. Like most other geese, the female covers the eggs with down from her breast.

When the molting season begins the Eskimo kill
these geese in common with others, capturing them by
means of nets set on the marshes, into which the molting birds are driven.   At this time the destruction of
the birds is very great.

This species in Norton Sound is called white-headed
goose, while the name applied to it by the Russians is
sa-sar-ka, meaning guinea hen, evidently from the coloring of the plumage.

TREE DUCKS.

Intermediate between the true geese and the ducks are the so-called tree ducks, belonging to the genus *Dendrocygna*. Of these, two species are found along our southern border, and occasionally afford some sport to gunners. They are rather duck-like in form, but have very large heads and feet, the tarsus being reticulate instead of scutellate, like the ducks. In other words, the skin of the tarsus is covered by small scales, looking like a network, instead of by broad, deep scales which overlap in front. This, it will be remembered, is a character of the geese (*Anserinæ*). Moreover, the tarsus in the tree ducks is equal to or longer than the middle toe, instead of being shorter than it. The lower part of the thigh is naked, and the hind toe is extremely long.

This group appears to have relationship with the Old World sheldrakes, and with the goose-like genus *Chenalopex*, rather than with either the ducks or the geese. They are birds of tropical distribution, and in the United States are found only along the southern border. One species is common in the West India Islands. None of them, however, is sufficiently abundant to be considered as furnishing gunning, but two of the three species belong in the list of our water fowl.

BLACK-BELLIED TREE DUCK.

Dendrocygna autumnalis (Linn.).

The neck, back and breast are cinnamon-brown, the forehead somewhat paler. Sides of head, throat and upper neck yellowish-gray. At the back of the head a black strip begins, which runs down the back of the neck. The middle of the back, rump, upper tail coverts, belly, flanks and under wing coverts are black; the wing coverts are yellowish, fading into ashy and grayish-white on the greater coverts. When it is closed the wing thus shows a white strip for nearly its whole length. The tail is blackish-brown, and the under parts yellowish-brown. The under tail coverts are white; the bill is red, changing to orange at the base; its nail is bluish; legs and feet whitish. The young bird resembles the adult, but its colors are duller throughout, and it lacks the black flanks and belly; they are grayish-white, barred with dusky; length, 19 inches; wing 9 1-2 inches.

In certain parts of Texas the black-bellied tree duck is not a scarce bird. It is found there in summer and autumn, and at this time of the year visits the grain fields, where some shooting at them may sometimes be had. Its name is well applied, for it perches in the trees without difficulty, and walks about on the branches as if much at home. In fact, it is said to pass the hours of daylight largely in the branches of trees, and to do its feeding and traveling chiefly at night. This duck nests in the hollow trees, and there deposits twelve to fifteen eggs, without forming any nest. When hatched the young are said to be carried to the water in the mother's bill.

It is easily domesticated, and when once tamed associates with the fowls of the farm on perfectly good terms. When tamed it is said to be very watchful, and to utter a shrill call at the approach of any individual or at any unusual sound.

In Texas, where the bird is most common, it is known as the tree duck, corn field or long-legged duck, while in Louisiana the common appellation for it is fiddler duck, from the clear call-note that it utters at night when in flight. It frequents the old corn fields which have been overflowed, and from such places it may be started in pairs, often giving good shooting. Its flesh is highly esteemed.   Some of the local names used in South America and in Mexico are applied to it by reason of its call-note.

Mr. Xantus took a single specimen of this duck at Fort Tejon, in Southern California, but this is the only specimen known from that State.   In Mexico and Central America they are common.   Dr. Merrill states that these birds reach Fort Brown, Texas, from the South in April.   Most of them depart again in September or October, but some stay until November.

FULVOUS-BELLIED TREE DUCK.

Dendrocygna fulva (GMEL.).

The brown tree duck is a more northerly species than the preceding, and is found in Mexico and northward through parts of California and Nevada, as well as in Texas and Louisiana. The head, neck and lower parts are deep reddish-yellow, darkest on top of head, and changing to reddish on the flanks, the longer feathers being streaked with pale yellow; middle of neck whitish obscurely streaked with black. A distinct black stripe runs from the head down the hind part of the neck. The upper parts are brownish-black, the feathers of the wing being tipped with chestnut. The upper tail coverts are white; the belly and lower tail coverts yellow-ish-white; the bill is blackish, and the feet and legs are slate-blue; the length is about 20 inches; wing, 9 1-2 inches. The colors of the young are somewhat duller, and the wing coverts lack the chestnut.

The fulvous tree duck, known as the yellow-bellied fiddler in Louisiana, and the long-legged duck in Texas, is quite common there at certain seasons. Its habits do not vary greatly from those of the black-bellied tree duck. Like that species, it spends much of its time in fresh water lakes and sloughs, feeding on the grasses that grow there, and it also visits the corn fields at night in search of grain.

The flesh of both these species is said to be very delicious, and is eagerly sought after.* The birds are shot only by being stumbled on or by lying in wait for them as they come into or leave the corn fields.

This duck is exceedingly unsuspicious and readily permits approach, so that many of them are killed. When crippled, however, their strong legs enable them to run very fast, and, like all ducks, they are expert hiders, getting into the grass and lying there without moving. The bird is also a good diver, and if it reaches the water is not likely to be captured. It is said never to be found on the salt water, but confines itself entirely to inland pools, rivers and swamps.

---

*On this point compare Robert Erskine Ross in "California Duck Notes," *Forest and Stream,* July 26, 1902.

THE TRUE DUCKS.

The ducks may always be distinguished from their relatives, the geese, by characters already indicated. The tarsus, that is to say, the naked portion of the leg, between the joint where the feathers end and that where the toes begin, is covered in front by broad, overlapping scales, instead of by a naked skin, ornamented with small hexagonal scales. The ducks are usually smaller than the geese. They are also, as a rule, more highly colored, though this brilliancy prevails more in the males of the fresh-water ducks than in the sea ducks. Nevertheless, this is not the invariable rule, for the males of all the mergansers, and such species of sea ducks as the eiders, the harlequin, the butter-ball and long-tailed duck are extremely showy and beautiful birds. As a rule the ducks have shorter necks and legs than the geese.

It has long been known to naturalists and to a few gunners that in the mallard and some other ducks the males assume during the summer a plumage very different from that which they commonly wear during the autumn, winter and spring, and not unlike that of the female. This is not generally known, and even by ornithologists has not always been understood. Recently, however, in the Proceedings of the Academy of Natural Sciences of Philadelphia, for the last quarter of

1899, Mr. Witmer Stone, in a paper entitled "The Summer Molting Plumage of Certain Ducks," has discussed the subject in a very suggestive way.

Mr. Stone calls attention to the fact that in only one of our ducks—the old squaw—does the adult male possess a distinct winter plumage which is different from the breeding dress, that the old males of all our other ducks remain in the same plumage from the time they arrive in autumn till their departure northward in spring, and intimates that, judging by analogy, we should suppose that since these ducks show no tendency toward a change of plumage when they leave us in the spring, they must retain the same feathers that covered them during the winter until the end of the breeding season, when a complete molt should occur and a new dress be assumed exactly like the one just shed.

It is known, however, that this is not the fact, and, as stated, the "plumage after the breeding season" has been described in some species. The first record of this peculiar summer plumage in the male ducks is found in the supplement to Montagu's "Ornithological Dictionary," 1813, under the head of "The Pintail (*Dafila acuta*)." The observations made on some domesticated birds are given as follows: "In the month of June or beginning of July these birds commenced their change of plumage, and by degrees after making a singular mottled appearance, especially on the part of the body which was white before, became by the first week in August entirely of a brown color. The beautiful bronze on the head, the white streak on each side of the neck, and all the white beneath, as well as the elegant scapulars, had entirely vanished, and to all appearance a sexual metamorphosis had taken place. But this change was of short duration, for about the latter end of September one of the males began to assume the masculine attire   *   *   *   and by the middle of October this bird was again in full plumage."

Twenty-five years later the naturalist Waterton described a similar molt in the male mallard, and as time went on, other species were found to undergo like changes. In Mr. Ridgway's "Manual of North American Birds," a number of species are given as having a peculiar summer plumage resembling the female. Such are the mallard, blue-wing and cinnamon teal, the gadwall, widgeon, pintail and scaup. On the whole, however, very little is said in the books about this change.

Mr. Stone's examination of four species of eider ducks brought back from the Arctic by Mr. E. A. McIlhenny, and taken near Point Barrow, in the late summer or early autumn, leads Mr. Stone to believe that in all ducks where the plumages of the male and female are markedly different we may expect to find this double molt and a dull summer plumage in the male. He points out that this summer plumage is in no sense a nuptial dress, and that while it may begin to appear before the young birds are hatched, it is not seen until after the mating season is over, and is distinctly a postnuptial dress. The change is chiefly restricted to the head, neck, breast and scapulars; in other words, to those parts which are most conspicuously colored.

A very important point in connection with this summer plumage is that the annual molt of the flight feathers does not begin until it has been fully acquired, and that as soon as the new flight feathers have become strong enough to be used, the dull plumage, as well as the remainder of the old plumage, is lost, the molt of the body feathers proceeding in the usual way. In other words, this dull plumage lasts only during the period while the birds are unable to fly, for, as is well understood, ducks molt the quill feathers of their wings all at once, and for a time lose the power of flight. . Now at such a time a dull plumage would naturally be useful in rendering the bird inconspicuous, and thereby protecting it, and Mr. Stone believes this to be the explanation of this curious summer molt. He adds that the feathers of this plumage are very poor and loosely constructed, like the "first" plumage of young birds, which is only a temporary summer dress.

Mr. Stone quotes European authors who have described eider ducks of different species in this dress, but have called them young males, evidently not appreciating the meaning of the change. He then goes on to describe in detail this summer plumage in four species of Pacific eiders and in the red-breasted merganser, from which it appears that up to July the nuptial dress of the male is usually retained, but that by the latter part of August and in early September this "summer molting plumage," as Mr. Stone calls it, is fully assumed.

NON-DIVING DUCKS.

SUB-FAMILY *Anatinæ*.

As has already been said, the ducks are divided into three sub-families. Of these the first is the *Anatinæ*, or fresh-water ducks. One unvarying character of this group is that it has the hind toe simple, while in all the sea or diving ducks it is lobed, or provided with a loose membrane or flap. The feet of the fresh-water ducks, as a rule, are smaller than those of the sea ducks, formed more for progression on land than for swimming. The fresh-water ducks feed in shallow water, gathering their food from the bottom by stretching down the neck, or by tipping up the body, as do also the geese and the swans. They do not dive for food, though they often do so to escape from danger when wounded. As a rule they feed on vegetable matter, from which it results that their flesh is very palatable. As it is a fact, however, that all ducks are indiscriminate feeders, in cases where the fresh-water ducks have access to animal food their flesh readily acquires an unpleasant, fishy taste. There are thirteen or fourteen species of fresh-water ducks found in North America, most of which are familiar to gunners. Naturalists are by no means agreed as to the proper nomenclature to be applied to the different species in this group, but for the purposes of this work it will be sufficient to take that adopted by the American Ornithologists' Union in its revised Check List of North American Birds.   It is to be noted, however, that the order in which the species are arranged is not that of the Check List.

MALLARD.

Anas boschas LINN.

In autumn, winter and spring the colors of the mallard are those of the common domestic duck, which is its descendant. The head and neck are brilliant metallic green, sometimes showing golden and purple reflections, according to the light's reflection. About the neck, below this green, is a narrow ring of white, usually broken at the back. The back is brown, or brownish-gray, finely waved with grayish-white, as are the inner scapular feathers, which darken to rich brown on the wing. The speculum, or wing patch, is violet, with metallic reflections, crossed near the end with a black bar, and tipped with a white one. The rump and upper tail-coverts are black, and the tail white, each feather being grayish along the shaft. The breast is deep glossy chestnut, and the other under parts gray, waved with narrow black lines. The under tail-coverts are black. The bill is yellow-green, with a black nail, the eyes dark brown and the feet orange. The length is about 2 feet and the wing from 11 to 12 inches. The summer dress of the male closely resembles that of the female, but is darker. This plumage is assumed in June and is lost again in August, when the winter dress is resumed.

The female is colored much as the female of the tame duck; the feathers generally are dusky, with broad, pale yellow or buff edges. On the upper parts the dark color predominates; on the lower, the buff; often almost to the exclusion of the blackish streaks. The wing patch is colored as in the male, as are the bill, feet and legs. The chin is almost white and the throat is buff.

No one of our ducks has a wider range than the mallard, which, as has been said, is the progenitor of the common domestic duck. It is found over the entire northern portion of the world; and, in America, as far south as Mexico, while in Europe it breeds in Southern Spain and Greece. It is believed to be common throughout Asia, except in tropical India, and it is more or less abundant in Northern Africa. Although a migratory bird, the mallard may usually be found throughout its range in winter, provided there is open water, and so a place where it may feed. In many places in the Northern Rocky Mountains, where the thermometer often goes to 30 or 40 degrees below zero, mallards may be found throughout the winter living in warm springs or along swift streams, where the current is so rapid that the water never freezes. Thus it is seen that the winter's cold has little to do with the migration of the mallard—or, in fact, with that of many other ducks—and that, if food is plenty, the birds can bear almost any degree of cold. It is the freezing of the waters and thus the shutting off of the food supply that forces these inland birds to move southward.

In the New England States the mallard is not a common bird, but in the Southern States, the interior and California it is extremely abundant.

In the northern interior the mallard is shot from early October until the waters close in November, and all through the winter it is abundant in the Southern States. Here it feeds in the marshes along the salt water, in the rice fields and along the sloughs and streams throughout the interior, and becomes fat and well flavored and is eagerly pursued. It comes readily to decoys and if one or more live ducks are tethered with the decoys to call down the wild birds, they are quite certain to respond and to offer easy shooting to the gunner. Formerly the mallard bred in considerable numbers within the limits of the United States, though it has never been a common bird at any season on the Atlantic coast north of New York. Yet it used to breed in great numbers in Illinois, Indiana,

Wisconsin, Michigan and Minnesota, as well as in the prairies of the further West and about alkaline lakes and pools on the high central plateau. Now, most of the birds proceed further north to breed, and Canada, the Hudson's Bay country and the shores of the Arctic Sea are all occupied by it during the nesting season. Dr. Brewer states that "it has been known in rare instances to nest in a tree, in such cases occupying a deserted nest of a hawk, crow or other large bird."

The mallard is one of our typical fresh-water ducks. It is rarely or never found on salt water, but, on the other hand, is common on the lagoons along the southern Atlantic coast which are brackish. Here it associates with many other fresh-water ducks and is frequently seen flying in company with black ducks, sprigtails, widgeons and other species.

The mallard rises from the water by a single spring, almost straight up in the air, and then flies upward at a sharp angle, until it has reached a height of thirty or forty feet, when it flies rapidly away. Its speed on the wing is considerable and when coming before the wind it is necessary for the gunner to make considerable allowance to hit it. When the mallard rises on the water it usually utters several loud quacks of alarm, and when associated in companies, as it usually is, the birds keep up a more or less continuous conversation. When flying, its attention is readily attracted by an imitation of its note, and this call, made either with the mouth or with an instrument known as a duck call, is often used to lead it to observe the decoys. If it can be made to see these, it is extremely likely to come to them.

This species readily hybridizes with certain other ducks. A hybrid supposed to be mallard and muscovy duck is common. So also is one between the mallard and the black duck, and of these I have killed a number. They bear a general resemblance to the black duck, but the head and neck are much darker and show glossy reflections. Moreover, the crissum or anal region is jet black, as are the upper tail-coverts, and the male is likely to possess the recurved tail feathers which characterize the mallard drake.

Many years ago, in Carbon county, Wyoming, I killed a male hybrid between the mallard and pintail. In form it resembles the male pintail, but its head is blackish green, with metallic reflections, almost the color of the male shoveller. Its breast is chestnut and its back much like that of a mallard. The general effect is that of a male pintail with mallard coloring.

Perhaps no one of our North American ducks is so well known as the mallard, and yet it has comparatively few common names. It is called greenhead, wild drake, wild duck, English duck, French duck and gray duck, or sometimes gray mallard for the female. In Canada the name stock duck was formerly common, referring evidently to this bird as a progenitor of the domestic duck. The French Canadians call it *canard Français* or French duck. Mr. Trumbull calls attention to the old but now obsolete duckinmallard, a word supposed to be a corruption of duck and mallard, duck being the female and mallard the male. The word is thus the equivalent of duck and drake, it having been the custom, seemingly, to speak of the species by this double name.

BLACK DUCK OR DUSKY DUCK.

Anas obscura GMEL.

Under the general name "black duck" are included two species and one sub-species so closely alike that only a careful comparison will distinguish them.

They are birds similar in size and form to the mallard, but very different in color. The black duck is brownish-black or dusky, all the feathers edged with pale grayish or yellowish. The head and neck are streaked with yellowish. Of this there is least on the top of the head and the hind neck, which are sometimes nearly black; most on the sides of head and throat.

These last are sometimes almost buff, without any
streaking. The speculum, or iridescent wing patch,
is sometimes metallic-green and sometimes violet,
edged with black. The bill is yellowish-green and the
nail dark, while the feet are orange-red, the webs
dusky. Length, 22 inches; wing, 11. The sexes are
essentially alike.

Since the first edition of this book was published,
Mr. William Brewster has described (*Auk* xix, p. 183,
April, 1892) a new form of black duck (*A. obscura
rubripes*). It is slightly larger than the common form,
has the dark feathers of crown edged with gray or
yellowish, the dark markings on foreneck and sides of
head coarser and blacker, bill yellow, tarsi and toes
bright red. Its distribution is apparently northern
and western.

FLORIDA DUSKY DUCK.

Anus fulvigula RIDGW.

The general color above is brownish-black, as in the black duck, but the feathers more widely margined with yellowish, giving a generally paler cast to the bird. The chin and throat are always plain unstreaked buff, these being finely streaked in the black duck. The speculum is green, sometimes tipped with white, which may then form a bar across the wing. The bill is olive-yellow and there is a triangular spot of black at its base, near the angle of the mouth. The legs and feet are orange-red. The length is about 20 inches and the wing 10. The female is somewhat paler than the male.

The Florida duck is an altogether lighter colored bird than the dusky duck and there can be no question as to its specific distinctness nor of the ease with which it may be distinguished if the differential characters are borne in mind. These consist (1) in the altogether paler coloration, the under parts being buff, streaked with dusky, instead of the reverse; (2) the plain buff cheeks, chin and throat, these parts being thickly streaked in the dusky duck; (3) the black spot at base of upper mandible, next to corner of mouth; (4) the green instead of violet speculum.

MOTTLED DUCK.

Anas fulvigula maculosa (Senn.).

The mottled duck resembles the Florida duck in the characters given above, except that the cheeks are streaked instead of plain, the speculum violet instead of green and the general coloration rather darker—mottled rather than streaked. It is described by Mr. G. B. Sennett as follows: Top of head blackish-brown, margined with very pale buff. Chin and throat isabella color. Cheeks, buffy white, with narrow streaks of dark brown. Feathers of breast, wings, upper parts and flanks blackish-brown, margined with pale buff. Under parts buffy white, each feather with a broad

97

blackish-brown mark near the tip, giving a decidedly mottled appearance. Under tail-coverts blackish, with outer margins of inner webs reddish-buff; those of outer webs buffy white. The four middle tail feathers blackish-brown, the others brownish. Under surface of all tail feathers light gray. The speculum is metallic purple, its feathers tipped with white. Length about 19 inches, wing 10 inches.

These three forms are so much alike that it is not probable that the average gunner will be able to distinguish them apart. They occupy different regions, and while their ranges probably overlap, it is not likely that the southern forms are ever found much beyond the regions which they are known to inhabit.

The dusky duck, better known as black duck, is the commonest of the fresh-water ducks of Eastern Canada, New Brunswick, Nova Scotia and the New England coast, but when it gets as far south as the Chesapeake Bay and North Carolina it finds there its relative, the mallard, in numbers as great as its own and associates with it on terms of equality.

The black duck, while feeding almost exclusively in fresh water, by no means avoids the sea coast. On the contrary, in the New England States it spends most of the day resting on the salt water and only visits the inland streams, swamps and marshes to feed during the night. In these localities it does not disdain such salt-water food as it may pick up, and in the early morning at low tide I have seen great flocks of these birds feeding on the sand beaches and mud flats off Milford, Conn., where their chief food must have been the winkles that are so abundant there.

The black duck is not common in the interior, though it has been reported from near York Factory. Dr. Yarrow has reported it from Utah, but these birds were perhaps mottled duck (*A. f. maculosa*). I, personally, have not seen it west of Nebraska, and then only on a very few occasions. The specimens then noted may have been mottled ducks. It is occasionally taken in Iowa and Minnesota, but so seldom that most duck shooters do not know the species. Occasionally a man, whose experience extends over fifteen or twenty years of gunning there, will say that he has seen a bird two or three times. It has been reported as breeding in great numbers about forty miles north of Winnipeg, Manitoba.

In mild winters the black duck remains throughout the season in Massachusetts and Connecticut, but sometimes, if the cold is bitter and long-continued, the ice covers its customary feeding grounds, and its food becoming very scarce, it grows so thin that gunners refuse longer to kill it. At such times it sits off shore in the sea, or, if the ice extends very far out from the shore, upon the ice, and almost starves to death. We have once or twice seen birds caught in muskrat traps which were nothing more than skeletons covered by feathers.

In New England the black duck is considered one of the most acute of all our fowl and is very difficult of approach. They usually refuse to notice decoys, and, owing to their keen senses and constant watchfulness, are not shot in great numbers. The gunners believe that their sense of smell is very keen, and will not attempt to approach them down the wind, believing that the ducks will smell them.

The black duck rises from the water in the same manner as the mallard and its note is not to be distinguished from the mallard's. In the Southern States, where they feed chiefly on grasses and rice and wild celery, they are very delicious, but on the New England coast they are sometimes found to be very inferior table birds.

In the South the black ducks often congregate in flocks of several hundred, resorting especially to little flag ponds in the marshes which they especially affect. Here they appear to have lost much of the suspiciousness which they show further north and often come readily to decoys, responding as easily as the mallard to the quacking of duck, man or duck call.

More than almost any of its relatives the black duck seems to be a night feeder, and all night long its cries may be heard through the marsh; yet it is, of course, well known that all ducks feed at night, especially when there is a moon, and the very common belief that the black duck does this more than others may be without foundation.

The black duck is frequently domesticated and does well in confinement, and it readily interbreeds with the mallard, either the wild or the domestic. Domesticated birds are frequently used as decoys, and with great effect.

While the black duck breeds chiefly to the north of the United States, nevertheless many rear their young in Maine, New Hampshire, New York and even as far south as North Carolina, though there is, of course, a possibility that the birds breeding there may belong to the next species. The nest is usually built on the ground, concealed in high grass or rushes, and the eggs vary in number from six to eleven or twelve. They are grayish-white, with a very faint tinge of green. Mr. Geo. A. Boardman, of Calais, Me., however, reports that he once found a dusky duck's nest in a cavity of a leaning birch tree about thirty feet high. The young, from the time they are newly hatched, are expert in hiding, and at the approach of danger make for the shore and conceal themselves among the grasses.

The Florida dusky duck, while very similar to the black duck, may easily be distinguished from it if the characters already mentioned are kept in mind. The general differences are much paler color and absence of streaks on the cheeks, chin, throat and fore-neck, besides a difference in the markings on the bill. This bird was long considered to be a pale southern race of the black duck, but of late years has been considered a valid species. Its range is a very restricted one and is confined apparently to Southern Florida.

In habits it does not differ greatly from the ordinary black duck, except so far as its surroundings necessitate a difference. During the winter it resorts

for food to the fresh-water ponds during the day and
at evening flies to the shores about the islands, where
the night is spent.   The birds mate in late winter and
early spring and the broods are hatched in April.   The
nest is placed in heavy grass or vegetation, which is
often so thick as to conceal the eggs.   Often the nests
are placed at the foot of a palmetto or other bush.   It is
said that many of these nests are destroyed by the burn-
ing of the grass, which takes place each year in certain
portions of Florida in order to make way for the fresh
grass for the cattle.

The eggs of this species are said to be similar to those
of the ordinary black duck, but are a little paler and not
quite so large.   It is altogether probable that all the
black ducks killed in Florida may belong to this species.

The mottled duck described by Mr. Sennett as a sub-
species of the Florida duck, closely resembles it.   The
cheeks, however, are somewhat streaked with brown, as
in the ordinary black duck, though the throat is unstreaked and the general appearance of the bird is
spotted or mottled rather than streaked. The difference
in color of the speculum in these three forms of black
duck is a real one, and of importance.   It denotes the
average effect of color independent of changes due to
the angle at which the light strikes them.

Very little is known about the habits of this sub-
species, which appears to be confined to Eastern Texas
and Louisiana, and to extend its range north as far as
Kansas.

GADWALL.

Anas strepera Linn.

The general colors of the gadwall duck are gray, most of the feathers being nearly white, crossed by narrow bars of black or blackish brown. In the adult male the head and neck are pale brownish-white, thickly speckled with black or blackish-brown. The top of the head and back of neck are often rusty brown and the throat is yellowish, sometimes dotted with brown. The breast and back are buff, or nearly white, marked with dark slate brown or even black bars. The back, scapular feathers and sides, white, with cross bars of black; the lower part of the back still darker changing to absolute black on the upper tail-coverts. The long scapular or shoulder feathers are fringed with reddish-brown; the greater coverts at the bend of the wing bright chestnut. Speculum white, edged beneath with velvety black, and with broad patch of same in front, between the white and the chestnut. Belly and under tail-coverts black; tail gray, fading to white at the edges; the rest of the under parts white. The bill is bluish-black and the legs and feet yellow, with dusky webs. The adult female is much like the male, except that she is duller throughout and she generally lacks the black of the full plumaged male. Usually there is no chestnut on the wing, but the speculum is white and the bird may be known from any other fresh-water ducks by this character. The young are still more dull in color. Often the speculum is indistinct, but there is usually enough of it, with the bill, to identify the species. Mr. Gurdon Trumbull was the first to call attention to the presence in highly plumaged males of a well-defined black ring, extending almost around the neck, between the lighter feathers of the head and neck and the darker ones of the breast.

The gadwall duck is distributed over almost the whole northern hemisphere, being found alike in Europe, Asia, Africa and North America. At the same time it is not an abundant bird anywhere, apparently never occurring in large flocks nor even in frequent small ones.

In North America, however, its distribution is general, but is chiefly westward. Still it has been found breeding on the island of Anticosti, in the Gulf of St.

Lawrence, New England and Long Island, and to the south of this, generally along the Atlantic coast. A female was captured in Bermuda in 1849.

The gadwall is not uncommon in Illinois, Minnesota and generally through the Mississippi Valley, and formerly bred to some extent over the whole country. It is said to be common in California in winter and has been taken on the Pacific coast of Mexico, as well as in British Columbia. Its chief breeding grounds, however, appear to be north of the United States, although no doubt to some extent it passes the summer in the high mountains of the main range from Colorado northward.

The male gadwall is a very handsome bird, particularly striking in his combination of quiet yet effective colors. There are some things about the species which remind one strongly of the widgeon. Often a large flock of widgeons may include a small number of gadwalls, and often the gunner will see from his blind a small flock of birds approaching him, which at first he imagines to be widgeons, but which, when they have come closer, prove gadwalls.

It is difficult to understand why the gadwall is so scarce a bird. It is true that in his ornithological report of the Survey of the Fortieth Parallel Mr. Ridgway tells us that he found it by far the most numerous duck during the breeding season in Western Nevada, where, in the valley of the Truckee River from the base of the Sierra Nevada Mountains to Pyramid Lake, it outnumbered all other species together. Yet there appears to be no region known where it occurs in great flocks, like those better known species with which it commonly associates, as the widgeon and the pintail, and, by comparison with other species, gadwalls are very seldom killed. So far as we know, this bird ought to be on the increase. It seems to differ from most ducks in not being gregarious and in preferring to keep in pairs or very small companies, perhaps made up of the members of a single family. It pays little attention to decoys, and, in my experience, seldom comes to them, although occasionally shot when flying by.*

The gadwall has a number of common names, of which two of the most familiar are gray duck, applied also to two other species, and creek duck, which is used along the Atlantic coast. Besides this it is known as speckle-belly, from the dark markings often seen on the under plumage; blaten duck, which is nearly a translation of its Latin name; Welsh drake and German duck, given by Giraud and probably now obsolete. Its similarity to the widgeon is indicated by its names, widgeon and gray widgeon, used along the southern Atlantic coast, and in England it is sometimes called sand widgeon.

The nest of the gadwall is built on the ground and is a mere depression, lined with dried grass or leaves, and sometimes with down. It is usually near the water's edge and well concealed. The eggs are of a pale creamy yellow.

---

*See lengthy correspondence on this subject in *Forest and Stream*, Vol. lviii, January and February, 1902.

EUROPEAN WIDGEON.

Anas penelope LINN.

This species, so familiar in the Old World, is a not uncommon straggler in North America. It has been killed in so many different places that it is important that it should be described here. In the adult male in autumn and winter the head and sides of neck are bright rufous, almost the color of the head of the male redhead, but without the metallic gloss, or still more like the head of the male green-winged teal. The forehead and crown of head are white, often shaded with rufous, so as to be cream color or even pinkish. The chin is white; throat and part of the front of the neck black. Often there is a cluster of small blackish or greenish feathers behind the eye and on the back of the head, and sometimes the sides of the head are minutely streaked with dusky. The breast is purplish gray; the sides, flanks and back waved with cross-bars of black and white, the effect being somewhat like that of the same parts in the male green-winged teal. The tertiaries, or long feathers growing from the third bone of the wing, are gray on their inner webs and velvety-black, edged with white on the outer. The wing-coverts are white and the speculum or wing-patch brilliant metallic green, sometimes changing to black at the extremity. The upper and lower tail-coverts are black, the other under parts white, the wings and tail brown, the tail often edged with white. The bill is bluish, its nail black, and the legs and feet gray. The length is about 18 inches, wing between 10 and 11 inches.

In the female the head and neck are yellowish-red, dotted with black or greenish spots and sometimes the top of the head is altogether black. The general color of the upper parts is brown, the feathers being edged and barred with whitish. The wing-coverts, instead of being white, are merely tipped with white, while the speculum is dull black or even in the young sometimes grayish. The under parts are white, as in the male.

The female of the European widgeon is not always to be easily distinguished from certain plumages of the American bird, but its bill and general aspect will always identify it as a widgeon, and a specimen about which there is any doubt should always be preserved for submission to an ornithologist.

This species belongs to the Old World, yet has been found over much of the New. It occurs regularly in Alaska and breeds there, and, no doubt, it is due to this fact that it has been killed in California, Illinois, New York, Pennsylvania, Maryland, Virginia and Florida. I have killed it in North Carolina, but it occurs there so seldom that it is not at all known to gunners, and my boatman when he picked up this bird took it at first for a redhead and afterward for a hybrid.

Its habits, as observed in the Old World, do not greatly differ from those of the American widgeon, and it is said to be as numerous in certain parts of Europe as our bird is here.

During the molting season the male loses his bright colors, which, however, are regained in the early fall.

AMERICAN WIDGEON, BALD-PATE.

Anas americana GMEL.

The male bald-pate has the forehead and crown of the head white, margined on either side from the eyes to the back of the head by a broad band of metallic green, the two bands meeting behind and sometimes running a little way down the neck. The head in front of the eyes and the sides and upper neck are white, thickly dotted with black. The throat is nearly white; the lower neck, fore-breast, back and sides lavender or purplish-gray, sometimes quite rich. The feathers of the sides are cross-barred with fine lines of black; the back is finely waved with lines of paler, changing to distinct lines of blackish and white on the lower back; the upper and under tail-coverts glossy black; the tail brownish-gray; the wing-coverts broadly white, some of them tipped with black, so as to make a black bar across the wing. The speculum is green and black; the lower breast and belly white, which extends up on the sides of the rump. The bill is light bluish, with a black tip, and the feet are somewhat darker, with still darker webs.

This is the color of the most highly plumaged males, and from this there are all gradations down to the much duller female, which entirely lacks the green head-patch, the large white wing-patch, and in which the speculum is very much duller, being merely blackish, with a white border in front. The general aspect of the female is streaked and speckled with blackish brown and whitish, becoming darker on the breast and sides of body. The upper parts are grayish and the under parts nearly white, the under tail-coverts being barred with black and white. Young males usually have the breast purplish-gray, the speculum brilliant, and traces of white wing-coverts.

The bald-pate or widgeon is widely distributed throughout America and is found in winter as far south as Mexico and even Central America. It is an occasional straggler to Europe, but is found there only by accident. At the present day it is merely a winter visitor to the United States, except in certain portions of the West, where a few widgeons may still breed on the high central plateau or on the flanks of the Rocky

Mountains. It is not commonly found in New England, yet Mr. Boardman has reported it as found near Calais, Me., and it occurs occasionally on Long Island. Further to the south, however, in Chesapeake Bay and on the coasts of North and South Carolina, it is a common bird in winter, occurring in great flocks and eagerly sought after for its flesh, which is very highly esteemed.

The widgeons reach the United States usually in the month of October, and great numbers of them winter in the Southern States. On the Atlantic coast they are constantly found associated with other species of fresh-water ducks, as well as with the canvas-backs and the redheads. It is said that they especially seek the company of the canvas-backs when these are feeding, and that they rob them of the grasses and celery which they bring up from great depths, which the widgeons could never reach. At all events it is certain that they associate with the canvas-backs, and no doubt they feed largely on the leaves of the plants of which the canvas-backs eat the roots. Certain it is that at these times and in these places the flesh of the widgeon is so excellent that it cannot be distinguished from that of its larger and more famous companion.

The widgeon is regarded as one of the shyest of our ducks. Of it Mr. D. G. Elliot, in his admirable book on the "Wild Fowl of North America," says: "The widgeon is one of the wariest of our ducks, suspicious of everything, and not only is unwilling to approach any spot or object of which it is afraid, but by keeping up a continuous whistling alarms all the other ducks in the vicinity and consequently renders itself very disagreeable and at times a considerable nuisance to the sportsman. However, its flesh is so tender and palatable and it is such a pretty and gamy bird that one is inclined to forgive many of its apparent shortcomings. The usual note of this duck is a low, soft whistle, very melodious in quality, and when on the wing the members of a flock keep continually talking to each other in this sweet tone as they speed along. They fly very rapidly and usually high in the air in a long, outstretched line, all abreast, except perhaps the two ends are a little behind the center bird, who may be considered the leader. When only moving from place to place in the marsh, and but a short distance above the ground, they proceed usually without any order or regularity, reminding one sometimes of a flock of pigeons. The pinions are moved with much quickness and the long primaries give a sharp-pointed shape to the wing that causes the birds to be easily recognized. Flocks composed of a number of widgeon and sprig-tail are often seen, and the combination is a very unfavorable one to a sportsman hoping for a quiet shot at close range.

"As the birds approach the decoys some widgeon will whistle and edge out to one side, as much as to say, 'It may be all right, but I don't like the looks of it,' and he will be followed by another suspicious member. Then the pintails become uneasy and begin to climb and look down into the blind, and the patient watcher sees the flocks too often sheer off to one side and pass by. But should there be some birds present, as often happens, which are heedless of all warnings or suspicious utter-ings, and keep steadily on, with the evident intention to settle among their supposed brethren, then, as they gather together preparatory to alighting and the sports-man rises in his ambush, suddenly the air is filled with darting, climbing birds, who shoot off in every direc-tion, but generally upward as if the flock was blown asunder, and all disappear with a celerity that is aston-ishing, and, to a nervous sportsman, with results that are mortifying."

Notwithstanding this watchfulness, widgeons often come very nicely to decoys, and a passing flock, espe-cially if it be small, may frequently be turned from its course by a low, soft whistle and will swing into the de-coys and drop in a series of beautiful curves until they are almost over them.   Then, however, the gunner must waste no time in selecting his bird and holding properly on it, for the widgeon is able to get out of danger with considerable speed.

This species is extremely common in California, where it is eagerly sought after.   In the Mississippi Valley region it is not so abundant nor so greatly esteemed, for there the mallard, on account of its greater size, is preferred.

The breeding grounds of the widgeon include the whole of British America and Alaska, but its summer home is rather in the western portion of North Amer-ica and away from the seacoast.   The eggs are creamy white in color.

Among the names given by Mr. Gurdon Trumbull, in his excellent work so frequently referred to, are green-headed widgeon, bald-head, southern widgeon, California widgeon, white-belly and poacher. Other names are bald-face, bald-crown, wheat duck and smoking duck.

EUROPEAN TEAL.

Anas crecca LINN.

This is a European species, occurring only casually in North America. It very closely resembles the common green-winged teal, but lacks the white bar on the side of the breast, has the black and white markings of the back and sides much heavier, has the inner webs of the outer scapular and sometimes part of the outer webs, white or yellowish, and the forehead bordered on either side by a pale-buff line. The female is so similar to the female green-winged teal that only an expert ornithologist can distinguish between the two. The European teal is found occasionally in the Aleutian Islands, and it has frequently been exposed for sale in the New York markets with other ducks shot in the neighborhood. The most important distinguishing mark between these two very similar birds is the white bar on each side of the breast, which is so noticeable in our green-winged teal, but absent in the European species.

In December, 1900, two of these teal were killed near Merrick, L. I., N. Y., by Mr. Sherman Smith.

European observers tell us that this teal is abundant over the Old World; that it breeds in Great Britain and Ireland and is common over Lapland, Russia and Northern Asia. It is readily domesticated.

GREEN-WINGED TEAL.

Anas carolinensis GMEL.

The adult male has the head and neck reddish-chest-nut and a broad band of metallic green on either side, running from the eye to the back of the neck, where the two meet in a tuft. The under side of this green band is margined with a narrow line of buff; the chin is black; the breast is reddish cream-color, dotted with round or oval spots of jet black. There is a collar round the lower part of the neck; the sides of the breast, back of lower neck and of the body are finely waved with lines of black upon white ground. The back is similarly marked and the lower back is brownish-gray. The upper tail-coverts are dark, margined with

118

white, and the tail feathers gray, edged with white. On the side of the breast, in front of the bend of the wing, is a broad white bar. The tips of the last row of wing-coverts are margined with yellowish. The speculum is black and green, margined with white. The outer scapulars are velvety-black. The belly and a patch on either side of the under tail-coverts are rich buff, the under tail-coverts black. The bill is dark, nearly black, and the feet grayish-black. The length is about 14½ inches.

The female is brownish, the feathers being generally margined with buff. The sides of head are whitish, speckled with brownish. The wing is like that of the male, but the speculum is somewhat smaller and duller. The breast is usually more or less spotted and the under parts are white, with faint indications of spots.

The green-winged teal is found over the whole of North America, from the Arctic Sea on the north to the Gulf of Mexico and Central America on the south. It occurs also in Cuba. It is one of the most beautiful of our ducks and is highly esteemed by gunners.

Unlike many of our better known fresh-water ducks, the green-winged teal is rather common in New England, as well as in the interior and to the southward, and wherever found it is a great favorite. It flies with astonishing speed, but with great steadiness, and often the flocks are of very great size and fly so closely bunched together that they resemble more a flock of migrating blackbirds than of ducks. At such times, if they suddenly become aware of the presence of the gunner, the bunch flies apart like an exploding bomb and the birds dart in all directions and at such a rate that it takes a quick shooting to catch them. On the other hand, if the shots can be fired into this close mass the havoc created is very great; ten, twenty or thirty birds sometimes being killed by the discharge of two barrels.

While the green-winged teal is much at home on the water and is a good diver in times of danger, it is also very much at home on the land, over which it runs with considerable speed.

Although this species breeds chiefly to the north of the United States, its nests have been taken in Wisconsin, Iowa and on the prairies and in the mountains of the West. I have seen it in Montana, Wyoming and Colorado, accompanied by young, and I recall one occasion in North Park, Colorado, where I spent a very pleasant half hour watching an old female and her young as they busily fed in the narrow stream near where I sat. The mother bird at length discovered me, and though not greatly alarmed, she promptly led her flock of eight tiny young ashore, where, in a long line, with the mother at the head, they promptly trotted into the bushes and concealed themselves.

The green-wing is a more hardy bird than the blue-winged teal and is often found on warm springs and streams in the North long after the ice has closed most of the quiet waters. I have seen it in Connecticut in the early winter, when almost everything was frozen up.

The nest of the teal is commonly placed not far from the water, in high grass or sometimes among a tussock of rye grass, or I have even found it on top of a dry ridge, under a sage brush at quite a long distance from any stream. The eggs are small and apparently a little rounder than duck eggs usually are. The number in a nest varies from ten to fifteen.

BLUE-WINGED TEAL.

Anas discors LINN.

The adult male has the top of the head and the chin black; a white crescent-shaped band, edged with black, extends from the forehead above the eye down to below the bill; the rest of the head is dark lead-color, sometimes with glossy purplish reflections. The long scapulars running back from the shoulder are black, streaked with buff. The back and upper parts generally, dark brown and dull black, spotted, barred and streaked with buff. The lower back is dull brown; the smaller wing-coverts at the bend of the wing sky-blue, as are also some of the long shoulder feathers. A wide bar of white across the wing, above the speculum, which is green, separates the blue and the green. There is a

122

narrow line of white at the extremity of the speculum and a patch on either side of the tail. The lower parts are light chestnut, thickly speckled with black. The under tail-coverts are black, as is also the bill. The eyes, legs and feet are yellow, the latter with dusky markings.

The female is always to be known by the blue markings on the wing, though the brilliant green speculum is often wanting. The chin, throat and base of the bill are white, marked with blackish, and the head and neck streaked and speckled with dusky brown. The other parts are dark brown, speckled with dusky brown. The bird is slightly larger than the green-winged teal.

The blue-winged teal is often called summer teal, and this gives a hint as to one of its habits. It is apparently a bird of more southern distribution than the other teals and is almost the earliest of the migrating ducks to make its appearance. The first to arrive are commonly found on our streams in late August or early September, and persons who are pushing through the marshes in search of rail very frequently start little bunches of blue-wings from the open places. It may be imagined that such birds have not come from a great distance. Indeed, the blue-winged teal breeds at many points in the West, and would do so more frequently were the birds permitted to make their northward migration without being disturbed by gunners.

The blue-wing is common throughout Eastern America, but in the West its place is chiefly taken by the cinnamon teal, a closely related species. In its northward migrations the blue-winged teal is found summering on the Great Slave Lake, and Mr. Dall tells of having seen it on the Yukon, and it has been reported from other points in Alaska. It breeds also in Northern New England, as well as near the prairie sloughs of some of the States of the Central West. The nest is placed on the ground, among reeds and grasses, and is usually, but not always, near the water. It is lined with down from the mother's breast, and when she leaves the nest she covers the eggs with this down and over it places more or less grass. The number of eggs is said to be from eight to twelve.

During the winter these birds reach Mexico and Central America and are commonly found in Florida and the Gulf States. They feed in great numbers in the southern rice fields, where they are reported to be caught in great numbers by means of traps set by the negroes. Teal are abundant in the low country about the mouth of the Mississippi, where they are known to the creoles as printannierre and autonnierre, according to the season in which they are seen.

The teal frequently travel in very large flocks, and the. speed with which they move and the closeness with which they are huddled together have become proverbial among gunners. They come up readily to decoys and not infrequently a large flock may come in without warning to a heedless gunner and drop down among his stools before he sees them. When he stands up to shoot, the teal leave the water as the mallard does, by a single spring, and dart away in all directions, coming together again and going on in a close bunch. If a flock is seen flying by, they may sometimes be attracted by a soft, lisping note, and if they see the decoys they are likely to drop in among them. The blue-winged teal is fond of running about over mud flats and sifting them for food, and in localities where they are abundant a place such as this is one of the very best in which to tie out for them.

As with the green-wing so with this species—great numbers may be killed by the single discharge of a gun, provided it is properly aimed. Audubon speaks of having seen eighty-four birds killed by the single discharge of a double-barreled gun.

CINNAMON TEAL.

Anas cyanoptera VIEILL.

In the adult male the top of the head is blackish-brown, while the rest of the head, the neck and lower parts are bright chestnut. This color grows darker on the belly, until it is quite black on the under tail-coverts. The scapulars, or shoulder feathers, and a part of the back, are chestnut, the feathers having paler edges and the long ones a buff central stripe; these are also barred with black. The smaller wing-coverts and the outer webs of some of the scapulars are sky-blue. The middle coverts are dark, tipped with white, and the speculum is dark metallic green. The tail is blackish, the bill is black, the eyes yellow or orange and the feet are bright yellow, with touches of dusky. The female is very much like the female blue-winged teal, but is larger and some-what more richly colored. The belly is usually dis-tinctly spotted. Length, 17 inches; wing, 7½ inches.

The cinnamon teal is a western species. It is rarely found as far east as the Mississippi Valley, though it has been taken in Florida, but such birds are mere accidental wanderers. The cinnamon teal becomes abundant after the main Continental Divide is crossed and is a common breeder and migrant all through the Rocky Mountains and in California. In summer it is found as far north as the Columbia River, and probably breeds freely all through the Western United States. I have found its nest in Wyoming placed under a small sage bush, thirty or forty yards from a little mountain stream that was nearly dry. It had eleven eggs, ivory-white in color, and there was no down in the nest nor any appreciable lining.

In his account of the cinnamon teal, published in the "Birds of the Northwest," Dr. Coues paints one of those charming word pictures which make his writings such delightful reading as well for sportsmen as for naturalists. He says of it: "I never think of the bird without recalling scenes in which it was a prominent figure. I have in mind a picture of the headwaters of the Rio Verde, in November, just before winter had fairly set in, although frosts had already touched the foliage and dressed every tree and bush in gorgeous colors. The atmosphere showed a faint yellow haze and was heavy with odors—souvenirs of departing flowers. The sap of the trees coursed sluggishly, no

longer lending elastic vigor to the limbs, that now
cracked and broke when forced apart; the leaves
loosened their hold, for want of the same mysterious
tie, and fell in showers where the quail rustled over their
withering forms. Woodpeckers rattled with exultation
against the resounding bark and seemed to know of
the greater store for them now in the nerveless, drowsy
trees that resisted the chisel less stoutly than when they
were full of juicy life. Ground squirrels worked hard,
gathering the last seeds and nuts to increase their winter's store, and cold-blooded reptiles dragged their stiffening joints to bask in sunny spots and stimulate the
slow current of circulation before they should with-
draw and sink into torpor. Wildfowl came flocking
from their northern breeding places—among them
thousands of teal—hurtling overhead and plashing in
the waters they were to enliven and adorn all winter.

"The upper parts of both forks of the Verde are
filled with beavers that have dammed the streams at
short intervals and transformed them in some places
into a succession of pools, where the teal swim in still
water. Other wildfowl join them, such as mallards,
pintails and green-wings, disporting together. The approach to the open waters is difficult in most places
from the rank growths, first of shrubbery and next of
reeds, that fringe the open banks; in other places, where
the stream narrows in precipitous gorges, from the almost inaccessible rocks. But these difficulties overcome, it is a pleasant sight to see the birds before us—
perhaps within a few paces if we have very carefully

crawled through the rushes to the verge—fancying themselves perfectly secure. Some may be quietly paddling in and out of the sedge on the other side, daintily picking up the floating seeds that were shaken down when the wind rustled through, stretching up to gather those still hanging or to pick off little creatures from the seared stalks. Perhaps a flock is floating idly in midstream, some asleep, with the head resting close on the back and the bill buried in the plumage. Some others swim vigorously along, with breasts deeply immersed, tasting the water as they go, straining it through their bills to net minute insects, and gabbling to each other their sense of perfect enjoyment. But let them appear never so careless, they are quick to catch the sound of coming danger and take alarm; they are alert in an instant; the next incautious movement or snapping of a twig startles them; a chorus of quacks, a splashing of feet, a whistling of wings, and the whole company is off. He is a good sportsman who stops them then, for the stream twists about, the reeds confuse and the birds are out of sight almost as soon as seen.

"Much as elsewhere, I presume, the duck hunter has to keep his wits about him and be ready to act at very short notice; but there is double necessity on the Verde. The only passages along the stream are Indian trails, here always warpaths. In retaliation for real or fancied wrongs—or partly, at least, from inherent disposition—these savages spend most of their time in wandering about in hopes of plunder and murder; this, too, against each other, so long as the tribes are not leagued in common cause against a common enemy. On the day I have in mind more particularly we passed a spot where lay the bodies of several Apachés. From the arrows still sticking in them we judged afterward that they had been killed by a stray band of Navajos. But this was not what we thought most about at the time. We were only four together and this was close by the place we designed to spend the day in hunting and fishing. Contemplation of the decaying Indians was not calculated to raise our spirits, for though, of course, we knew the danger beforehand and meant to take our chances, it was not pleasant to have the thing brought up in such a way. We kept on through the canyon a little more cautiously, talked a little more seriously and concluded to look for game in places where there was the least likelihood of an ambuscade. I confess that the day's sport was rather too highly spiced to be altogether enjoyable, and suspect that others shared my uncomfortable conviction of foolhardiness. However, the day passed without further intimation of danger. Game was plenty and the shooting good. Out of the woods and with a good bag, we were disposed and could better afford to laugh at each other's fears."

The habits of the red-breasted teal do not differ markedly from that of the eastern relative, which it so closely resembles.

The true home of this species seems to be in Southern North America and South America, and it is found in Chili, Patagonia and the Falkland Islands. It is a bird that gives great shooting to western sportsmen.

SHOVELLER.

Spatula clypeata (LINN.).

The male shoveller has the head and the upper neck very dark glossy green, with violet reflections, an entirely different color from that of the mallard, almost black. The lower neck and breast are white; belly and sides rich chestnut brown. The under tail-coverts and vent are black, bordered by a gray line, a patch of white at either side of the rump. The back is dusky brown; the upper tail-coverts black; the long scapulars, or shoulder feathers, streaked with black and white; the wing-coverts are light blue, the last row tipped with white, forming a narrow band across the wing, and back of this is a bright green speculum nar-

rowly bordered by white.   The tail is whitish, blotched
with brownish-gray.   The expanded bill is black, the
eyes yellow and the feet orange-red.

The female is colored very much as is the female
mallard, but has the blue wing-coverts and the green
speculum.   The belly is sometimes pure white.   The
bill is orange or brown, often speckled with black.   The
feet are orange.   Length, about 19 inches; wing, 9 to
10 inches.

Young males of different ages have the plumage
generally like the female, but as they grow older the
head and neck are mottled with black and the under
parts are often chestnut.   Whatever the plumage, the
shoveller may be recognized by the great expansion of
the bill toward the tip, which gives it the name spoon-
bill.   This bill has a fringe of very slender, close-set
lamellæ, which are long yet flexible, and are admirably
adapted to the process of sifting out food from the fine
soft mud in which the shoveller delights to feed.

This species is one of the most widely distributed of
all the ducks, being found throughout the whole of the
northern hemisphere.   In North America it is nowhere
a very abundant duck, but, at the same time, is frequently met with throughout the South and West; yet
it never appears in great flocks, as do the black duck,
mallard, widgeon and the teals, but rather in small, occasional companies, though I have seen a flock number-
ing nearly a hundred.   This, however, is unusual.

On the New England coast and Long Island the
shoveller is quite an uncommon bird, but further to the

southward, as in Maryland and North Carolina, it is
frequently killed. In many of its ways, as, of course,
in its appearance in some respects, it resembles the teals,
but it is much less gregarious in its habits. The shoveller breeds from Texas to Alaska, and I have frequently found the nests in Dakota, Montana and Wyoming, usually near prairie lakes, often under a bunch
of rye grass or a sage brush and usually fairly well concealed. There are usually a few feathers and some down
in the nest, which contains eight or ten greenish-white
eggs. The female sits close, but when startled from
her nest flies away without sound and soon disappears.

The young, when first hatched, do not show the peculiar shape of the bill possessed by the adult, this being
a later development. Young birds of the first season,
when killed in the fall, will be found to have the bill
very flexible, so that it can be bent in every direction.
The shoveller is a fine table bird, but because of the
small numbers that are killed it is not very well known.

Mr. Trumbull gives as the names for this bird the
blue-winged shoveller, red-breasted shoveller, shovel-
bill, broady, butler duck—"the bird being so called because of its spoon-like bill, and with reference to a well-
known general in the civil war"—cow-frog, spoon-billed
widgeon, spoon-billed teal, mud-shoveller and swaddle-
bill. In Louisiana the bird is known as mesquin. The
note of the shoveller is a weak quack, somewhat like
that of the green-winged teal.*

*Compare "California Duck Notes," by Robert Erskine Ross,
Forest and Stream, Vol. lix, p. 67, July 26, 1902.

PINTAIL.

Dafila acuta (LINN.).

The male pintail has the head and upper neck wood brown, darkest on the crown, often with greenish, reddish and purple reflections. A part of the hind neck is black; lower down it becomes grayish, finely barred with dusky, gray and white. The front of back and sides are waved with very fine cross bars of white and black. Most of the wing is gray or brownish. The speculum is green, in some lights coppery, margined with white, tawny and black, and with a cinnamon-colored bar in front. A line beginning at the back of the head and passing down the side of neck is white, running into the white of the fore-neck and under parts. The long feathers growing from the third bone of the wing are pale gray, with a black strip down the middle. The long scapulars, or shoulder feathers, are black, edged with whitish. The upper and under tail-coverts are black, touched with white on the outside, forming a line of white. The tail feathers are mostly gray and brown, but the long central pair, which are narrow and pointed, and extend far beyond the others, are black. The bill is bluish-gray, eyes brown, and the legs and feet gray. Length, 26-30 inches; wing, over 10 inches.

The female is one of the plain grayish ducks, resembling in a general way the female mallard, or the female green-winged teal. The ground color of the upper parts is rusty or whitish, streaked with dusky or brownish. The chin and throat are whitish; the wing-coverts brownish-gray, edged with white. The under parts are white, streaked with dusky. The bird is always to be distinguished by its bill and its feet.

The pintail is a bird of wide distribution, inhabiting the whole of the northern hemisphere, from Alaska on the west to Japan and Northern Kamschatka on the east. In America it is found all over the country, at different seasons of the year, from ocean to ocean, and from the shores of the Gulf of Mexico to the Arctic Sea. In winter it is found in Cuba also. Although breeding in Alaska, on the Mackenzie River, and in Greenland, it is also a summer resident of the Western United States, and breeds in considerable numbers in Dakota, Idaho, Montana and Wyoming. I have found their nests there in the middle of June, the young not yet having made their appearance.

The pintail is not very abundant in autumn on the New England coast, though it is found occasionally in Maine and Massachusetts, and in somewhat greater abundance in Connecticut, where it is known as pheasant. On Long Island it is more common during the migrations, and when we reach the coast of Virginia and North Carolina it is one of the abundant ducks. Here it often associates with the mallard and black duck, and when the birds fly to and fro from their feeding grounds, a small bunch may contain four or five mallards, two or three black ducks and an equal number of pintails. On the other hand, little flocks made up only of pintails are often seen.

In the first volume of the "Water Birds" Dr. Brewer gives the following abridgment of Mr. Kennicott's account of the pintail in the north: "The summer home of the pintail is within the Arctic region, farther to the northward than that of any other of our fresh-water ducks, comparatively few breeding south of Great Slave Lake. In their spring migrations to the northward they move in immense flocks, which only disperse upon their arrival at their breeding grounds. A few reach that lake about May 1, but the main body arrive about a week or so later, and mostly pass directly on across the lake to the northward. On the Yukon the first specimens were seen in the latter part of April, and before the 10th of May they had arrived in immense flocks, which remained some time together in that vicinity before passing farther north or separating to breed. At this time the birds were fat, and their flesh delicious, much superior to that of any other duck, except the widgeon. At the Yukon the pintails are the latest in nesting of any of the fresh-water ducks, and generally hatch a week or two after the mallard. He found them breeding in the same grounds and at about the same time, with *Fulix affinis,* though they do not associate with that species. He always found their nests in low but dry ground, under the shelter of trees or bushes, though never among thick, large trees, and not more than two or three rods from water. They never build on hummocks in the water, nor on high land, but always just upon the edge of a marsh or lake. The nest is usually placed at the foot of a willow, among grass rather than leaves or moss, and is extremely simple, being composed of merely a few bits of broken dry grass and sticks, but well lined with down. The eggs are from seven to nine in number, and rather small in size."

Mr. E. W. Nelson, whose studies of northern birds are so interesting, has given a graphic account of the breeding habits of the pintail, and, among other things, calls attention to an act by this duck curiously similar to the well-known drumming of the snipe. The bird falls from a great height, with wings held stiff and curved, and producing a sound which at first is low, but gradually grows louder, until, as the bird reaches the ground in its diagonal fall, the sound becomes very loud. A man who has had a bunch of canvas-backs or black-heads sweep down over him as they prepare to alight, can well imagine what this sound is like. The cry of the pintail in autumn and winter is a low, lisping whistle, but at other times it is. said to utter a sound something like the quack of the mallard, and also one similar to the rolling note produced by the black-head.

The pintail is quite a shy bird; its usual flight is high in the air, which gives it an opportunity to inspect the country for signs of danger. Often, however, if the weather is favorable, these birds come well to decoys, and are easily killed.

There are few more graceful species than this. The long pointed wings, the slender form, terminating in a long neck and tail, and the swift flight, make the bird a very beautiful one.

This species rejoices in many names, and some of them given by Mr. Trumbull are pied gray duck, gray widgeon, sea widgeon, split-tail, sprig-tail, spike-tail, picket-tail, sea pheasant, water pheasant, long neck, sharp-tail and spindle-tail.

WOOD DUCK.

Aix sponsa (LINN.).

The adult male has the head and long thick crest rich green and purple, with brilliant metallic reflections. A narrow line of white starts from the upper angle of the bill, passing over the eye, and continuing down into the crest. Another wider line starts behind the eye and runs down into the under part of the crest. The throat and upper neck are white, sending out two branches, one up behind the eye, another back behind the head, partly enclosing the violet black of the lower back of the head. The lower neck and breast are rich chestnut glossed with purple, dotted in front with triangular

spots of white.   The back is purplish-black, with glossy
reflections, as are also the upper wing-coverts.   The
shoulder feathers and tertiaries are black, with blue,
green and purple reflections, and the longest of the tertiary feathers is tipped with white.   On the side of the
breast, just in front of the wing, is a broad white bar,
and below it, another bar, which is black.   The sides
and flanks are finely waved with black lines on a brown-
ish-yellow ground, many of the feathers having a bar
of black, bordered with white at the extremities.   The
under parts are pure white, but the under tail-coverts
are glossy black.   The upper tail-coverts are long, fall
over the tail on either side, and are rich with metallic
reflections.   The bill is deep red, with a black spot near
the base, a white spot on the side, a yellow border to
the base, and with a black nail.   The eyes are bright
carmine red, surrounded by orange-red or scarlet eye-
lids.   The legs and feet are yellow, with dusky joints
and webs.

The adult female is generally gray, or greenish-gray,
but her markings, in a general way, resemble those of
the male.   She has the crest, but not so much of it as
the male.   The throat and under parts are white; the
breast and sides greenish-gray, dotted with white markings; the upper parts are more brownish, and have
purple and bronzy reflections.   The secondaries are
white-tipped.   The bill is dusky, and there is a narrow
line of white all about it.   The length is about 19 inches,
wing 9½ inches.

The wood duck is easily the most beautiful of North

American ducks. It is commonly compared with the mandarin duck of China, but it is larger and its dress is a little more highly colored, and while more rich, is yet more simple.

This is a bird of the South, and breeds everywhere throughout the Eastern and Southern United States, in suitable localities. Unlike most of our ducks, it is not a migrant to the far North, though it has been found as far North as latitude 54 degrees, but it confines itself pretty well to the United States, and further to the southward.

The wood duck is a bird of swamps and small inland waters, and is notable as being one of the few species which always nests in trees. Sometimes it takes possession of a hole excavated by a great woodpecker, or it may adapt a hollow in a trunk or branch to its use. It is very much at home in the timber, and threads its way among the tree-tops at great speed. The eggs are often laid on the bare wood that forms the floor of the cavity which it occupies, but, as incubation goes on, the mother plucks more or less down from her breast to cover them. When the young are hatched, if the nest is over the water, they crawl to the opening and throw themselves into the air to fall into the water. If, however, the nest is at a distance from the shore, the mother carries them to the water in her bill. When the young ducks are hatched their claws are exceedingly sharp, and they are great climbers. They thus have little difficulty in making their way to the mouth of the hole.

The wood duck is often kept in confinement, and is a beautiful pet. There are many records of its having been bred in captivity.

While a great many wood ducks are shot, they are nowhere sufficiently numerous to make it worth while to gun especially for them. Those that are killed are taken chiefly by accident, when they fly near to decoys put out for other fowl. Being shot at all seasons of the year they are becoming very scarce and are likely to be exterminated before long.

DIVING DUCKS.

SUB-FAMILY *Fuligulinæ.*

Under this head are included what are commonly known as the sea ducks, deep water ducks, or diving ducks, birds more fitted for a continuous life on the water than those heretofore described, and which, as a rule, derive their sustenance from water deeper than that frequented by the shoal-water ducks.

As pointed out in another place, these birds have larger feet than the shoal-water ducks, while the legs are placed further back. These characters make progression on land more difficult, but assist markedly in swimming and diving. All the birds of this sub-family may be known by having a web or lobe hanging down from the hind toe. This web or lobe is absent in all the fresh-water ducks. The sea ducks or diving ducks are supposed to spend most of their time on the salt water, but this is a rule to which there are a multitude of exceptions, and many of the species of this sub-family resort to inland waters to rear their young. Some birds commonly regarded as exclusively marine are found at all seasons of the year on great bodies of fresh water, as the Great Lakes and Yellowstone Lake in Wyoming.

As stated, most of the members of this sub-family procure their food by diving, and bring up from the depths of water fish, mollusks and grasses of one kind and another. Many of them are, therefore, not delicate food, although, on the other hand, the far-famed canvas-back, which belongs to this group, is one of the choicest of our ducks.

There are various strongly marked anatomical and other differences within the group, which do not require consideration here. They are described at length in various ornithological works.

Mr. Elliot has pointed out that, as a rule, the notes of these birds are harsh and guttural.

While the fresh-water ducks usually spend their time in the marshes and in fresh-water ponds during the day, the sea ducks, as a rule, resort to wide stretches of open water, where in moderate weather they rest during the middle of the day, resorting to their feeding grounds at evening, and sometimes feeding during the night and well into the morning.

RUFOUS-CRESTED DUCK.

Netta rufina (Pall.).

The adult male has the sides of head and throat pur-
plish-brown, darker on the throat, and changing to
pale reddish at the front and base of the crest, becoming
paler toward the tips of the feathers. The lower half
of the neck, with a narrow strip running up the back of
the neck to the head, the breast, belly, lower tail-coverts,
upper tail-coverts and rump, black; darkest on the neck
and breast, and with greenish reflections on upper tail-
coverts. Back, grayish-brown, growing darker toward
the rump. The scapulars, or shoulder feathers, brown-
ish-yellow. Speculum, white tipped with gray. The
bend of the wing, white, as are also the primaries, except the tips of some of the outer ones, which are gray-

ish-brown.   The sides and flanks, white, indistinctly
marked with brownish bars.   The tail is grayish-
brown; the bill and feet red.   There is a full, soft crest
on the crown of the head.   Length, 22 inches; wing,
10 inches.

The female has much less crest than the male, and it
is brown.   The rest of the head and neck, and the lower
parts, generally, are pale ashy, darker on the breast and
sides.   The upper parts are grayish-brown.   Those portions that are white in the male are faintly marked in
the female, or do not show at all.   The speculum is
white, as in the male, but much duller.

This is an Old World species, very doubtfully attributed to North America.   It may be questioned
whether it has ever been seen here in life by an ornithologist, but specimens have been found in the New
York markets for sale, with other ducks which were
known to have been killed near that city.   No sportsman is likely to meet with it, but it is introduced here to
complete the list of North American ducks.

CANVAS-BACK DUCK.

Aythya vallisneria (WILS.).

The adult male has the top of the head and the feathers immediately about the base of the bill and chin, black; the rest of head and neck are reddish-brown, what would be called in a horse, mahogany bay. The lower neck, fore-back and breast, black. The back, lower breast and belly, white, very finely waved with black bars; whence the name, canvas-back. Primaries, black. The tail, black, with a grayish cast; bill, black; iris, red; feet, lead color.

The female has those parts which in the male are red, brown and black, wood-brown, with touches of whitish behind the eye, and on the fore-neck. The plumage, generally, is grayish-brown, the tips of the

147

feathers often being whitish, and vermiculated with dusky. The length is 20 to 22 inches.

Of the American ducks, the canvas-back is easily the most famous. Its flesh depends for its flavor entirely on the food that the bird eats, and since for many years it was chiefly killed where the so-called wild celery abounds, the reputation of the canvas-back was made by the individuals that fed on this grass.

As a matter of fact, it may be doubted whether in waters where this plant is abundant the canvas-back is any better than some of its fellows of the duck tribe, such as the redhead or the widgeon, which subsist largely on the same food. But the fame of the canvas-back is now too firmly established ever to be shaken, and it will continue to be regarded, as it has so long been, as the king of our ducks.

The canvas-back is an American species, and has not even any close relatives in the Old World. In winter it ranges south as far as Central America, but confines itself to no portion of the country, being equally abundant on both coasts, and in the interior as well. I have killed it on the Atlantic coast, as well as in Southern California; and during the migrations it is abundant in Montana, and generally throughout the interior.

Years ago the canvas-back bred in the Northern United States, toward the west, probably in Minnesota, certainly in Dakota and Montana, but, as with so many other species, the settling up of the northern country has destroyed its breeding grounds, and it now, for the most part, passes far to the northward to breed. Dr.

Dall found it breeding at Fort Yukon, in Alaska. Mr. Ross met with it on Great Slave Lake; and other northern observers have detected it throughout the fur countries. Besides this, Captain Bendire found it breeding in Oregon, and Dr. Newberry believed that he had obtained evidence of its nesting in the Cascade range. The nest of the canvas-back is large and well built, and is lined with down and feathers, plucked from the breast of the mother bird. The eggs are grayish-green in color and number from seven to nine.

On their return from the North the canvas-backs reach the United States late in October or early in November. They are hardy birds, and it seems that it takes cold weather to drive them southward. On the New England coast they are very rare, though a few used to be killed there. On Long Island they scarcely ever occur of late years, nor are they found in great numbers on the Virginia coast. In North Carolina, however, and along the open broad waters which fringe that State and South Carolina, canvas-backs are very abundant. They used to be so, also, in the Chesapeake Bay, but continual gunning and the destruction of their feeding grounds by frequent floods, which kill the plants on which they subsist, have made them there much less abundant than they used to be. The shooting grounds in Chesapeake Bay and Susquehanna Flats, which a few years ago afforded such good gunning that they were bought or rented at fabulous prices, are no longer so much frequented by the birds, and have become much less valuable.

Like many others of our game birds, the canvas-back during the last few years has learned a good deal. Always a shy and wary bird and difficult of approach, it has learned to avoid the shores, and perhaps is gradually learning to avoid the bush-blind. As its diving powers are great and it is not obliged to fly over the land to get to its feeding grounds, it spends its time in great rafts, on the shallow open waters of such sounds as Currituck, Pamlico, Core and Albemarle, feeding safe from danger, and during the morning and evening hours taking its exercise by flying great distances up and down the sounds, high in air, far above the reach of any gun. It is only in dull and rainy weather, when the wind blows hard, that the canvas-backs come in from the open water to seek the shelter of a lee of the marsh, but when such weather comes and the gunner is properly located, the canvas-backs will come to his decoys as readily as any other ducks. In the same way, when—as happens usually at least once each year—a cold snap closes the waters of the sound, leaving only a few air holes, where warm springs or swiftly moving currents keep the waters open, the canvas-back and other fowl resorting to these open spots may be killed in great numbers. On such an occasion, in January, 1900, I saw canvas-backs in numbers greater than I ever beheld before. An account of this flight, published in *Forest and Stream*, is as follows:

"I have recently had an opportunity of being brought into what I may call close association with the greatest of all the wildfowl, the superb canvas-back duck, and

within the last ten days have seen more of these birds
and at closer quarters than during any season for many
years. The locality was Currituck Sound, and the
sights that I saw were witnessed by several others, old
gunners, who agree with me that so great a flight of
canvas-backs has not been witnessed for many years.

"The first few days of shooting had about it nothing
very startling except that one-half the bag of ducks
consisted of canvas-backs. The first day was cold, gray
and lowering, with a keen breeze from the northwest,
and occasional spatters of rain, changing later to snow,
which in the afternoon fell heavily. It was an ideal
gunning day, and the birds came to the decoys in beautiful style, so that the first seven or eight canvas-backs
were killed without a single miss, and for a brief and
happy hour I was deluded into the belief that at last
I had learned how to shoot ducks. The rude awaken-
ing from this cheerful dream came soon afterward, and
was thorough. I do not imagine that I shall ever again
be deceived in this way.

"The second day's shooting was not markedly different from that of the day before, except so far as the
weather was less favorable, and so the number of canvas-backs secured was very much less. Saturday was a
lay day, on which there is no shooting, and when we
arose we found that the continued cold weather had at
last had its effect and the sound was frozen over. There
were many large air holes, however, crowded with
birds, but the cold continued. The next morning many
of these air holes had frozen, others had grown smaller

and the natural result was that the ducks, geese, swans
and blue-peters which occupied the open water seemed
crowded together as thickly as possible.   Much of the
day was spent on top of the club house, studying the
waters with the glass, watching the movements of the
birds, marveling at their inconceivable numbers.   All
around the horizon, except on the landward side—that
is to say, for 270 degrees of the circle—birds were seen
in countless numbers.   Turning the glasses slowly
along the horizon from northwest to north, east, south
and southwest, there was no moment at which clouds of
flying fowl could not be seen in the field of sight, and
yet, notwithstanding the numbers of birds seen on the
wing, the air holes seemed to be packed with fowl, and
great bunches of geese and swans stood and walked
about on the ice.

"Away to the north were three large air holes, two of
which were white with canvas-backs, while in the third
one, geese were the prominent fowl, although many
canvas-backs were constantly leaving and coming to it.
Off to the southeast, at the south mouth of the Little
Narrows, was quite an extent of open water occupied
by a horde of geese, two large bunches of blue-peters
and some thousands of common ducks.   In the Little
Narrows, a deep but narrow channel flowing close by
the house, were great numbers of ducks feeding, and indeed on that Sunday one might have sat on the boathouse dock and killed from thirty to fifty birds as they
traded up and down the Narrows.

"In the afternoon three or four of us walked down to

Sheep Island Point, not ten minutes' distance from the house, where there was an air hole. In this at the moment of our arrival swam fifty or sixty ducks—hooded mergansers, ruddies, mallards, whistlers, butter-balls and perhaps a dozen canvas-backs. Three or four hundred yards to the north was another small air hole, perhaps four or five acres in extent, which was crowded with canvas-backs. We sat down in the fringe of sedge about 60 or 70 yards from the nearest air hole, which had a length of perhaps 150 feet and a breadth of 100. The live birds in this air hole would make good decoys, and we hoped that if the fowl began to fly some of them would alight near us. Two of the four men were provided with good field glasses.

"We had not been waiting many minutes, when what we had hoped for took place. A bunch of 200 birds rose from the further air hole, and after swinging about a few times, dropped down in the one close to us. These were immediately followed by other bunches, and these by others; so that often two or three flocks would be swinging about in the air at one time, and all of them with our air hole as their objective point. They descended into it by companies of fifties, hundreds and two hundreds, and before long the open water was so crowded with the fowl that it seemed as if it could hold no more, and as if the birds that came next must necessarily alight on the backs of their comrades.

"Soon after the birds alighted they began to dive for food, and, probably one-half of them being under water at any one moment, room was made for other incom-

ing birds to occupy. The splashing of the diving ducks
made the water bubble and boil, and the play of the
birds as they sometimes chased each other made the
scene one of the greatest possible animation. Presently
something occurred to attract their attention, and all
stretched their necks up into the air and looked. I
think I have never seen anything in the way of feathered animal life more impressive than this forest of
thick necks, crowned by long, shapely heads of rich
brown. After their curiosity was satisfied they began
again to feed and to play. It is impossible to convey to
one who has not witnessed such a sight its interest and
fascination. . Here within gunshot—and when seen
through the glasses appearing within arm's length—
were twelve or fifteen hundred of the most desirable
duck that flies, entirely at home and living for the
benefit of the observers their ordinary winter lives.

"Looking with the glasses over the smooth ice away
to the northward, we could see flying over the ice, or
resting on it, fowl as far as the eye could reach. From
the level of the ice where we sat, the ducks, resting on
the water, appeared only as indistinct lines. The geese
were, of course, larger and darker, and made distinct
black lines; while some very distant swans, resting on
the ice, were magnified by the illusive effects of the mi-
rage, so that they looked like detached white houses.
While we sat watching the canvas-backs, two or three
small flocks of geese swung around over the air hole,
but finding no spot where they might moisten the soles
of their feet, they alighted on the ice just beyond it.

"We sat and watched the fowl until the increasing chill of the air and the sinking sun warned us to return to the house. As we arose without any precautions the canvas-backs at once became alert, and as we pushed our way among the reeds away from the shore the whole mass rose with a mighty roar of wings and a splashing of water that made one think more of the noise of Broadway when traffic is heaviest than anything else that I can recall.

"That night it was again cold, and in the morning the Little Narrows was closed by ice, except for a few air holes, and the open water in the sound was still less. The ice was not yet sufficiently strong to bear a man, and yet it was too heavy to be broken through by a boat. Numbers of the shore gunners endeavored to get out to the air holes to shoot there, but none, I think, succeeded. Those of us at the house shot at various nearby points, with moderate success, one man making the great score of sixty-six canvas-backs, besides some other ducks.

"That night after dinner one of the party stepped out on the porch of the house to look at the weather. The night was clear and cold, brilliant stars twinkled in the sky; through the branches of the trees over the boathouse corner, and reflected in the placid waters of an air hole in the Narrows, shone the crescent of the young moon, embracing between its horns the dull globe which was yet to grow. The scene was odd and beautiful, like a stage effect of some mediæval scene. As he stood there, delighting in the beauty of the night, yet nipped a little by the keen frost, a curious sound—like that made by a river running over the pebbles of a shallow— came to his ear. It recalled to the veteran salmon angler the murmur of the Restigouche as through forest and open and deep pool and murmuring shoal it hurries on its way to the Bay of Chaleurs. He wondered what could cause this sound in this place, and above all on such a night, and, walking down to the boat house, passed through it and stood on the dock. Here the explanation of the sound was plain. The air holes which during the day had enlarged were crowded with feeding canvas-backs, and the murmur of the water was neither more nor less than the splashing made by the fowl as they dived for food.

"The freeze lasted for some days longer. The birds were abundant; but the weather, clear, windless and toward the last warm, was much against the gunning, since the fowl did not fly. Nevertheless one or two men at different times had good shooting—some of them better than they had ever enjoyed before or expect ever to have again. This shooting was largely at canvas-backs, since very few common ducks were shot. The freeze having closed their feeding grounds, they sat about on the ice, unwary and inert, waiting till the waters should open again, and in the meantime starving. Under such circumstances no one cared to kill them. On the other hand, the canvas-backs taken were unusually heavy and fine birds.

"Across the sound, on the waters of a neighboring club, very great shooting was enjoyed, though they secured practically no canvas-backs. On the other hand, they made enormous bags of geese and swans, something which no one can regret, since the geese and the swans at Currituck Sound are so numerous that they eat up vast quantities of the food which might better be consumed by the ducks. There are men long familiar with these waters who declare that the geese and the swans are constantly becoming more and more abundant and that ultimately they will occupy these waters to the exclusion of more desirable fowl. This, however, is not likely to occur in our time, and the prophecy may be classed with another, made twenty years ago by one of the most eminent ornithologists of this country, who declared that fifteen years from that time the blue-peter would be the game bird of Currituck Sound. The years have come and the years have gone, but there are still a few canvas-backs left, and it is possible that when our children tie out in Currituck Sound in just the right weather they, too, may kill a few of these glorious birds."

The food of the canvas-back, from which it takes its specific name, and to which it owes its delicious flavor, is the so-called wild celery, which is really a water grass. It grows both in fresh and brackish water, and is common at various points along the sea-coast, and also in the fresh waters of the interior.

This plant, like many others, has a variety of common names. Some of the most familiar in different localities are "tape grass," from the tape-like appearance of the long leaves; "channel weed," as it fre-

quently grows in channels where the water flows, not
swiftly; "eel grass"—this name arises, it is said, by Dr.
Darlington, from the habit which eels have of hiding
under the leaves, which are usually procumbently floating under the water's surface. The appellation "wild
celery," a local term applied originally perhaps only by
gunners and watermen at Havre de Grace and vicinity,
is, like many vulgar synonyms, a misnomer, as this
plant is in no particular related to celery, which by
botanists is known as *Apium*. Wild celery, or, as it is
more generally known along the coast, eel grass, is not
confined to the Chesapeake Bay or to the sea-coast. It
is found in the Brandywine Creek, growing in slow-
running water, and in many other interior waters. The
scientific name of the plant is *Vallisneria spiralis*
(Linn.), the generic name being given in honor of An-
tonio Vallisneri, an Italian botanist. It is a diœcious
herbaceous plant remarkable on account of its mode of
fertilization. It grows entirely under water, has long
radical grass-like leaves from one to three feet long
and from one-quarter to three-quarters of an inch wide.
The female flower floats at the surface at the end of
long thread-like spiral scapes, which curiously contract
and lengthen with the rise and fall of the water. The
male flower has very short stems or scapes, from which
the flowers break off and rise to the surface to fertilize
the pollen of the attached floating female flowers.

The canvas-back is one of the swiftest of all our
ducks. It is commonly said that they fly at the rate of
ninety miles an hour, but, of course, this is a mere

guess, since no accurate observations have ever been made on their flight. It is certain that they proceed at great speed, and the novice at canvas-back shooting is very sure to shoot behind them until he has had a great deal of practice.

The canvas-backs start from their southern home toward the north early in March and follow the coast and the interior northward, often reaching northern waters before they are generally open. On the breeding grounds they are practically undisturbed.

REDHEAD DUCK.

Aythya americana (EYT.).

In general aspect like the canvas-back, for which it is often mistaken. The adult male has the feathers of the head full and puffy. The head and neck are bright reddish-chestnut, often glossy with coppery reflections; the upper part of back, lower neck, breast and rump, and upper and under tail-coverts, black. The back, shoulder feathers of the wing, sides and flanks, whitish, cross-marked with black lines, slightly wider than in the canvas-back, thus giving the whole plumage a darker tone. The speculum is pale bluish-gray, bordered with black above and tipped with white. The primaries are dusky, some of the inner quills being dark slaty-gray. The tail is dusky. The bill is pale blue, black at the tip, the eyes yellow, and the feet are bluish-gray. The abdomen is white.

The female is a plain brownish duck, almost white on the forehead, chin and sides of the head. The lower neck, sides and flanks are brown, as are the lower parts generally, but the lower tail-coverts are white. The speculum is as in the male.

Like the canvas-back, the redhead is a bird of general distribution through North America. It is very common in migration on the Atlantic coast, as well as in the interior and on the Pacific coast. Mr. Ridgway found it common and evidently breeding at Sacramento, Cal., in June, 1867, as well as in Nevada, where he saw beautiful decoys made of its skin by the Piute Indians. It is said not to reach Alaska in summer, but is found breeding throughout the Hudson's Bay country, east of the Rocky Mountains. Formerly it bred in great numbers in the United States, in Michigan, Wisconsin, Minnesota, Dakota, Montana and Wyoming, but the continual persecution to which the redhead, with our other ducks, is subjected in spring has driven it from many of these ancient breeding grounds. There are some localities, however, in the Middle West occupied by gunning clubs where spring shooting is not allowed, and here the redhead and some other varieties of ducks stop and breed, with the result that in the autumn the club members have shooting far better than they ever did when spring shooting prevailed. Birds that have been bred on the grounds are gentle and wonted, and act as decoys to their relatives migrating from the North, calling them down and giving them confidence that here, at least, is a place where they may be free from persecution.

In winter the redhead is found as far south as Mexico and Southern Texas, but is more common further to the northward, and, indeed, goes but little south of the region where open water is found. It is abundant during the migrations on Long Island, but is not common on the New England coast. Each autumn and winter, however, redheads are shot in great numbers on Great South Bay, but rarely or not at all on Long Island Sound. On the eastern shore of Virginia, in Chesapeake Bay, and on the sounds along the coasts of North and South Carolina the redhead is very abundant, and it spends the winter in great numbers in these waters, leaving them only when, as usually happens once or twice each winter, it is driven further south by the occurrence of cold weather, which freezes the sounds. In such places, in all sorts of weather, they may be seen, high in air, trading, as it is termed; that is to say, flying long distances far above the water, as if examining the ground before they determined to alight. The great flocks of birds that do this trading are usually canvasbacks and redheads.

The redhead is said by northern explorers to breed throughout the fur countries, and they have also been found breeding near Calais, Me. The nests are usually built close together, in colonies, generally near the water, and are somewhat more substantial than ducks' nests often are. The eggs are almost white, and are usually ten or twelve in number.

In many of its habits the redhead resembles the broad-bill or black-head. It comes up to decoys quite as gently as that bird, when it has once made up its mind to do so, and when about to alight the birds crowd close together, and thus offer the gunner an opportunity to kill several at a time. When only wounded the redhead dives and skulks well, and is not always to be recovered. After diving and swimming a long way under water it comes to the surface, and perhaps shows only a portion of the bill, swimming off so low against the wind that it is not likely to be detected.

The flesh of the redhead is excellent, and when it has been feeding on the same food, it cannot be distinguished from that of the canvas-back.

The redhead is a near relative of the European pochard, which it closely resembles, though easily distinguished on comparison.

This species is sometimes called the red-headed broad-bill, red-headed raft duck, and, oddly enough, Washington canvas-back.

BROAD-BILL.

Aythya marila nearctica STEJN.

The adult male has the head, neck and fore part of breast and of back, black; the feathers of the head and neck with a greenish gloss; rump, primaries and tail, brownish-black; the speculum, or wing mark, white; middle of back and sides, white, cross-lined with black and white. The under surface of the body is white, marked on the lower belly with narrow blackish cross-lines and black beneath the tail. The bill is broad, pale bluish-lead color, with a black nail; the eyes yellow; the legs and feet gray; the length, 18 to 20 inches.

The female has the front of head, immediately around the base of the bill, white. Those parts which

in the male are black are in the female brown. The
back is much darker, faintly marked with zig-zag white
lines. The bill is darker.

. Many widely different opinions are expressed as to
the value of the broad-bill as food, and those who de-
bate this question are both right and both wrong. In
other words, the flesh of the broad-bill, as of most
other ducks, is sometimes good and sometimes bad, depending on the food which it eats. Along the New
England coast, where, to a great extent it feeds on shell-
fish and other animal matter, the broad-bill is not a delicate bird, but further south, where its food is largely
vegetable, and where its name is changed to black-head
and blue-bill, it is a most excellent fowl. In the interior, too, it lives chiefly on vegetable matter. There
it is known as the scaup duck, blue-bill, raft duck, big
fowl duck, and is eagerly sought after. However,
the tendency of this bird appears to be toward the sea-
coast. It is abundant in California, where many are
killed, but it does not seem to go as far south as its
relative, the little black-head, and winters on the New
England and New York coasts and in New Jersey, being, in my experience, rather rare as far south as Virginia and North Carolina, where the little black-head
is very abundant.

The broad-bill is a species of wide range, being
found throughout North America, as far south as Central America, and also in northern portions of Europe
and Asia. It formerly bred in some numbers on the
northern prairies, and I have found its nests in North

Dakota and Montana, though some of these may have been those of the next species. Dr. Dall found it breeding in Alaska, and it is supposed to breed generally through northern North America, in the British possessions.

The nest of the broad-bill is usually placed close to the water; it is little more than a depression in the ground, among the grass, lined perhaps with a few spears of bright grass, and with down from the bird's breast. The number of eggs is six or eight; they are grayish-white in color, and when the mother leaves them are usually covered by the down.

The broad-bill is abundant in Long Island Sound and on the Great South Bay, where it is shot in great numbers from batteries. It reaches our coasts late in October, and is usually found associated together in considerable bodies, which, however, are likely to break up into small flocks in rough and stormy weather.

LITTLE BLACK-HEAD.

Aythya affinis (Eyt.).

Exactly similar in color to the broad-bill, but smaller. The gloss on the neck is likely to be bluish or purplish, instead of greenish. The length of this species is about 16 inches, as against 18 or 20 in the preceding.

These two species were long regarded as the same, and, indeed, as yet there seems to be no definite character to separate them, except that of size. On the New England coast, during the migrations, the two are often found associated together, and this is true to a less extent further to the southward. At the same time the difference between them is well recognized by ornithologists and by gunners generally, and is expressed in the common names applied to this species,

167

which Mr. Trumbull and others give. Some of these are little broad-bill, little black-head, little blue-bill, river broad-bill, creek black-head, river blue-bill, marsh blue-bill, mud blue-bill, mud broad-bill and fresh-water broad-bill.

Notwithstanding the fact that most of the little black-heads are readily to be identified by their size, there is considerable variation in the species and sometimes these birds almost equal the broad-bill in their meas-urements. It is stated that the adult males can be easily identified, no matter what their measurements may show, by the metallic gloss of the head feathers, these being always green in the broad-bill and blue or purple in the little broad-bill. This metallic gloss, therefore, would seem to be considered by some naturalists a specific character.

This is one of the most abundant birds of the south-ern seacoast, being found, in winter, from New Eng-land south to Florida, and even beyond that, to the West Indies and Central America. It is found, indeed, over the whole of North America, and, while breeding chiefly north of the United States, it is yet found in Minnesota, Dakota and Montana.

Owing to its similarity to the greater broad-bill, it is not always easy to determine just what the range of this species is. Some Alaska explorers give it as breed-ing in that country, while others declare that of the many broad-bills seen by them none belongs to this spe-cies. However, east of the Rocky Mountains the nests have been found throughout British America, usually placed in swamps or near lakes, very simple in construction and lined with down.

The little black-head is one of the swiftest fliers and most expert divers of all our ducks, and the task of retrieving one that has been wounded, unless one is provided with a good dog, is not always an easy one. This species is quite as much an adept at skulking and hiding as its larger relative, and, on the whole, is very well able to take care of itself. The flesh is usually very delicate, yet the very reverse of this may be true in localities where it has had an opportunity to feed largely on shell-fish.

Black-heads seem to be equally at home in shoal water and in deep; they can dive as well as the canvasback, and yet they are quite willing to puddle about through the edge of the marsh and to pick up a livelihood in company with the fresh-water ducks.

RING-NECKED DUCK.

Aythya collaris (Donov.).

The adult male has back of head and crown loose and puffy, at times showing almost as a crest. The head, neck, breast, upper parts and under tail-coverts, black; the head sometimes glossed with purple and the back with greenish. There is a more or less distinct chestnut or reddish-brown collar around the middle of the neck, and a white spot upon the chin. The speculum is bluish-gray; sides of body waved with white and blackish lines. The under parts are white. The bill is dark grayish blue, with a black tip, and a very pale (in life nearly white) band across it, near the tip; the eyes are yellow.

The female does not show the neck ring and the bill

is less plainly marked. The black of the male changes to brown in the female. The fore part of head, all about the base of the bill, is nearly white. The lower parts of the body are white, sometimes marked with brown or brownish-gray, growing darker toward the tail. The length is 16 to 18 inches.

The female of the ring-necked duck is very similar to that of the redhead, but the former is darker, except about the bill, where the pale markings are much paler, often almost white. The difference in the bills is characteristic, that of the female ring-neck being much the shorter and broader.

The ring-necked duck is by no means so abundant as many of our other species and is quite commonly confused with the little black-head, which it closely resembles in habits. In fact, as a rule, gunners do not distinguish between the tufted duck and the little black-head, and when counting up their score at the end of the day always refer to this species as a black-head. Its common names indicate this confusion. It is called ring-necked scaup, ring-necked black-head, marsh blue-bill, bastard broad-bill, ring-billed black-head, ring-billed shuffler, and sometimes it is called creek redhead because of its resemblance to that species. I have also heard boatmen, who had happened to notice the red collar about the bird's neck, call it a hybrid between a black-head and a redhead.

The ring-necked duck is found sparingly throughout almost the whole of North America. Its chief breeding grounds are north of the United States, but it probably

used to breed also in suitable localities on the plains, and
its nests have been taken near Calais, in Maine, as well
as in Wisconsin and Minnesota.   Its nest is built usually in thick cover, close to the water, and is a neater
structure than most ducks' nests.   The eggs are usually of a grayish ivory white and number from eight to
ten.   This species is occasionally taken on the California coast and also on that of New England, but it is nowhere common.   Even in the South, in that paradise of
ducks, Currituck, Core and Albemarle sounds, these
birds are few in number.

They decoy well and are easily killed when they come
up to the stools, although very swift fliers.

It is said that this bird is more abundant on our inland waters than on the sea-coast.   Even there, however, it can never be called an abundant species.   Its
flesh, under favorable circumstances, is excellent eating,
and if it were more abundant it would be one of the
most desirable of our fowl.

GOLDEN-EYE, WHISTLER.

Glaucionetta clangula americana (BONAP.).

The adult male has the head somewhat puffy, but the feathers longer on the back of the head, forming more or less of a crest.   The head and upper part of the neck are dark glossy green, with purple reflections and a roundish and sometimes oval white spot just back of the bill and below the eye.   The lower neck, fore-back, scapulars and wing-coverts, with the secondaries and most of the under parts, pure white; the back, long scapulars, and the base of the secondaries, black.   The long feathers of the wings and their coverts are blackish.   The tail is ashy-gray; the bill black; eye yellow; legs and feet yellowish-red. The total length is about 20 inches.

The female has the head and upper part of the neck brown. There is a white ring about the lower neck, and the upper breast is gray. The back is blackish-brown. The white on the wing is chiefly confined to the secondaries. The under parts are white; the tail is dark brown; bill sometimes yellowish, but more often brownish; legs and feet as in the male.

The American golden-eye has been separated by naturalists from the bird of Europe and called a variety, on no better ground than that it is slightly larger than the Old World form. Naturalists are not agreed on this point, and sportsmen are not greatly interested in such fine distinctions.

The golden-eye is a bird of wide distribution, breeding throughout the northern parts of the Northern Hemisphere and in winter pursuing its migrations as far south as the Southern United States and even beyond to Cuba. It is a bird familiar to all sportsmen, but from the standpoint of the epicure it is not highly regarded. It has been found breeding as far north as Alaska and undoubtedly is scattered in summer, in moderate numbers, all over the British possessions. It breeds in Maine and also in Massachusetts, but probably not south of that. I have found the golden-eye common, in summer, in the high Rocky Mountains, not far south of the parallel of 49 degrees, but am unable to say whether it was this or the next species.

The golden-eye is one of the few tree-breeding ducks, choosing for this purpose some hollow limb or broken-off stump in which to lay its eggs; these are pale grayish-green in color and are said to be from six to eight. Concerning the breeding habits of this species, the veteran naturalist, Mr. Geo. A. Boardman, said in *Forest and Stream:*

"Fifty years ago we used to have six different tree ducks breeding on our river: Barrow's golden-eye and the buffle-head (*albeola*) rare, but the common golden-eye, the American merganser, hooded merganser and wood duck abundant. About fifty years ago pickerel were put into our waters, which soon put an end to most of our wild ducks breeding, as the pickerel ate up all the chick ducks except in the few lakes or ponds that were free from pickerel. Near to Calais are several ponds and lakes that are free from those fish, and the tree ducks bring their young to those lakes for safety.

"I was at the Kendrick Lake, and a lad that lived near by was with me. A duck (whistler) came flying low toward us, when the lad threw up his hat with a shout, when the old duck dropped a young one that fell near us that was at least ten days old. The old one went for it so quickly I almost lost it, but I got it and put it in my pocket for a specimen. We were near the lake, and the old duck also, when we saw she had four others in the water. The boy said if we keep quiet she will go away and bring others, or if she is afraid of us very much she will take those across the lake or to the other lake. They were getting near to some water grass, when the old duck made a flutter, caught one and went across the lake; it was hardly two minutes before she returned and took another.

"I don't think she took them by her mouth, and the one she dropped, if it had been in her mouth we should have seen it. Mr. Eastman, father of the lad, said they often took their young from one lake or river to another if they thought them in danger, and said he had seen them bring the young from the nest to the water and then in their bills, but, to go any distance, or if they are any size, carry them pressed to the body by the feet, and the boys often by a shout made them drop their young. They brought me several different kinds afterward, wood duck, whistlers and hooded mergansers, but no young of the large merganser."

In a recent number of the *Auk* (Vol. XVII (N. S.), p. 207, July, 1900) Mr. William Brewster has given a most interesting account of the nesting habits of this species. The article is illustrated by admirable photographs.

The whistler, as it is frequently called, although resorting to the fresh waters during the breeding season, is much at home on the salt water in autumn and winter. It is an expert diver and feeds largely on shell-fish, and when it can obtain them, on small minnows. On the other hand, it readily eats grain and frequents the wild rice fields of the interior and the fresh marshes of the coast, and when it has lived on grain for some time its flesh is very good eating. The name whistler, so commonly applied to it along the sea-coast, is given because of the quivering, whistling noise made by the wings while the bird is flying, which is often recognizable long before the bird itself can be seen. Other names for this species are golden-eye, from its yellow iris; conjuring and spirit duck, from the rapidity with which it dives; brass-eye and brass-eyed whistler, whistle-wing, merry-wing, great-head, bull-head, iron-head, cob-head and cub-head.

While the whistler is one of our most beautiful ducks, it is not highly regarded by those who have an opportunity to kill better fowl, and, like the little dipper and ruddy duck and the mergansers, it is often allowed to pass over the decoys without being shot at. It is not a bird that decoys readily, and, as a rule, offers little sport; but at many points in New England and Canada, where better ducks are rare, its pursuit offers some reward to the gunners.

BARROW'S GOLDEN-EYE.

Glaucionetta islandica (Gmel.).

Adult male extremely similar to the golden-eye, but larger and with the head and upper neck bluish-black, with purplish reflections instead of greenish, with the spot at the base of the bill, and in front of the eye, triangular or crescent-shaped, and with very much less white on the wing, this usually being confined to two long bars with a short, black bar between them.

The female is much as in the ordinary whistler. The collar about her neck is narrower than in the whistler; the white on the wing is less and is crossed by a black bar. The grayish on the breast, sides and flank is wider in this species than in the whistler.

178

Barrow's golden-eye is much less common than the ordinary whistler. Like that species it is a northern bird, but it appears to be much less abundant in Europe than even in this country. I have frequently seen, breeding in the lakes in the high Rocky Mountains, golden-eyes which were probably of this species, but I was never so fortunate as to have any of them in the hand. Like the whistler, Barrow's golden-eye breeds in trees, laying eight to ten eggs, grayish-green in color. Mr. C. W. Shepard found this duck breeding in Iceland, where, in the absence of trees, it built its nest in holes in the cracks and crevices of the lava. Barrow's golden-eye has been found in Alaska, on the Yukon River, and at Sitka, and specimens have been taken at other points in the north. Mr. Boardman believed that this species breeds in the woods of Calais, Me., though as yet their nests have not been discovered. Mr. Nelson states that it is a winter resident on Lake Michigan, and is probably found generally in winter through the interior wherever there is open water. A number of specimens have been taken on the coast of Massachusetts. Mr. Elliot has found it quite abundant on the St. Lawrence River, near Ogdensburgh, and has frequently killed it there over decoys. He says: "The birds would fly up and down the river, doubtless coming from and going to Lake Erie, stopping occasionally in the coves to feed and floating down with the current for a considerable distance, when they would rise and fly up stream again. My decoys were always placed in some cove or bend of the stream where the current was least strong, for I noticed the birds rarely settled on the water where it was running swiftly.   This duck decoys readily in such situations and will come right in, and, if permitted, settle among the wooden counterfeits.   They sit lightly upon the water and rise at once without effort or much splashing.   The flight is very rapid and is accompanied with the same whistling of the wings so noticeable in the common golden-eye.   In stormy weather this bird keeps close to the banks, seeking shelter from the winds. It dives as expertly as its relative and frequently remains under water for a considerable time.   The flesh of those killed upon the river was tender and of good flavor, fish evidently not having figured much as an article of their diet."

BUFFLE-HEAD DUCK.

Charitonetta albeola (LINN.).

The adult male has the head and upper neck black.
From behind and below the eye a very broad white band
or patch extends backward to the ends of the feathers.
The black of head and upper neck is brilliant with
metallic reflections of green and purple. The feathers
of head are long and loose, giving it a puffy appearance,
and they can be raised so as to make the head seem very
large. The back is black, fading to ashy on the upper
tail-coverts. The tail is gray, with whitish edges. The
lower neck, entire under parts, greater wing-coverts,
outer scapulars and some secondaries, white. The quill
feathers of the wing are gray, the bill is lead color, the
eyes brown and the feet flesh color or lavender.

181

The head of the female lacks the extreme puffiness of the male's. She is generally a dark lead color, or slaty, very much paler below, has a white patch on the side of the head behind and below the eye, and a white wing patch formed by the outer webs of the secondaries. The bill is dark lead color and the feet and legs grayish-blue.

The male buffle-head is one of the most beautiful and active of North American ducks and is also one of the most abundant, especially along the sea-coast. It is confined to North America and is scattered over most of the continent, from the extreme North to Mexico. It is said not to be common in Alaska, but sometimes to occur on the Aleutian Islands, and Dr. Stejneger found it in winter also about the Commander Islands, on the Asiatic side of the Pacific. The buffle-head breeds throughout much of British America, nesting in hollows in trees, and its nests have been found on the Yukon River, as well as in many other localities in the North. Mr. Boardman believes that it breeds near Calais, Me., and young birds, still unable to fly, are said to have been killed at Pewaukee Lake, in Wisconsin.

The butter-ball is an extremely restless and busy bird, and in the dull times of the duck shooting, when the weather is still and no birds are flying, it is very likely to dart over the gunner's decoys and startle him by its unexpected presence. However, the butter-ball is so small, and also so swift of flight, and so expert in diving, that not very many of them are killed. They are by no means shy and often come readily to the decoys, among which they alight, feed, and after swimming about for a short time will fly off again. The dipper flies very rapidly, quite equaling in this respect the black-head, which is known for its speed on the wing. Usually it alights without checking itself at all and strikes the water with a splash, sliding along the surface for some little distance. Mr. Elliot's remarks on the diving of this species are well worth repeating. He says: "As a diver the butter-ball takes rank among the most expert of our ducks, disappearing so quickly, and apparently with so little exertion, that it is almost impossible to shoot it when sitting on the water. When alarmed, with a sudden flip up of its tail and a scattering of a few drops of water, it vanishes beneath the surface, appearing almost immediately at no great distance from where it went under, and either dives again at once or takes wing, which it does easily and without any fuss. Sometimes half a dozen of these birds will gather together in a sheltered piece of water and be very busy feeding. A few will dive with a sudden jerk, as if drawn beneath the surface by an invisible string, and the others will quietly swim about as if on the watch. The first that went under water having returned to the surface, the others dive, and so it goes on for a long time. Occasionally all will disappear, and then the first one to rise seems much disconcerted at not finding any one on watch and acts as if he were saying to himself that if he 'had only known their unprotected state, he would never have gone under.'"

Mr. Elliot states also that the flesh of this duck is very palatable and is excellent when broiled. In this species, as in others, the food regulates the excellence of the flesh.

Mr. Gurdon Trumbull gives among the names for this very well-known species the buffalo-headed duck, little brown duck, spirit duck, conjuring duck, dipper, robin dipper, dapper and dopper, die-dipper, marionette, butter-ball, butter-duck and butter-box, diver, wool-head, scotch duck, scotchman, scotch dipper and scotch teal.

OLD-SQUAW, LONG-TAILED DUCK.

Clangula hyemalis (LINN.).

Male, in winter, with broad strip running from the base of the bill, back, including eye, to about the ear, pale gray; at the ear darkening to black, which fades again to pale gray on the side of the neck; top and back of head, throat and lower sides of head and upper neck, all about, white; breast, back, upper tail-coverts, wing and long feathers of tail, black, the outer sides of the tail fading to white. The secondaries are reddish-brown; scapulars, pearl-gray; under parts, white.

In the male, in summer, the pale gray line running back from the bill, including the eye and parts of cheek, are as in winter, but the remaining parts of head, neck, breast and upper parts generally are deep brown or even black. The feathers on the fore-back and the scapulars are margined with tan. The other upper parts are black, or blackish-brown, with some grayish on the secondaries. The four middle tail feathers are black; the breast and part of the belly are dark brown, and the rest of the under parts white. The bill is black, crossed by a bar of orange, and the feet are black.

The female, in winter, has the head, neck and lower parts white, marked with dusky on forehead and crown, as well as on the ears, chin and throat. The upper parts are brown, many of the feathers being bordered with grayish. In summer the head and neck are more gray and the general plumage darker.

The old-squaw, as it is commonly called on the New England coast, is one of the commonest of our winter birds, and is found on both coasts of America, as well as of the Old World. It is a beautiful bird, active, noisy and hardy, going little further south than it is obliged to to procure food, although occasionally it extends its migrations as far as Florida and California. In Europe it is sometimes found, in winter, in the Mediterranean Sea.

The old-squaw breeds in the Arctic regions and has been found in Spitzbergen, Nova Zembla, Iceland and Northern Alaska, as well as in Hudson's Bay. It commonly associates, even on the breeding grounds, in great flocks; and I have seen them in Alaska in June and July, hundreds together. They commonly breed on the waters of fresh-water pools, making their nests under low bushes, or among coarse grass, close to the water. The eggs are given as being only five to seven in number. The nest is made of grass and weeds and is invariably lined with down, which is of fine quality, apparently not much inferior to that of the eider duck.

On their return from the North the old-squaws do not reach the New England coast until the weather has grown quite cold, long after the different varieties of scoters have come and established themselves in their winter home. Here they congregate throughout the winter in vast numbers, associating with the scoters and the eiders and yet often keeping very much by themselves. The old-squaw is one of the most expert of divers and it used to be stated—and may be believed—that in old times it could not be shot on the water with a flint-lock gun. Even now it frequently dives so rapidly as to apparently escape the shot, and instances are given of where a bird, shot at when flying low over the water, had dived from the wing and escaped uninjured.

The common name of this species refers to its noisy habit. It is continually talking while on the water, and the flocks, when flying, frequently utter their musical cry. In almost all localities the bird takes its name from this call, which is difficult of imitation. Perhaps the Canadian syllables, *Ca cá-wee,* imitate the note as well as anything that has been attempted. *South south southerly* is supposed to represent it, but hardly does so. The old-squaw is remarkable for the rapidity and the irregularity of its flight. A flock starting low over the water, to go in some direction, will zig-zag hither and thither, constantly uttering their mellow cry and reminding one, in their swift and darting flight, of the flocks of wild pigeons which used to be seen in the olden times.

Beautiful and active bird though it be, the old-squaw is unfit for use on the table. It is always fishy, and no treatment with which I am acquainted will render its flesh palatable. It feeds chiefly on shell-fish, and its flesh tells the story.

In the spring, when the birds are preparing to take their flight to the North, they prepare themselves for their long journey by extended flights; as the local gunners call it, "trying their wings." Late in the afternoon they rise from the water in great flocks and circling high in the air, fly about for hours, performing many beautiful evolutions. The migrations are usually performed by night and perhaps at no very great height above the ground. At all events, I recall that some years ago, in a New England village near the Sound, the weather-vane one morning in April was observed to be missing from one of the churches. A search revealed it lying on the ground near the building, bent and broken, and not far from it was the body of a male old-squaw, which had flown against the vane with such force as to break off the iron pivot on which it swung.

HARLEQUIN DUCK.

Histrionicus histrionicus (LINN.).

The general color of the male harlequin is leaden-blue, marked with black, white and chestnut, as follows: Space between base of bill and eye, with a strip extending along the crown, a round spot near the ear, a narrow strip extending from below the ear a short distance down the upper neck, a narrow collar around the lower neck, a bar across the side of breast, in front of the bend of the wing, a part of the scapulars and tertiary feathers, tips of some of the greater wing-coverts, a spot·on the lesser wing-coverts and a round spot on either side, just before the tail, white. The collar about the neck, the bar on the side of the breast, bordered with black. A strip from the forehead to the back of the neck, black, bordered with rufous. The rest of the head and neck is dark lead color, sometimes almost blackish, and with glossy reflections. The rump, upper and·under tail-coverts are black; quills of the wing and tail, dusky; sides and flanks, bright tan, inclining to reddish. The bill and feet are bluish-gray; length about 17 inches.

The adult female has the space between the eyes and bill and a spot behind the ear, white; the rest of the head and neck are dark brown, darkest on top; wings and tail blackish; the other parts reddish-brown, except the belly, which is white.

The harlequin duck is one of the most striking and beautiful of our ducks. It is one of our most northern species and not very much is known about it. On the Atlantic coast it is seldom found south of Maine. It is a bird of the Old World as well as the New, and, in fact, is found over the northern portions of both hemispheres. British ornithologists, however, have declared that it is only a straggler on the European continent, but that it occurs regularly in Iceland and Eastern Asia. On the other hand, we know that it is commonly found during the summer in the northern Rocky Mountains, and I have seen the birds, evidently mated, in the Sierra Nevadas, in June. There, Mr. Ridgway tells me that it breeds as far south, at least, as Calaveras County, California.

All through the summer months in Northwestern

Montana harlequins may be seen spending their time, in small numbers, on lakes, often in the high mountains, where the melting waters from the glaciers form curiour little mountain tarns at the edge of the timber line. Its nest has not been found in this country, and only twice in Europe; once by Mr. Shepard, who states that he found it breeding in Iceland "in holes in the trees," while the Messrs. Pierson state that they found them also in Iceland in holes in the banks. It is altogether probable that in the northern Rocky and Sierra Nevada mountains the harlequins breed in trees, while in Alaska they very likely breed in holes. In the summer of 1899 harlequins were seen abundantly on the salt water in Alaska, but all those taken were males. They were very common in Prince William Sound and at many points in the Bering Sea. An interesting account is given in the *Zoölogist* for 1850 on the breeding in confinement of a pair of this species in Melbourne Gardens, Derbyshire. Eight eggs were laid, which were hatched about the middle of June, and several of the young ducks reached maturity. Some of the names given for this duck by Mr. Gurdon Trumbull are painted duck, mountain duck, rock duck, lord for the male and lady for the female, and squealer.

LABRADOR DUCK.

Camptolaimus labradorius (GMEL.).

In the adult male the head, upper neck, upper breast and wing, except the long quill feathers, are white. A strip on the crown, running down over the back of the head, a collar about the neck, the back, rump, quills of wing and tail and entire under parts, black. The cheeks are sometimes tinged with yellowish. The long scapulars are pearly-gray and the tertiaries have black margins. The bill is black, with some orange at the base and along the edges; the feet are grayish-blue. The bill is somewhat expanded near the tip.

192

The female has the plumage of a general brownish-gray tint. The tertiaries are ashy-gray, edged with black, and the secondaries, white, forming a distinct wing patch. The bird is about 20 inches in length.

The Labrador duck, or, as it is sometimes called, the pied duck, is one of our North American birds which has already become extinct, and this only within a comparatively few years. It was a bird of the sea-coast and was formerly not uncommon along the Atlantic, as far south as New Jersey, yet it seems never to have been very abundant. Giraud, who wrote in 1843, said of it: "This species is called by our gunners 'skunk duck,' so named from the similarity of its markings to that animal. With us it is rather rare, chiefly inhabiting the western side of the continent. In New Jersey it is called 'sand-shoal duck.' It subsists on small shell and other fish, which it procures by diving. Its flesh is not considered a delicacy. A few are seen in our market every season."

In the years 1871, '72 and '73 specimens were occasionally exposed for sale in the New York markets, but even at that time the bird had become so rare that ornithologists were on the watch for it, and as soon as a specimen was exposed for sale it was bought up.

The pied duck was a strong flier and apparently well able to take care of itself, and its practical extinction took place before gunning was practiced on any very great scale. It was not especially sought for as a table bird, and no satisfactory reason has as yet been advanced for its disappearance. The number of speci-

mens of the bird now existing is very small, probably
not more than sixty in all, of which about two-thirds
are in this country.   A very beautiful group of Labrador ducks is to be seen in the American Museum of
Natural History, in New York, where five specimens
have been handsomely mounted in their natural surroundings.

STELLER'S DUCK.

Eniconetta stelleri (PALL.).

In the adult male, most of the head and upper portion of neck are satiny white; the space between base of bill and eye and the tuft running across the back of the head, dark olive-green. The space about the eye, chin and throat, and band about the lower neck, the middle of the back, the long shoulder feathers, tertiaries and secondaries, glossy blue-black. The rump, upper tail-coverts and tail, somewhat duller black. The scapulars are streaked lengthwise with white, while the tertiaries have the inner webs of the feathers fully white, and the secondaries are tipped with white. The wing-coverts, some of the scapulars and the sides of the back are white. The quills of the wing are dull black, while the lower parts are rusty-reddish, darkest in the middle of the belly and fading on the sides and breast to buff. The dusky of the belly darkens toward the tail, until it becomes dull black. There is a spot of blue-black on the sides below the bend of the wing. The bill and feet are grayish-blue.

The adult female is generally reddish-brown, speckled with dusky or black. There are two narrow bars across the wing, formed by the tips of the greater coverts and of the secondaries. The speculum is brownish; under parts light brown, spotted with brownish-black; the back sooty-brown.

This very handsome duck is found in America only on the coasts of Alaska. It frequents the coast of Asia, however, and has been taken in Russia, Sweden, Denmark and Britain. It appears, however, to be only a straggler in Western Europe. It is distinctly an Arctic bird and more numerous in Alaska than in any other region. The nest is built on the ground, among the grass, and is well concealed. It is said to breed on St. Lawrence Island.

The species is one that can interest only Alaskan sportsmen, but it is an exceedingly beautiful bird.

SPECTACLED EIDER.

Arctonetta fischeri (Brandt).

In the adult male the space immediately about the eye is silky white, bordered by a line of velvety black, before and behind. The feathers between the eye and the bill are stiff and extend over the bill almost to the nostril. At the base of the bill they are white, changing to dark green, which grows paler toward the black bar before the eye. The crown, back of the head, running down a little way on the neck, pale olive-green. Beneath the space around the eye a strip extends back to meet the olive-green, which is deep dull green. The head and neck, except as stated, are white. All the lower parts, including the upper breast, are pale leaden-gray; while the whole back and wing, except the greater wing-coverts, the tertiaries and a patch on each side of the rump, are yellowish-white. The bill is orange, deepest along the edge, and pale on the nail. The eyes are pale blue or bluish-white. The feet and legs are yellowish.

In the adult female the head generally is buffy, streaked with dusky. A strip of brown runs from the bill before the eye to the top of the head. The throat is very little streaked or spotted. The general upper parts are tawny, barred with black. The belly and the region under the tail is grayish-brown. The length is about 20 or 22 inches.

The spectacled eider is another Alaskan bird of which not very much is known. It is a dweller in the far North, its range seeming to extend only from the mouth of the Kuskokwim River to Point Barrow, where it breeds. Another observer, however, gives it as occurring much further to the South, and says that it breeds among the Aleutian Islands, where it is a resident, although shy. The nest is built in the grass, not far from the water, and the eggs are from five to nine in number. Mr. Nelson, who has spent so much time in Alaska, and is very familiar with this bird, sounds a note of warning about it, saying that it might readily be so reduced as to become very rare. It is an extremely local bird, and with a narrow breeding range, and with the attacks continually made on it for food by the Eskimo it has every prospect of becoming scarce.

It is to be noted that the autumn plumage of male and female in this species are very nearly alike, dark brown with black mottling, and that the breeding dress does not appear to be assumed until toward spring.

It is said that the flight of this bird is unusually swift, much more so than that of most other eiders, and that they usually fly low over the water.

COMMON EIDER.

Somateria mollissima borealis A. E. BREHM.

The adult male of the common eider duck has the crown deep black—split behind in the middle line by a strip of white or greenish-white—and reaching forward from the eye to the bill. The upper part of the back of the neck and the feathers back of the ears are pale green. The rest of the head and neck, with the fore-breast, back, scapulars, wing-coverts, tertiary feathers and sides of rump, white, often tinged with yellow or creamy buff. The breast is sometimes pink tinted. The other under parts, the greater wing-coverts, secondaries, middle of rump and upper tail-coverts, black; quills of the wing and tail, brownish-black; bill, dull orange-yellow; legs and feet, orange.

The adult female is generally of a reddish-brown color, mostly barred with black, but the head and neck are merely narrowly streaked with black. The crown of the head is darkest. The under parts are a grayish rather than reddish brown, with darker bars. The tips of the secondaries are white, forming two bars across the wing. Length about 22 inches.

The eider duck inhabits the northern shores of both coasts of the Atlantic. In winter it is found in more or less abundance along the New England coast, and I have seen it killed as far south as Long Island Sound.

The eider breeds in Labrador, and to the northward, and in many parts of Europe is almost a domestic bird. The down, which is plucked from the breast of the female, for the lining of the nest, is a valuable article of commerce, and in an earlier chapter something has been said about the way these birds are protected and their down secured in Norway and Iceland.

When seen along the coast of Southern New England the eider is often found associated with the scoters, there commonly known as coots, and when killed it is usually shot out of flocks of these birds.

Mr. Gurdon Trumbull notes as names of this bird, and of the next, the terms sea duck and drake, shoal duck, Isles of Shoals duck and wamp (this being of Indian origin, probably from wompi, white).

AMERICAN EIDER.

Somateria dresseri SHARPE.

In this species the colors of both sexes are precisely
like those of the preceding.   The differences between
the two lie chiefly in the manner in which the feathers
of the front of the head meet the naked portions of the
bill.   In these eiders, on either side of the forehead a
branch of the naked skin of the bill runs up into the
feathers, which border it above and below.   In the case
of the common eider these branches are narrow and run
up nearly to a point, but in the American form they are
broad and terminate abruptly and bluntly.   In the common eider, therefore, the feather patches running down
into the angles between the naked skin are broad, while
in the American eider they are narrow.   There is also

some difference in the shape of the bills in the two species, that of the common eider appearing slightly straighter and more slender, while in the American bird the upper outline of the bill in profile is slightly concave. Slight as are the differences between the two, they appear to be constant and to be of specific value.

The American eider is the commoner of the two along the American coast. It is said to be found in winter along the Atlantic as far south as the Delaware River, but this perhaps only in winters of unusual severity. The American eider sometimes goes inland, and has been taken on the Great Lakes and in adjacent States, but there it is only an accidental straggler.

Its breeding grounds are in Labrador and from there to the Bay of Fundy. The nest is on the ground, very often on small islands, at a little distance from the mainland, and is formed of moss, weeds and twigs. Often it is under the shelter of some little low-growing evergreen, or in the open ground, behind the shelter of a rock. The eggs are few in number, only six, and are usually deposited on the soft layer of down with which the nest is lined. When the mother leaves the nest she covers the eggs with this down. The young are dark mouse-color when first hatched and are at once expert in swimming and diving. As soon as the females begin to sit, the males leave them and assemble in flocks in the open water. The eggs are said to be of two colors—one a pale greenish-olive, the other much browner; the paler egg is sometimes spotted and splashed with darker.

The eiders are deep-sea feeders and subsist chiefly on small shell-fish, which they bring up from the bottom, often at great depths. They gather together in large flocks, and when they rise on the wing do so gradually, running and flapping along over the water for some distance, much after the manner of the scoters. In fact, in many of their ways these birds remind us much of scoters.

As might be inferred from their food, eiders are not desirable table birds, the flesh being usually fishy and very rank.

PACIFIC EIDER.

Somateria v-nigra GRAY.

The plumage of the adult male is extremely like that
of the two preceding species, though the bird is somewhat larger, with a broader and deeper bill. The black
of the crown extends forward in the white strip beneath
the forehead branch of the bill, but does not reach as far
forward as the nostril. In the male there is a large
V-shaped black mark on the throat, as in the king eider,
but in this species the V-shaped mark is longer and narrower than in the king duck. The color of the bill is
deep orange, almost orange-red, fading toward the tip,

which is yellowish-white. The legs and feet are brownish-orange.

The female is pale brown on the head and neck, darkest on the crown, streaked everywhere with blackish. The upper parts are reddish, barred with black. The length is about 22 inches.

This eider is the common Pacific coast form, found in the North Pacific, Bering Sea and on the coast of Siberia. It is scarcely, or not at all, known south of Alaska. In the Arctic Ocean it is found as far east as the Coppermine River. It breeds throughout much of this range, not only in Alaska, but on the shores of the Arctic Ocean. The nests are variously placed, sometimes at quite a distance from the water; at others, close to it. They are sometimes on little islands, and are abundantly provided with down. In Alaska the breeding ground is often in the marsh and sometimes the place chosen is close to human habitation. The male is reported as assisting in building the nest and as constantly associating with the female during the time of incubation, though he himself takes no share in that labor. The food of this eider is generally mussels and shell-fish, which it brings up from the deep water.

When the young are hatched, early in July, the old birds begin to molt. The natives pursue the ducks in their canoes, striking at them with their spears. It is said that they do not kill many. Like the other eiders already spoken of, the fall plumage of the male is closely like that of the female, and we are told that the young males only attain their full adult breeding dress at the commencement of the third year. The Pacific eider is a large and handsome duck, weighing from four to six pounds. It is said to be loath to fly in stormy weather and to avoid rough water, resorting to the beach during wind storms or else taking to sheltered bays and inlets, where the water is quiet.

KING EIDER.

Somateria spectabilis (LINN.).

In the adult male the feathers about the base of the bill, a small spot below and behind the eye, and a large V-shaped mark on the throat, black. The whole top and back of the head, running down to the nape of the neck, pearl-gray or bluish-white, darkest below, where it sometimes changes almost to black. The sides of the head, running back from the bill below, pearl-gray, and a patch over the ear sea-green, fading into white above and behind. The rest of the head, neck, middle of the back, most of the wing and a patch on either side of the rump, white; the breast deep buff or cream-color. The greater wing-coverts, scapulars, or shoulder feathers, and primaries, brownish-black. The scapulars and tertiary feathers are falcate or sickle-shaped, bending downward over the primaries. The hinder portion of the back, rump, upper tail-coverts and under parts, black; the tail is brownish-black.   Except in the breeding season, the bill is shaped much as in the ordinary eider duck, but in spring there is a large, square, soft swelling on the bill, extending down nearly to the nostrils.   The feathering in the median line extends down further on the top of the bill than it does on the sides, in this respect differing markedly from any of the other eiders.   The bill is reddish-orange, and the legs and feet similar, but slightly paler.   The length is about 23 inches.

The adult female has the plumage buff or tawny, streaked on head, chin and throat with darker, the streaking being most abundant on the top of the head. The breast and sides are somewhat paler, with black bars across the feathers.   The back and shoulder feathers are blackish-brown, tipped with yellowish.   The wing feathers are mainly black or blackish-brown, the greater coverts or secondaries being tipped with white, to form two narrow bars across the wing.   The tertiaries are reddish on the outer webs.   The rump and upper tail-coverts are tawny, barred with black; tail, black; breast and belly, blackish-brown; under tail-coverts, reddish, barred with black.   The bill is greenish-gray and the feet yellowish.

Like some of the other eiders, this is a bird of circumpolar distribution, and is found in both continents. It appears to be everywhere much less abundant than other birds of the genus and is found chiefly in the far North, although it sometimes occurs on the New England coast.   It has been found in Long Island Sound and on the New Jersey coast, as well as on one or more of the Great Lakes and on some of the far inland rivers. It appears to be nowhere a very abundant species, but is found in the Arctic Sea, on both coasts of America, and is not uncommon in Alaska. All the Arctic expeditions report seeing it and many have found its nest. It is resident in Greenland and it is said that it occasionally breeds as far to the southward as the Bay of Fundy.

Mr. Charles Linden reports it as having been taken, on a number of occasions, on Lake Erie, and Mr. Nelson gives it as a visitor to Lake Michigan and to other parts of Illinois and Wisconsin; while the Smithsonian Institution possesses specimens shot on Lake Erie and others secured on the Illinois River.

In Alaska Dr. Dall has found it, though not south of the Bering Sea. It occurs, however, in the Bering Sea, on both the American and Asiatic coasts, not far south of Bering Straits.

The king eider breeds far to the northward. Its nest is entirely simple, merely a hollow in the ground, in which pale green eggs are deposited, over which the female bird commonly places a layer of down.

From what has been said of its range it will be seen that the king eider is not likely to come within the reach of the gunner, except as a very rare straggler. It is one of the most beautiful of ducks, and the male, if killed, can at once be recognized. This species feeds chiefly on shell-fish of various descriptions, and, as may be imagined, is not a desirable bird for the table.

AMERICAN SCOTER.

Oidemia americana Sw. AND RICH.

In the adult male the entire plumage is deep black; the neck shows faint purplish reflections; the fore part of the bill and a line running back to the feathers, along the cutting edge, black; the remainder of bill, from before the nostrils, much swollen, and bright orange in color; the legs and feet are black.

The adult female has the bill entirely black. Above, the plumage is dark grayish-brown; the feathers of the cheeks, back and scapulars often tipped with paler; the lower parts are more nearly gray. The length is about 18 inches.

The scoter is a bird of very wide distribution, being found on both coasts of North America, as well as on many inland lakes. On the Pacific coast it ranges from the Arctic to Southern California and on the Atlantic at least as far south as the Chesapeake Bay. Mr. Audubon, on the other hand, says that the scoter ranges along the entire southern coast and that it is found as far south as the Mississippi River.

On its southward migration the scoter reaches Southern New England late in September, and often in open winters remains there through the whole season, taking its departure for the North in May. When, however, the weather is cold, and the shore blocked with ice, it moves further southward to open feeding grounds, returning northward as the ice disappears.

Alaskan travelers have found this species as far north as Norton Sound, where it breeds, as well as on the east coast of Labrador. This species, with other scoters, also breeds in some of our inland lakes, nests of these birds having been found on some of the larger lakes in Dakota and the birds having been seen in abundance on the Yellowstone Lake, in Wyoming, all through the summer.

The scoter on the New England coast is usually found associated with the white-winged and the surf scoters, which commonly outnumber it in the flocks.

All these scoters are characterized by curiously swollen and more or less hollow bills, which are highly colored. All of them are known along the eastern seaboard as "coots."

AMERICAN VELVET SCOTER.

Oidemia deglandi BONAP.

The adult male has the bill expanded into a prominent knob at the base on the top. At the sides the bill is sunken, as if hollowed out. This knob, with the base of the bill and its margin, are black. The sides of the bill in front are red, changing to orange and then to white near the tip. The plumage is uniform black, often very deep or often brownish throughout. There is a small white spot behind the eye and the secondaries are white.

The female is uniform dirty gray, the wings darker than the body. The secondaries are white, as in the male. The length is about 21 inches.

One of the commonest of the winter sea-ducks is the velvet duck, more often called the white-winged coot. It is found on both coasts and also on the Great Lakes and some of the inland rivers in winter. It comes down to the New England coast late in September and spends the winter there in company with the other coots and the eider ducks. It is exceedingly abundant and is shot by the various methods described in the chapter on sea shooting. While migrating, or while taking long flights, it flies high above the water, often out of gunshot, but from such heights I have sometimes seen it brought down, either by the expedient of shooting or shouting at it, or sometimes I have seen a gunner scale his hat high into the air, when the whole flock would dart 20 or 30 or 40 yards directly downward toward the water and then continue their flight. Usually the birds, when flying from their roosting to their feeding grounds, pass but a few feet above the water, moving along with a strong, steady flight.

The white-winged coot feeds almost exclusively on small shell-fish, which it brings up from the bottom, and the flesh is very far from palatable. The gunner on the New England coast who kills them, usually parboils them for a time, and then bakes them, the result being a dish that is eatable, but is thought by many to lack character.

The velvet ducks breed in Labrador and to the northward as far as the Barren Grounds. The nest, often made among underbrush or low woods, is a hollow in the moss, lined with down, and contains seven or eight eggs. This species, like the old-squaw and other coots, spends much of its time, late in the spring, in preparing for the long flight that it must make to its summer home. The hours from three o'clock in the afternoon until dark are spent chiefly on the wing, and often it is not much before the first of June when the last of the coots leave the New England shore.

On the Pacific coast this species is found in winter as far south as Southern California and in summer to the Bering Sea. In the month of July I have seen them on the Gulf of Georgia in vast numbers, the birds being, no doubt, chiefly males, the females nesting somewhere in the vicinity.

The coots are regarded as exceedingly tough and hard to kill, and the gunners along the New England coast who shoot them commonly use very large shot, often 3's, and sometimes 2's. Birds that are only wounded, dive and skulk with great skill, and if there is any sea on the water, are likely to escape notice and not to be recovered. Often they dive, and apparently never come to the surface again, and it is believed that they cling to weeds at the bottom and remain there until dead.

Some of the names given for this species by Mr. Trumbull are May white-wing or great May whitewing, pied-winged coot, bell-tongue coot, Uncle Sam coot, bull coot, brant coot, sea brant, assemblyman, channel duck.

VELVET SCOTER.

Oidemia fusca (Linn.).

In the adult male the bill is much swollen near the gap, but is not much elevated at the base. The general color is orange or reddish, crossed on each side by a diagonal black line, running from above the nostril obliquely to the side of the nail. The plumage is brownish-black, with a small patch behind the eyes, and a white speculum on the wing.

The female is sooty-gray, paler beneath, and with a white speculum.

The velvet scoter is scarcely to be considered an American bird, being only an accidental visitor to our shores. It is an Old World species, which has, however, been taken in Greenland. It is not a bird to be considered by the sportsmen, who will never meet with it.

SURF SCOTER, SKUNK-HEAD.

Oidemia perspicillata (LINN.).

The adult male is deep black above, changing on the lower parts to a very dark brownish-black. There is a white patch on the forehead, cut off squarely behind the eyes, and running out to a point a little beyond the gap of the bill. On the back of the head and neck there is another white patch, cut off squarely in front and running down to a semi-circular ending on the back of the neck. The bill is swollen at the base, white and red in color, with a squarish patch of black on either side near the base. The nail is horn-color. The feet are orange, with dusky webs.

The adult female is brownish-black everywhere, becoming sooty or almost lead-color below, and sometimes almost white on the abdomen. The bill is black, but little swollen, and, of course, the black spot shown in the male is not apparent. The bird's length is about 20 inches. Mr. Ridgway states that sometimes in the adult male there are other white marks than those described, and sometimes one or the other of the white patches on top of the head is wanting, but these conditions are very unusual.

This species, which is known as surf duck in the books, is commonly called by gunners coot, sea duck, skunk-head and also sometimes hollow-billed coot. It is peculiar to America and in habits and distribution does not differ markedly from our other coots. It is said to breed on the Arctic coast and to proceed southward as far as Bermuda. It is also commonly found on the Great Lakes and is not infrequently killed by gunners on the marshes to the south of them. Mr. Audubon found it breeding as far south as Labrador, in fresh-water marshes, and the nest was rather more substantial than that of many of the sea-ducks, being well built and lined with down. It contained five eggs, of a cream color. Nests found by Mr. MacFarlane on the Anderson River contained eight eggs.

While vast numbers of coots winter on the New England coast, and seem to thrive there, numbers apparently equally great proceed further south, wintering in the mouths of the Delaware River and in Chesapeake Bay and out at sea. In these regions, however, where there are so many better ducks, they are not much pursued, and, on the whole, it may be said of these coots, and of the old-squaw, that they are not rapidly growing fewer in numbers.

Besides the names already given, Mr. Trumbull tells us that this duck is called horse-head and bald-pate, off the coast of Maine; patch-head, patch-polled coot and white-scop, at other points on the New England coast; muscle-bill, pictured-bill and plaster-bill, snuff-taker, spectacled-bill coot and spectacle coot, blossom-bill and blossom-head, butter-boat-billed coot; while the females and young are called, at various points, pishaug, gray coot and brown coot.

RUDDY DUCK.

Erismatura rubida (WILS.).

The adult male has the crown black, which color runs down on the back of the neck; the side of head, including cheeks and chin, pure white; the entire upper parts, reddish-chestnut, except the wing-coverts; the middle of the rump and lower back, greenish-brown, freckled with paler. The quills of the wing and tail are brownish-black; the under parts are silvery-whitish, something like the breast color of some of the grebes. The under tail-coverts are white; the bill and feet grayish-blue; length, 16 inches.

The female is much duller; the upper part of the head is dark brown, paling on the sides of the head.

Often there is a white strip below the eyes, running almost from the base of the bill to the back of the head. The chin is white. The throat and neck are brownish-gray, fading to silvery on the breast and belly. The upper parts are grayish-brown, mottled and·speckled with reddish. The wings and scapulars are dark brown; the quills of tail and wings as in the male; the bill is bluish, often blackish, and the legs and feet, bluish-gray. The young male is still duller.

The ruddy duck is found throughout North America, and is one of the gentlest and most unsuspicious of our birds. It is resident in Northern South America, and yet it frequents the northern portions of the continent as far as the 58th parallel. It is abundant in California and equally so on our South Atlantic coast and occurs often in Massachusetts during the spring migration.

The ruddy duck, although it takes a long time to rise from the water, is a strong flier. It is, however, very much at home on the water, a rapid swimmer and a very good diver. The ruddy is a most gentle and unsuspicious little bird, and appears to pay no attention to the gunner, though he may be standing in plain sight, as it darts down and splashes into the water among the decoys. Until within a few years, gunners in our South Atlantic waters never shot these little birds, which were accustomed to come to the decoys and feed among them and then swim or fly away unmolested. Of late years, however, this has become a fashionable bird for the table, and, bringing good prices, is eagerly sought after by market gunners.   Great numbers are therefore killed each season now, where formerly they were almost unmolested, and the result has been a very noticeable reduction in the numbers of these little birds.

The ruddy duck has a great number of common names, most of which refer to its physical peculiarities or to its great gentleness.   Thus it is called sleepy broad-bill, sleepy-head, sleepy duck, sleepy coot, sleepy brother, fool duck, deaf duck, booby and booby coot, paddy and noddy.   From its tail it is called stiff-tail, spine-tail, quill-tail coot, pin-tail, bristle-tail, heavy-tailed duck, stick-tail and dip-tail diver.   From its supposed toughness, or the difficulty with which it is killed, come such names as hard-headed broad-bill, shot-pouch, stub and twist, hard-head, tough-head, hickory-head, greaser, steel-head, light-wood knot and perhaps hard tack.   There are a great number of other names, for which the reader must be referred to Mr. Trumbull's excellent volume.

MASKED DUCK.

Nomonyx dominicus (LINN.).

The adult male, in full plumage, neck all around, back and sides, dark cinnamon-brown, the back and sides with the feathers broadly streaked with black; the front of head, including chin, cheeks and crown, black, this color extending nearly to the back of the head. The lower parts are rusty, but the feathers of the side are streaked with black. The wings are brownish-black, with a white speculum. The under tail-coverts are brownish, spotted with black. The tail is dark brown; the bill blue, and feet blackish; length about 15 inches.

The female has the head black, with one or two brownish streaks running back from the bill. The chestnut is paler, verging to yellowish, and spotted with black; the sexes are thus much alike, but the female is very much duller.

The masked duck is found in North America only as a straggler, for it belongs in the tropics. It is a common West Indian and South American species. It has been taken on Lake Champlain, in New York, in Massachusetts, in Wisconsin, Texas and Mexico. It does not appear to be anywhere an abundant species, as is its near relative, the ruddy duck. We are told that it does not seem to be at all at home on the land, and that when it walks it is in some degree supported by its long, stiff tail. Gunners should be on the watch for this species.

FISH DUCKS.

SUB-FAMILY *Merginæ.*

The mergansers, or, as they are often called, the fish-ing ducks, may be distinguished from all others of the *Anatidæ* by their narrow and round (not flattened) bills, always provided with sharp, backward-directed, tooth-like lamellæ. Except for their bills, they are like the sea-ducks. They are birds of handsome plu-mage, always provided with a crest, which in the male may be enormously enlarged and very striking, as in the hooded merganser, or merely puffy, with brilliant iridescent hues, as in the goosander. The mergansers feed almost altogether on small fish, which they cap-ture by diving, and as a consequence their flesh is not at all desirable. Our species are widely distributed over America.

225

AMERICAN MERGANSER.

Merganser americanus (Cass.).

The adult has the head and upper neck greenish-black, with brilliant metallic reflections, the head being puffy and the feathers slightly longest on the back of the head. The back is black, fading to ashy-gray on the rump and upper tail-coverts. The primaries and secondaries are black, but the rest of the wing is chiefly white, crossed by a black bar. The under parts are white, tinged with salmon color, rosy or pinkish, which does not last long after death. In old skins, the breast feathers often become barred with ashy. The tail is ashy-gray, with bill, eyes and feet bright red. Length about 26 inches.

In the female the head and neck are reddish-brown, and there is a long crest on the back of the head, much more marked than in the male. The chin and throat are white, the upper parts gray. About one-half of each secondary feather is white, forming a speculum on the wing. The primaries are black, the flanks and tail gray. The lower parts are pinkish salmon-color in life, fading to white. The bill and feet are red.

Valueless as food, the great merganser is certainly one of our most beautiful and graceful birds. It is a close relative of the goosander of Europe, and was long considered to be the same bird. The differences on which they are separated are very slight. The merganser is a resident of the extreme North in summer. It is found in Alaska, though apparently not very common there; and, in fact, it does not seem to be a very common bird anywhere, both the other species exceeding it in numbers. It is one of our most hardy birds, and one of the last to go South in the autumn; and, indeed, it will remain about air holes in the rivers, where it can fish, long after most other ducks have taken their departure for the South.

It is well established that the goosander breeds in the hollows of trees, wherever trees are accessible, though some observers who have reported nests of this species from the far North, beyond where timber grows, state that it builds its nest upon the ground in the ordinary manner of many of the salt-water ducks.

Definite information as to the breeding habits of this merganser was first given by Mr. Geo. A. Boardman, of Calais, Me., to whom ornithology owes so much. In *Forest and Stream* he has said:

"Many years ago I was up at Grand Lake Stream salmon fishing, when I saw a large duck fly into a hole high up in a large birch tree. The log drivers said it was a sheldrake and had nested there many years. I was anxious to see what kind of a merganser it was. After the log drivers' day's work was done one of them by driving spikes managed to get up. The old bird flew out, and he brought down one egg, and said there were seven more. I then got the man to arrange a noose over the hole, and the next morning we had the old bird hung by the neck and the eight eggs were new to science. The log drivers said they had seen the old bird bring down the young in her bill to the water. Several years later Mr. John Krider, of Philadelphia, went with me to the same tree and collected the eggs. He was a well-known collector. Mr. Audubon was mistaken in his account of the nesting of this merganser, since he describes it as nesting on the ground among rushes, in the manner of the serrator, having a large nest raised 7 or 8 inches above the surface."

Often, while travelling along streams in uninhabited parts of the country, one may come upon a mother merganser and her brood of tiny young and may drive them before him for miles along the stream, the birds keeping well out of his way, and the mother watching over them with the tenderest care. It is a curious sight to see these little downy creatures run, as it seems, over the surface of the water, at the same time flapping their

tiny featherless wings, but making extraordinary progress.

While the goosander, like others of its kind, feeds
almost exclusively on fish, it is said that in the autumn
its flesh is not noticeably bad, but that in spring it is exceedingly rank and oily.

RED-BREASTED MERGANSER, SHELDRAKE.

Merganser serrator (LINN.).

The adult male has the head greenish-black, with some metallic reflections of violet and purple. The crest is a ragged one, chiefly on the back of the head; the feathers are irregular, but few of them being long. There is a well-marked white collar around the upper neck, below the black. The lower neck and breast are pale pinkish brown, streaked with black from above downward. The back and inner scapulars are black; the lower back and rump, grayish, waved with black and white; the tail grayish-brown. The wing is chiefly white, crossed by two black bars. The primaries are brownish-black, and the outer webs of the inner secondaries edged with the same color. On the side of the breast, in front of the bend in the wing, is a patch of white feathers, margined with black. The sides are barred with black and white, and the rest of the under parts white. The bill, eyes and feet are bright red. Length about 22 inches. In this species the nostrils are situated near to the base of the bill, whereas in the goosander they are nearly half way between the base and tip of bill. This character will enable the observer to distinguish the two.

The adult female has the top of the head and crest reddish-brown; the sides of head and neck somewhat paler, fading to white on the throat. The upper parts are dark ashy-gray; the sides almost the same, but somewhat paler. There is a white patch on the wing, divided by a black bar. The under parts are white, often with a pinkish or salmon tinge in both sexes, but this is by no means always present. The bill, legs and feet are like those in the male, but perhaps a little duller.

Like the goosander, this species belongs to the Northern Hemisphere at large, and is found in Europe, China, Japan and other islands of the Pacific. Mr. Shepard found it breeding in Iceland, in company with Barrow's golden-eye, and Old World observers generally have reported it as abundant in the North. It occurs regularly as a resident in Greenland, and, of course, in North America is quite a common species. It has been reported, in summer, from Alaska, and from Maine, and breeds in both sections. Mr. Mac-

Farlane found it also breeding on the Anderson River, in the far North. The nest is reported to be closely similar to that of the black duck, and the parent often lines it with down plucked from her breast.

Like the preceding species, the red-breasted merganser is a tough and hardy bird, well fitted to endure our northern winters, and not proceeding southward so long as there are any open waters in which it can gain a livelihood. It spends much of its time on the salt water and associates more or less with the winter sea-ducks of the New England coast, but more perhaps with the whistlers than with others.

The red-breasted merganser feeds altogether on fish, and for this reason has no value whatever as a table bird. Mr. D. G. Elliot, in his excellent work on North American Wild Fowl, gives a graphic description of their fishing, which is well worth reproducing. He says: "When engaged in fishing, by their rapid diving and manœuvring beneath the waters, they cause the small fish—if the schools are of any size—to become widely scattered, and many rise close to the surface. The gulls take advantage of such opportunities, and pounce upon their luckless finny prey from above, and then, with ducks diving into the depths and gulls plunging from above, the scene is a very lively one. I remember on one occasion watching a number of this merganser engaged in fishing in a cove, when their movements attracted to them a large flock of Bonaparte's gull (*Larus philadelphia*), which hovered over the ducks for a moment and then began to plunge head foremost into the water, one after another, in rapid succession, emerging, frequently with a small fish in the bill. The mergansers paid no attention to their fellow-fishermen, although at times a plunging gull would come perilously near one of the saw-billed gentry as he rose from the depths; and what with the rising and disappearing mergansers, and the air above them filled with the forms of the darting gulls, executing all manner of swift and graceful evolutions, the scene was very spirited and full of animation."

The red-breasted merganser is swift of wing, and as might be imagined, an expert diver. It frequently comes in very gently to decoys, dashing along at great speed, until it reaches the point where it wishes to alight, and then, without checking its flight, throwing itself breast down upon the water, and sliding over it for some distance. After alighting, it looks about for a moment, alternately raising and depressing its crest, and if it sees nothing to alarm it, goes to work fishing. There is no reason for shooting it, as it is worthless for food.

Among the common names applied to this bird, in different sections of the country, are sheldrake, saw-bill, fisherman, pied sheldrake, shelduck and big saw-bill.

HOODED MERGANSER.

Lophodytes cucullatus (LINN.).

Adult male has the head, neck, back and scapulars, black. The very long full crest is pure white, margined with black. The wing-coverts are gray, fading to ash color behind, and the greater coverts are black at the base and tipped with white, showing a distinct black and white band across the wing. The secondaries are white, the basal portion black, which gives the effect of two wide white wing-bars, bordered in front by two narrow black wing-bars. In front of the wing, on the side of the breast, are two black and two white bars, crescent-shaped. The sides and flanks are rusty-brown, or tawny, growing darker toward the tail, and crossed by fine, black lines. The under parts generally are white; the under tail-coverts streaked with dusky. The bill is black, eye bright yellow and the feet yellowish. Length about 18 inches.

In the female the head and crest are reddish-brown, and the upper parts are grayish-brown. The chin and throat are white; the flanks grayish-brown. There is a patch on the wing, white, crossed by a black bar, and the under parts generally are white. The bill is yellowish, darkening to brown on the margin and on the nail.

The hooded merganser is one of the most striking of our North American ducks. It is exclusively a North American species and occurs in Europe only as a straggler. Throughout the whole of North America, however, it is generally distributed, and seems to be no less abundant, for example, in Nebraska than it is on the Atlantic or Pacific coasts.

The hooded merganser breeds over much of the country, in suitable localities. Mr. Boardman has found it breeding abundantly in Maine, where its nests were always found in the hollows of trees, the cavity being usually lined with grass, leaves and down. He has related the following curious incident in regard to the breeding of this bird:

"On one of my collecting trips my attention was called by the log drivers to a singular contest between two ducks—it proved to be a female wood duck and a female hooded merganser—for the possession of a hollow tree. Two birds had been observed for several days contesting for the nest, neither permitting the other to remain in peaceful occupancy. The nest was found to contain eighteen fresh eggs, of which one-third belonged to the merganser, and as the nest was lined with the down of the merganser it appeared probable this bird was the rightful owner of the premises."

Mr. Audubon stated that the hooded merganser bred in Kentucky, Ohio and Indiana; and Dr. Bachman believed that it breeds in South Carolina. It certainly breeds in Florida. During its migrations, the hairy-head, as it is often called, is common in New England, and generally all along the coast, at least as far as South Carolina. In the marshes of Currituck Sound I have seen them in great numbers, sometimes in flocks of over one hundred individuals.

The hooded merganser is a bird of exceedingly swift flight, and may often be taken at a little distance for a canvas-back or black-head, as it flies swiftly toward one. It is an unsuspicious bird, coming up readily to decoys, striking the water with a swift rush and, for a few moments after alighting, swimming about alertly, as if to observe its surroundings. Usually it flies with great directness, and is not easily frightened into changing its course. The hooded merganser is an extremely expert swimmer and diver, and it is a beautiful sight to watch a small body of them, as one sometimes may, when they are feeding without knowledge of the presence of an enemy. At such times the startling plumage of the male is seen to very great advantage, and one is greatly attracted by the beauty of his plumage and the grace of his motions.

This bird rejoices in a variety of names, of which water-pheasant, hairy-crown, hairy-head, saw-bill diver, little saw-bill, swamp sheldrake, spike-bill and cock-robin are the most familiar.

The smew, *Mergus albellus,* was reported by Audubon to have been taken in Louisiana, near New Orleans, in 1817. The bird was a female. Since that date no specimens have been reported as taken within the United States. If the bird ever occurs on this continent it is only an accidental straggler. It is perhaps more likely that in the case of the specimen taken by Audubon there was some mistake of identification. However, the description is given here, taken from Mr. Elliot's "Wild Fowl": "Adult male, general plumage, white. A large patch at base of the bill, including the lores and eyes, lower portion of nuchal crest, middle of the back and two crescentic narrow lines on side of breast, outer edge of scapulars and rump, jet black. Upper tail-coverts, gray; edges lighter. Middle wing-coverts, white; greater coverts and secondaries, black, tipped with white. Primaries, blackish-brown. Tail, dark gray. Sides and flanks undulated with fine black lines on a gray ground. Bill, bluish; nail, lighter. Iris, bluish white. Legs and feet, bluish lead color; webs, darker. Total length, about 16¾ inches; wing, 7 6-10; culmen, 1¼; tarsus, 1⅛.

"Adult female.—Head and nape, chestnut brown; lores and cheeks, brownish black. Throat and sides of neck, white. Upper parts, brownish-gray, darkest on the rump; some feathers on back tipped with ashy gray. Sides and flanks, brownish-gray. Under parts, white. Tail, brown-gray."

Male.

Female.

THE SHOVELLER.

Reduced from Audubon's Plate.

PART II.

WILDFOWL SHOOTING.

A GOLDEN-EYE NESTING PLACE.
Photographed by Wm. Brewster. (See p. 176.)

WILDFOWL SHOOTING.

If it be true, as has often been said, that the enjoyment taken in any sport is proportioned to its difficulties and hardships, then we may readily comprehend why wildfowl shooting is popular. To be sure, there are other reasons; the rewards are sometimes great, and though no description of shooting is more uncertain than this, yet as man is a hopeful creature, and usually believes that he will be fortunate, even though all his fellows are unlucky, men continue to go duck shooting, even though the measure of success with which they are usually rewarded may be very meagre. One good day, or one successful expedition, will long remain fresh in the duck shooter's memory and will lure him on to make trip after trip, year after year, in the confident hope that some time this good fortune will come to him again. In the faith that his success will repeat itself, he gladly endures cold, hunger, wet, and even danger, over and over again.

As the finest weather for duck shooting is what is usually denominated foul weather—that is windy, cloudy, or rainy, often with snow squalls and a temperature so low that ice forms—the gunner must always go prepared to suffer some discomfort. If his shooting is done from a boat and in a place where the wind has any sweep he is sure to get wet and may even be swamped; or if it should happen that he guns in a locality where there are wide flats which may be overlaid by a skim of ice, too thick to be pushed through with a boat, yet hardly strong enough to bear one's weight, there is danger of a wetting, if not of something worse; for the mud is deep and sticky, and he who is once mired in it will escape only with difficulty and discomfort.

In old times it was taken for granted that the duck shooter should be uncomfortable, but of late years we have largely changed that. The older gunners who in their youth thought nothing of shivering all day in a thin coat under the icy wind, or of standing for hours waist deep in the water, when the flight was on, or of lying out where the flying spray reached them and froze as it touched their garments, now do none of these things. They provide themselves with thick, warm clothing, and with overgarments of rubber. They take lunches with them and sometimes even carry small stoves in boat or blind by which to warm their food or themselves if the weather becomes too bad.

But with all these added comforts has come one great drawback which outweighs them all; this is the great scarcity of fowl. In old times, given suitable weather conditions, duck shooting on most of our waters was likely to be successful. Now, even with the best of weather, the chances are against success.

In the pages that follow I have endeavored, by means of description and accounts of shooting trips, to give a fairly accurate notion of most of the methods by which ducks are killed in North America. These methods vary to some extent with the different localities in which they are practiced, and they grade into one another so that it is not always easy to draw a sharp line between two methods of the sport. I have tried to cover the whole country and thus to make the volume of interest and of use to duck shooters wherever they may be.

SWAN SHOOTING.

Swan shooting can hardly be characterized as a sport, for the few swans that are killed are shot chiefly by accident, when they fly over points where gunners are concealed waiting for ducks, or at times when, with the geese, they come up to goose decoys. Most of those killed during the winter are secured in the Chesapeake Bay and on Currituck Sound, where they winter in considerable numbers, flocks of two or three hundred sometimes being seen. On the occasion of a freeze, even larger numbers gather together, looking, as they sit along the marsh or in the air holes, like great drifts of snow.

Swans are sometimes shot when standing on the shore of the marshes; this can only be done when the wind is blowing hard on the shore. Under such conditions the gunner is sometimes able to land at a distance from the bird, and to creep through the reeds, within gunshot, since the swan cannot hear him on account of the wind.

Swans decoy readily, and occasionally the professional gunners have a few wooden swan decoys on the house boats which they inhabit and in which they move from place to place, but nowhere, so far as I am aware, is the shooting of swans made a business. One or two of the ducking clubs on Currituck Sound have small stands of live swan decoys which have been captured

244

from time to time, which they occasionally tie out when they go to shoot geese, but on the whole the number of swans killed each year is very small, and does not nearly equal the young bred each season. There seems good reason for believing, therefore, that the swans are holding their own, if not increasing, and in many of the localities where they pass the winter, professional gunners aver that the swans are now more numerous than they were in old times.

Swans do not dive, but bring up their food from the bottom by reaching down with their long necks and tearing off the grass with their powerful bills. They are wary birds and not easily approached. Sometimes they sit on the water long enough for a boat to sail up within shot of them, but this is unusual. They rise from the water slowly, flying a long way before they fairly get up into the air, paddling with their great feet, and striking the water with the tips of their strong wings, so as to make a great noise. As they can rise only against the wind, advantage is sometimes taken of this fact to sail down on them, and a shot may then be had. When changing from one feeding ground to another, or from the feeding to the roosting ground, they usually fly high, provided the weather is calm and bright; but if the wind blows hard, or it is raining or snowing, they often pass along within easy gunshot of the marsh, and it is on such occasions that they are chiefly killed. Each flock usually follows the course taken by its predecessor, and if the gunner happens to be in the line of flight, and the weather conditions are propitious, he may have several shots during a morning or an afternoon. I recall having seen one man, a number of years ago, pull down three great swans from the sky just as the sun was setting.

The note of the common swan is very different from that of his western relative. It is a plaintive, rather high-pitched call, often repeated, and can be fairly well imitated by blowing into the neck of a wide-mouthed bottle. On the principal shooting grounds of the South the boatmen are familiar with the call-note of the swan, and imitate it faultlessly. This skill often gives the gunner an opportunity for a shot which he would not otherwise have.

Mr. D. G. Elliot, in his admirable work on the "Wild Fowl of North America," has this to say about the notes uttered by the wounded swan: "The song of the dying swan has been the theme of poets for centuries and is generally considered one of those pleasing myths that are handed down through the ages. I had killed many swans and never heard aught from them at any time, save the familiar notes that reached the ears of everyone in their vicinity; but once, when shooting in Currituck Sound over water belonging to a club of which I am a member, in company with a friend, Mr. F. W. Leggett, of New York, a number of swans passed over us at a considerable height. We fired at them, and one splendid bird was mortally hurt. On receiving his wound the wings became fixed, and he commenced at once his song, which was continued until the water was reached, nearly half a mile away. I am perfectly familiar with every note a swan is accustomed to utter, but never before or since have I heard any like those sung by this stricken bird. Most plaintive in character and musical in tone, it sounded at times like the soft running of the notes in an octave:

> " 'And now 'twas like all instruments,
>   Now like a lonely flute;
> And now it is an angel's song
>   Which makes the heavens be mute,'

and as the sound was borne to us, mellowed by the distance, we stood astonished and could only exclaim: 'We have heard the song of the dying swan.' "

Occasionally, if a cygnet should become separated from the flock with which it has been feeding, it shows itself very gentle, and can sometimes be called up to a bunch of goose or even of duck decoys. I have seen this happen, the bird coming in close to the water and passing over the decoys. It then turned and flew over them once again, when it was killed by the gunner.

A wounded swan is very difficult to recover. These birds cannot dive effectively, but can and do swim, so as to lead the pursuing boat a long chase. When crippled, they usually swim right up into the wind's eye, and as they can swim faster than a boat can be rowed, they often escape.

The cygnets of both species of our swans are gray, and these young birds should always be chosen when the opportunity for a shot presents itself. Swan shooting, however, as already remarked, is largely a matter of accident, and while I have known of ten being killed in a day, at a goose box, I have also known of whole seasons to elapse without a single shot being had by men who were devoting themselves to duck and goose shooting.

It is well for the duck shooter to carry with him, besides the cartridges of B or BB shot, with which he will provide himself, on the chance of getting a shot at a flock of geese, a few cartridges of T or OO buckshot, for long shots at swans.

Although swans are such large birds, and rise with difficulty from the water, they nevertheless fly with great swiftness, and the gunner must recollect this, and must shoot well ahead of them. If the swans are flying against the wind, he should aim at the bird's head, remembering that a single pellet striking a swan in the neck is quite as likely to be effective in bringing it down as two or three shots which may strike it in the body. If, however, the bird is flying down wind, and high up in the air, the gun should be held somewhat in advance of the point of the bill. Allowance must always be made for the great size of the bird. It would seem to the novice as if a mark such as this could scarcely be missed, but this very size and the swiftness of the bird's flight are likely to deceive.

As swans are usually shot overhead, they sometimes fall almost in the gunner's blind, or, at all events, very close to him. It is an impressive sight to see one of these great birds, struck with a fatal charge, come tumbling to the earth. Its great size, its broad expanse of wing and its long neck make it appear even larger than it really is, and when it strikes the ground it does so with a thud which seems to shake the marsh.

I once killed and weighed an American swan which turned the scale at 25 pounds; how much larger they may grow, I do not know.   At all events, they are royal birds.

GOOSE SHOOTING.

The wild goose has long been proverbial for his shyness and wariness, and he well deserves the reputation that he has gained, and yet sometimes he is found to be "as silly as a goose." So that the gunner who follows the geese enough to see much of them, will find that at one time great acuteness and at another a singular lack of suspicion are present in the ordinary wild goose. Few birds are more difficult to approach than these, and yet few come more readily to decoys or are more easily lured from their course by an imitation of their cry.

Constantly pursued for food, their experience, almost from the egg shell, has taught them suspicion. On the breeding grounds in the North, at the time when the young geese are well grown, but as yet unable to fly, great numbers are killed by Indians and Eskimo, who, assisted by their dogs, drive the birds out of the shallow pools in the marshes, where they dwell, and spear them with their bone tridents, or catch them in nets, or kill them with sticks. In the same way many of the adults also are destroyed during the molting season.

Several instances have occurred where swans and geese—killed by gunners in the United States—still bore in their bodies evidences of having been wounded by the aborigines of the far North. The United States

250

National Museum has a number of examples of this kind, where the birds' bodies have been pierced by long arrow heads, which remained in the wound and were covered up in its healing. Many years ago there was figured in *Forest and Stream* the wing of a swan which still bore, lying between the radius and ulna, a long copper arrow head, which must have been shot into the bird somewhere in the far Northwest. The old wound had healed, and the bird when killed was in good condition.

Notwithstanding the annual destruction by the natives, there are always left vast numbers of geese to take their flight southward at the approach of winter, but when they reach the northern confines of the United States they find awaiting them a horde of gunners bent on their destruction.

ON THE STUBBLES.

In the interior, and especially on the high plains of the wheat-producing belt of Manitoba, the Dakotas and Nebraska, geese are shot in two principal ways.

Of these, the more common is shooting them in the grain fields from which the crops have been harvested, to which the birds resort for food. They pass the night in lakes or rivers, not far from the feeding ground, and in the early morning take their flight to the stubbles, there to feed during the day. The gunners prepare as blinds, or places of concealment, pits dug in the fields, the earth being carried away to some distance and scattered over the ground, so that there shall be no fresh soil exposed to attract the attention of the flocks and render them suspicious. About the pits are set up the decoys, which usually consist of sheet-iron profiles of geese, on sharp-pointed iron standards implanted in the ground, so that when seen from the direction from which the birds are coming, they look like a flock of geese standing on the ground. On these, and on his power of calling, the gunner, hidden in the pit, depends.

He is in his blind by daylight, and soon after this the flight begins. If he has had time to study the habits of the birds, his blind is placed directly in the line of flight, between the roosting and the feeding ground, and his decoys are likely to call down to within gun-shot many of the passing flocks. Sometimes, if two or three men are shooting together, they will dig their pits about a gun-shot apart, and at right angles to the line of the birds' flight. In such a case they plant their decoys midway between the pits, with the result that the flocks which come down to them are likely to offer shots to the occupants of the two pits between which they fly.

While most of the birds killed are likely to fall at once, there will still be many which, struck by one or two pellets, or hit too far behind, will carry off the shot, and, gradually lowering their flight, will come to the ground a long way from the pit. It is important, therefore, that each flock shot at should be watched as it goes away, in order that birds hard hit, but still able to proceed for some distance, may be seen to separate themselves from the flock and to come down. Unless very carefully marked, such birds are likely to be lost to the gunner, unless he is provided with a dog.

At every lull in the flight, it is the practice to leave the pit and go out to gather the dead geese; and toward the middle of the day, when the morning flight has ceased, the more distant ground should be carefully looked over by the gunner, and, if practicable, systematically hunted out with a dog. The result of this search will often add largely to the bag.

Sometimes, instead of digging pits in the stubble fields, the gunners conceal themselves in the straw stacks which may still be standing in the field, and do their shooting from them. The straw stacks having been there before the geese came in the fall, are familiar objects to the birds, and cause them no alarm. Often they pass close over them or feed on the ground near them. Where these stacks are used for hiding places, the decoys are scattered around them in the most convenient situation.

It is not common for the passing flocks to alight with the decoys in the stubble fields; usually by the time that the birds have approached close to them, the decoys are recognized as deceptions, and the flock turns off.

Goose shooting in the wheat stubbles is also practiced in parts of Washington. Pits are dug and decoys put out, just as in the stubbles of Dakota and Nebraska, and the birds come readily to the decoys.

ON THE SAND-BARS.

Sand-bar shooting, which was formerly practiced with great success on some of the larger rivers of the West, especially on the Platte, is somewhat similar in character to the shooting on the feeding grounds, except that it takes place early in the morning and late in the afternoon, when the birds come to the river to drink, as well as to provide themselves with the sand and gravel which are as necessary to them as food. The blind may be a hole dug in the sand-bar, or perhaps a pile of drift-wood and trash, in which the gunner conceals himself. The decoys are similar to those used in stubble shooting, and are placed between the water and the blind. The birds usually come in each day at about the same hour, and so regular are their habits that one familiar with a locality could almost set his watch by their arrival. In this shooting the birds are much more disposed to come to the decoys than in stubble shooting, and often appear to wish to alight with them.

The birds commonly killed in this form of shooting are the Canada goose, Hutchins's goose, the white-fronted goose, or prairie brant, the blue goose and the snow goose.

If the geese are no longer killed on the Platte River in their old numbers, they have not altogether deserted that stream in their southern journey. They still resort to it, but overshooting has taught them caution, and the methods by which they are killed have wholly changed. At the present time they go into the river late, pay no attention whatever to decoys, and have become so wary that shooting them on the sand-bars is hardly attempted. When they rise they no longer circle about, but at once get up in the air as high as possible, keeping directly over the middle of the river, and so usually out of shot of concealed gunners. Many and bitter have been the complaints of late years by the men who used to go goose shooting to this famous ground, but the birds have learned their lesson well, and it may be doubted if sand-bar shooting will ever again be practiced on the Platte with any great degree of success.

The geese now killed in the vicinity of that river are secured chiefly by stubble shooting, much as they are captured in Dakota, and a recent account of these methods is given in the following article contributed to *Forest and Stream* in 1899, by a writer who signs himself "Invisible." He says:

Readers who have been there need not be told of the past glories of duck and goose shooting on the wide-flowing Platte in Nebraska, but to those who have not hunted on the once famous river, a description of the stream, the country and the methods employed to bag the wary honkers may be interesting.

The Platte is a shallow, wide stream from one-half mile to one mile wide in some places, and the bottom is entirely of sand. In late April and in May and June it rises or gets on a "boom," as it is generally called. Then the water is from three to six feet deep in all the main part of the river, and in the main channel from ten to

even fifteen feet in some particular places. A beautiful
valley, smooth and level as a floor, stretches away for
miles from both sides in some places, and in others only
on one side, when the high bluffs come up to the bank.
Beyond this level valley are the high lands, irregular
lines of sand bluffs, and on the high table-land beyond
is the feeding ground of the great army of geese and
ducks that frequent the Platte every spring and sometimes in the fall. Geese and ducks are not as plentiful
here now as years ago; while there are a good many
birds here every favorable spring, there is not one to
the fifty there used to be in years gone by. Ten and
fifteen years ago fifteen to twenty geese were a common
thing for one man to kill in one day, or even in a half
day's hunt. A friend claimed to have killed fifty-two
geese one afternoon from 2 o'clock to sundown, and no
one who knows the man or the numbers of birds doubts
the claim. But these are past supplies, never to be seen
on the Platte again. At the present time on stormy
days, if a hunter is in a good place, he may be able to
bag in the course of a day ten, or maybe fifteen or
twenty, geese, and as many ducks. But these days and
chances are, indeed, very rare. Very much oftener the
hunter comes in with one goose and a few ducks, or if it
be a bad day he comes in empty-handed.

I live within one day's drive of the river, and in the
spring a party of four or five go to the old Platte for a
two or three weeks' hunt and a general good time.
Landing at the river about 4 o'clock in the evening,
after a good drive of thirty-five miles, we are made wel-

come by an old friend who lives about forty rods from the river; we put up our team and then commence to pitch tent, for we come prepared to camp out. While working around camp we see long strings of ducks and geese come sailing leisurely in from their feeding grounds out on the bluffs and in the valley; old-time memories are revived, and we all work with a vim to get the tent up and banked and ditched around; we carry hay to make our bed, and then get supper. When this is all done it is too late to do any shooting. Shells are gotten out, guns are examined, hunting suits are laid out handy, and everything is put in readiness for an early start in the morning. While all this was going on, ducks and geese have been alighting in the river, and several hundred geese are out on the sand-bars, making merry music for our ears. The musical honk-a-honk is heard after it gets dark, as some tardy members come in to their roost on the sand-bars.

We go to bed with the intention of having goose for dinner next day if Dame Fortune shall see fit to send a flock our way. We all arise next morning before daylight, eat a hasty breakfast, don dead grass color suits, and, with a dozen decoys each and a gun, sally forth, going out where we know they feed in a corn or wheat field. Arriving at the field, we dig a pit, place the loose dirt where it won't be conspicuous, then put out the decoys, and settle ourselves comfortably and await the coming of a flock of honkers, or perhaps ducks. We are in sight of the rim, and pretty soon we see some rise up and start for the feeding grounds. We watch every movement made by the flock. They rise high up as they clear the river bank and head directly for us. We crouch low in the blind with guns in readiness, and goose-call to our lips. They don't see the decoys, for it is not very light yet. As they come nearer they come down a trifle; yes, they see the decoys. The leader sets his wings and drops below the others, and they sail gracefully for the decoys. But, alas! they turn, about the time we are sure we have a shot, and by a graceful sweep go by to one side out of range, and alight just back of us about 150 yards.

However, we settle down as we see another flock get up out of the river. They go up and start out on the same line with the other flock. They head directly for the other flock on the ground behind me, and, reassured by seeing the others there, they drop down within 40 yards of the ground, and come almost directly over me. I rise with gun in hand, four reports in quick succession, and three noble Canada geese fall to the ground; and one other starts, then rises and starts on, but one more shot and he comes tumbling down to earth. The fun has started in earnest. The geese come out in small flocks, and the guns are booming in every direction. In two hours the flight has ceased, and we gather up our geese and decoys and start for camp. We sum up at camp: four guns have bagged eleven geese and five ducks in the two hours' shoot.

The next day the wind blows hard from the north, and snow is falling in large flakes. It is cold; but we start out to try our luck about 2 o'clock in the afternoon.

We separate and take up position in the willow thickets that abound along the river bank. With the river on the north of us, feeding grounds are a great deal closer on the south side, so, contrary to their regular habits, the birds come out with the wind, and come back flying low, but with no good results; so I concluded to get in a good sheltered place and wait for some to come over, if I had to wait all day. They flew on all sides, ducks and geese both, some barely clearing the ground. Just to the south of me was open ground for about 200 yards, then a high bluff with some trees growing on the sides and rising above the table land above. My patience was nearly exhausted, when just behind these trees came a flock of mallards. I did not see them till they rose to clear these trees. As I stood in a thick stand of willows, they never saw me, but came on just a little to my left about 40 yards high. They looked big and grand. I could distinguish all their fine colorings as they came closer. I rose up and made a double on two fine drakes that were nearest to me. Having retrieved these, I had not long to wait before a lone pintail came along, and I had a fine shot at him. Shooting was good until dark. I bagged seventeen ducks and one brant. One of the other boys got sixteen ducks, and the others all had a respectable bag of ducks.

We had another stormy day while on this trip, and these two days were my best, in fact the only days when we bagged very many ducks. We got geese almost every morning and evening until our return home.

Ducks do not seem to decoy on the feeding grounds

here, but on some ponds of still water they decoy splendidly, and good bags may be made on any decent day.

After the geese had, in large measure, been driven away from the Platte, good shooting was had on the Arkansas River. The method of gunning on this stream was to choose an island as near the centre of the river as possible, where there was a good sand-bar for decoys, within thirty or forty yards of the island, and to dig a pit and shoot the geese as they came in to the decoys. Often the shooting was very good here, and frequently the bag was a mixed one, for ducks frequently came up within shot, lured by the goose decoys. In this shooting, bags of from 25 to 40 geese and 15 to 20 ducks were often made.

WITH LIVE DECOYS.

Except in a few places in the East, goose shooting is hardly at all practiced, and to the gunner of the northeast coast a goose is the greatest of all feathered game. By accident a few are killed every year at various points on the New England coast, but at one or two places in Massachusetts, and from Maryland southward, many geese are killed annually.

In these localities it is desirable and almost necessary, however, to use live goose decoys. These are set out within gun-shot of the blind, and their movements and vociferous calling lure down their wild relatives, which often alight among them, and begin to fight or to play with them.

In the South the most common method is to have a water-tight box built on some shoal, or at the edge of some sandy beach, in a place where the geese are accustomed to congregate. Such a box is commonly four feet deep, and is, of course, open at the top. Usually it is large enough for two men, who are provided with a seat, and with a shelf in front, on which they can place ammunition. A fringe of grass or bushes is tacked about the edge of the box, projecting only six or eight inches above it, through which the occupants can watch the geese as they draw near.

On a good goosing day, long before it is light, the men go into the goose-pen and capture the live decoys, which are placed in coops, each one large enough to hold two or three birds. The coops are then transported to the boat, if the journey to the box is to be made by water, or are put in the wagon, if the box is close to the shore. The goose stools, on which the tethered birds are to stand, are put in the boat; then the gunners, with their arms and ammunition, enter it, and the start is made for the box. If it should happen that the box has not been used for a long time, or if the previous day was stormy, with a high sea, the box may be found to be full of water, in which case it must, of course, be bailed out. The gunners, with their arms, ammunition and lunch, take their places in it, and the men go off to leeward to set out the decoys. Usually the water is so shoal that they can wade about in it without going over the tops of their high rubber boots. If it is deeper than this, the chances are against much shooting, for the wild geese are pretty well informed as to the depth of the water, and if it is too deep for them to feed they are not likely to alight. On the other hand, the water must be deep enough for them to swim easily.

The number of decoys put out is usually not less than six, nor more than fifteen. Whatever the number, the geese are set out in the form of a V, the angle being toward the box. Each goose is provided with a stool, which consists of a sharp-pointed stake, four feet long, sharpened at the end, and topped with a round or oval piece of board, eight or ten inches across. When the sharp end of the stake is firmly implanted in the mud of the bottom, the board table should be two inches under water. Immediately below the table there is fastened to the stake a slender leather strap, from three to four feet long, terminating in two branches, each of which has at its end a running noose, which is put around the goose's leg and drawn up snug, yet not too tight. As each stool is planted in the mud, the man who tends it goes to the boat, takes a goose from the coop, fastens it by both legs to the strap, and throws it on the water. As soon as the bird has been put out it begins to bathe, and for a time is busily engaged in ducking, shaking itself and swimming about, so far as its strap will permit. After it tires of this, it is likely to swim up to the table, climb on it and stand there preening itself. The best caller among the decoys is usually put at one end of one of the lines or off to one side, and the goose to which this gander is particularly attached at the other end. After the decoys are tied out, the men go away and hide their boat, and then take a position on the shore, as near as possible to the blind, where they can watch everything that is done.

If the weather is right for goosing, it is usually not long before a flock of the birds are seen coming. The decoys are likely to recognize them as soon as any one, and as soon as they see them they begin to call. If the decoys are properly set, the approaching geese will answer, and will usually lower their flight and prepare to alight with them. It is a common practice to allow them to do this, and then to fire one barrel at the birds on the water and another as they rise. If they swim up to the decoys in a long line, as they often do, the gunners, by aiming at their heads and necks, may often kill a large number on the water, and then, shooting with judgment, as the birds begin to rise, may get a number more. By this means, in favorable localities, more than a hundred geese are sometimes killed in a day, and not infrequently, with the geese, a number of swans may be taken, since the swans resort to the same feeding and roosting grounds that the geese occupy.

There is little to be said in praise of the altogether common practice of allowing geese to alight and shooting them on the water. It, of course, largely increases the count, which, in fact, is what many men shoot for, but there is certainly little satisfaction to be derived from killing with the shot-gun on the water a bird as large as a goose, and the better sentiment of the best class of gunners will favor shooting at the geese as they are about to alight, and then giving them the other barrels as they go away.

While much of the goose shooting on the South Atlantic coast is done from boxes planted on the shoals or the beach, it is sometimes done from sand-bars, locally called "lumps," in which pits are dug and these surrounded with a fringe of bushes or sedge. Shooting from such a shelter with a stand of live decoys is described by Mr. E. J. Myers in *Forest and Stream* in the following words:

Into the blind, because the skiff has already faded out of sight in the gray mist, and amid noisy splashing and washing one old gander is already stretching his long neck and straining the leather thong which ties him to the stake driven in the shallows out of sight. Out of the duskiness and gray shadows come muffled sounds as of the heavy wing strokes of the flying geese, that resolve into nothing as we settle ourselves down to patiently wait. Brighter grows the daylight from behind the sandy ridges dividing the ocean from the sound, and the great bars shooting to the zenith light the watery waste into vermilion and carminated blood, and, a glowing red ball of fire, up comes the sun. Involuntarily made a sun worshiper, I rise; when Hayman roughly pulls me down, and points with gun barrels directly at the sun just suspended over the rim of the horizon. Lo! there, as if they were issuing from its glowing, incandescent mass, a V-shaped dotted line is

spread across its face—the apex in its heart and the
ends reaching far out. "They are coming this way.
How swiftly they fly! Are they high or low?" But the
old gunner says not a word, as if miles away they could
hear the hoarse whisper, and lets his hand weigh heavily
on my shoulder for utter silence. On they come, nearer
and nearer; but, oh! how high. No use, they are too
high even for the 10-gauge; but hear that old renegade
decoy gander *honk-honk* as he tries to lure his wild
brethren to their death—the only thing, I suppose, the
white man taught him. From above the leader echoes
honk-honk, and we are afraid to move; but they go on,
and I stare at Hayman, who mutters, "Too high," and
peers between the brush of the blind as time goes on.

"See there!" But my eyes detect nothing across
the stretch of waters. "Low down on the water, coming from the lighthouse." "Too much for my eyes,"
I am about to say, when I see the whirling forms just
over the water, coming directly toward us. "Aye, they
will light," as the whole twenty decoys begin to flutter
and *honk-honk,* and then the heart stops beating and
the breath bates as the geese alight and begin swimming toward the decoys.

"Mark"—"fire"—three wild geese float on the water.
Up and at them—the second barrels bark and another
goose falls as the others wing away.

Out on the sand, Hayman takes some twigs and
fixes the dead geese as if they were sitting on the sand
—to me they look just as if they were alive, sitting
upon the nest.

"Great Jupiter! look at that, Hayman." For across the heavens, line after line, reaching from the easterly horizon to its westerly rim, came successive flocks as we crouched low down in the blind. Countless myriads moving onward, and then Hayman's hand fell heavily on my shoulder, backing, forcing me lower to the sandy floor. Far over our heads a flock was circling—sailing around and around, answering with noisy greetings the *honk-honk* of the captive renegades luring them to their doom—noisy converse between the clouds and the sand. Lower and lower they come, and just as they are about to light something frightens them, and then up rises Hayman; and I, needing no prompting, let the iron dogs bark for two that came tumbling almost in the box. A third one tumbled on the water and began fluttering away. Hayman sprang into the water and put two shots into it before he got the goose, nearly a quarter of a mile away. Away went the others, and then, "See, that one is badly hurt," said Hayman, as one bird seemed to be sinking slowly from the flock, flying away off in the distance. Lower, at first, three or four geese seemed to stick to the wounded one; but as he sank lower, the others went back to the flock, and the doomed one sank lower and lower, falling slowly to the sound, the life-blood ebbing away—badly, maybe fatally hurt, too far for us to get it. Deserted, abandoned and left to die.

So we went on until we had twelve before noon, and then the largest flock of the day settles about 600 yards away on the shoals, the water barely high enough to reach their breasts. The decoys honked to them in vain, and then I rose them with the Winchester and got one straggler going low as they flew over our heads. More real enjoyment in that one feat than in anything that happened that day.

So the hours waned and the day went by, and about 4 o'clock the signal, four shots, brought Bobby with the coops to the lump to take us back. We were all out of the blind on the lump with half the decoys in the box when a flock came right at us. Hayman and I sprang down in the blind and grasped the guns, while Bobby crouched behind the coop and squeezed the old rene-gade decoy gander until he honked as never honked he before. I named him Simon Gerty, after the old white renegade on the Ohio, who in the dime novels figured with Daniel Boone.

Heard one ever the yarn before, that the geese came and settled down among the decoys with coop and boy on the lump? Bobby's shrill voice, wild with eager im-patience, "kill 'um," spoiled the intended slaughter, but we got two, making fifteen geese.

Sport enough for the day, and wading across the water we got into the skiff and sailed back to the Brant. A bath and a smart rub down, and dinner all ready. And then, as the boys cleaned the guns and hung up the fowls, I stretched out on the deck, enjoying a *dolce far niente,* the priceless satiety of a sportsman who has had one fair day without mar or spoil.

On certain large lakes in Massachusetts, which are

regularly visited by the geese on their migrations, the practice of shooting over live decoys has been carried to its highest perfection.   Here are used not only live decoys tethered in the water and on the beach, but birds are kept also on the shore behind the stand, which, on the appearance of a flock of wild geese, are tossed into the air, and fly down to the captive decoys in the water.

On a little hill behind the stand a man sits concealed in a blind ready to throw the fly-geese, which are taught to fly out, circle about and finally alight in the water. As each one of these birds is thrown, the tethered birds on the beach and in the pens set up a loud honking, and the combination of the calling and the flying birds usually brings the approaching flock to the water. They do not always alight near the decoys, but even if they are quite a distance from shore, the flying birds and those seen on the beach are likely to draw them in.

A very clear idea of the success which attends this mode of decoying at Silver Lake, where one stand of live decoys numbers about 200 birds, can be had from an account of it published some years ago in *Forest and Stream,* which **reads** substantially as follows:

On the afternoon of November 15th, Charles and I went to the lake with our traps.   On the way we met William, the crack shot, and were told by him that the boys had killed eighteen geese that morning.   Our blood was up at once, for we had not forgotten the last hunt.

After supper we stood in the sand, when from out of the sky came the faint, long honk of geese.   There they are, and George stirs up the decoys. Old One Wing hears the call and straightens out for work. Soon the whole point is in one grand roar. The wild geese swing over us, and we can just make out the line of black rushing through the air. They wheel out over the lake, honk a few times, and we hear them no more. In a little while, as we look up the lake, we see a flash, then three or four, and then come the reports of the guns. Men at a stand on the east side of the lake have shot, and now the air is full of geese. We try to stop some of them, but it is of no use; so this ends the fun for the present.

It is now about 12 o'clock. Add, Tom, Herb and I are in the stand. George has turned in, having been up two nights. There is a light ripple on the water. The moon shines brightly, and we are saying that it is an ideal night for birds, when Herb says, "What is that just inside the blocks?" Tom looks with glasses, and says, "Ducks; about fifteen." They come nearer and are almost near enough to shoot, when there comes, *honk, honk, honk* right over us. There are fourteen geese, with wings crooked, scaling to our decoys. Have you ever seen them? and didn't your blood tingle? Something startles them, and they whirl to the north, going toward the place where the other shot was fired.

As the boys had been up nearly all of two nights, I offered to stand watch to-night. As I stood there looking at the water, it came to me why this place was called Silver Lake. The moon shining on the water, which was stirred to a little ripple by the breeze, made it seem like a lake of silver, and I thought it well named. The geese decoys had settled for the night, with only now and then the low growl of an old gander, which would be quickly answered by one of his goslings on the hill. The faint hoot of an owl comes to me from the eastern side of the lake, while from the southern end I hear the quick quack-quack of some ducks which have just lit. Then the soft call of the decoys at the new stand comes to me from afar off and startles me from my dreams, causing me to stir up the decoys and almost sending me in to wake the boys before I knew what it was. As I get over my excitement and find that my heart is not in my mouth, I hear the boom of a volley of guns at Oldham Pond; then in a short time another, and right upon it three reports from the new stand. I go into the air about a foot, and see Oliver, and Herb close at his heels, bareheaded and hair standing on end. "Great Scott! Have the British landed?" from Oliver, while Herb is saying: "What's the matter, Fred; are you trying to blow us up?" I explain matters, and as it is after 3 o'clock we decide to turn in and let the lake take care of itself. Nothing thus far. But our time is coming.

In the morning about 8 o'clock George said: "I am looking for a large flock of geese to-day." He had gone to feed the decoys, when Gene said: "There are geese." We pressed the button, and in a minute all were in the stand. "There they are," said George. "I never saw so large a flock before." As they came out over the lake the new stand let out their flyers; then

Gunner's Point let theirs go; and when George and Herb pulled on them, the way those goslings went from the hill was a caution. The wild ones see the flyers and hang, then crook, and then scale toward the water. They head into the wind, then wheel and come in the wind, then settle in the lake, and there they are. "Four acres of them," says George. I shall never forget how those geese looked coming in. Talk about pictures, it was the prettiest one I ever saw. Such a large flock of wild ones, with about 300 decoys flying around the three stands, was enough to open any sportsman's eyes. The gunners at Gunner's Point break about a dozen from the bunch, but do not shoot at them; the rest come toward us. George says: "They can't help it." We get fifty near enough to shoot; then another flock of twenty came, and eight lit with our decoys. Charles and I were going to attend to these, but they swam away before George could get the rest as he wanted them. We rushed up beside Add and George, and as George said, "Get on to them," we rose up over the stand.

Geese everywhere; where shall I shoot? I see four together, with some more in range. I hold on the four. "Are you ready? Fire!" What a roar from the guns, and also from the wild geese and decoys. Twenty-seven dead and wounded geese. We are not to shoot flying; but William, from force of habit, shoots, and says he knocked his goose. Well, the world was full of them, and some must have flown into it. They circle around the lake and alight everywhere. Ten come with our decoys. We "get on to them," and kill nine. In a few minutes six alight with the decoys at the north end. We go up there and kill them all. Now they shoot at the new stand, then at Gunner's Point, and about a hundred alight in the lake in front of us. We get out the boat and pick up the game, then hustle after the flyers. As we are driving them in we see one among them looking rather wild. "Close in on them, boys. That is a wild one," says George. It proves as he says, and we had driven in a wild one. He will make a decoy another season. After we got the flyers in I hear Add say, "Here comes a single goose; nail him, Fred." I grab a gun, shoot twice, and the goose flew on. * * *

After dinner we try for the flock which is in the lake in front of us. Tom sees a flock of seven coming. They alight with the others. After a time thirty-six start to come on. They get almost near enough to shoot, when they turn and swim away as fast as they can. What's the matter? We are no longer in doubt, for a man comes in to the stand, having walked around the shore.

Soon we see another large flock coming, fully as large as the first. They come over, and we throw on them; it does the business, and they alight. I would like to know how many geese there are in the lake now. We drew about sixty, but could only get twenty-two together. Thomas gave the word, George not being there. We killed twenty-one. George came into the stand just as we fired, and we had the laugh on him. By this time it was dark. The geese were honking all over the lake. We drew on six, and killed them all. I would rather not say anything about the next shot, but perhaps it will be as well to give the bitter with the sweet. There must be some hitch, and here it was. Eleven geese near enough, all hands in the stand, and as George said "Get ready!" some one shot. We all fired at the break of the gun, but only got three. George was mad, and the way he talked left no doubt in any mind what his opinion was of the man who shot. * * *

We find that we have made a record for the stand, sixty-eight geese in twelve hours being the most ever killed in the same time at any stand at the lake.

In Great South Bay, Long Island, and in Shinnecock Bay there are still a few stands of live wild geese, and some birds are shot there every year. As a rule, the shooting is done from boxes sunk in the points of the marsh or in bars, and twenty-five or thirty geese are tied out as decoys. The old gander, or honker, is usually put quite a distance off to one side.

Under some conditions the geese come down to the decoys here as in other places along the Atlantic coast, but sometimes it happens that old and suspicious birds will take the bunch down to the water far out of gun-shot. When this happens, it is the part of the tender, who is well off-shore in his catboat, to "swim" these geese up to the decoys. He must work backward and forward near enough to them to urge them toward the boxes, and yet not so close as to cause them actual alarm or, indeed, suspicion. As in most other places where geese are shot, the attempt is usually made to shoot the first barrel at the birds on the water and the second at them as they rise. The "swimming" of geese requires great judgment and perseverance and a good knowledge of the points and bars of the bay. Often it takes hours of careful work to get the geese up to the right place, yet very often it is successfully done, and the desired shot is had.

DRIVING.

During the winter, geese frequent many of the wider rivers running into the Chesapeake Bay and into the brackish water sounds on the coasts of Virginia and North and South Carolina. Here they are often shot by a method of driving which is graphically described in an account written by Mr. L. J. Picot, who has practiced it, and published in *Forest and Stream*. It is as follows:

That part of the Roanoke River which flows through Warren County, and between the upper portions of Halifax and Northampton counties, North Carolina, has long been a favorite feeding place for the wild geese. As soon as the first biting frosts come in October great flocks of geese take up their winter abode in these waters. Huge boulders or rocks in midstream furnish them roosting places at night, without fear of danger of invasion from man or beast. These rocks are always situated between swift-running, though shallow, water, rendering their approach by night almost impossible. The river is a succession of falls for several miles. In the clefts of the rock, hollowed out by long friction, lodge quantities of various berries, acorns and rich nuts, floated from up-stream. There, too, is the tender watercress abundant. This—the berries and nuts—is the food of the wild goose. The river is a quarter of a mile wide, unnavigable save for a light flat-bottomed canoe, such as is generally used by fishermen and sportsmen in small streams. There is nothing to disturb the serenity of the geese save the gun of the sportsman. They are so little hunted that they disport themselves in the gurgling waters or sit on the rocks, not heeding persons or vehicles passing along the road on the river's bank. Often they present an easy mark for rifle-shot, which is almost sure to bring down one or more, as they are huddled so close to each other. One sturdy old gander stands sentry to the main flock. With vigilant eyes, one foot updrawn in his feathers, he gives notice of approaching danger by a loud *honk-honk*. They take his advice promptly and leave for another feeding place, generally in the falls, higher up or lower down stream, depending entirely on the direction from which the danger comes. One great comfort to the hunter is that their flights are very rarely over a mile at the longest, and he can soon have another pop at them.

The romance of rising in the weird and misty light of the morning, without any breakfast or hot punch, and sneaking to the river's bank, is entirely left out in our plan of goose hunting on the Roanoke River. There is no crawling through mud and briers for a half mile. The geese wait for you to get your breakfast, and dinner, too, if you want it, before you pay them your respects in the manner which I shall presently describe. You just ride along on the bank of the river as you might if you intended going to church or a funeral on a quiet Sunday morning in the country. You try to strike the stream at the lowest part, where the geese frequent, and follow up the water's edge until the geese are sighted, and at some points you can see them for a mile or more. It is always necessary to have two men, and it is better to have a party of three to make a successful hunt. More than this number overloads a boat, and lends a cheerful prospect of a good ducking in the rapids by standing on a smooth, half-sunken rock.

We take a boat, usually kept just above or below where we expect to find the geese, and paddle to one of the hundreds of small islands in the river, from six feet in circumference to several acres. We select a small island, dry and full of driftwood, débris of bridges swept away in freshets, and soft grass. We select a small island, because the birds, wary of the shore, will not approach so close to a large one as to a small one. Here we are perfectly secreted by bushes and driftwood, not at all cramped in posture, while waiting for a shot. The dry grass or a log gives choice of a seat. The man in the boat, who is to be the driver, then scuds along the bank furthest from the grass, so as not to alarm and put them to flight. As soon as he passes them sufficiently far to make them believe he has gone on some other business up the river, he heads his boat directly for them, just drifting with the stream, and often whistling a merry tune so as to attract their attention without doing so too suddenly. The geese watch the bearing of the boat, and when it floats toward them they swim away from it. The man in the boat is an old hand and knows full well when he can push away. If they show signs of restlessness he paddles away, pretending not to notice them. The object, as seen at once, is to start and keep them swimming with the current. Once set them fairly to moving, and here comes a solid quarter of an acre of geese swimming gracefully with the undulations of the water right down to the muzzles of our guns.

How we tremble with excitement and impatience! You whisper through chattering teeth to your neighbor to keep quiet till you shall say "Fire." The distance on the water deceives an inexperienced eye, and your neighbor wants to shoot, but you beg him to hold on yet, and wait until they are within thirty or forty yards. One gives the word to fire to the right and the other to the left; two barrels in the water and two shots as they rise; and such flapping and beating the water was rarely ever seen before. You rush, delighted, from your hiding place to yell to the man in the boat to gather the dead and wounded birds, and there may be anywhere from four to a dozen. If there are some only wing-tipped, here is fun indeed, for a goose uses his feet for all they are worth, and, aided by the rapid current, makes good time in search of a hiding place in the rushes of an adjoining island.   An extra boat now comes in well.   A dog is nowhere.   Once carried past the island, he cannot swim against the current.

The so-called white brant, which for many years have spent the winter or a part of it on Delaware Bay, are very wary, and are shot with difficulty or by accident.   The most successful way of obtaining them, however, is to paddle up to them among the ice.

When the ice is breaking up in the spring the gunners get into a boat on which ice is piled, the men themselves wearing white clothing, or being covered with sheets and keeping as much as possible out of sight.   The man in the stern manages the oar which propels and directs the boat, which is sometimes thus sculled right in among the flock.

In the Sacramento Valley, in California, the wild geese, on their southern migrations, arrive early and stay late.   One of the first localities to be visited by the geese in that neighborhood is Fisherman's Lake, which lies only eight miles north of Sacramento.   Although occasional small bunches reach the Sacramento Valley in the very last days of August, most of them do not come until about the middle of September.   Usually, however, by September 12th or 15th, large numbers have arrived, and a record kept from 1876 to 1887 shows the earliest arrival noted to have been August 14th, while in 1880 the earliest birds did not come until September 17th.

BRANT SHOOTING.

FROM A BATTERY.

Brant are shot from batteries in very considerable numbers, and this mode of securing them does not greatly differ from ordinary duck shooting from a battery. There are two principal methods practiced in various places, which means only that for each the battery is set out in a different situation. The commoner method is called shooting on the tide. The battery is rigged in the usual way on the feeding grounds of the brant, in shoal water under the beach. For a single battery eighty decoys would be used, while for a double battery the number might be increased to a hundred. The decoys are disposed much as in shooting ducks from the battery, as shown in the diagram in the account of that sport.

Usually, the battery is rigged out near high water. As the tide begins to fall, the brant leave their off-shore grounds and strike in to the beach, in order to be there when the water has become shoal enough for them to feed on the grass growing on the bottom. Sometimes they come in small numbers, in pairs or in bunches of half a dozen to fifteen, and then offer very pretty shooting. At other times they may come in great bunches of several hundred or a thousand, and puzzle the gunner, who knows that if he shoots at this big

bunch none of them will come back, and he yet fears
that he may not get another shot so good.

The other method of shooting them is to rig out
the battery on the off-shore flats, near the deep-water
channels.   To such places the birds resort to sit and
rest, when the tide is rising and they can no longer
feed.   At such times the gunner's tender with the sailboat will work back and forth to leeward of the birds,
approaching just near enough to disturb them, but not
to frighten them, and trying to make them take wing
and fly on a little way, so as to go down with the next
bunch of birds.   In this way a skillful boatman will
drive the different flocks two or three hundred yards,
not further, pushing them along by easy stages until
some of them go down to the decoys about the battery.
The work is difficult and slow, and requires great
judgment and experience, and it is by no means always
possible to handle the birds as one wishes to.

Usually the southern brant begin to work up north
in February, and reach the coast of Virginia, north of
the mouth of the Chesapeake Bay, late in February.
The birds that have wintered on the Virginia coast
are by this time moving north, and reach the Great
South Bay in small numbers early in March, though
they do not become abundant until about the 20th.
By the 15th of April most of the brant have left the
Great South Bay, and by the 20th or 25th of April they
take their final departure from the Massachusetts coast,
where they are not seen again until October.   Their
movements depend greatly on the wind.   Sometimes

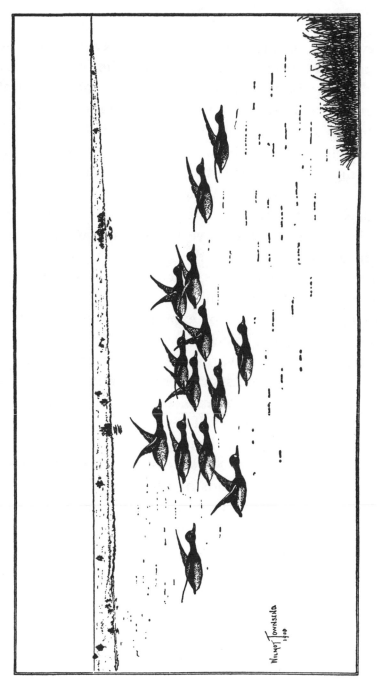

A CANADA SPECIAL.

they collect in surprising numbers in favorite localities, seemingly waiting for favorable weather conditions. If the spring is stormy and cold, with gales from the north, northwest and northeast, the brant remain here, growing more and more numerous; but should a southwest wind begin to blow, the birds may all disappear in a night. Sometimes they linger in the Great South Bay until the first days of May, but they cannot be depended on to remain so late.

Brant were formerly very unsuspicious, and came with great readiness to the decoys set out about the battery; but of late years, since they have been so persistently gunned, they, like other birds and mammals, are learning the lesson of experience, and often do not decoy readily, and sometimes not at all.

In some places in various Atlantic coast waters, the tides and the currents sweep together masses of grass and seaweed in particular places, which are called seaweed banks or bunks. These are often piled up so that the surface of the heap is within a few inches of the top of the water. Where such bunks are formed near the feeding grounds of the brant it is often possible to rig out a battery, and to lie there and shoot them in very tempestuous weather; at times, in fact, when a battery could not live in deeper water. At such times the brant are uneasy, flying about and seeking shelter, and come to decoys more readily than at other times. The gunner who is fortunate enough to find such a place, and to get rigged out there, is likely to have exceedingly good shooting.

Mr. C. R. Purdy, whose long experience as a brant shooter entitles him to speak with all authority, has kindly contributed the following notes on brant shooting in the Great South Bay:

"Brant shooting in the Great South Bay is entirely confined to the spring months. Although a few flocks pass through in their southern migration, they never stop in the bay in any numbers. In the spring, however, they select these waters as a resting place on their return to their northern breeding ground. A few scattering flocks drop in the bay about the middle of March, and from that time on, the flight improves each day until about the first week in April, when it is at its height and the fowl are in the bay in great numbers.

"If we could have in the fall the same number of brant that we have in the spring they would furnish magnificent shooting, but, arriving as they do in the spring months after being shot at all winter in southern waters, they seem to be familiar with all the devices used by man for their capture, and it is only by hard work and under extremely favorable circumstances that even a fair bag can be made. My average, as I find on looking over the score book, is from thirty to thirty-five birds a week, and my best day in fifteen years was forty-seven brant.

"Brant prefer to feed on the shoals immediately under the beach, and as they cannot dive for their food they wait until the ebb tide is partly down, when they can readily reach the young marine grasses by dipping. It is in such places that the gunner rigs out his shooting outfit, which usually consists of a single battery with from seventy-five to eighty brant decoys, or a double battery with ninety to one hundred. Some gunners do not use so many brant decoys, and fill out with duck decoys.

"When the flight of brant starts for the beach the birds will continue to fly during the greater part of the ebb, or until all those that have been living on that shoal have come in, but they have a bad habit, acquired in the South, of rising high in the air to see what lies beyond the decoys they are approaching, and in this way they are very likely to discover the poor wretch in the box, who, in his efforts to get lower down out of sight, is trying to shove himself through the bottom of the battery.

"Young birds, which can be recognized by the scattering white spots under the wings, are not so suspicious and decoy much better. When a flock does come in well, an experienced gunner will usually wait until the birds lap—as is their habit—and as many as eleven have been killed by two barrels.

"The old eel-grass on the shoals will often collect until it forms almost a small island with the top just below the surface of the water. These are called by the gunners seaweed bunks, and vary in size, some being only large enough to protect the battery, and make a lee for it, while others are fifty or sixty feet across. When a bunk makes up on a good brant shoal, the gunner who rigs out under it may remain in his battery, even if it should come on to blow heavily, when a battery could

not live on an open flat. In the heavy wind the brant
do not rise high as they do in light weather, but hug
the water and decoy readily.

"Often brant will be found in scattered bunches
along the edges of off-shore flats—called middle
grounds by the gunners—and in the channels. There
they swim about, picking up driftweed, often taking
to wing and flying short distances and again alighting
as soon as they get sight of a tempting lot of grass.
At such times good shooting may be had by rigging
out as near as possible to the place where the birds are,
and by carefully sailing boat to leeward of the brant,
when they can gradually be worked up to the decoys.

"Brant are sometimes held in the bay by thousands
when the wind is unfavorable to their northern flight,
and if the wind changes suddenly and blows from the
southward, they will leave in a body and usually on
the flood tide. Many a time I have sat on the side of
the box and watched the procession go by, flock after
flock, cackling and talking. Decoys are then useless,
as they pay no attention to them. Now and then a
flock will stop in their onward flight to fly around in
a circle—to see if their steering gear is all right, as
the gunners explain it. When they reach the east end
of the bay, the birds mount high in air and are gone for
another year."

The following spirited account of brant shooting
from a battery behind a seaweed bunk was also kindly
written for me by Mr. Purdy:

"It's no use talking," said the captain, "these old brant are getting too well educated for us." His remarks were drawn out by a bunch of 500 or 600 brant that we had discovered, living at Flat Beach, and for which we had rigged with the result of killing only seven. Although bunch after bunch had headed for the decoys, they had a bad habit of rising in the air when about two gunshots from the rig, to see whether there was anything dangerous beyond the nice-looking lot of decoys we had out.

"If there had only been more young birds, I think they would have done better," the captain continued. "I don't know what we had better do next. I suppose we might as well go east, as far as Old House Flat, and look around."

So we got sail on the sloop and stood east. We had been working with the brant since the 20th of March, and it was now the 3d of April, but as yet the big flight of birds had not come on. We had been picking them up, some days three, and others seven or eight, and the season's score looked as if it would be slim. But still we had a good comfortable thirty-foot sloop, with a large cabin and plenty of good things to eat; and we could afford to wait and see.

We reached Old House Flat about dark and anchored close under the beach.

"I don't like the looks of the weather," the captain remarked, as we were tying up the sails. "I am afraid we are in for an easter." After supper we went on deck to take a last look at the weather, and things did not look promising for the next few days' shooting. The wind had pulled in to the northeast, and a heavy scud was driving across the moon. So, paying out more chain, we turned in, to be lulled to sleep by rattling blocks and the dull boom of the surf on the beach.

The alarm clock got us out at 4 o'clock next morning, and after breakfast we went on deck to look about. It was still dark, and the wind was northeast, blowing hard, almost a gale. This meant too much sea on the flats for a battery. I resigned myself to a day of reading in my bunk. But by seven o'clock the ebb tide began to make and the captain announced his intention of taking the sharpie, and going ashore to collect driftwood for the stove. He had been gone about a half hour, and I was dozing over my book, when I heard the scraping of the sharpie alongside, followed a minute later by the captain's head being thrust in the cabin door.

"The quicker we get a move on us the better," he said. "There is a good seaweed bunk in shore to the east of us, and any quantity of brant are going in to the beach."

That was enough for me. I was out of the bunk in a minute and on deck with the glasses. I could make out one hundred brant or more on the flat, about a quarter of a mile to the east of us, and several bunches were swinging around to the windward of the sloop and heading in shore. We wasted no time. The stops were thrown off the head fender of the battery, and

the sloop's stern shoved around with a pole, until she
lay broadside to the sea, when the centreboard was
dropped, to hold her there. This made a lee for the
battery, and it was launched over the side. It was so
rough that the battery could not carry the iron duck
decoys when clear of the boat. So seven of them
weighing twenty-five pounds each were lowered into
the stool boat, followed by my eight and ten gauge
guns in rubber covers, with two rubber bags containing shells for the guns. Then I threw in the old
gunning coat for a pillow, and the rubber blanket
for the bottom of the box, and taking the battery
in tow of the stool boat, using the anchor rope of
the head fender for a tow line, we succeeded after
twenty minutes' hard poling in reaching the seaweed
bunk.

A seaweed bunk is nothing more than a large mass
of seaweed, worked together by the tides until it forms
almost an island which may vary from ten to fifty feet
across, with the top a few inches below the surface.
Our bunk we found a good one, thirty or more feet
wide and forming a splendid shelter for the battery. It
was the work of only a few minutes to throw the head
fender anchor under the lee of the bunk, straighten
the battery down wind, and drop the tail stone. Guns
and traps were put in the box and the decoys thrown
out. We were using eighty brant with a single battery, seven or eight decoys were dropped across to
windward of the head fender, and a double line down
each side of the battery, close enough together to

break its outline. The rest were scattered between a point fifteen yards distant on the left hand of the battery and forty yards to the leeward.

Leaving me in the box, the captain started back to the sloop to exchange the stool boat for the sharpie, as he would have to tend the battery from the shore; the shoal water and the direction of the wind preventing the use of the sloop. After getting the sharpie he rowed over to tell me that he was going to put up the brant that we had seen going in to the east.

At last then I was alone, with only the wooden decoys bobbing and moving around me. I dropped down the side fender and walked around to wet down the battery deck. The old gunning coat was doubled up on the head board, the rubber blanket spread on the bottom of the box, covers taken from the guns, which were loaded with No. 2 and BB shot for the eight-gauge, and No. 4 and No. 2 for the ten, and with the ten-gauge on my right hand and the eight on my left, the muzzles sticking over the foot of the box, and with the shell bags between my feet, I lay down to wait for something to happen.

I wondered if the captain had started the birds yet, and I rolled partly over and looked back. No; he had not gone far enough up to get on the other side of them yet. So I dropped back and began to follow the course of a three-masted schooner which was going west, outside the beach, under lower sails. Suddenly the air back of me was filled with the sound of tearing muslin. I caught up the ten-gauge and twisted around to take a **part in the** disturbance. A bunch of shell duck had cut down to the decoys back of me and were gone before I could get around to them. The next minute I was just as well pleased that I had not shot, for the captain had started the brant, and they were coming down the shore. There seemed a very large squad of them; too bad they could not come in smaller bunches at different times! I hugged the bottom of the box close, and began to toss up in my mind whether to try the eight-gauge first or the ten, or had I better let them alight, or would it be better to have them bunch in the **air.** I was considering these things, when, to my horror, I saw the whole flock going past me to the leeward, and not noticing the decoys. That would not do. So off came my old black soft hat, and flirting it with a quick motion along the edge of the box, I called brant talk as loud as I could. How quickly they noticed it! The head part of the bunch lifted in the air and caught sight of the stool.

In an instant everything was changed. The head birds had turned for the decoys, and the rear birds were mounting the air to see where they were going, and, finding out, fell in behind. They were all talking at once and were hugging the water where the heavy wind was least felt. "They will come in like chickens," I thought, "and if I work those two guns all right we will have something to look at to-night." Along they came, a regiment of them, beating slowly against the wind. How big they looked! Soon the half-dozen birds in advance reached the decoys and dropped in, and the others were over the tail part of the decoys, when something alarmed them. It was useless to stay down out of sight any longer, and I seized the eight-gauge and aimed at a thick bunch of birds to left hand. How they tumbled out! Those No. 2 shot did great work; five shut up dead, and more were coming, dropping until four more had fallen, making nine, and another looked as if he were badly hurt. I watched him to see whether he would drop out further to the windward.

The captain came rowing down like a steamboat, to gather in the birds. He shot over the cripples and we owned our nine brant. I stood up in the box to receive the captain's congratulations and was staggered by his question: "What was the matter; weren't they near enough?"

"Near enough! Of course. Didn't you pick up nine?"

"Well, then, you must have had buck fever. Two guns in the battery and only fired one shot at a crowd of brant like that! You're a great one for an old duck shooter!"

But no matter, we had no time to indulge in regrets, we felt that we must take advantage of the ebb and get what birds we could. The captain had just gotten nicely out of the way, when seven brant came in from off shore, and four stopped in the lower part of the decoys.

Picking up my ten-gauge, I scored a clean miss on the three flying birds with the first barrel, but managed to kill two with the second, and, catching up the eight-gauge, I stopped two others as they started out of the decoys.

After a look around and seeing nothing on the wing, I sat on the edge of the box for a while, when a low k-r-r-k from the lower part of the decoys caused me to look quietly that way. A single brant was swimming through the rig. It is strange how sometimes they will come up and alight when you are sitting up, and at other times you cannot get them near decoys when you are hidden well. I made sure of gathering in our solitary friend, for I wanted to get out of the thirteen hole.

Soon another flock came in sight, off shore, and I got down in the box to watch them. I wished they would not get around so far back of me, for this turning one's self into a corkscrew by trying to peek backwards in a battery is not agreeable. They did not show up on the other side of the box for some time, but at last I saw them up to the windward. They had dropped in, and were going to swim in to the beach. There was nothing to do but to lie close. Five minutes passed and an old black duck came over the box and looked down in my face. I imagined I could detect a leer in his cunning old eyes, as if he knew I would not shoot at him with those brant coming down. It seemed to me as if by this time the brant must have drifted down before the heavy wind. I rolled over a little and looked and saw one swimming down just outside the decoys, and the rest were almost at the head

fender. I decided to let that single fellow get down
a little further and to take the eight-gauge and swing
around on the other chaps, and take the single one in
as he started up. When he was far enough down, I
swung around with the eight-gauge and took a careful aim at the waterline of the nearest bird of three
sitting together, but they jumped as I pulled and I
scored a blank, the second barrel stopping one bird.
Now for the single one! He didn't lead up according
to programme, but climbed down wind and was now
a long shot off. I sent both barrels on the ten-gauge
after him. The first hit him hard, but it looked as if
he would carry it off; but no, he set his wings and scaled
in toward the sharpie, and then let himself down gently
—a cripple. A puff of smoke rose from the sharpie and
a moment later his brantship was tossed rudely on to
the stern seat.

The captain shoved slowly toward the battery, picking up the dead, and was soon within talking distance.

"We will have rain soon; it is getting thick off there
to the east," was his first remark. "You didn't do
much with that last bunch," was his second. But
just then a boat going in to the beach to the west of us
put up a big cloud of brant and the captain started
back for the shore. I stood on the deck to look around
while he was rowing away, and off shore of me to the
east and west I could see the white tails of brant,
bobbing up and down on the waves. Our easter was
doing big work and the brant were stopping in the
bay, tired out by facing its force.

More birds were coming now and the shooting went on briskly as they came up, flock after flock. I made some rank misses that I felt I could explain to myself; but I knew that it would be pretty hard to do so to that dark object sitting in the sharpie on shore, with a powerful pair of field glasses glued to his eyes.

Forty-seven brant lay in the bottom of the boat when down came the rain in torrents. We tried to stand it long enough to bring the score to fifty, but the shower bath on my upturned face was too much for me, and we reluctantly gave it up and rowed back to the sloop. Those forty-seven noble birds were stowed away, the rig picked up, rubber boots and wet clothing taken off, and with dry clothes, feet in old comfortable slippers, a stiff hot Scotch to take the chill out of the bones, we loaded our pipes and proceeded to talk it all over.

"Well, what do you think of to-day, Cap?"

"I would like to have made it fifty," he replied, "but if we do half as well to-morrow I will be satisfied."

We came near it, but that is another piece of history. The day behind the bunk had always remained my big day at brant, and, with the great increase of batteries and the brant growing wilder each year, I know only too well it will never be duplicated, at least in the Great South Bay.

BAR SHOOTING.

At one or two points only, along the Atlantic coast, is brant shooting practiced from boxes on sand-bars with live decoys. For many years, however, this has been the only successful method of securing these birds at Cape Cod, where three clubs, known as the Monomoy, Providence and Manchester, have long existed, and have occupied the branting ground on terms of entire harmony.

For more than forty years, Mr. Warren Hapgood was a prominent member of the Monomoy Club and an enthusiastic brant shooter, and many years ago he contributed to the columns of *Forest and Stream* an extended and admirable account of this shooting, which is in part given below. It will be observed that in its essentials bar shooting for brant does not very markedly differ from goose shooting from boxes, but the conditions which prevail at Cape Cod are so very different from those existing where geese are shot, and the brant themselves have so many peculiarities not shared by the geese, that brant shooting, as practiced here, requires a description by itself. In the article above referred to Mr. Hapgood says:

Brant shooting is a peculiar kind of sport that but few have indulged in. There are many obstacles in the way. The haunts of the birds are few and isolated, their feeding grounds limited, their sojourn brief; nor can any degree of success be achieved without the proper appliances, such as a house to live in, boats, boxes, bars, live decoys and a skillful hand to manipulate them. When, however, all these are obtained, no spring shooting on the coast of New England gives greater satisfaction, or better rewards the energy and skill of the sportsman. The birds are large, weighing three and a half pounds, numerous, and, gastronomically, have no superiors. They are not distributed universally along the Atlantic shores, as are Canada geese, black duck, coot and other aquatic birds. At the easterly end of Massachusetts is the nice, old-fashioned town of Chatham, and some three miles away to the southward of this is the island of Monomoy, a mere belt of sand running still further southward six miles.

Facing eastward from Monomoy, one sees the broad Atlantic, where "they on the trading flood ply, stemming nightly toward the pole." It is no uncommon occurrence for a fleet of a hundred sail to be seen at anchor or struggling against wind or tide to reach a port, and many a gallant ship has been wrested from her course by the storm king and tossed upon the beach as a mere toy. After an easterly gale, one of the objects of intense interest to tourists is the matchless grandeur of the spectacle of "hills of sea, Olympus high" that dash themselves in thunder upon this sand-bar, again and again to be absorbed in the bosom of the refluent wave. On the westerly side of the island, stretching up and down some miles, is what is called "Chatham Great Flats," over which the water flows, varying from two feet to almost nothing, according as it is full or neap tide.

Adjoining these flats, on the southerly or westerly side, is deep, blue water, where grows an immense quantity of common eel grass (*Zostera marina*), upon which the brant feed; and this is the great feeding grounds for these birds on Cape Cod. So attractive is this locality that thousands of these little geese assemble here every spring to "feed and batten," preparatory to the long journey, via Prince Edward's Island, to their breeding grounds at or near the North Pole. It will be understood that the marine vegetable that proves so savory a morsel to the brant grows in water five or six feet deep at high tide, and, as these birds are not divers, they can only feed at low or nearly low tide. Then, as the flood tide drives them from their feeding grounds, particularly when it is breezy, the birds become uneasy and scatter about in little "pods" or flocks, evidently seeking other feeding grounds or more comfortable quarters, where they can rest till the tide ebbs so they can return to the feast. It is during this period —from about half flood to half ebb tide—that the brant are flitting about over the flats and likely to catch sight of and be lured to the decoys; and it is during these four or five hours each day that the shooting is done.

The time for the brant to arrive from the South in spring varies considerably. A warm, forward spring brings along the brant in considerable numbers by the 1st of March; whereas, a backward season will hardly make good shooting before the end of the month, and by the 25th of April so few remain as to offer the sportsman no inducement to pursue them further, though it is quite probable a few straggling flocks may be seen as late as the 1st or even the 10th of May. During this period they are constantly coming and going,

especially when the wind is to the southward and westward. It will be readily observed that the shooting
season at best only extends over a period of four or five
weeks. They rarely stop at this place in autumn on
their way south, and, if they do, are not fat or fit for
table use. The birds, on arriving in the spring, enter
the bay from the west in flocks or gaggles—varying
from a few individuals up to several hundred—at no
great distance from the mainland, sometimes passing
directly over, not deigning to stop, even though their
food is abundantly spread out before them and thousands of their less suspicious brethren are feeding there,
while other flocks will gradually lower themselves
down, swing around once or twice, then plunge into the
liquid element. All the migratory birds that follow the
coast line must of necessity pass this point both spring
and fall. Sometimes they lift and go over Nanset Bar or
Monomoy Island, and sometimes they pass around the
southerly end of the island, Cape Malabar, but the great
mass rise to a safe altitude, strike a "bee line" east by
north, and pass directly over this strip of land. We
have often remarked that the leader of each flock must
have a pocket compass placed in the top of his head, so
unerringly do they steer.

One would naturally suppose, on seeing these birds
constantly feeding at any locality along the shore, it
would be easy enough to kill them. There are many
such places up and down our coast, but for reasons very
few birds can be killed. At the mouth of Bass River,
many brant linger and feed through the entire season,

but there are no "flats," no points where boxes can be planted and successfully worked; the water is too deep, the shore too bluff, and the brant feed only at low tide. A box might be placed on the feeding ground, and operated for a short time during each low tide, but the depth of water in the immediate vicinity would prevent the recovery of cripples, an important item in brant shooting; and, moreover, all our experience teaches us that shooting at these birds on their feeding ground soon drives them to other quarters, from which they would never return. The same conclusion was arrived at on examining the harbor of Nantucket. It will be found, even at Chatham, that before any shooting can be done, a vast amount of hard work is to be performed. The feeding grounds and flats are so far from the town that living there is not practicable, and a shanty or house must be built on the island. Boxes are to be made, pens constructed for holding the live decoys, and a well dug for fresh water. This "well" arrangement is a curiosity to the uninitiated. The island, where the shanty is located, is not over two hundred yards wide, but of undulating surface, i. e., composed of little hillocks and valleys or basins. If a hole three feet deep be dug in one of these basins, and a common flour barrel inserted, it will, on the flood tide, partially fill with pure, soft water, and will continue to rise and fall with each tide. The reason of this is that rain falls upon this porous sand and percolates till it reaches salt water, which, being of greater specific gravity, holds or buoys up the fresh water.

The planting of the boxes is a job no one man can perform. A water-tight box, large enough to accommodate three persons, must be about six feet long, three and a half wide, and two and a half deep. One half of this is buried in the flats; the other is hidden by sand being wheeled and piled up around it. Nor is this all—a bar twenty or thirty yards long and two feet high must be made and maintained, for the decoys to run on and for the wild ones to assemble upon. The sand must be taken at low tide from some little distance, so as to leave the flats and bar moderately smooth and natural.

There is an enormous tendency in this Cape Cod sand to seek a dead level. Three hundred wheelbarrow loads may be to-day piled up to form a bar, which a high tide and wind will to-morrow send back to its normal condition of inherent dead level. Early in the season, before the bars are consolidated, every high wind and tide does more or less damage to the bars, which must be repaired before the box can be used, as no brant will come near when it is in sight. Almost every newcomer volunteers a plan for preserving the bars, such as bags of sand, brush or stone deposits, piles driven around, concrete and canvas coverings. Some of these have been tried, but, on the whole, without success.

Another desideratum in branting is live decoys. No visionary enthusiast need lay the flattering unction to his soul that without these, or with wood decoys alone, he will meet any degree of success. Decoys are usually obtained in the course of shooting by being slightly wounded in the wing, when a phalanx is amputated and the bird is added to the gaggle. The little captives will, when placed in a pen with the old ones, commence eating· corn, their usual diet while in captivity, and, although they probably never before saw a kernel of corn, they thrive well on this simple bill of fare. Presumably, in their normal condition, they never see fresh water, and yet, in bondage, this is their only beverage. Nor do they seem to suffer by the change. Another peculiarity about them in captivity is that they have no sexual intercourse, lay no eggs, exhibit no incubating desire, are cold, dignified and reserved, especially toward other fowl, nor do they ever become fully domesticated.

All through the earlier history of branting at this place, and up to about 1862, the business was carried on by 'longshoremen, who associated themselves together, for convenience, in unorganized clubs of from three to six persons. In 1863, a club called the Monomoy Branting Club, consisting of four resident and fourteen non-resident members, was organized. A little later another club was formed, and still later a third; but neither of these has been as successful as the first, probably from the fact that the most available shooting points were occupied before they entered the field. Of all the immense flats we have previously described, not more than four or five points are worth occupying, and from a single one of these—the "Mud Hole"—about as many brant have been killed as from

all the others combined.   This point has been for nearly
half a century occupied by one family, father and sons,
until their interest was merged in the Monomoy Branting Club.   Fifty years ago, when flint-lock guns were
in use, the boxes were partly covered over, to prevent
the diving fowl from catching sight of the flash, and
thus escaping.

The guns were run out through embrasures, and this
method necessitated the order, "Ready!—one, two—
fire!" It was discovered, however, when the birds were
with the decoys, that they were not so easily frightened, and all this roofing-in arrangement was dispensed
with, more particularly after the invention of percussion caps.   As we have been connected with the Monomoy Branting Club from its birth, our remarks hence-
forth will have reference more especially to the doings
of that organization.

In forming the club, it was arranged that the non-
resident members—persons living in Boston or vicinity
—should build and furnish a shanty, provide boats,
boxes and the necessary tools for carrying forward the
enterprise, while the resident members—whose homes
were at Chatham—should make and keep in repair the
boxes, do boating, cooking, taking care of the decoys,
and generally looking after the welfare and interests
of the non-residents.   We are happy to add that the
plan has worked admirably, and to the entire satisfaction of both "the high contracting parties."   It is for
the time being a sort of co-partnership, the non-residents paying a stipulated sum for board and privileges,

sharing equally with the residents in all the game killed. A shanty, or house, 12x16 feet, was built and furnished. This, however, was found, a few years later, to be too small for the convenience of the members and invited guests, and it was enlarged to double its original capacity, giving ample room for reading, sleeping, dining, cooking, storage, etc.

We will now suppose the shanty to be in perfect running order, three boxes—the "Mud Hole," "North Bar" and "Gravel"—generously bestowed in their respective bars, fifteen live decoys in the pen at the sunny side of the shanty, ready for use.

As the day has been calm, the bars are in good condition, and the prospects are favorable that Monday morning will usher in a week of grand sport. It will be high tide at 7.15 A. M., and the boxes must be occupied by 5 o'clock. The alarm-clock, which acts as a sort of reveille, is set at 4 o'clock, and brings every man to his feet. A hasty repast is improvised, while each gunner adorns himself with his coarse, heavy wool clothing, oil suit, long boots and woolen mittens. Three decoys are placed in each basket, and it is astonishing with what precision the residents will seize the particular birds that are to be worked on the same line, as there is no perceptible difference in the size, plumage or voices of the sex. The boxes are distant from the shanty as follows: "North Bar," about a mile; "Mud Hole," half a mile, and "Gravel," one-third of a mile. As the North Bar is lowest, the tide, of course, reaches it first; and as the distance from the shanty is greater, Reno, who is as constant at the box as the North Star to the Pole, must start first. He takes with him S. and H. The high tide of the previous night had filled the box, which must be bailed out ere it can be entered. The decoys are then fettered and allowed to run out upon the bar, and as the water is making around us,. they rush down for a morning bath, which they seem to enjoy exceedingly. Washy, who has for some years managed the Mud Hole, is accompanied by M. and the doctor, while George, with W., occupies the Gravel. The parties have scarcely got well placed when a small "pod" of brant come flitting along toward the North Bar, and four out of seven were knocked down by S. and H., and gathered. "What is that black spot away down to the southwest?" asks Reno, after gazing steadily for a few moments in that direction. "It looks like a large flock of brant," he continues, the spot still holding his eager eyes. "Yes, it is a flock of brant, and they are heading for us," he adds. As the flock comes on and on, nearer and nearer, "Yes," he exclaims, "they are making directly for us. Now they turn! There—there they go, right for the Mud Hole," his face elongating at the sight. "Now," says S., "they have all lighted within two hundred yards of the box, and, as the tide is still flowing, they will be likely to swim in and give the boys a splendid shot." Sure enough, they soon catch sight of the decoys on the bar and commence swimming for that point. Only one head is now seen above the bar. The resident who manages the decoys keeps his eyes steadily above the

edge of the box to observe what transpires and report
to his companions, who crouch down out of sight,
especially when birds are approaching. As the brant
assemble upon and around the bar, the observer will notice these heads, and he understands the leader has sig-
nified to his associates that now is the best time to
shoot, and that they must very gently raise their heads
so as to look out for the most desirable groups to shoot
at, and yet not to cross the fire of the others. The order is now presumed to be given: "Ready—one, two—
fire!" The first discharge should be simultaneous, the
second at will. Then the box is suddenly vacated, and
such a splashing and dashing after cripples, which are
captured first, and afterward, on the way in, the dead
birds are picked up. "A big shot," says H. "About a
dozen," mutters Reno, who is never sanguine. "More,"
says S. "Can tell better when we arrive at the shanty,"
continues Reno. At this moment several sea duck
(*Somateria mollissima*) come puffing along and attempt to pass the North Bar, when, quick as thought,
the three guns were aimed, and three eiders were floating on the flood, while a fourth was struck hard, but
managed to escape.

The tide is fast making over the bar, now "boring"
up, now falling off again. "Shall we be driven?" asks
H. "If it continues to flow hard we probably shall,"
responds Reno. Again it "bores," and a wavelet enters
the box. The decoys are now unfettered and placed in
the basket. Another wave forces the party to mount
the top of the bar. Here is the dread alternative, either

to retreat to the shanty or stand on the bar for a long
hour, till the tide ebbs so that they can re-enter. As
the road lies between the Mud Hole and Gravel, and
so no shooting can be done at either during the passage,
it is decided to stand it out. Usually on being driven
when the Gravel is untenanted they "fleet" thither. At
high tide, when the wind blows fresh, the birds are
skipping about pretty lively, and some very good shots
are likely to be made. A flock of about twenty brant
drew near the Mud Hole, and was greeted by a salute
of six guns, and seven dead were left to be gathered,
beside one "wing-tip," which gave Washy a hard pull
to overhaul.

As soon as the tide ebbed so that the North Bar could
be bailed out, the party re-enter, put out decoys and
proceed to business; nor were they long idle. "Is that
a little black cloud or flock of birds away down there
toward Harwich Point?" asks H. Reno, although remarkably vigilant, is not particularly long-sighted, and
did not at first take in the situation; but after a while
the little spot, as it moved slowly along, apparently
close to the water, attracted his eye. "Oh, yes, I see,"
and the little dark cloud grew bigger and bigger as
nearer and nearer it came. "Yes, it is a large flock of
brant coming right for our bar," giving the decoy line
a jerk at the same time. On, on they come. "Down,
down!" he cries, and two of the heads disappear.
"They are now very near," he continues. "There they
swing around; now we have them; they are all in the
water." The two heads, after a few minutes of awful

suspense, are slowly raised, and two pair of astonished eyes behold a hundred and fifty brant swimming hither and thither, coquetting and playing together, entirely innocent of danger. Gradually they work their way along to the southward of the box, spreading about, some quite near and others more remote. At length they come together very handsomely within forty yards of the box. "Now is our time," whispers Reno. "Are you ready?" he nervously continues. An affirmative response is made, and he gives the order, "Put over! One, two—fire!" Bang! bang! go the six barrels; splash! splash! go the three pairs of long boots. The dead and wounded are gathered in with all possible despatch, and but for one cripple the work would have been quickly done. This one, however, gave Reno a fearful jaunt.

Away went our black-footed hero, paddling for dear life toward the North Pole, and away went Reno in pursuit. The pursuer had not the benefit of a long pair of legs, though he had excellent pluck, while the pursued was blessed with a splendid pair for the work before him. Now the brant seemed to gain on his pursuer, and now Reno on the object of his pursuit. S. and H. watched with breathless anxiety this little episode incident to branting. These birds are not divers, but stand up bravely till their pursuer is quite near, when they plunge in and swim under water; but they make slow progress, and are then easily captured. Placing his bird under his arm, he slowly returns. "Big shot," says S. "How many?" inquires Reno, as he jumps into the box and puts the decoy in the basket. "Twenty-three," instantly rejoin both S. and H., "and one cripple, which makes twenty-four," "and this beats any shot of the season," he rejoins, at the same time seating himself and commencing to fill his pipe. After such a big shot a great many wise remarks are volunteered, a great many suggestions made which are to apply to the future, but the future always brings with it an enormous amount of vitality. As this conversation was vehemently progressing a flock of seven brant came up behind the box, caught sight of the decoys, swung round twice; but as the tide was nearly off the flats, and as they rarely light except in water, it was thought best to "give it to them." Four fell dead, while a fifth dropped too wide out to be recovered. This was the last shot, and as the other parties had long since gone in, Reno concluded to "take up." The dead birds are tied in bunches, and thrown over their shoulders or across the guns, and, amid mutual congratulations, the party proudly set out for the shanty.

Only four shots were fired at the Gravel. At first a flock of nine brant came and alighted near the point of the bar, and as they "bunched up" five of them were murdered in cold blood. Then a pair whirled round over the bar, apparently reconnoitering, but this temerity cost them their lives. The third shot was at a big loon (*Gavia imber*), by George, and he was handsomely knocked down at eighty-three yards. A lone sheldrake closed the morning's work, and the party retired. As soon as Reno entered the shanty he asks:

"How many did you get, Washy, at that first shot?"
"Seventeen and two decoys," was the cool reply. "I
hardly thought you got as many," rejoins Reno.
"Ought to have had thirty," growls Washy; "and we
should if I could have kept the doctor down." And
they all gathered around the breakfast table, as full of
chatter and merriment as a pack of monkeys. "What
does the morning's work foot up?" asks H., as the
record must be entered in the journal. "Well, here it
is: Mud Hole, 27; North Bar, 32; Gravel, 7; a grand
total of 66 brant." The evening tide is worthless, and
there will be no more shooting till Tuesday morning.
That night a fresh breeze sprang up from the southwest, bringing along a great many brant, and, moreover, doing some damage to the bars; but there is no
time in the morning for "sand rolling," and they must
be hastily patched up for the nonce.

Tuesday morning, all hands up at 4 o'clock, lunch,
and start for the boxes in the following order: First
Reno, with W. and the doctor, for the North Bar; next,
Washy, at his old haunt, the Mud Hole, with M. and H.
as companions, and, last, George and S. occupy the
Gravel.

As the birds enter the bay mostly from the westward,
the boxes all face that point of the compass. Scarcely
had the last party put out the decoys, deposited the basket in the box, and comfortably seated themselves,
when a flock of about seventy-five brant came pushing
their way along up from the southward and lighted in
the dark water near Mud Hole.

"Will they swim up with the tide?" asks M.

"Fine chance for them—it is flowing rapidly," Washy answered, as the brant were playing, chasing each other and picking up floating eel grass.

Now they turn and head for the bar, now sag away again. Again the birds set toward the box. "Down, down!" cries Washy, and he alone is the "observed of all observers." On again they come, swimming hither and thither within a hundred yards of the three throbbing hearts. Now again they halt, then retreat, as though they were suspicious all was not right. At last one old "honker" starts for the live decoys, which have to be occasionally jerked by the check-cord to make them "show wing."

"Yes," says Washy, "he is coming right on to the point of the bar, and the whole flock are following."

At this juncture of affairs another flock of forty sprang up from the westward, shimmered along, swung round and lighted with the main body. "R-ronk, r-ronk," ring a hundred voices; "Ruk-ruk," as many more—and such tumult and confusion! The guide quickly conveys the cheering intelligence that many of the brant are so far on the bar as to get "toe-hold," and the others are in moderate proximity. These birds are quite vigilant, and any sudden movement would instantly send them beyond the possibility of a hope of recovery.

"Raise your heads slowly," says Washy, and the two heads are gradually elevated to the level of the third, when lo! the bar is dark as Erebus with the waving mass. A few moments of nervous consultation as to the best group for each to fire at, and the guide whispers, "Get ready!" Just at this moment the birds spread suddenly about and frustrate the plans, producing dreadful uncertainty for a few seconds, but they soon "bunch up" again, and the word was given: "Put over! Ready! Fire!" The smoke of six guns wreathes its way heavenward; out jump the two—splash! splash! —away they go. Washy takes a breech-loader along with him to knock over any wing-tipped birds that cannot otherwise be gathered. One "old honker," with just a little bit of a muscle of the carpus pricked by a stray pellet, is pulling foot for the dark, deep water off Harding's Beach. No non-resident would undertake to chase a strong bird half a mile, and, if he did, he would certainly fail. The motion of the waves over the white sand brings a dizziness to one not accustomed to this work, and makes him feel every moment as though he was about to "topple over headlong." Far different is it with the guide or leader, who has spent his whole life upon the water. Away goes our little winged hero, following closely is our stalwart guide. Further on and further still they go, almost out of sight. On the way out Washy had gathered two or three dead birds, which he still held in his hand, and when within about a rod of the live bird he throws one of the dead, to frighten the living, so that he will dive and turn two or three somersaults in a bewildered condition, so that his pursuer rushes forward and captures him. In the meantime the dead and wounded had been gathered, the bar smoothed off, ready for another crack at them.

"How many?" asks Washy, as he stops to take breath.

"Nineteen and two decoys—twenty-one all told," quickly responds H.

"Well done," says Washy, and it seemed to give him a heap of comfort as he placed that decoy in the basket.

"But look, you," says M.; "there go nine right up for the North Bar."

"Precisely!" ejaculates Washy, hardly yet recovered from his long tramp. Puff, puff! Away out in the dim distance rises the smoke, and the flock is reduced to four. Not much time elapsed before a brace of black ducks (*Anas obscura*) were swimming in for the Gravel. The guns were brought to bear, and in a few minutes they were quietly reposing on the bottom of the box. The brant had for some time been feeding in the channel between Monomoy and Nanset. The regular feeding ground extends from near the Mud Hole to the inner point, a distance of two miles. In passing from one to the other, as they do on each tide, feeding in the channel at high tide and at Inner Point at low tide, they are very likely to receive a salute as they pass in review before the boxes. A shot from the Gravel started a large flock from the inner harbor, and as they lifted and moved majestically along westward, it was like a huge black cloud, so thick and dark. On it moved toward the Gravel, and, strange to say, notwithstanding the water was quite shoal, and in some places nearly off the flats, they all dumped down a little distance from the bar. Some were within gunshot of the box. What was to be done? A thousand brant, all within 180 yards of the two well-charged guns! As the tide was fast leaving the flats, and the birds could walk around anywhere, and, moreover, as they began to stretch up their necks and show signs of suspicion, it was thought best to fire as soon as they should come together and offer a favorable opportunity for a good shot. This they soon did, and George gave the order, and the other two guns belched forth fire and smoke. Easy task to gather up the thirteen dead birds that lay upon the water. Scarcely was the shot made on the Gravel when Washy's eye seemed to be riveted to the western horizon. After a few minutes, as if almost doubting the correctness of his own eyes, he says:

"There is a flock of sea ducks coming this way, I think. No, they are brant," he continues, with much straining of the visual organs. After a few moments' pause, he bursts out again: "I declare, they are *Soma-teria mollissima,* coming right straight for the box!"

"They look to me more like brant," says M.

"No," remarks Washy; "don't you see how steadily they fly, and so close to the water?"

On they came till within about eighty yards of the box, when their keen eyes caught sight of some movement—most likely the nervous motion of cocking the guns and getting ready for the reception. They all suddenly wheeled to the southward with as much precision and regularity as a file of soldiers. A grand fusillade of six guns ensued, but only one bird was left to remind the gunners of the wariness of these sea rovers.

The tide was now ebbing fast, and George had taken up his decoys and retired. A pair of brant came down by the North Bar directly for the Mud Hole, and as they approached, seemed to slacken up, as if to inspect the works or be introduced to the decoys, and as they drew close together were both let down by the unerring aim of Washy, with a single gun. Then a lone brant was despatched by M. A single sheldrake, which, as the tide was off the flats, was easily gathered, and this ended the morning's sport at this bar.

The wind, which at early morn was southwest, a little later veered to westward, blowing fresh, and doing much damage to the bars, which must be repaired before they are in working condition, and the residents, with such as would volunteer, went out after dinner for that purpose, with barrows and shovels. The bars are likely, on a high tide and strong westerly wind, to be shifted from the front to the rear of the box, but, as the party cannot wait for the next east wind to transport it back, it must be done by main strength. Roll-boards are laid from a distance of two or three rods, the barrows are filled, rolled upon the boards, and are dumped upon the bar, then leveled to give it an even appearance, and the work is done. On this particular occasion the Mud Hole received one hundred and seventy-five of these raw recruits, and it is splendid exercise—almost equal to dragging a hand-sled up a long hill, with a prospect of a "coast" down again. It is also an excellent specific against dyspepsia, strengthens the muscles, expands the lungs, purifies the blood, and brings in its train that sweet repose—that blessed slumber—entirely unknown to indolent persons. The bars are now in good order and ready for the morning's sport.

It is observed on the branting grounds of Cape Cod, Mass., that in seasons when there are few young brant there is practically no shooting. The old birds that visit Cape Cod year after year become perfectly familiar with boxes, bars, boats, batteries, decoys, and other contrivances used by gunners for their destruction. The birds seem to understand perfectly what the little piles of sand, with the brant decoys and the wooden decoys about them, mean, and give the place a wide berth.

If, however, the young predominate in a flock, they will come to the decoys, even though to do so they may have to separate themselves from the main bunch. Often they will succeed in turning the flock and in drawing some or all of the old ones after them. When this happens, the birds sometimes come up in such numbers that the gunner may knock over twenty or more at a shot.

In order to complete the history of the Monomoy Branting Club up to the year 1900, Mr. William Avery Cary, the able secretary of the club, has very kindly furnished me with the accompanying memorandum of the consolidation of the three clubs at Monomoy, and of the somewhat changed methods prevailing there at the present time. He says:

Up to June, 1897, the shooting was carried on by three clubs, the Monomoy, Providence and Manchester, so-called, during a season of five weeks, the Monomoy taking three weeks and the Manchester and Providence one each. At that time the membership of the Monomoy proper was only fifteen. On the date mentioned such of the Providence and Manchester members as were left took shares in the Monomoy Club, the number of shares being increased to twenty-five and the number of boxes to five.

The feed having changed so that the birds did not come in to shore as in the past, we were obliged to push the boxes further out, and where it became necessary, on account of the strong tides and the high waves and strong winds, to cover some of the boxes with canvas, thereby precluding the use of live decoys, except in the very mildest of weather. We then found that they were not acting satisfactorily under the unnatural footing of canvas.

The birds gradually became more shy, and appreciating that they were of a gregarious nature, we largely increased the number of our wooden decoys, so that where we used to have twenty-five or fifty birds to a box we now have about two hundred decoys, which has materially helped our scores.

DUCK SHOOTING.

PASS SHOOTING.

Of all methods of duck shooting, that known as pass shooting is perhaps the most difficult and the most sportsmanlike. The gunner stations himself at some point where the ducks are likely to fly, and shoots them as they pass over him. This point may be between two lakes or two portions of a single lake, or between roosting and feeding ground, or perhaps only near some lake at which the birds stop on their migrations. At all events, most of the shooting is overhead at swiftly flying birds, and great skill and judgment are required to make a satisfactory bag.

Sometimes the gunner stands behind some cover of bushes, or he may sit or kneel in a pit dug in the ground, or at times, if the birds are newly arrived, and so are unsuspicious, he may stand out in plain view. However he may be concealed, if the shooter has been fortunate enough to secure a position in the direct line of flight, he will have interesting shooting, and will probably receive some new ideas as to the swiftness with which a duck passes through the air.

Graphic accounts of this method of shooting have often been published. One of the best of these which has appeared in recent years, is from the pen of Mr. E. Hough, in *Forest and Stream*, in which he describes

317

a day's shooting, in 1897, in North Dakota, as follows:

At the head of the Dead Buffalo Lake there is a narrow strip of water separating it from a smaller lake above, and between this little sheltered basin and the wide, deep water, where the wild celery grows, there is a more or less constant flight of ducks. We put out our team and hastened quietly as we could down to this fly-way, seeking not to alarm the birds till we had taken our stand on the ridge between the lakes, where the rushes grow much higher than a man's head and run out almost entirely across the narrow channel. One of the dogs ran on ahead of us, and even before we could run over to the pass, there arose an enormous black cloud of ducks, which began to stream over the pass and to spread out over the big lake below.

Each of us had his pockets full of shells, and before we had deployed as skirmishers across the pass the pockets began to empty. The ducks came in a constant stream, without intermission for many minutes, nearly all of them low and almost in our faces, and with that velocity of flight seen nowhere except on a duck pass. The four of us, with shouts and calls and eager vociferations of "Mark! mark! mark!" poured in such fire as we could. Mr. Bowers cut down his first two birds after his regular style, and Gokey, wading out into the middle of the channel, began to fold up birds with the smoothness of the old-time shot. I came near stopping my own gun to watch the sport of duck shooting on the pass, which I consider to be one of the most difficult and exciting forms of shooting. High up in the air the passing bird would suddenly close up, its head falling back, and come down like a stone with an excellent great splash. For the Chief, I can say he was diligent, and often I saw him cut down his duck, sometimes dropping it at his feet as he stood on the dry ground. Both the Chief and myself were raw at first on the pass, but after the flurry we got down to it and shot with our average of badness, I suppose. All of us killed ducks, many ducks, so many and in such mingled fashion that for a time no one could tell whose duck it was that fell out of the flight under the pattering fusillade. The retrievers were busy wading and swimming, and we, too, at times, paused to pick up a bird or so. In half an hour the flight slackened, and we stopped to take account. Many of our birds fell back of us in the water, and unless killed stone dead such birds were as good as lost; for they would dive and disappear as soon as they got to the water. We could see that many of our ducks were canvas-backs and redheads. I shall make it short by saying that the first hurried flight did not last long, and that during the day, which came off very hot, the birds did not move much, Gokey very wisely declining to go out and stir them up, as he said that would drive them off their feeding beds and cause them to leave the lake. The evening was still, and the birds did not move as we had expected. Moreover, we were most of us tired and sleepy, and not disposed to kill everything in sight. After we had picked up our dead and found such of the cripples as we could, we had somewhere between thirty and forty ducks, I believe, nearly a dozen and a half of which were fine fat canvas-backs and redheads. This we voted plenty good enough for us.

Not so Gokey. Both he and Bowers declared we had seen no shooting at all. They held conference, and soon announced that on the following day we must be prepared for a long ride. We were to go to the famous Chase Pass, about twenty-four miles northeast of Dawson, and to see what both these gentlemen declared to be the best flight of ducks in the whole country.

Here again I am obliged to say that the representations held out did not begin to equal the reality. The Chief and myself have traveled a little in this big country of America, and have seen ducks all the way from British America to Mexico, yet never, even on the Gulf coast of Texas, did we ever see so many ducks, such comfortable, obliging ducks, and ducks so accessible and incessant. It was a wonderful sight of wildfowl— one of those sights which make the unthinking say that there are "just as many ducks now as there ever were." Gokey said this was always a great place for ducks, but that this year the birds were more numerous than for many years previous, thanks to high water and to the license law, which cut off the non-resident market shooting and reduced that of game hogs who knew no moderation. Gokey said that up to the past two years it was a daily sight at Dawson station to see the entire platform lined with ducks waiting for the train to bear them out of the State. He said that in warm weather it was no unusual thing to see two or three wagon loads of spoiled ducks hauled out into the country and dumped into a coulee. He seemed to take comfort in the hope of better things. Both he and Warden Bowers are assured of the wisdom of the non-resident act, whatever the non-resident himself may think about it. I think both the Chief and myself would be disposed now to say that if a shooter can in any way afford it, it would pay him better to pay his $25 in North Dakota, where he can get some shooting and where the birds are not being destroyed in such quantities for the markets, than to go to some more liberal but more illy-stocked State for a sporting trip. I know this license law has stopped much shooting and cut off much non-resident travel to North Dakota, for the gun stores of St. Paul and Minneapolis complain that it has hurt their trade with sportsmen who outfit for shooting trips to the Northwest. Even the railroads don't like the law, for it lessens their traffic. The ducks, however, are to be congratulated upon it, and so are those whose fate enables them to get a look in at one of the greatest remaining sporting grounds of America.

It was 11:45 in the morning when our long ride over the easy prairies came to a pause at the famous Chase Pass. From the high ridge which rims in this valley we looked down and saw two great lakes, each reaching away four or five miles from the point of view, each perhaps half a mile or more across. Between these two bodies of clear water there stretched a high ridge of hard, dry ground, apparently a quarter of a mile across from water to water, and about 40 feet above the surface of the water at the summit of the ridge. There was a light wind moving, and the water was rippled and moving, so that we could see no ducks at first. As we drove down nearer to the bank we caught sight of thousands of black, bobbing figures, all over the whole face of the waters. In shore, and now not over a few hundreds of yards from us, there rested upon the bars literally a black mass of ducks, thousands upon thousands. This is not the enthusiasm of a man who has never seen many birds before, but is the literal and calm truth. I never in my life have seen so great a body of wildfowl at one time. Soon the birds began to soar up and circle blackly about, and in time the air was dark with a countless multitude of circling, twisting and turning fowl, each bunch with a different direction from the others. It was enough to drive one crazy.

Neither Bowers nor Gokey showed any signs of losing his mind, though I feared for the Chief. For my own part, I have a vague recollection that I stood upon one foot while the team was being turned out and the deliberate preparations made for the hunt.

"Take plenty of shells," was about all the advice Warden Bowers had to offer. "You'll need them all, for you won't kill every shot."

So we took each a back load and hurried off to the pass over which the birds were streaming. We had been told that on this pass, no matter what the weather, the ducks fly all day long. This we did not believe, but set down as "ag'in natur'." Yet we found it true this day at least, though the morning started in very fair and warm.

We found that a series of pits had been dug along the ridge, a few feet below the summit, deep enough so that the shooter would be concealed when he crouched down. In these pits we saw many old shells, but these were weather-beaten and showed to be those of last year. We were the first to shoot on this wonderful pass in the wonderful duck year of 1897.

Gokey took the furthest pit, Bowers next to him, then myself, then the Chief, who thus was furthest to the left as he faced to the west, from which direction the first flight came. We hurried under many passing flocks as we trotted into the firing line, and as soon as we got located each began to shoot. The ducks were most accommodating, and came to us at first in a vast mass, out of which it was next to impossible to pick out any individual birds. The speed of the flight was terrific, and the hiss of the wings cutting, low and close or whispering high overhead, was never absent from the ear. Nor was there absent the steady cracking of the guns. Gokey's regular double report, mingled with the cornsheller activity of Bowers' repeating Winchester, smote my ear on the right, while nearby on the left the sharp crack of the Chief's little 12-gauge sounded incessantly. Not one shot out of four landed its game, but, none the less, there was a series of heavy thumps all about us, more especially to the right of the firing line, where the two Dakota men were in action.

After a while we had a little let up and I looked over

to see how the Chief was getting along. I then had about a dozen ducks piled up in my pit, most of them belonging to Bowers, I presume, but when I approached the Chief he was sitting with his head in his hand, gloomily looking down at a hen spoonbill which he had chased into the grass and killed with a stick.

"What's the matter, Chief?" I asked him, kindly and like a perfect gentleman.

"The truth is," said he sadly, as he looked up from the hen spoonbill, "I can't land on 'em. Now, I've been holding for the solar plexus of about 4,000 individual ducks that have sashayed across here, but I can't seem to land on 'em. When I lead they—don't misunderstand me—they duck, as it were. They ain't there. How about that? Are these things too good for everybody? How did you fellows happen to get any? Did you shoot into the flock and hit another flock?"

I explained to the Chief that I got ducks by watching closely where Mr. Bowers was shooting and then shooting into the same flock with him. He regretted that he was so far out of the way of this sort of assistance that he could not avail himself of anybody's skill but his own, and he hadn't any.

The Chief and I then concluded to visit a while, and we shot together out of his pit for a few rounds. By this time the birds had begun to come back from the east, and now the fun grew yet more fast and furious. The flocks would start from the eastern lake high up in the air. "Mark east!" would come the warning down the line, and each man would get below the level of the ridge. As the birds approached the high ground they would drop rapidly and come over the pass parallel with the ground and very low. They would roll over the top of the little ridge beyond us, dip down into the coulee across our front, disappear for a moment, and then come surging and boiling and whistling up in a long, swift, feathery wave over the crest of our breastworks, hissing almost into our faces as they swept on out toward the water. Never was such an exciting situation in the world!

Never in all my life did I see such shooting. It was a glimpse, a glance and then a swift wheel to get a fair shot at a disappearing bunch almost over the edge of the reeds which lined the water's edge behind us. Sometimes the ducks flew almost into our faces. Often we dodged down to escape what seemed an imminent danger of losing a hat or a head. Twice I shot ducks ahead of me which fell thirty feet behind me. Once I had a fat duck come crushing into the pit beside me, and once I dropped a teal against the bank of my pit. A more perfect embodiment of a hot corner on ducks never existed. It was almost bewildering in its tension. It was a delirium of ducks.

The Chief and I shot from his pit together, and after a time we both began to improve, coaching each other on the lead as the different flocks came by. I could see that he was stopping his gun when he fired and holding about six feet ahead on birds where he should have led twenty. I could see the line of his smoke cut in apparently a dozen feet behind the bird which he thought he was leading almost too much. He did an equal service by me, and soon we began to acquire the lead, a distance which seemed utterly absurd at first. The pile of birds at our pit began to grow. At lunch time the Chief had become a finished performer on the pass. A very nice-looking farmer lady came out with a very nice-looking lunch, and as she drove up, the Chief and I rose and cut out four ducks from a passing flock, just to show the lady how it was done. Alas for me! I fell down on my next chance, but the Chief killed a pair out the next flight over. Then, as we gathered at the reed bed for luncheon, he cut down a high single, and a moment later yet another. I saw a glance of triumph come into his eye. He had caught the knack of it.

At lunch we paused now and then to kill, or try to kill, the ducks which continued to pour over. Mr. Bowers told me that he and some friends once killed fourteen ducks at that same spot while they were eating lunch one day. I think we dropped half a dozen or so before we had cleaned up the lunch. A bountiful and well-cooked one it was, and to have it thus brought down warm from the farmhouse was the last touch of comfort on this dry, comfortable and absolutely ideal fly-way. A good part of our lunch was made up of four grouse, which we had picked up along the road; almost the only grouse we saw in this part of the coun-try, where they are very scarce this year.

After our lunch we resumed position in the skirmish line, minus Gokey, who had a headache and did not shoot for a while. It was an old story with Gokey, and it did not take him long to kill the twenty-five birds which make the limit *per diem* for a shooter in the State of North Dakota. With the Chief and myself it was different. We got a good deal bigger run for our money than anybody else, because we shot worse. It now began to be a struggle of courtesy between us all. "I never touched that bird; it's yours, my friend," I would say to the Chief. "Your bird, sir," he would reply, with equal courtesy; and so we would argue over it.

Bowers and I nearly scared the Chief to death by covertly piling up a lot of our birds in front of his pit and then proceeding to count them before him. We made it out to be twenty-nine birds, and the warden told him it would cost him $400!

It would seem that one should soon kill his limit on a flight like this, and so he can, even though he be new at the sport of pass shooting—the hardest shooting in the world, and not to be compared with the easy work of shooting over decoys. Yet I have noticed that even the best shots will spoil 100 shells to pick up twenty-five ducks on a pass like this, and it takes a little while to shoot 100 shells, especially after the first flurry is over and one steadies down and behaves like a shooter, picking his shots and taking care. We had shot a little over a couple of hours before we thought it best to rectify our rough counts of individual bags and to go after the birds which had fallen dead back of us in the reeds. Bowers and I went over the crest of the ridge to look for some birds we had killed on the hard ground, and while we were there we saw the prettiest bit of shooting done on the trip.

The Chief was then alone in the pit over which the main flight was passing, and he had his eye on the birds. He took toll out of everything that crossed. Five times we saw him rise and fire at flocks and small bodies of birds, and each time he got meat. Once he killed all three of three ducks that went over down wind, high and fast, a handsome bit of work. Twice he dropped his double out, and out of five accepted chances he did not miss a shot. It was good enough fun to sit and watch this, and Bowers and I both concluded we had no more advice to offer him. When we got to his pit we found him radiant and hugging to his bosom the light 12-gauge, with which he was now thoroughly in-fatuated. He expressed himself as for once absolutely satisfied with the world. "Did you see me deflate that last un?" he asked cheerfully.

When we picked up our birds we found that, count-ing a half dozen birds we had given the farmer's wife, we had our limit, or so near it that we did not care to go closer—ninety-eight birds in all. Thereupon came up human nature, as the Chief and I both realized. It was the first day we had had outdoors with a gun for a long time, and the best chance to kill a lot of ducks either of us had ever had in all his life. I confess that my per-sonal wish was to kill some more. I wanted to try just one or two shots more. I wanted to see if I could kill a double out of the flock just heading for us. I wanted—well, I admit I wanted to go ahead and shoot a lot.

But this we did not do, and after we saw the awful pile of game we had when we got it together, every one of us was mighty glad we had killed no more, even the question of the law aside. All of these birds, except those eaten by ourselves, were taken to Fargo and there disposed of, Mr. Bowers and myself laboring faithfully till we had them all given away. It is sure we killed enough. How many we could have killed had we all shot all day long as steadily as possible I should not like to say. I believe we could easily have fired from 500 to 600 shells apiece and have killed perhaps one-fourth or more of that number of birds apiece. But what a butchery that would have been, for even our one party. What a butchery it would be for many parties, taken for not one day, but for many days. I never had the lesson of moderation more forcibly impressed upon me. It was not at first pleasant, I admit, and I vaguely found the customary excuses for doing what I wanted to do, just as human nature always finds such excuses; but once the temptation was overcome we each of us felt happy. We are each ready to say that the killing of twenty-five ducks on a red-hot pass is fun enough for one day for any man, and that the law is a good one and should stand and be respected. This limit is one which should be set in every gentlemen's shooting club all over the land. It is enough. It is at the moment hard to realize it, but it is enough. Stop at twenty-five, and you feel bad at the time, but good after a while.

So we went away long before evening, while a cold

storm was blowing up, and while over the greatest duck
pass of the Northwest the long black streamers of the
flight were growing thick and thicker.   Into the night,
over roads made softer by a drizzling rain, we drove,
reaching town late, but very well contented.

Precisely similar to pass shooting is that mode which
is sometimes practiced in the East and called bar
shooting.

Less than 100 miles from New York, in the harbor
of a New England town, is a little island which at low
water is connected with the mainland by a long bar.
On either side of this bar are feeding grounds for the
ducks, and in autumn, winter and spring the birds at
morning and evening fly between the two feeding
grounds and so between the island and the mainland.
When the tide is low, in the morning or at evening, the
gunners often gather on this bar, and, stationing themselves a gunshot or more apart, wait for the ducks to
fly.   The birds are chiefly scoters of two or three kinds,
old squaws, a few broadbills in spring and always a few
whistlers and buffle-heads.   Sometimes, if the weather
is entirely calm, no birds at all will fly across the bar;
at other times, if it is stormy or foggy, there may be
quite a flight—half a dozen flocks of old squaws, as
many of coots, one or two small flocks of broadbills and
scattering whistlers and dippers, with rarely a black
duck.   Sometimes the coots, if the breeze is gentle, will
fly across at considerable height, too far off to be
reached by shot, and then occasionally they may be

brought down within gunshot by the shrill yell of one of the gunners or even by a shot fired at them. It is curious to see a dozen of these great birds turn almost completely over at the unexpected sound and dash down toward the water.

The gunners in this shooting do not make use of any blind, but crouch low on the stones of the bar, keeping motionless and out of sight until the birds are nearly over them. In such shooting I once saw a man cut down two eider ducks out of a flock of coots passing over him.

Similar to this is the shooting which is practiced in New England on the hills which separate the wide, open waters from some more sheltered bay or lake to which the birds may wish to resort. In quiet weather when the birds do not come in until a long time after dark, this shooting is practiced only at night. But on stormy days the flight of ducks and geese often begins two or three hours before dark, and black ducks, pintails and geese may fly from that time until darkness has shut down, and some may be killed. If the wind is from a quarter where the birds are obliged to face it they often fly very low and the shooting is then extremely easy, if their course brings them within range of the gunner.

If they are shot at night it must be a cloudy night with a moon. On a bright moonlight night the birds cannot be seen unless they pass very near to the gunner, and even then he is likely to have only a glimpse of them, while if a bright moon is shining behind clouds the diffused light renders the whole sky so light that duck or goose can be seen quite a long way off and the gunner has little difficulty in knowing just when and where to shoot.

Twenty years ago this method of shooting was practiced to a considerable extent in New England and with not a little success. It was not very uncommon for a good shot to kill in an evening two or three geese and perhaps five or six ducks. We imagine that of late years much less of it has been done, particularly as in many States all night shooting is forbidden.

At certain points on the South Atlantic coast, notably at Carroll's Island, in the old time, overhead shooting, as it is called there, has been practiced for many years. This came in after the fowl, through much pursuit, had become wild and no longer came to decoys at the points. At first these overhead birds used to fly within range, but as they were shot at more and more they took to flying higher. Where at first ordinary 10-gauge guns were used, 12-pound 8's presently became necessary. Later, heavy 8-gauge guns, weighing from 16 to 19 pounds, were used, and finally single-barrel 4-gauge guns, weighing from 19 to 22 pounds and shooting BB or even larger shot, were fired at these flocks, which looked almost like bumble bees as they passed over the land. Often the sport was good, and we know of a man who killed in three days 117 canvas-backs and red-heads from these overhead flocks.

SHOOTING IN THE OVERFLOW.

Wildfowl shooting in the timber is practiced in many parts of the South at seasons when the rivers overflow their banks and spread over the low wooded country through which they pass. Sometimes the shooting is done in the pleasant autumn months, when the October haze covers woods and fields with its light veil, or, again, it may be followed in early spring, when the winds howl noisily among the tree tops amid rain and snow flurries. Suitable conditions for timber shooting do not always prevail, for very often neither spring nor fall overflow takes place. When, however, the Mississippi River does break out of banks in the autumn and covers much of the low country, making more accessible the acorns and the roots and the shoots that the birds like so well, great sport may be had in the overflowed lands, to which all the fresh-water ducks resort, though the most of them are mallards.

When such conditions prevail, if the gunner can choose a stormy, windy day, when the birds find it uncomfortable to sit out in the broad, open waters, and can find a place in the timber where the ducks are feeding, he is likely to have great shooting. Of course, he must go thither in a boat, and usually two men go together—one to paddle and the other to shoot.

On the way through the timber many shots will be had at birds sprung from the water by the approach of the boat, but when the spot is reached where the ducks have been feeding, a dozen or twenty decoys will be thrown out, and a blind built for the boat. Often this consists merely of a few branches stuck in the mud by the vessel's side, or it may be practicable to push it into tall grass or reeds, which will form a natural blind. Whatever spot is chosen, the gunner must have plenty of elbow room for himself and his companion, for there is no greater handicap in shooting than being cramped.

Usually the birds that have been feeding in this place, and which have been driven away by the boat's approach, will very soon begin to come back, and will come in very gently to the decoys, offering extremely pretty and easy shooting. Besides this, on a day such as described, small bunches of birds are continually flying about over the timber, looking for places where the feed is good, and seeing the imitation ducks floating on the water, at once lower their flight to secure their share of the good things their companions are feeding on.

Often, if they are permitted to do so, the ducks will alight among the decoys, and sometimes those that are particularly gentle will even begin to feed with them; but the lack of motion in the wooden stools soon renders them suspicious, and they spring into the air with a sharp quack, only to be cut down before they fairly get on the wing.

If by chance, while good shooting is being had on such a day, the wind should suddenly die down, it will be found that the shooting ceases almost at once, for the birds then cease to fly and resort to the open water and sit there until dark.

RIVER SHOOTING.

River shooting is practiced with great effect in many parts of the country where narrow streams, flowing through deep beds, permit the gunner to walk along their winding course, and to shoot the ducks as they rise before him. In the same way, in the South, and indeed in many portions of the country, from the Southern States to California, river shooting is practiced by paddling along narrow streams, keeping close to the banks, and shooting the ducks as they get up. In this last form of the sport two men are usually required, one man sitting in the bow with his gun, the other handling the paddle in the stern. Usually the gunners take turns, one paddling for an hour, and then being relieved by his companion, and shooting for an hour. In the narrow sloughs of Ohio, Illinois, Indiana and Minnesota the same sport is practiced. During the migration, these sloughs, which are often bordered by wild rice, or, at all events, produce abundant vegetable food, are resorted to by the ducks, and often the stream's course is so tortuous that the birds rise not more than twenty or thirty yards before the boat. Shooting of this description is usually easy, since the birds spring into the air and give the gunner a straightaway or climbing shot. On the other hand, many crippled birds are likely to be lost, as they fall on the land or in the thick grass or weeds of the bank. For this reason a well-trained dog—a setter, pointer, or water-dog—is of great assistance, since he is sure to find many birds that would otherwise be lost.

This is a favorite method of shooting in many parts of the South, and men who practice it are enthusiastic about it. Such an one is the writer of an account of "Duck Floating on the Tombigbee River," in Southern Alabama, printed in *Forest and Stream* over the signature P. B. M., which reads as follows:

I closely scanned the river below me as it lay glistening in the morning's sunlight. With my spyglass I looked under the overhanging willows and into the little nooks and corners along the shore. Very soon a fine flock of mallards emerged from under the willow that had hidden them from our view. One by one they came out and gazed without any signs of fright at the green floating mass that our boat appeared to be. As soon as the plumage of these birds was plain and the bright emerald green of the drakes' heads was distinct (for by this time the current had silently carried us near to them) I, with one barrel on the water and the other on the wing, killed seven of these fine fowls and received most gracefully the compliments of Kirk upon my skill. All sportsmen know how animating a good beginning is in a day's sport and how the expectation of killing more game lends a keener zest to the pursuit.

So it was with us as the gentle Bigby bore us down its current to as glorious a day's shooting as ever fell to mortal lot. More mallards swam out from under willows and so many were killed that the bottom of our boat was covered, and I was covered, too, with Kirk's compliments. I made quick double shots right and left and capped the climax of Kirk's good opinion by calling his attention to two ducks thirty feet apart, promising to kill both at one shot on the wing, which I did in spite of his assertion that "it can't be did."

Below Camber's, where the river was eddy, the sharp brown nose of a beaver was thrust up above the water's surface, and his curiosity was rewarded by a load of BB shot. The beaver sank out of sight, leaving the water red with blood. My guide told me he would soon rise, but not to fire until he told me. In a few seconds the animal slowly rose to the surface and swam to the shore. As he crawled up on the bank I obeyed my companion's order "to fire," and killed the beaver. Before the smoke of my gun had cleared away, a quick stroke of the paddle carried the skiff to land, when, leaping out, Kirk seized the beaver, preventing his rolling into the water, and threw him into our boat.

Of all modes of locomotion that of gliding down the smooth current of a river in an open boat is the most delightful; it soothes the senses and quiets the nerves in a way indescribable. Softly floating down the current of that river so rich in Indian lore, with a sky overhead like Italy's, I thought of the dusky old chiefs, Tombecbee and Tishabee, whose names "are on our

waters still," whose hunter's shout made these grand
old woods ring.   These red men, like me, once drank
in the beauty of this scene, where the mock orange trees
bloomed and the golden water-grass filled the river's
edge, while visions of the happy hunting grounds came
to them.

We reached Houston's Island, where hundreds of
ducks were feeding, a sight to gladden any sportsman's
heart, as their bright plumage glistened in the sun.
Here Kirk, by skillful paddling, brought me into close
range, and more victims fell to our guns.   Here on this
island, my guide tells me, is where Sam Rowe, the bar-
keeper, with his little Winchester, killed his big buck
from the deck of the boat, whose horns ornament the
boat, and upon which horns Sam "hangs many a tale"
for the amusement of the passengers.

We drifted along under the high, white cliffs of Bluff
Port, and just below Kirk discovered, standing on the
heights, a flock of turkeys.   We allowed our boat to
float directly under them, so as to be concealed.   Then
my companion went ashore, took off his shoes and tied
his rifle to his back with his suspenders, and ascended
the cliff in a zigzag fashion.   Almost as soon as he
reached the top the sharp crack of the rifle told the
doom of a big gobbler that was thrown down to me.
Kirk's gobbler took away all appetite for killing mallards, but not for lunch, so we kindled a fire and fell
upon our eatables with a hearty zest, while I was enter-
tained with hunting stories.   We got adrift again and
floated lazily on, not caring much for the ducks that we

would sometimes drift upon so noiselessly that we would catch them asleep upon logs, with their heads tucked under their wings. Our boat was nearly full, and often we did not disturb the slumbers of the solitary old drake as he enjoyed his siesta on a log.

As we pass Spring Bluff we hear the mellow notes of Steve Brown's horn vainly endeavoring to call back his dogs from the pursuit of a deer. The deer's crossing place on the river was only a quarter of a mile below, and Kirk took his place quickly in the middle of the boat, seized his oars and pulled hard and fast that we might intercept him. We were just in time to see a big buck take to water, and a few pulls on the oars brought us in range of him. Kirk threw up his rifle, took steady aim and fired, but only wounded him. We could travel faster than the deer in water, and the skiff was soon alongside.of the deer, and Kirk took him by the horns. A deer sinks like lead when shot dead in water, and we had to manœuvre well to get him to the shore. Kirk proposed to mount and ride him ashore, as we were towed along, but to this I objected, thinking it best to gain a little time for Brown's dogs to come. The dogs soon arrived, and seeing the situation of things swam out to our assistance. With their aid the deer was killed, landed, disemboweled and was soon lying with our game in the boat.

We were soon adrift again, and long shadows on the Bigby's bosom told us that the day was closing. Away below we heard the welcome sound of the "Clara's" double whistle. As the current carries us down, our game is counted: Thirty-seven mallards, six teals and one deer and turkey are our trophies. Two great black columns of smoke are now just below, and the steamer sweeps around the bend in full view. The broad, good-humored face of Captain Ham greets us from the roof as he calls out, "What do you want?" In reply I seized a dead mallard by the legs and waved it in the air. The alarm whistle was blown and the engine slowed, and as we ride the waves alongside, our friends, the officers, welcome us with hearty greeting. Old Captain Bennett, the mate, seized our rope as we threw it aboard; then I was jerked on the steamer by the arm and our boat hauled up. We return the Captain's compliments on our skill by presenting him with the turkey, while good old Sam Rowe must needs treat us all around, except the Captain.

In spring, when the snows are melting and the weather is wet, the narrow streams from which one may expect to jump ducks are likely to be bank full, and when this is the case the man who is walking along them for ducks must often use considerable care and skill to approach within shot without being seen. This is often very difficult and requires much creeping through mud and water, and even then may fail.

In California, and on some western rivers, a modification of "floating" takes place. The gunner, without a companion, occupies a low, flat boat, which rises but little above the water; sometimes the flat deck of this boat is fitted up with hooks or loops by means of which

weeds, grass or branches of trees are fastened to it, so
that when seen from the level of the water the boat
looks merely like a mass of drift stuff coming down the
stream.   The gunner, when he reaches the point where
he intends to begin to shoot, ships his oars, and passing
a sculling oar through the hole in the stern of the boat,
lies on his back and slowly sculls the vessel with the
current.   His eyes are just above the mass of the trash
on the deck, and he is able to scan the surface of the
stream before him.   If he sees ducks he directs the boat
toward them and slowly approaches to within shot.   If
he is careful, the birds are not likely to take the alarm
until he has come as near to them as he wishes to.
When he rises, the birds take wing, and he fires.

Floating for ducks is likely to be practiced at any
time in spring or fall, but it is quite obvious that it is
likely to be more successful in the early winter, after the
quiet ponds and slow-flowing sloughs are frozen, than
when all the water is open.   If, for example, the
weather in the Northern States should have been cold
for a few days, late in November, so as to close much
of the feeding ground, and there is a swift-flowing
stream that has not yet been frozen, good shooting is
usually to be found there.   It will be had, however,
only at the expense of considerable suffering from cold,
but it is sure to be good.   An account of such a day's
shoot, written by Mr. E. Hough for *Forest and Stream,*
is worth quoting:

It was very cold; our boat was calked by the fingers

of the frost and could not leak a drop. We shivered
under our heavy coats. Far and wide the bottoms
were a sheet of ice, for winter had caught old Skunk
"out on a high," though the water was now within the
banks, ice being on either shore, and the meagre current
in the middle looked blue-black and forbidding in the
morning light. A cold wind whistled through the
trees, and the whole scene was so dismal that it was
with feelings almost of foreboding that we stepped
aboard and shoved off, heading eastward, where a faint
gray streak told of the coming day. Fifteen minutes
passed in silence as we sped on down the racing current.
Then a sharp whizz greeted our ears as a solitary spike-
tail crossed from the right. We dropped two empty
shells in the bottom of the boat, and the duck went right
on; a double miss to begin on. Now an old mallard
starts from under the willows and he comes down dead
all over. Two more follow and meet a like fate. Then
they start up by the hundred, from under the ice,
among the willows, from the dry ground. "Shoot!
shoot!" my companion cries, and as fast as I can work
the top-snap I comply. Half our ducks fell on shore,
and before we could break through the ledge of ice
many of the cripples were lost beyond recovery, sometimes creeping off a hundred feet beneath a sheet of ice,
where a man could not follow them.

We now exchanged places, and Virgil took the bow
with both guns, it being our agreement that but one
should shoot at a time, we not caring to add another to
the list of accidents from careless shooting in boats.

As we rounded a bend I noticed my friend trying to catch a sight on a big mallard which was swimming ahead of him. "Trying to shoot on the water, are you, hey?" said I; "see here——" "No, I am not. He's dived twice. Hold on! Whoa! Back water! Confound him; there he goes again!" And that duck was never seen again. After several such experiences we concluded to shoot on sight. With few exceptions the single ducks would dive instead of flying. It was most provoking to get within thirty yards of a fine duck and then, just as you expect to see him start up to meet an honorable death, see him settle down in the most approved hell-diver style, till his eye just showed above water line, and then dive to shot. These "slinkers," as we called them, were all mallards, though I have seen redheads do the same thing. They were nearly all uninjured, so far as we could see. Sometimes we could see two or three skulking along the edge of the river with their heads down, trying to escape notice till they could hide or dive. The day was very cold, ice formed on our oars so thick that we often had to stop and pound it off, and it struck us that the birds were possibly too numb to fly or had their wing tips frozen fast. A friend afterward suggested that these were all crippled birds, driven in by the freeze, but some of their actions and their numbers precluded the idea with us, though the shooting had been very heavy that fall.

Meantime imagine us gliding down the swirling current, between long rows of ice-laden, creaking willows, now running full before the wind, now rounding a bend to meet a row of whitecaps which dashed an icy spray in our faces, now pulling straight away, now veering quickly to escape a sunken log or projecting ice ledge. We scarcely knew our familiar stream in its changed appearance. Sometimes we ran through the woods for miles without knowing where we were.

The black and angry clouds, the ice fields, the strange sounds in the woods and the swiftly moving vistas of the ever-changing, restless river made up an effect which will not soon pass away. It was novel, it was glorious, this boating with the mercury below zero and the river narrowing slowly. Would I have changed my uneasy seat in this winter panorama to hunt any other game on foot or on horseback, or play any fish beside a summer pool? By no means. Such fascination I have never known.

It was the last day of the season and all the ducks in the country were crowded along that narrow channel, and no one else was there to molest or make afraid.

Whang! went Virgil's gun. "I got that old slinker that time," said he. Sure enough. We could see his red feet paddling against the transparent ice as he vainly tried to dive. We had learned to believe it as honorable to shoot a duck diving as one flying.

At noon we landed, stretched our limbs and ate our frozen lunch. We had now nearly as many ducks as we thought it honorable to take. I realized that if we would catch the evening train we must hasten. So cautioning Virgil not to shoot any more, I took the oars, and we flew down stream at a lively rate. Running thus for some time in silence, except an occasional "Port a little! straight away!" from my companion, I was startled by the double report of his gun, followed by the whistle of a flock of mallards as they passed up stream. Two ducks lay stone dead upon the water. "Thought you weren't going to shoot any more," said I. "Well," said he, a little ashamed, "I couldn't help it; the old gun would come up, and I had to hold her, you know." We changed again before long, and I made a righteous resolve not to shoot another duck, and allowed several to pass unsaluted. Finally an old drake came shooting along by the river. "It would be a sin," thought I, "to kill that duck, for we have a plenty. Shoot him? No. That's not so easy, though. I don't know—I guess—just watch me drop him as he crosses." Now, is not that an intense moment, when the gun comes just against the shoulder and the duck seems glued to the end of the barrel? Every intervening object is blotted out; you can see nothing but the duck, and he falls to the crack of the gun as if you had struck him dead with a concentrated eye glance. But, alas! alas! for my principles. I had killed another duck!

We now left both guns unloaded, and one taking his seat in the stern with the paddle and the other at the oars, we went ahead in grand style, and in due time reached our journey's end. Here we pulled out our boat and locked her to a tree, but happening just then to meet a native with a train, we concluded a hasty bargain by which he was to haul our boat over to the station for the sum of one dollar, the roads being, as he said, powerful bad.

Virgil started ahead with all the ducks he could carry and I followed with the rest, together with the guns and coats. At the station we were the wonder of all observers, there appearing to be a general desire to see "the two fools who had come all the way from Metz right in the dead of winter." We reached home in good season, having made the round trip in one day. That night we divided up with several families, and the next day some of our game appeared upon tables where possibly ducks were rarely seen.

This hunt, we thought, paid us well, not so much in the game as in that we felt that we had surprised Nature in a new mood, one which she had gotten up for herself and intended no one else should see. It was audacious in us to tempt her in such a mood; but in the memories of the day our audacity was rewarded.

From still another section, and of another season, is the account which follows, also taken from *Forest and Stream:*

The air is damp with a heavy fog that has settled low upon the earth, the long grass hanging over the narrow road being as wet as from a rain. The birds are not yet awake. Even that early riser, the thrush, has not opened his eyes. We tread, single file, the winding path that leads from the road down the wooded river bank to the boat.

Dan takes his position in the bow. It is my turn at

the oars, and off she slides into the water. The fog seems to have grown denser. It is impossible to distinguish objects over a dozen boat lengths away. Five, ten, fifteen minutes are tipped off by the dip of the oars; still the fog hangs about us like a thick veil, denying even a glimpse of the shore for which we were steering.

"Say, old man, how's this?" cries Jim, pointing to a stake we have almost collided with. I feel much provoked, for I recognize our starting point. We have made a circuit. Jim produces a small compass attached to a watch-chain; we take our bearings carefully and try again. This time the trees come out of the fog to meet us, for we have made the opposite shore. The boat glides on just out of reach of the overhanging bushes. A great blue crane flops out of a tree above us, and, with a harsh cry that startles Dan, disappears in the fog.

Easy now. Here is the narrow stream leading up through the marsh. We change positions, Jim moving up to the bow with his gun, while I settle in the stern to paddle. The first bend, and no ducks. The stream now is scarcely wider than the boat. Water bushes are bent aside to enable us to pass, taking care not to disturb an ugly-looking wasp nest with its wicked owners asleep on the outside. I give the boat a shove around the next turn. Up rise several ducks. Bang! bang! goes Jim's gun. A clean miss with the first barrel, but the second drops its victim all in a heap, as limp as a wet dish-rag. Another comes out of the wild rice at my very elbow. The paddle slips into the water as I reach for my gun, and down comes the duck with a splash. Dan is overboard attending to business, and quickly retrieves the birds. Nice fat fellows they are. Here comes a straggler returning through the mist. Jim has his eye upon him and makes a very creditable kill. Dan splashes off through the weeds and water and retrieves, with the duck held firmly in his mouth. He climbs into the boat, and with muddy feet and dripping hide carefully squats upon the middle seat, where somebody will have to sit at the oars. Dan never neglected to place one or more of his feet on that seat every time he entered the boat, provided they were wet or muddy. Jim and I argued with him earnestly and often against this weakness, and now and then with the broad end of the paddle, but all to no purpose. So after a bit I would laugh when it came Jim's time to occupy the muddy seat, and Jim would giggle when I had to make a blotter of myself.

Back down the stream we turn to the left and add another duck to our string. The fog is lifting now, a light breeze swaying the rice and cat-tails. The blackbirds are awake, chattering over their breakfast and making sociable visits from one flock to another. Clear as a tinkling bell comes the *pink-pink* of the reed birds. A tall crane stands out in the water across the creek, foraging for his morning lunch. I produce my pipe and light up, while Jim makes himself useful at the oars. Half a mile up the creek we strike the mouth of another stream that zig-zags across the marsh. I take the post of honor this time. We are not fairly into the

stream before a plump-looking duck comes out of the
rushes, but drops back as the smoke curls away from
my gun. Quiet now, for a loud word would frighten
the ducks that are probably feeding under that clump
of water bushes ahead, whereas often they will not
take wing at the report of a gun unless very near them.
We approach with great caution, for this is one of our
favorite spots, though the ducks have a trick of going
out on the wrong side of the bushes—undoubtedly the
right side for them, the bushes being so high that the
ducks are out of range before they show above them.

This time we try a new dodge on the feathered inno-
cents. Jim steps out upon the marsh while I proceed
with the boat. If they only come this way, well and
good. But, no; the fates are against us. Out they go
as the boat jars the bushes, but further up than usual,
and only one, most likely a youngster, falls a victim by
separating from the flock.

We have time for one more stream ere the tide low-
ers. I give Jim the bow, and tell him to shoot straight
and take his time about it, for this is the boss stream
of the creek. He stands up in the narrow bow ready
for action, the hammers of his gun lying back like
the ears of a horse about to bite. That rascal, Dan, is
on the seat again; but this is not the place or time to
rebuke him, for the stream is deep and the boat un-
steady. I paddle noiselessly around the bend. The
expectation becomes almost painful. With fluttering
of wings, up rise two beauties. Jim swings his gun and
leans to one side. Dan thinks it a good time to get off

that seat, and does it so expeditiously that with the
report of the gun both Jim and the ducks disappear, he
having lost his balance by the recoil of the gun and
Dan's untimely move. He clutches frantically at the
air, but it avails him not. There is a resounding
splash, and Jim's feet are hanging on the edge of the
boat, while his body is in the water. He holds the gun
at arm's length above the water, the muzzle wobbling
suggestively in a line with my head, as he endeavors
to dislodge his feet. I think, "Good Lord, if he should
pull that trigger!" and forget to offer him any assistance in my anxiety to get out of range of that gun barrel. But in less time than it has taken to tell it, Jim is
on his feet in water up to his middle, indulging in such
roars of laughter as to nearly frighten the ducks into
spasms, and sending them scurrying out of the creek
as if the devil himself was chasing them. You may be
sure I laughed with him. It makes me smile to this
day when I think of Jim hanging by his heels, head
down, in that little creek.

This mishap spoiled our shooting, but we succeeded
in stopping a couple of ducks as they passed out. Putting up a small sail, we sped down the Chipoax and
Lorne, fairly well satisfied with our bag of seven ducks.

To me, Chipoax Creek was a joy forever, and really
possessed no mean beauties when viewed at high water.
It sweeps in graceful curves through the green marsh,
its course as crooked as a blacksnake's track, now running under a steep bank from which the trees reach
down their branches as if to drink, and further on, its

waters playing about the trunks of huge cypress trees standing well out from the shore. But when the tide went out, how marked the change! I have seen the very walls of its muddy channel laid bare, while on either side great, gray, slimy flats come out of the water, their glistening surface broken here and there with decaying snags and dotted with little patches of tangled grass. But it is not my desire, O Chipoax! to revile you because your waters leave you uncovered, for many is the time that you have floated my boat and offered up your treasures with unstinted hand. Long may your tides flow in and out and your channel remain unchoked by débris of the sea.

IN THE WILD RICE FIELDS.

Scattered over the northern country, between the Hudson River and the Missouri, are many thousands of reedy swamps and shallow lakes, and great stretches of wet meadow-land, where the wild rice grows. In the spring, so soon as the water is warmed by the genial rays of the advancing sun, the tiny pale green spears show themselves above its surface, and, all through the hot summer, grow taller and stouter, until, when August comes, the tasseled heads begin to bow with the weight of the flowers, and, a little later, the soft, milky grain appears in a waving crop. In the good old times, before the white man's foot had explored every recess of our land, or his plough furrowed every prairie, or

his crooked gray fences disfigured each landscape,
these rice fields were the homes of innumerable wild
creatures.

On their borders the herons built their nests, and in
the open waters, among the stalks, they did their fishing. In and out among the stems, the wild ducks and
grebes swam in daily journeyings, while the rails and
the coots ran or waded or climbed among the stalks,
undisturbed. Here the muskrat had his home, living,
in the summer, perhaps, in a hole on some higher piece
of ground, and, in winter, building for himself, from
the reeds and the stems of the rice, a house, solid, substantial, and impervious to the cold. Here, too, lived
the mink, taking his daily toll of fish or frogs from the
water, sometimes killing the muskrat, and, now and
then, feasting greedily on the eggs or the young of
some bird, whose nest he had despoiled.

Among the rice or the reeds, the blackbirds built
their hanging nests of grass, supported by three or four
natural columns, and all through the heat of the June
days the mother bird brooded her pale blue, black-
streaked eggs, swinging easily to the movement of the
rice stems, like the sailor in his hammock at sea. More
solid and substantial were the houses built by the
marsh wrens; round balls of grass, deftly woven about
a stalk of the rice, roofed over as well as floored, and
with only a narrow hole for the passage in and out of
the tiny owner. Sometimes a single pair built half a
dozen of these nests, near one another, before making a
habitation that pleased them, and those that they had

left were taken by the bumblebees for homes in which
to do their housekeeping.

Rarely, in such marshes, might be found the nest of
the great gray goose; the female brooding her eggs on
a solid nest placed on a foundation of reeds and grass,
the faithful gander not far from his mate, ready, at an
instant's warning, to fight bravely in her defense,
should prowling fox, or coon, or wolf, approach his
home. Then, after the yellow goslings were hatched,
the pair led them, by well-known paths, hither and
thither through the rice fields, telling them where the
best food was to be found, where danger might lurk,
and teaching them how to live their lives.

But it was when autumn came, and the ripened
grain, loose now in its husks, began, as the breezes
blew, to drop down into the water below, that the
greatest accessions came to the life of the wild rice
fields. Now, from the north, singly and by tens, and
hundreds, and thousands, came flying the hordes of
waterfowl which had been hatched and reared toward
the borders of the Arctic Sea. Their numbers were
beyond belief, and such as no man of the present day
can hope to see again.

Flock after flock, they came dropping down into the
marsh, until the open spots were crowded with their
dark bodies, and from the concealment of the reeds,
where no water could be seen, tumultuous clamorings
told of other thousands hidden there. In those days,
when ducks were food for the infrequent dwellers of
those regions, the single discharge of a gun would sup-

ply the hunter with birds enough for several days; then, no one thought of shooting ducks or geese, except to eat, and, indeed, ammunition was often far too valuable to be wasted on birds. Indians have told me that, when camped on the borders of the wild rice lakes of Minnesota and Manitoba, it was their common practice to enter the water, and, fixing a chaplet of grass or rushes about the head, to wade very slowly close to the flocks of unsuspecting fowl, and, seizing them by the feet, to draw them, one by one, beneath the water, until enough birds had been obtained to satisfy their wants.

To such lakes and sloughs, where the birds regularly came to feed on their migration, the gunners of years ago used to resort, and, taking their station on some point of land, or on a muskrat house, or in a boat concealed in reeds, to have, without the use of decoys, such shooting as to-day is hardly dreamt of.

Much further to the west, in the arid region, now and then a marsh is found, where reeds and tall tasseled grass, somewhat resembling the wild rice, grow, and, during the migration, unusually good shooting may be had in just this way. Much of this is almost precisely like pass shooting, and, unless the gunner has had considerable practice, he is likely to make bad work of it. Shooting such as this taxes the skill to the utmost. It is as different as possible from shooting over decoys, where, commonly, the birds, preparing to alight, check their flight, and give opportunity for deliberate work. But these birds darting into the wild rice fields are, almost all of them, going as fast as they can fly. The shooting must be quick, yet the man who flatters himself that he is a quick shot in the brush will miss almost all his birds. There is required, for success, a mingling of quickness and deliberation, and a knowledge of how to hold on the ducks, which is only to be attained by much practice. As a rule, those birds which, when alarmed, strive to rise straight up in the air, like the mallard, the black duck, the widgeon and the teals, are more easily killed than straight-flying birds, such as canvas-backs, redheads and bluebills, which, no matter what they may see to alarm them, do not alter their course, but merely fly the faster. The bird which checks its onward flight and tries to rise higher—which flares, as it is termed—can be overtaken and passed by the muzzle of the gun, which is not always the case with the darting, diving ducks.

A gunner of great experience, whose advice is well worth taking, and who is very skillful at these swift-flying overhead birds, states that, rising to his feet well before the bird gets to him, he aims at the point of the bill, and, following the bird until it is nearly, but not quite, above him, he then moves the gun a little forward and pulls the trigger. The bags which this man makes confirm his statement that this is a good way to hold on these overhead birds.

A stirring account of the abundance of the wildfowl in the wild rice fields of the West, thirty years ago, is given in an article from the graphic pen of Mr. T. S. Van Dyke, contributed a dozen years ago to the columns of *Forest and Stream,* from which the paragraphs given below are taken. To the gunners of the present day, this picture may seem too vivid and highly colored, but many men have seen flights of fowl as great, and can confirm Mr. Van Dyke's account, if such confirmation were needed. This is the story, as he tells it —a story of the last days of the muzzle-loading shotgun:

It was a bright September afternoon, the day after my arrival at Henry, that my friend and I were paddling up the crooked slough that leads from Senachwine to the Illinois River. Wood ducks, mallards and teal rose squealing and quacking from the slough ahead of us, but he paid no attention to them, and I soon ceased dropping the oar and snatching up the gun and getting it cocked and raised just as the ducks were nicely out of range. When we reached Mud Lake—a mere widening and branching of the slough at the foot of Senachwine—we drew the boat ashore. Huge flocks of mallards rose with reverberating wings from the sloughs all around us and mounted high, with the sun brightly glancing from every plume. Plainly could I see the sheen of their burnished green heads and outstretched necks, the glistening bars upon their wings, the band of white upon their tails, surmounted by dainty curls of shining green.

There were already in sight what seemed to me enough of ducks to satisfy any one. Long lines of black dots streamed along the blue sky above Senachwine, up the Illinois and over Swan Lake—between the river and Senachwine—while from down the slough, up the slough, from over the timber on the west, and the timber along the river on the east, came small bunches and single birds by the dozen. Shall I ever forget that big mallard that bore down upon me before I was fairly hidden in the reeds? He came along with sublime indifference, winnowing the air with lazy stroke, bobbing his long, green head and neck up and down, and suspecting no danger. As he passed me at about twenty-five yards, I saw, along the iron rib of the gun, the sunlight glisten on his burnished head. I was delightfully calm, and rather regretted that letting him down was such a merely formal proceeding. If he were further off, or going faster, it would be so much more satisfactory. Nevertheless, he had to be bagged, whether skill was required or not, so I resigned myself to the necessity and pulled the trigger. The duck rose skyward with thumping wings, leaving me so benumbed with wonder that I never thought of the other barrel.

But little time was left me for reflection, for a wood duck, resplendent with all his gorgeous colors, came swiftly down from the other direction. Every line of his brilliant plumage I could also plainly see along the gun, for I was as cool as before. Yet this gay rover of the air never condescended to fall, sheer, rise, or even quicken his pace, but sailed along at the report of each barrel as unconcerned as a gossamer web on the evening breeze.

I concluded to retire from the business of single shots and go into the wholesale trade. This conclusion was firmly braced by the arrival of fifteen or twenty mallards in a well-massed flock. They came past me like a charge of cavalry, sweeping in bright uniform low along the water, with shining necks and heads projecting like couched lances. I could see four or five heads almost in line as I pulled the first trigger, yet only one dropped, and that one with only a broken wing. As they rose with obstreperous beat of wing, I rained the second barrel into the thickest part of the climbing mass, and another one fell with a broken wing, while another wabbled and wavered for a hundred yards or more, then rose high and hung in air for a second, then, folding his wings, descended into a heavy mass of reeds away on the other side of the main slough. Meanwhile, my two wounded ducks, both flattened out on the water, were making rapid time for the thick reeds across the little slough, and both disappeared in them just as I got one barrel of my gun capped.

So it went on for an hour or so. There was scarcely a minute to wait for a shot, yet in that hour I bagged only four or five ducks.

While gazing a moment into the blank that despondency often brings before me, two blue-winged teal shot suddenly across the void. With the instinctive quickness of one trained to brush shooting, I tossed the gun forward of the leading teal about the same space that I had been accustomed to fire ahead of quail at that apparent distance. The rear duck, fully four feet behind the other, skipped with a splash over the water, dead, while the one I had intended to hit skimmed away unharmed. I had fallen into the common error of tyros at duck shooting, viz., underestimating both the distance and speed of the game.

Some of my friends, who had never been west of the Alleghanies, had often said that there was no sport in duck shooting; that it took no skill to stop a clumsy duck in clear, open space, and that the duck was not a game bird, anyhow, etc. How I wished for the presence of some of those friends that evening as old Phœbus entered upon the home stretch and his glowing chariot neared the gate of gilded clouds. The number of ducks increased by the minute. They came with swifter and steadier wing and with more of an air of business than they had shown before. Those hitherto flying were nearly all ducks that had been spending the day in and around Senachwine and its adjacent ponds and sloughs. But now the host that during the day had been feeding in the great corn fields of the prairie began to move in to roost, and the vast army of traveling wildfowl that the late sharp frosts in the North had started on their southern tour began to get under way. Long lines now came streaming down the northern sky, widening out and descending in long inclines or long, sweeping curves. Dense bunches came rising out of the horizon, hanging for a moment on the glowing sky, then massing and bearing directly down upon us. No longer as single spies, but in battalions, they poured over the bluffs on the west, where the land sweeps away into the vast expanse of high prairie, and on wings

swifter than the wind itself came riding down the last
beams of the sinking sun. Above them the air was dotted with long, wedge-shaped masses or converging
strings, more slowly moving than the ducks, from which
I could soon hear the deep, mellow honk of the goose
and the clamorous cackle of the brant. And through
all this were darting here and there and everywhere,
ducks, single, in pairs and small bunches. English
snipe were pitching about in their erratic flight; plover
drifted by with their tender whistle, little alarmed by
the cannonade; blue herons, bitterns and snowy egrets,
with long necks doubled up and legs outstretched behind, flapped solemnly across the stage, while yellow-
legs, sand snipe, mud hens, divers—I know not what
all—chinked in the vacant places.

When I shot the last one of the two teal ducks instead of his leader, I thought that I had discovered the
art of missing, and fondly imagined that the skill I had
acquired by shooting in brush would now show my
friend Everett something worthy of his notice. How
the bright bloom of that youthful conceit wilted under
the fire that now consumed my internal economy! The
nerves that felt but a slight tremor when the ruffed
grouse burst roaring from the thicket, now quaked like
aspens beneath the storm that swept over me from
every point of the compass. There I stood, the converging point of innumerable dark lines, bunches and
strings, all rushing toward me, at different rates of
speed, indeed, but even the slowest fearfully fast.
There I stood bothering with a muzzle-loader, loading

it with trembling hands, fever heat and headache from its recoil under the heavy charges I was vainly pouring into it, with the last duck that had fallen swimming away only wounded, half afraid to reshoot it because my ammunition was getting exhausted, yet knowing that it would surely get away if I did not reshoot it; painfully conscious, too, that my chances of hitting a well duck were fragile compared with the certainty of a shot at the cripple; there I stood, delighted yet bewildered, ecstatic yet miserable.

Never did Nature make a fitter background for such a display as appeared when twilight sank over the earth. The sky was one of those rare autumnal skies, on which light is shattered into a hundred tints, when, above the horizon, all is clear-cut in sharp outline, and over all below it lies a pallid glow that intensifies all brilliant colors, but throws a weird, sepulchral gloom upon all sombre shades. From the departed sun a broad, rosy light radiated far away into the zenith, while the clear sky on the east was changed by the contrast into pale gold tinged with faded green. North and south, the deep blue changed into delicate olive tints, shading into orange toward the centre of the great dome. On the west were cloud-banks of rich umber, fringed with crimson fire; on the east, long banks of coppery gold, and aloft long, fleecy streams of pale, lemon-colored vapor. Over such a stage now suddenly poured a troop of actors, that made the wonders of half an hour—aye, ten, five minutes ago—seem a mere puppet show.

Hitherto the ducks had all come from the level of the horizon. But now, from on high, with a rushing, tearing sound, as if rending in their passage the canopy of heaven, down they came out of the very face of night. With wings set in rigid curves, dense masses of bluebills came winding swiftly down. Mallards, too, no longer with heavy beat, but with stiffened wings that made it hiss beneath them, rode down the darkening air. Sprigtails and other large ducks came sliding down on long inclines with firmly set wings that made all sing beneath them. Blue-winged teal came swiftly and straight as flights of falling arrows, while greenwings shot by in volleys or pounced upon the scene with the rush of a hungry hawk. In untold numbers the old gray goose, too, came trooping in, though few came near enough to give us a fair shot. Nearly all of them steered high along the sky until over Senachwine Lake, or Swan Lake—a little below us to the northwest—then, lengthening out their dark strings, they descended slowly and softly in long spiral curves to the bosom of the lake. Brant, too, dotted the western and northern skies, marching along with swifter stroke of wing and more clamorous throats, until over the water's edge, then slowly sailing and lowering for a few hundred feet in solemn silence, suddenly resumed their cackle, and, like a thousand shingles tossed from a balloon, went whirling, pitching, tumbling and gyrating down to the middle of the lake. Far, far above all these, and still bathed in the crimson glow of the fallen sun, long lines of sandhill cranes floated like flocks of down in their southward flight, not deigning to alight, but down through a mile of air sending their greeting in long-drawn, penetrating notes.

Myriads of ducks and geese, traveling from the north, swept by, far overhead, without slackening a wing. Far above us, the mallard's neck and head, looking fairly black in the falling night, could be seen outstretched for another hundred miles before dark. "Darkly painted on the crimson sky," the sprigtails streamed along with forked rudders set for a warmer region than Senachwine. Widgeon sent down a plaintive whistle that plainly said good-bye. Bluebills, wood ducks, spoonbills and teal sped along the upper sky with scarcely a glance at their brethren who chose to descend among them. And far over all, with swifter flight and more rapid stroke of wing than I had deemed possible for birds so large, a flock of snowy swans clove the thickening shades, as if intending to sup in Kentucky instead of Illinois.

Yet, of those that tarried, there were enough for me. With tremulous hand, I poured my last charge into the heated gun, and raised it at a flock of mallards that were gliding swiftly downward, with every long neck pointed directly at my devoted head. *Wheeooo* shot a volley of green-wings between the mallards and the gun; *ksssss* came a mob of blue-wings by my head as I involuntarily shifted the gun toward the green-wings; *wiff, wiff, wiff,* came a score of mallards along the reed tops behind me, as, completely befuddled with the whirl and uproar, I foolishly shifted the gun to the blue-wings. As I wheeled at these last mallards, after making a half shift of the gun toward the blue-wings, they saw me, and turned suddenly upward, belaboring the air with heavy strokes, and just as I turned the gun upon them a mass of bluebills, with the sound like the tearing of forty yards of strong muslin, came in between, and just behind me I heard the air throb beneath the wings of the mallards I had first intended to shoot at. The gun wabbled from the second mallards to the bluebills, and then around to the mallards behind me—each chance looking more tempting than the last —and finally went off in the vacancy just over my head that the mallards had filled when I raised it.

You who think you know all about duck shooting, if you have never been in such a position, have something yet to learn. Excitement and success you may enjoy to the full, but while your ammunition lasts you know nothing of the pleasures of contemplation. Amid the shock, and jar, and smoke, the confusion of even loading the quickest breech-loader, and retrieving the ducks even with the best of dogs, you see nothing compared to what you may see without a gun. As I dropped the worthless gun upon a muskrat house, and sat down upon top of it, the whole world where I had been living vanished in a twinkling, and I found myself in another sphere, filled with circling spirits, all endowed with emotions, hopes and fears, like those that Dante saw in Paradise.

There, indeed, was the great sea of being, but all one vast whirlpool that engulfed the soul of the poor powderless "tenderfoot," while his ears were stunned with the whizz and rush of wings all around his head, with the thump and bustle and splash of ducks alighting in the water before him, the squeal of wood ducks, the quack of mallards, the whistle of widgeon, the *scape* of traveling snipe, the grating squawk of herons, egrets and bitterns, the *honk-honk* of geese, the *clank-a-lank* of brant, and the dolorous *grrrroooo* of the far-off sandhill cranes.

Such was the effect that these myriads of birds had on the young fellow, inexperienced in duck shooting, who was then first introduced to the sport; yet it was but a short time before he became as skillful in stopping the on-rushing birds as those who had been at it much longer, and these are some of the pictures that he paints of his autumn spent along the Illinois River:

Though ducks in the West do not come to decoys in the autumn as well as they do in the spring, there are still many days when they come quite well, especially wood ducks, teal and bluebills. Many a time during the middle of the day we pulled the boat into a blind of reeds and willows, and set out decoys in the open water a few yards outside the brush, and many a time did I have to drop the roasted snipe or pumpkin pie and snatch up a gun as the air began to sing beneath descending wings. And many a time, when yielding to the soporific influence of a heavy lunch on a soft Indian summer day, did I suddenly start from the

land of Nod just in time to hear my comrade's gun
from the other end of the boat, to see two or three
ducks come whirling and splashing below, while the
rest of the flock were towering nicely skyward just as I
got hold of a gun.

What camp-fires roared along the Illinois in those
days! It saddens me to think that such days may come
no more for me. Driftwood piled as high as we could
throw it, shot a glare across the river until the dead
cottonwoods upon the other side looked like imploring
ghosts with arms stretched heavenward, and we could
almost see the white collars on the necks of the geese
that passed high above us. Bunches of mallards, wood
ducks, sprigtails, etc., hung around the fire, with every
color glowing brightly as in the evening sun, and
naught was needed save a string of trout or a deer to
make the scene complete. Cold, and all other jars that
shiver this mortal crockery, were banished there, and
all thought of the whole outside world went whirling
away into the vortex of flame and sparks that streamed
skyward through the tree-tops. Little did I hear of the
song or jest or the laughter that almost woke the
echoes from the eastern bluffs. For by some strange
principle of suggestion, some mysterious mental connection, the whole outer circle of darkness was to me a
picture gallery upon which I could lie and gaze by the
hour. The walls of that dark rotunda beyond the fire
were for me full hung with the brightest scenes of the
new life I had entered, and they drew with them by association all those that I had passed through before.

There, again, was the bright sky, swept by long strings of whizzing life, widening out and streaming toward me in swift descent; and by its side was the old dog, rolling with happy gallop over the buckwheat stubble, slackening into a cat-like tread as he swings to leeward of the clump of brush in the corner of the field, stiffening into rigid faith as he crawls under the fence and enters the tangled woods beyond. There, again, was the stately mallard, or more gorgeous wood duck, relaxing his hold on air and falling a whirl of brilliant colors, or the wary old goose, with drooping neck and folded wing, coming to earth with impetuous crash; and by their side the catbrier brake or hemlock-clad slopes, where the wintergreen fills the air with its fragrance, while the ruffed grouse shoots like a shaft of light among the dark ranks of tree trunks. And bright among them all were those autumn days, when the bloody sun struggles down through smoky air, and the whistle of the woodcock's wing in the sapling grove sends through the heart a more tender thrill than ever. Succeeding years have hung many a new picture in the dark rotunda that surrounds the camp-fire; but none of them, in all the freshness of youth, shines with more brilliancy than still through the mist of years shine those around the camp-fires on the Illinois.

Though the morning flight of ducks is often very heavy, it generally lacks that tumultuous intensity of presence that characterizes the evening flight. Beginning with the first gray of morning, when a lonely mallard, perhaps, comes winging his way slowly out of the circle of darkness around you, crosses the open sky above in dim outline, doubles up at the report of your gun, and sinks at your feet with a sullen whop, the flight increases with every new beam of light that struggles through the misty morning. They fall no longer from above, as in the evening, and stream in from every other quarter of the horizon about as much as from the north. There is less rush and bustle, but they move with steadier march. They are not shot by you in volleys like projectiles from some uncontrollable impulse, but they move with more majestic sweep and more as if they had some inkling of what they were about. At the first report of your gun the air throbs beneath the beat of thousands of wings, and a wild medley of energetic quacks, dolorous squeals, melodious honkings and discordant cackling, as the myriads of ducks, geese and brant still roosting in the ponds rise in a clamorous mob. Again, for a few moments the tyro may lose his wits as the vast horde breaks into a hundred divisions, each circling perhaps a dozen times through the lightening sky and streaming over his head without remembering or caring that it was from that spot that the fire just spouted skyward. As the fire again leaps upward, the circle of sky overhead is cleared for an instant, as the ducks sheer and climb the air out of danger's reach; but in another moment it is thronged again with rushing wings. Beware, now, how you waste your fire upon this flock of teal just emerging into the gray, for you can hear the mallard's heavy wings, a hundred strong, beating the dark air close behind them. Beware how you waste your fire even upon the mallards, for upon the right the deep-toned honk of the goose sounds most thrillingly near. But, alas! how can the tyro reason calmly when the hiss of a sailing flock of mallards is heard just behind his head before his premises are thought of, and his conclusion is rudely hastened by a deep, dark line of bluebills pouring out of the remnant of the night upon his left?

This lasts, however, but a few minutes. As soon as dawn has fairly begun, the wildfowl travel wider and higher; you must keep yourself well concealed and do your very best shooting. For an hour or two, and often longer, the flight may be strong and steady, and then it will shade gradually off until you may find yourself waiting fifteen minutes for a shot. The evening flight rises by rapid steps to an overpowering climax, while the morning flight tapers away into all the flatness of the anti-climax.

One scarcely needs to be told that neither the morning nor evening flight is always during duck season such as I have described it. There are days when ducks will not fly as they will on other days, though they still throng both lake and slough in myriads. At such times the flight of those that do move is more over the face of the water than elsewhere, and then I have had rare sport from a big barrel sunk almost to the edge in the mud and water of Swan Lake, a little below the foot of Senachwine. Through a fringe of reeds around the edge of that barrel I have watched great flocks of mallards skim low along the water, until the long, green necks glistened within ten yards of the barrel. Then, as I suddenly rose to my feet, what a glorious medley of flashing bars on terrified wings, of shiny cinnamon breasts, white-banded tails, with curls of burnished green, red legs and beaded eyes, rose whirling and quacking upward! There, too, I have watched the geese winding slowly down out of the blue sky until near the centre of the lake, then, with set and silent wing, and every honking throat hushed as if in death, every neck and head immovable, drift slowly along a few feet above the water, until, as close as the corner of the ceiling where I sit writing, I could see their eyes sparkle in the sunlight. And then what an uproarious *wiff, wiff, wiff* of sheering wings, what a *honk-wonk-onk-kwonk,* and what a confusion of white collars and black necks, of gray wings and swarthy feet, would crowd upon my eye as I rose and looked along the gun!

It is sad to think that such scenes are fading fast into the things that were. There are, perhaps, parts of our country where the scenes of Senachwine twenty years ago are still repeated. But it may be doubted if they are repeated on so grand and varied a scale; and, even if they are, it will not be for long. The increasing interest in game protection will preserve many kinds of game to such an extent that our children's children may see shooting of some kind better than we now see. But no legislation can recall from the past the mighty hordes of wildfowl that once darkened the waters of the West, that dotted its skies and made its cornfields alive with roaring wings. Nor can any public sentiment, whether expressed in law or not, bring back the primeval solitude of those swamps and river bottoms which was such an important condition in such scenes as I have described. Those vast stretches of timber, broken only by ponds and their margins of mud and reeds, or by the long lines of the winding sloughs, those wide reaches of open land covered with wavy grass or reeds, cut with sloughs or broken by rush-fringed ponds of acres and acres in extent, over all of which one could see no sign of civilization save an occasional road, and hear none of the sounds of progress, save once in a while the far-off puff of the high-pressure steamer that was trailing its sooty banner along the distant sky, can never be restored.

CORNFIELD SHOOTING IN THE MIDDLE WEST.

In the fall of the year, after the crops have been gathered, and when the migrating birds begin to make their appearance, they resort to the cornfields to feed on the grain scattered about on the ground.

When harvesting the corn crop in Illinois it is the practice to drive a wagon through the field, and to pull the ears from the standing stalks and toss them into the wagon. Now and then an ear falls on the ground beneath the wagon and is not picked up, or strikes some portion of the wood or iron and knocks off a few grains, or a little loose corn sifts out through the bottom of the wagon box. This loose corn lying about, attracts the

birds, and both ducks and geese come to such fields to
feed.   Often, while gathering the corn, the men will
see a flock of ducks fly into the field, and after making
a circle or two, alight perhaps in some little pool of
water in a low spot.   Very likely the gun is standing
ready in the wagon, and one of the men takes it, and
having lined down the birds, creeps close enough to
them to get a pot shot as they are sitting on the water.
Or, if the harvest has been gathered, and it is seen that
the birds are regularly coming into the fields, the gunners may go out and lie down on the ground near the
feeding places of the birds, and perhaps get a number
of shots in a morning.   Such shooting, however, is
merely incidental—the picking up of a few birds when
the opportunity occurs.

It is after the weather begins to get cool, when the
little ponds and sloughs are frozen over, so that the
ducks can no longer feed in the shallow water at their
margins, that they seem most anxious to get into the
cornfields.   Often they will come in great numbers,
from distant open waters, and for a time will give sur-
prisingly good shooting.   A few years ago, when birds
were much more plenty than they are now, great
bags were often made in such situations.

In the pools which occur in almost every field, decoys
are often used.   Very frequently wild ducks' nests are
found and the eggs taken and set under a hen, so that
sometimes the whole brood is reared.   These in turn
breed the next year, and so a race of more or less domesticated ducks is established.   Sometimes the birds

of the first hatching go away in the autumn, migrating with the wild birds, and return again next spring to their northern home, apparently without having lost much of their tameness. If no decoys are to be had, the gunners call with the voice, or use duck calls.

Usually, even though no decoys are out, the ducks, in circling about over the cornfields before alighting, pass over the wet places to examine them, and so some shots are had. As soon as a duck is killed, the gunner, breaking off a stiff weed stalk, places the duck in the water, thrusts the stalk through the skin of the neck, and, pressing the other end into the mud, makes a life-like decoy. Other ducks coming in, see the decoys and come down to them.

The birds killed are at first chiefly mallards, but later in the season the brant come into the cornfield, though they generally alight where the corn grows small, so that they can see over it pretty well. The brant shooting in the cornfields is chiefly practiced in spring. The brant come along late in the spring, after the mallards have gone, arriving usually in great flocks, and alight in the middle of the big field. Sometimes these fields contain 160 acres—a whole quarter section, and as by spring the corn stalks have all been cut down, there is really no cover. The gunners must lie down in the furrows between the rows of corn stubble, and, making themselves as small as possible, wait for the brant to come within shot. Often they are obliged to shoot lying on their backs, and when the ground is hard and the gun heavily charged, the shock to the shoulder is severe. For this shooting, decoys are seldom used, except that occasionally the dead brant are set up with the weed stalks, as is done with the ducks.

In this cornfield shooting, as practiced in the middle West—that is to say, in Illinois and Indiana, it is not common to dig pits in the fields. Sometimes, however, on the sand bars or sand points in the river, gunners dig holes to lie in, but this is usually for shooting the Canada goose, a bird esteemed much more wary and harder to deceive than the brant. The birds called brant in that country are chiefly the white-fronted or laughing geese, with some snow geese and blue geese. They have a peculiar cackling cry, very different from the sonorous note of the Canada goose.

The shooting here described used to be practiced in the neighborhood of Green River and Rock River, in Illinois. Near the Green River was an immense marsh —known as St. Peter's Marsh—greatly frequented by ducks and affording good shooting in the season. It was a large tract, so wet and boggy that it was impossible for a man to walk on it. It was very soft, and would not support any weight. Here the birds bred in great quantities. In the neighboring valleys a favorite mode of shooting is to "jump" ducks. The gunner walks along one of the small sloughs, where the mallards breed, and from time to time flocks of eight, ten or a dozen spring from the water and fly off to another slough or pond. From each bunch that jumps up one or two birds may be killed, but no attention is paid to those that go off; they are never followed up.

In that country the season then opened on the fifteenth of August, and for two weeks there was good shooting at young ducks; then on a sudden all would disappear, and not a duck would be found until the advent of cold weather. The birds moved away North, as it was thought, only returning when forced South by the frost.

In shooting in the cornfields regular blinds of corn stalks were not built, but near the edges of ponds it was quite common to stick in the soft ground two or three rows of stalks, and to hide behind such a blind and shoot the birds that came in.

After the weather grew colder there used to be good shooting on the fly-ways along the sloughs, for if the wind was blowing hard against them the ducks flew low. They almost always followed the water, and could usually be shot from the shore. A friend tells me of shooting one evening, in an hour, over fifty teal. This was at what was known as the Big Slough; it is about nineteen miles long and one mile wide, and can only be crossed where it is bridged. The gunners stood on the points running out into the slough, and had their shooting from there. On the evening in question my friend reached the slough a little late and found all the points taken. It was perfectly still, and there was no wind to drive the ducks toward the points. At one place there was a long sand bar, which ran out into the slough; my friend waded out on this to a bunch of rushes which grew from the water nearly in midstream, and stood there in water about breast deep.

When the ducks began to fly, it was seen that they were all teal and that they were flying pretty low. While the shooting lasted it was active, and he gathered fifty birds. Besides these, there were, no doubt, many that were pulled down by the turtles, which during the shooting season make a fat living in that region by pulling down dead birds and cripples that are not recovered.

In some degree this fly-way shooting resembles pass shooting, but differs from it in that the birds commonly do not pass immediately overhead, but usually fly a little to one side and not very high.

Many of these small western rivers are crooked streams, and while as a rule the ducks follow the water, yet very often they cut across points; and where they do this very excellent shooting is to be had. The "whistlers" usually follow the stream. This is a local name for the "black jack," or tufted duck, said to be abundant there. Besides mallards, the more common birds were the widgeon, teal, butter-balls, and rarely the canvas-back.

Sometimes in that section geese and brant are hunted with horses; a horse is trained to feed gradually up near to the flocks, and the gunner walks behind him until within range. Sometimes, too, in shooting geese and brant, it is possible to creep down wind to within a hundred yards of the birds. Where this can be done and the birds can be approached near enough, the gunner, as soon as he sees that the birds are becoming uneasy, springs to his feet and runs toward them as fast as he can. As the birds must rise against the wind, they will sometimes come directly toward him for thirty or forty yards before turning to go away; meantime, the gunner has covered a good many yards, and just as the birds turn may succeed in reaching them with his shot.

Canada geese, white-fronted geese and snow geese resort to the cornfields as do the ducks, and often the gunner may return, after his morning shoot, with a very varied bag, which may perhaps even include a sandhill crane or two.

POINT SHOOTING.

No form of duck shooting is more pleasing and none more artistic than what is termed point shooting; and, when the weather is favorable, no form offers greater rewards.

The gunner's decoys float in the water, a short gunshot from his blind; the ducks flying by, see the decoys, and, if all the conditions are right, they are very likely to come in to them.

This shooting is practiced on various waters all over the country, the conditions varying more or less in different places. Thus, on the shores of some of the northern lakes and broad rivers the blind is built of stones laid up in the form of a wall, or, in winter, of blocks of ice. In the marshes of the South Atlantic ducking grounds stems of cane form the blind, or again in other places branches of trees or bushes may be used.

In the following pages I have described the chief features of this form of shooting as practiced on the waters of Currituck Sound, in North Carolina, a region with which I am familiar:

The sky was overcast and black; wind northeast, temperature 28°; prospect of snow or rain during the day. I had eaten a good breakfast, had struggled into the heavy outer clothing needed on a day like this, and was just leaving the house when the clock struck 6. This was in good time, for the sun did not rise until 7, and it would take us less than an hour to get to our point.

Down at the boathouse John was waiting in the skiff. Everything seemed to be there—guns, ammunition boxes, lunch kettle, my oil clothes—while from a little coop under one of the thwarts came the low chuckle of a live duck or two to be tied out with the wooden decoys.

The mast was stepped and we pushed out from the little dock, the wind caught the sail, the boat heeled over and began to glide swiftly along, with a pleasant ripple of water under the bow and a stronger gurgle under the stern. We had gone but a very short distance when the whir of wings and a splashing on the water warned us that we had disturbed some ducks; and a little later, vociferous quacking above the marsh which we were skirting told of black ducks frightened from their reedy resting places. Now and then, as we passed close to some point of land, the boat's way was checked for a moment as the tall growth of canes cut off the wind and the vessel resumed an even keel, while the sail for a moment shook in the still air. Again, when the point was passed and the breeze was felt once more, the skiff heeled over and darted forward like a good horse touched with the spur.

Already the sky was beginning to grow light in the east when we heard before us the clear, trumpet-like calls of geese talking to one another, and a moment later the louder tones and the splashing of water, which warned us that the birds had taken wing. In an instant the air resounded with their clamor, and now we could see them against the sky before, above us and on either hand—some of them almost within oar's length of us.

Still the guns remained in their cases and still I smoked my pipe, while John still tended sheet and tiller, for the law of North Carolina provides that birds shall not be shot except after sunrise and before sunset, and we respect the law.

Soon the geese are gone, and now we can see against the sky long lines and wedges of canvas-backs and red-heads winging their flight north or south to the feeding grounds which please them best, while through the quivering air falls the ringing whistle of a thousand wings.

Such are the sights and such the sounds that meet us under the breaking day as we cross the sound and enter a quieter bay, where the boat's prow touches the marsh and we have reached our ducking point.

We had been sailing over the waters of Currituck Sound, from which the low, sandy shore runs inland on a dead level for many miles. Much of this land is forest-covered, chiefly with tall trees of the Southern pine, whose straight, clean stems stand close together, often without any undergrowth, and remind one somewhat of the forests of the Northwest coast, if such small things may be compared with great. Here and there the land has been cleared and the stumps rooted out, the fields for a few years plowed and sown with corn or cotton or sweet potatoes, and then their cultivation abandoned when new growths of seedling pines spring up, and after a while the old fields start new forests again.

Most of the inhabitants of this country are to-day small landholders—farmers during the summer and fishermen and gunners in winter. They are a kindly, well-disposed people, truly Southern in the deliberateness of their actions, in their courtesy and in their hospitality. Many of the most intelligent and well-to-do of them barely know how to read and write. Although the winter weather here is often very cold, the houses are not built for cold weather, the chimneys are on the outside of the house, and the edifice itself is perched on stilts above the ground; either piers of brick or sections of thick pine logs supporting the timbers of the frame. At intervals of a few miles, at the edge of the road may be seen standing in the pine forest, churches at which the people gather on Sunday, for they are most of them regular attendants at church, this being the only form of entertainment and diversion which they have.

In the corner of some lot along the road, near each farm that one passes, may be noticed tiny shingled pent roofs, 6 or 8 feet long and half as broad, standing a foot above the ground and supported at each corner by a post. For several years, as I passed through the country, I speculated as to what these might be.

These roofs are shelters built over the graves of the dead, and there is surely a deep pathos in this custom of protecting from beating rain and drifting snow the last resting places of the forms of those whom we love so well. Many a mourning mother in her comfortable home, her heart rent with the anguish of recent bereavement, has suffered an added pang, as the storm beat upon the house, at the thought that the dear form which she has so often held in her arms lies in a grave out of doors exposed to all the fury of the tempest. It is a sweet thought in these simple North Carolinians to erect these shelters over the dear ones who have left them.

Some of these roofs are new, some are now gray and weathered, and others have still fallen to decay and lie in little heaps upon the ground. The generation by which they were erected has passed away. There are left now no loving hands to tend these old-time graves. Even the names of the dead are only vague memories or have been forgotten.

The dwellers on these little farms make fair livings

from their produce, which they ship by rail or by steamer to a market; or if by chance their crops fail, they turn to the waters of the sound to supply them with food or with money. For his canvas-back ducks the gunner receives $2 per pair, and the common duck and the fish find a ready market in a little city only forty miles away, which is reached by water transportation. So, really, the sound is the people's salvation, and to-day, just as it did centuries before the white man's foot touched this continent, it supports those who dwell along its shores.

These men, between the gathering of their crops in early autumn and the preparing of their land in early spring, spend much of their lives on the sound; so they are good boatmen, and, as a rule, know all the sloughs, leads and channels in these waters. Many of them are good shots, and from bush blinds and batteries kill, first and last, a great many ducks. They are also fond of hunting on the shore, chiefly with the aid of hounds, and sometimes follow the fox or drive the deer through lines of waiting men. They are a kindly people, and easy to get along with, the worst faults of the worst of them being drunkenness and a failure to respect the game laws.

Of course, there is a large negro population here, though it is said to be only 25 per cent. of the whole for Currituck County. As a rule, the negroes have made very little progress since the war. They still fail to appreciate the necessity of economy and the saving of money, and eat, drink and wear all that they earn. The number of negroes who have accumulated property and become landholders in the county is very small.

Currituck Sound is a long and shallow lagoon two or three miles wide, separated from the ocean by a narrow sand beach. The sound is bordered by low marshes, in which are many shallow ponds, leads and creeks, and is dotted with islands, also low. All this low marsh land supports a growth of tall cane, which in summer is bright green, turning yellow in the autumn.

In ancient times—there are men still living who can remember it—the water had nearby connection with the sea. There were inlets through the sand beach and the tide ebbed and flowed through these channels. Beds of oysters, clams and scallops flourished here, and even now the boatman who is unfamiliar with the channels may sometimes run aground on the old shell banks whose life has long departed.

Still longer ago the primitive dwellers on this coast drew a fat living of shellfish from the waters, and to-day at many points on the marshes of the mainland may be found heaps of shells which represent spoils gathered from the waters and carried to the camps, where the shells were thrown away after their contents had been extracted. Perhaps investigation of these shell heaps—true kitchen middens—might yield implements of this primitive time which would be of real interest.

The skiff's nose struck the soft marsh and Gunner sprang joyfully ashore, while the sail slatted furiously in the breeze. Then John ran forward, unshipped the sprit, rolled up the sail against the mast, and unstepping this and raising it on his shoulder, jumped ashore and carried it into the cane out of sight and left it there.   I handed out on to the marsh the different articles needed in the blind, until at length nothing was left in the skiff except her furniture and the decoys.   Then we carried the things up back of where the blind was to be made, and while I began to arrange matters there, John returned to the skiff and pushed it off to put out his decoys.

These were piled in the skiff on either side of the centre-board trunk, and there were perhaps in all seventy-five of them.   The lines by which their weights were attached were 10 feet long.   Using his pushing oar, John moved his boat about 20 yards from the point, and then thrusting the oar down into the mud, tied his painter to it by a clove hitch, and picking up the decoys began to throw them overboard.   He rapidly unwound the line from each, and then holding the decoy in one hand and the line about 2 or 3 feet above the weight in the other, he tossed them in all directions about the boat.   It seemed to be very quickly and carelessly done, but there was no lack of care in it.   When all that were needed had been thrown out it was seen that the head decoys were well up to windward of the blind, while the others were strung along from them to leeward, so that the last of the decoys were just a little to leeward of the blind.   About opposite the windward decoys, but a little inside—toward the marsh—from them, were put the three wooden goose decoys.   The finishing touch was to set out the live decoys—three in number, two ducks and a drake. For each live decoy there is a "stool," which consists of a sharpened stick 2½ feet long, surmounted by a circular or oval piece of board 6 inches across. Fastened to the stick which supports this board is a leather line 3 feet long and terminating in two loops, which are slipped over the duck's two feet and drawn tight so that the bird cannot get away, yet not so tight as to press unduly on the flesh.

Pushing his boat up to the head of the decoys and fastening it as before, John pressed the point of one of the duck stools into the mud until the little table on which the bird was to stand was 2 inches below the water's surface. Then opening the coop, he took out the drake, passed its legs through the loops, drew them close and put the bird in the water. It flapped away from the boat with frightened quackings, but recovering at once, began to bathe and to dabble in the water. The boat was now pushed to the tail of the decoys, and the two ducks put out there. Then John pushed the skiff along the marsh, hid it behind a little point, and soon was heard coming crashing through the cane toward the blind.

Meantime I had not been idle. I had brought everything to the blind, had set up in the ground the four forked sticks which were to support the two guns, had taken off the gun covers, opened the ammunition box, loaded one gun with duck cartridges and one with those for geese, had fixed the chairs, had broken an armful of cane and begun to repair the blind. In a short time, with John's assistance, the work was all done and I was standing in the blind waiting for the birds to come.

This, then, was the condition of things. The wind was northeast and I was facing south. The leading decoys were a little south of east of the blind, and the tail ones about south. Any birds coming from east, south or west would swing out in front of me and lead up over the decoys, and I ought to shoot at them just as they were passing over the tail decoys. My two guns, loaded and cocked, lay across their rests, muzzles to the left. Behind me was my chair, into which I would crouch if birds appeared. My clothing was. yellowish gray, harmonizing well with the surrounding vegetation. The top of the cane which formed the blind was broken off about breast high, so as not to interfere with the shooting.

As we approached the point in the morning we had disturbed a flock of 200 or 300 ducks and a small flock of geese, which had flown away unharmed to other feeding places. These birds we confidently expected would come back a little later, and now we began to watch for them with all our eyes. For a time, however, nothing came, and I studied the actions of the live decoys. These were having a very good time washing themselves, preening their feathers, and occasionally tipping up to feed on the bottom. After a while one and another of them swam up to its "stool" and clambered on it, standing there and arranging its feathers. From time to time the drake would call to the ducks and they would answer him, and when a buzzard or a blackbird passed over the water all three would call earnestly.

As I stood there watching the live decoys enjoy the water and their freedom from the coop, I heard John call "Mark to the east," and, turning, saw a single bird coming low over the marsh. Gently lowering my body until my head was hidden by the cane which formed the blind, I watched the simple bird's approach. John had given utterance to vigorous quacks, which had caught the bird's ear, and it had seen the decoys and was flying toward them. While it was still 100 yards distant the old drake saw it and saluted, and the ducks lifted up their voices in sonorous calls. This was too much for the lone black duck. He passed outside the decoys, well beyond gunshot, swung up into the wind, turned back, and with lowered flight and down-bent neck surveyed the decoys and prepared to alight. He swung over the live ducks and up toward the drake, and I jumped up, put the gun on him and pulled. Bang went the first barrel and bang the second; the duck climbed and climbed, and kept climbing; Gunner tore through the cane to see what had fallen and to bring in the bird; John made no comment and I said nothing either, though I had missed a shot that a ten-year-old boy ought to have killed.

I knew why I had missed the bird, though not how. I had let him get too far over the decoys and past me, and shot at him as he was going away, and not allowing for the velocity of his flight, had shot behind him. So my first shot for the season was a disgraceful miss.

I do not know how other men feel about missing,
especially about missing easy shots, but it plunges me
into an abyss of shame and mortification from which
I do not easily emerge.   At the best of times I am a
very bad shot, and often my missing makes me declare
that I will give up shooting altogether.   When, however, the time comes for me to get an outing again, I
forget all about my past misses and start forth as hopeful and as free from anxiety about missing as if I were
a good shot instead of being a villainously bad one.
So I mourned over this miss, and felt horribly ashamed
that John, and even that Gunner, had been witnesses
of my disgrace.

As I sat there thinking of this, John whispered
"Mark behind," and, turning my head, I saw a pair of
mallards—a big greenhead and a duck—almost over
me.   To grasp my gun and throw it to my shoulder
seemed but a second's work; but in a second a duck can
go a long way, especially down wind, and by the time
the muzzle of my gun was pointed in the birds' general
direction they had passed over us and were far beyond
the decoys.

In desperation I fired both barrels, and again I heard
Gunner rush to the water's edge, saw him look in vain
for something to bring in, and saw the ducks like a
pair of disjointed parentheses melt into the gray sky
and disappear.

"Those two came badly, sir," ventured John.   "Yes,
they came badly," I replied, "but we ought to have been
looking out for them."

Some little time elapsed without any further excitement, when suddenly—although we thought that we had been making good use of our eyes—a duck appeared quite close to the decoys, coming in as gently as one could wish. I very slowly bent to get my gun, resolved that this time, if it came, I would retrieve myself. On the bird came, looking only at the decoys; I rose up slowly, but he saw me and flared. I followed him, but gave the gun a little too much swing, and shot over him. Another miss.

Again despair seized me; and when a little later I missed an easy double at a pair of sprigs, which were alighting among the decoys, it tightened its grip. John said never a word in comment, nor did I. The trouble was too deep for words.

It is astonishing how much room there is in the air around a duck. I have seen the time when the birds were so thick in the air that it seemed as if it would be impossible to shoot a charge of shot through them without killing one or more, but how very easy it is to spare their lives. After a few more misses, John seemed to feel that I stood in need of comfort and consolation, and ventured the remark that there must be something the matter with my cartridges. I was shooting wood powder, and he asked if the shells were not old ones. They were old; but I knew very well that if the gun was held right the cartridges would do their work well enough, and—though I say it myself—I was too honest to attempt to excuse my lack of skill on the plea of poor ammunition.

It was not until after lunch that I got my first bird.
John and I had both become careless about looking out,
for it seemed useless to see the birds, as I could not hit
them. Suddenly a big black duck cut across the head
of the decoys, and, not seeing it until it had got by, I
threw up my gun and took a snap shot at it, and killed
it dead. It fell on the edge of the marsh and Gunner
brought it with much pride. John, too, was delighted,
and assured me that the shot was a good one, and that
I was getting onto them now. I shook my head
wearily, for I knew what an accident this success had
been. Still I presume that I was unconsciously a little
bit encouraged. At all events, we both kept a better
lookout, and a little later, when three widgeons came
by over the decoys, but not lowering to them, I doubled
on a pair with the right barrel and killed the third with
my left. This was a little better, of course, but still it
did not give me much courage. A little later, however,
when a pair of mallards came up the wind high up, and
I killed both, I began to take heart and really to feel
as if perhaps I could do something. The conceit was
quickly taken out of me, however, by three widgeons,
which stole in and alighted among the decoys unseen.
These I missed on the water with the first barrel, and
on the wing when they flew. They were not 25 yards
from me.

It was still early in the day—only 2 o'clock—and
there was time yet to kill a lot of birds if they kept
coming and—if I could only hit them. But there did
not seem to be much chance of my doing that. John was

encouraging, however, and regaled me with anecdotes of the numbers of birds that certain men whom he had accompanied had killed in the afternoon; and especially of one who only a few weeks before, after a day of very bad luck, had in an hour's shooting just before sunset run his score up to over thirty. I anticipated no such good luck, but I determined to endeavor to use greater care in shooting; to take my birds earlier, to hold further ahead of them, and not to shoot unless I felt reasonably sure that I was holding on each bird about as I thought I ought to.

Meditating thus, I was watching the sky to the south and east, when suddenly I heard from John the grating call of the canvas-back, followed by several loud honks, and sitting down I strained my eyes to see where the birds were to which he was calling. Peering through the stalks of the cane, I presently saw off to the right a single canvas-back coming with the steady flight that distinguishes these birds from almost any other ducks. He was an old male, white and handsome, and was headed straight for the decoys. John continued to call, and the bird had evidently made up his mind to come. We had a few canvas-back decoys out, and these with the geese were more likely to bring him; for, as is well known, canvas-backs will stool to geese as well as they will to their own kind. He came on swiftly and steadily, and at length, just as he was over the tail decoys, I arose, held about 2 feet in front of his bill and fired, and the noble bird fell. He had hardly struck the water before Gunner had plunged in, swam through the decoys and seized him, and in a few moments he was in my hand, and I was smoothing out his plumage and admiring the rich coloring of his head and neck, and the wonderful delicacy of his back plumage.

"Mark in front, high up," said John, before I had finished looking at the canvas-back. High up in the sky to the south of us I saw a pair of black ducks, which, in response to John's vigorous calls and to the invitation offered by the live ducks, rapidly lowered their flight, took a quarter circle to the west, and then coming down to about 6 feet above the water flew confidently on toward the blind, one about 2 feet behind the other. I waited till they were over the last of the decoys, rose to my feet and killed the first and then the second in capital style. They did not see me and never knew what had hit them. This was cheering.

From this time on until it was time to take up I shot fairly well—very well for me—and at night when we returned to the house I had twenty-two ducks, and believed that I had in some small measure effaced the feeling of contempt that John—and Gunner—must have for me.

I had other hours in the blind during my trip, and in some of them I did better than on this first day; in none worse, so far as missing went, though often I came in with a less number of birds.

Now and then, while we were sitting in the blind, John and I would be joined by one of the club watchmen, whose time is devoted to patrolling the marshes, driving off poachers, preventing night shooting, and

generally doing all in their power to preserve the shooting. These men are farmers in summertime, but
during the winter are glad to earn what they can by
watching the marshes; for this is a steady job, which
pays much better than fishing or gunning. They are
most of them old gunners, familiar from childhood with
these waters and their islands, and with all the ways of
the wildfowl. Constantly on the marsh and on the
water, they know just where the ducks are "using,"
and what are likely to be the best shooting points on
any given day. They are thus always consulted by the
men who are going to shoot on the marshes under their
charge, and their advice is usually taken.

The life of these watchmen is a lonely one. For six
days in the week they live on the marshes in little
houses built for them in the fall, but on Saturday
afternoons they report at the club and then go to the
mainland to spend Sunday with their families. Leading such a life, the watchman is delighted when one
of the club members comes to shoot on the marsh under
his charge, and often he spends most of the day with
the gunner, helping his boatman to tie out and take up,
assisting in retrieving the birds killed, and during the
quiet times sitting in the cane with the boatman and
gossiping. Some of them are silent men, but others are
great talkers.

The subjects which the two discuss are varied. Of
course the ducks and their actions are a fruitful theme,
but home matters claim a good share of attention; the
recent social events on the mainland, the last sermon

of the circuit rider; farming, past and future; marriages, sickness and death.

I heard one of them tell John a story which will perhaps bear repeating. He said:

"I never knew till the other day that coons went fishing."

"Why, of co'se they do," said John; "they mostly live on fish and crabs."

"No, that ain't what I mean. I mean fishing with a hook and line. The other day I was going up a little lead and I come to a bend, going slow and quiet, so's to see if they wus any ducks sitting in there. Just as I looked over the p'int I see an old coon a little ahead of me runnin' round on the beach this way and that way, like he was plum' crazy, and waving his paws. I watched him a little to see what he'd do, and pretty soon I see he was working around a little pool that had some minnies into it, and pretty soon he druv 'em up into a corner and he made a rush and swep' a lot of 'em ashore with his paws. I expected now to see him eat 'em, but he didn't; he just put 'em up where they couldn't get back to the water, and then he took one and trotted down to the water again. When he got there he stopped and looked about a little. When he found a place to suit him he stuck the minnie on one of his sharp claws and held that foot in the water. Pretty soon I saw from the way he acted that a fish was biting at the bait, and in a minute the coon jerked his paw out of the water and threw a little fatback out on the bank. He ran to it, carried it up on the marsh, and put it on a little patch of grass, and then went back and baited his claw with another minnie. Then he caught another fatback and put it up with the first one, and then went on fishing again. He kept this up until he had caught quite a number, and at last when he carried a fish to where the others was lyin' on the grass he set up and put his hands on his knees and looked at the pile of fatbacks, and seemed to be studyin'. Then he laughed right out and said: 'Ha, ha, ha! seven. Enough for supper.' That made me laugh out loud, and the coon grabbed up his fish and run off in the marsh."

"Huh!" said John. "Expect me to believe that?"

The lives of these marsh men are monotonous. The watchman rises with the dawn, and as soon as it is light clambers up to his post of observation—the roof of his house. This is only a one-story shanty, but standing here he can see over the cane which surrounds him and can look down into the larger bays, ponds and creeks which are within his jurisdiction. He can see if birds are sitting in these waters, and whether any are flying, and easily gets a notion of what is taking place in all the neighboring marshes. Day after day he watches the ducks, studying their habits and learning their ways, and no one can give better advice to the gunner as to where he should tie out.

Now and then a bit of excitement comes into the watchman's life, but it is excitement of a kind that he does not like. It is given in doses too strong for enjoyment. Occasionally the marshes are invaded by night shooters, who—with or without a light—scull up to rafts of sleeping ducks or geese and shoot them on the water, creating havoc in their close-packed ranks. When this occurs the watchman sallies out in his light skiff, and, knowing all the leads and short cuts, he usually has no difficulty in coming up with the poachers, whom he tries to drive away. On two or three occasions watchmen have been shot at by these gentry, though no one has ever been injured in this way. Several, however, have been badly frightened, and more than one has given up his berth under the stress of such a scare. Others, more courageous and wiser, put a bold face on the matter and give back threat for threat. Such persons the poachers speedily retreat from and avoid in future, for your true poacher is not a courageous animal. He does not enjoy a fight. Since the shootings that have recently taken place on these marshes the watchmen have taken to carrying shotguns and rifles about with them at night, and in the future the night shooters may expect a little shooting from the other boat.

Besides his work of guarding and patrolling, the watchman has little to occupy his time. Of course he does his own cooking, dish washing, wood chopping, and so on, and now and then he may be obliged to make a journey to the mainland for wood or water or provisions; but still he has plenty of idle time on his hands. Often he employs a part of this in trapping the minks, muskrats and coons which abound on the stands. The few skins that he may get he sells at the store, and the cash which he is paid for these goes a little way toward helping out the family living, or perhaps toward the expenses of next spring's farming operations.

Certainly, these men are not the least interesting of the inhabitants of the marsh.

The desirable wind for point shooting is one quartering from behind the gunner. This gives the birds abundant room to swing over the water and to come up to the decoys, offering a good shot to the man in the blind. Sometimes, however, it happens that after one has tied out with the wind just right and everything apparently favorable, the wind will haul more and more in front of him, or may shift suddenly, so that it blows directly on the point and in the gunner's face. One result of this is that his decoys, instead of riding in a long line head to tail, swing around and now sit in the water side by side, their bills, of course, facing the wind.

Worse than this is the fact that the fowl which come in can no longer swing over the water, but if they wish to alight to the decoys must swing over a marsh and come from behind the gunner and so over his blind. Thus they are quite certain to see him, or at least some of the strange objects that he has brought into the marsh; or if they do not see him, at least they come from behind him, and he is obliged to twist around and shoot at them when they are coming toward him and nearly over his head. For most men, I think, shooting of this sort is very difficult, and usually when such a shift of wind takes place it is better for the gunner to take up and move—if such a course is practicable—to some other point, where the wind is right.

One of the chief difficulties that I find in shooting at birds that come in from behind the blind is that a large proportion of them come quite low, and so are not seen until they are almost upon the gunner. By the time he gets his gun to his shoulder the bird is likely to be almost within arm's length. If now it flares and goes directly up in the air the shot becomes an easy one; but if, on the other hand, it keeps on over the gunner's head he has to twist around, and is very likely to shoot hastily at a straightaway, swift-flying bird, and to miss it.

I have never yet shot in a blind with a remarkably good shot—a man who took all chances and killed a very large proportion of his birds. I know that there are such men, but it has never been my fortune to see one of them shooting wildfowl.

Sometimes a bunch of birds coming low over the marsh at a tremendous rate of speed unseen may pass over a man's head with a sound which resembles the escape of steam from a large locomotive, and which, coming so unexpectedly, has a tendency to frighten one out of several years' growth. In my limited experience, canvas-backs and blackheads are the worst offenders in this respect, though occasionally an old black duck coming low down over the blind will startle one by the rustling of his feathers. On several occasions I have had a white-headed eagle come so near the blind that when I rose and shouted at him I could plainly hear his feathers creaking against each other as he threw himself nearly over on his back and scrambled through the air to get away.

It surprises one—though, of course, it is only natural—to see how many birds there are, which are not wildfowl, that come close to the blind entirely unsuspicious of its occupant. Hawks and sometimes, during gray days, owls hunt over the marsh, eager to prey on the blackbirds and sparrows whose haunt is here. Gulls often pass near the decoys, and occasionally one sees flying through the air a loon or a cormorant. Sometimes one of the latter may be seen perched over the water on a stake of some deserted bush blind. Eagles and buzzards, of course, and the ever-present crow, are constantly searching over the marsh and over the water, looking for dead and wounded ducks.

From the many ducks and geese that are so lost to the gunner the eagles and the buzzards no doubt gain a fat livelihood, and the clean-picked skeletons of wildfowl surrounded by the feathers are frequently seen in the marshes.

Besides these, in and among the reeds live blackbirds, sparrows, marsh wrens and rails, any of which will venture close to the blind. Sometimes a little Carolina rail in its peregrinations along the water's edge will even walk into the blind and gaze at its occupant with bright, dark eye, uncertain what he may be. It is amusing sometimes to see two or three men and a dog go crashing through the cane in hot pursuit of one of these little birds, who must laugh to himself at the clumsy efforts made by his pursuers to capture him.

Often a little whisp of snipe of two or three individuals pass within gunshot of the blind, or a single bird, like a bullet from the sky, may drop on some nearby point of the marsh, and run briskly about over the mud to the water's edge, probing with busy bill for food which is hidden beneath. In like manner now and then a killdeer plover or a pair of yellow-legs may fly in from beyond the marsh, and hurry along over the mud as if greatly pressed for time.

Herons, of course, are abundant in the marsh, and are of three sorts. The night heron—in New England called quawk—and the bittern are seen less often here than the great blue heron, which in these parts is known by an apparently unmeaning name—"forty gallons of soup." This bird is common here, and often comes close over the blind, or alights in the water near it.

It is interesting to watch one when it is fishing. Its huge wings and long straddling legs make a great commotion over the water when it alights, though there is no splash when it puts its feet down. The moment that it has folded its wings, however, it straightens its legs, neck and body, and for a long time stands bolt upright, absolutely motionless, looking for all the world like a straight, weathered stick standing out of the water. In this position it resembles anything rather than a bird, and its attitude is extremely ungraceful. The position and the entire absence of motion are due, I suppose, first to its desire to see whether any enemy is in the neighborhood; and second to give its prey, which may have been frightened by the shadow of its passing body, time to recover from this alarm.

After a period of stillness which may last five or six minutes, but seems to the watcher much longer, the heron, still holding its neck straight and stiff and its bill pointed somewhat upward, takes a cautious step and then stands still for a moment. Then, seemingly re-assured, it moves on with slow, careful steps, its head turned a little on one side, evidently searching the water for its food. It does not take the conventional heron attitude until it sees some little fish that is within reach. Then very slowly it draws in its neck and darts out its strong, keen bill, and usually captures its prey; not always, however, for I have several times seen one miss his stroke.

These are big birds, and birds, too, that one seldom has an opportunity to kill, yet it always seems to me a pity to shoot at them. They can be eaten, to be sure; yet no one who has ducks and geese to eat would be likely to prefer heron. Unless the gunner has some use for it, it does not, to me, seem worth while to kill any bird. Life is something so mysterious that it should not be lightly destroyed, and I have no sympathy with the wantonness which leads many shooters to try their guns on every robin, swallow, nighthawk or bat that may fly near to them. This is commonly done "for fun," or to see "whether I can hit it;" but it is all wrong.

Besides the birds of all sorts of which I have spoken,

and the water fowl, which are so conspicuous, and of which the lucky gunner secures a few, there are killed here occasionally birds that are altogether unexpected.

One of the most unusual of these was secured some years ago by a local gunner, who of course did not know what it was, but shot it because it looked so strange. This was a dovekie, or little auk, a bird of the Arctic regions, which is said to breed in Greenland, and which occurs in small numbers in winter off all the North Atlantic States. It is rarely seen south of New York, and, for all I know, its North Carolina occurrence may be a record.

The white brant, or snow goose, is found here every year in small numbers, one large flock living on the outer beach not very far from the Currituck Lighthouse. These birds do not seem to associate with the common gray geese, but keep by themselves, and feed largely on the marsh instead of in the water. Sometimes I have sailed within gunshot of this flock of 500, and their white heads appearing over the short marsh grass, which hides their bodies, have a very curious appearance. When fairly alarmed, they spring into the air and fly away with sharp, cackling cries, much less musical than those of the common Canada geese. They are seldom killed, I believe.

Now and then among the birds brought in by the gunners will be seen a curious duck, unlike anything known here, and which the ornithologist at once recognizes as a hybrid—something which is not very uncommon among the duck family. I have killed a male hybrid which was manifestly a cross between the mallard and the pintail, and have seen more than one hybrid between the black duck and the mallard.

I have heard of two or three strangers from Europe having been killed in these waters. These were English widgeons, usually found associated with the American bird, and recognized as something strange only after they had been killed and retrieved.

An abundant bird on the waters of Currituck Sound is that locally known as the hairy crown. This is the bird called in the books the hooded merganser. I have never seen these birds so abundant anywhere as here, and flocks of from 75 to 100 are sometimes seen. More often, however, the companies are much smaller.

If you see these birds coming a good way off, they will very likely fool you by their manner of flight, and you will at first say "Blackheads," and then "No, canvas-backs." Perhaps it will not be until they are almost within gunshot that you disappointedly exclaim: "Hairy crowns." These birds, though commonly they do not pay much attention to the decoys, come up without the least hesitation if they make up their minds to come, and alight in the water, swimming about with lowered crest and diving for food, quite unconscious that the decoys are shams. If you stand up in your blind and raise your gun they erect the crest in token of suspicion, and then may dive and swim under the water for a long way, or perhaps jump up and offer you a shot. It is only their swift flight that makes them hard to hit, for they fly very steadily. Sometimes, when a little flock is flying across at a distance, they can be called to the decoys by an imitation of their note, which is something like that of the blackhead—a guttural, grating croak.

The male hairy crown is a beautiful bird, with his elaborate livery of black, white, tan and delicate gray, but as hairy crowns are commonly regarded as worthless for eating, they are often allowed to pass unharmed by the gunner unless he is shooting for count, when he will try to knock down those that come to him, as each one retrieved counts as a duck.

The red-breasted merganser is much less common here than the hooded, but occasionally drops in among the decoys. Its local name is sawbill. The goosander I have never seen here, nor do the men with whom I have talked about it appear to know the bird.

During much of the day the music and clamor of the geese, softened by distance, fall upon the gunner's ear. It may be that in some channel not far from him great numbers of these birds are resting on the water, talking to each other, and often flocks of traveling birds pass up and down the sound, calling to each other or answering the salutations of other birds at rest. Often too a sailboat, passing through a great raft of geese, will put all the birds on the wing, and they rise in a thick cloud of dark specks against the sky, looking like a swarm of bees. When these birds have been so disturbed they often break up into small companies and fly here and there in different directions, seeking new resting places.

The man who sits all day in his blind is likely to have some of these moving flocks of geese pass near him, and sometimes they may fly so close that he will have an opportunity to shoot into them, and to pick a bird or two down from the sky. If he has a couple of goose decoys in the water, and if his boatman is a good caller, his chance for a shot is, of course, much better. It is extremely interesting to see the boatman call down a goose and to watch the actions of the deluded bird as it swings lower and lower in wide circles, and at length, with outstretched neck and hanging feet, comes up over the decoys to join its supposed comrades at their head. When the bird is distant the men fairly shriek out their calls, but as it gets nearer and nearer their voices are lowered, their heads are bent toward the earth, perhaps they place their hands or their hats in front of their mouths. The conversations which they hold with each other and with the goose are no longer shrill and loud-voiced honks, but are chuckling confidences which the supposed geese on the water are sharing with one another. The incoming bird still calls with loud, sonorous tones, as if anxious to attract the attention of the wooden decoys, but as he gets nearer and nearer, the talk of the men becomes still lower, until at last, when the gunner jumps to his feet and levels his arm, it ceases altogether.

Let no one imagine that because the goose is a great bird nearly 4 feet long, and apparently of slow and unwieldy flight, it is a matter of course that he will kill him. I confidently assert that there is nearly as much room in the air around a goose as there is around a duck, and unless your gun is carefully held you will shoot behind the bird. If you miss him with your first barrel you are very likely to miss him also with the second, which is likely to be fired with undue haste. If, however, your first barrel has done the work, and he falls to the water, your boatman is certain to offer you cordial congratulations which will warm the cockles of your heart.

Often it may happen that, while the goose does not come down to the decoys, he will alter his flight and pass over the blind within long range. In such a case your shot may perhaps fail to break any bone, and yet may mortally wound the bird, which, after making a wide circuit or a long flight, will at last come to the water stone dead.

The dogs used in this gunning are Chesapeake Bay dogs, brown or tan in color, and with coats long or short, straight or curly. They are admirable water dogs, and those which are well trained do work that is really marvelous.

To me these dogs look like the pure bred Newfoundlands which we used to see years ago, before the Newfoundland had been crossed with the rough St. Bernard, to give him the size which is regarded as essential for show purposes. I know that it is often said that the Chesapeake Bay dogs are a breed formed by crossing the Irish water spaniel with the Newfoundland, but I can see in the specimens that have come under my eye no trace of water spaniel character, except perhaps color, and every mark of Newfoundland. Even the color is not that of the spaniel, for we know that the original Newfoundland was often tan colored, or had tan points. The very small ears, the broad head, the short muzzle, the lack of feather on legs and abundantly feathered tail—the whole ensemble of the animal, in fact—to my mind point back to a Newfoundland ancestry much purer than anything we are in the way of seeing nowadays.

I prefer to believe the tradition which relates that the Chesapeake Bay dogs originated from two puppies rescued from a sinking ship which had sailed from Newfoundland and brought to Baltimore, and that these dogs are Newfoundland dogs of the old type, than which no more faithful, intelligent and vigorous breed ever existed. It may be that the race has not been kept pure, yet I think it has; for we see them generation after generation showing the same physical characteristics, the same splendid courage and endurance, and the same intelligence and love for the water.

I am told by a friend that these dogs can readily be trained to work to the gun in upland shooting, and that when so taught they display unexcelled nose and bird sense, and I regard them as most valuable dogs, and wonder that a breed so valuable has been so neglected.

The amount of work that these dogs will perform is very surprising. From just after sunrise until sundown, in cold, blustering weather, they will bring the ducks, swimming perhaps 75 or 100 yards for each one, or hunting through the thick cane for those that have fallen on the marsh.   Often each trip to bring a duck is made in part over soft mud, through which the dog must wallow, as it is too thick for swimming and yet too soft for walking; often the ice must be broken for a long distance to get to the bird; often the ice is too weak to support the dog, who breaks through every little while, and then must laboriously and carefully clamber out on the breaking ice in pursuit of a cripple which is moving along toward a distant marsh or toward open water.

I have often seen a dog bringing a bird over thin ice lie down on his belly with widely spread forelegs and drag himself along inch by inch, thus spreading his weight over as great a surface as possible so as to avoid breaking through.   Then, when a place was reached where the ice was stronger, he would carefully rise to his feet and trot along until the yielding ice again warned him that he must use especial care.   In a case where several trials had shown a dog that the ice would not bear him, and that it was a waste of time for him to try to travel on it, I have seen him advance by bounds, springing out of the water and coming down with all his weight on the ice, thus breaking a lane through it to the bird.   In this particular case the dog's stifles were so bruised by continual blows against the sharp edges of the ice that next day he was extremely sore and lame in both hind legs.

Another bit of ice work done by another dog seemed to me to show great intelligence.   A bird had been shot high in the air and had fallen heavily on thin ice 40

yards in front of the blind. It had gone through
the ice and did not reappear. The dog sent out
seemed disposed to cross the ice to the opposite marsh,
but, called back, found the hole through which the duck
had gone, but not the duck, though it was evident that
he smelt it. He made several casts about the hole, but
did not catch any scent, and then went back toward the
hole, but when 3 or 4 feet from it stopped, looked
at the ice and began to scratch. In a moment or two
he had made a small hole through the thin and soft ice,
and, quickly enlarging it, put his mouth down into
the water, pulled out the duck, and brought it to shore.
I believe his finding the duck—which had evidently had
life enough to swim a little way under the ice—was
pure accident; he happened to see it; but his digging
the hole in the ice showed wisdom.

These dogs have keen noses. They follow unerringly
the trail of a duck through the thick cane, and can trail
a crippled duck that has gone ashore on the marsh to
the spot where he landed by the scent that his body
leaves on the water. I have seen this done many times.
They understand perfectly the live decoy ducks, and
swim to and fro past them without in the least regarding them, though the decoys do not seem to like it if the
dog comes too close to them, and splash and quack at
a great rate until he has gone by.

If properly trained, I imagine that these dogs are the
best retrievers in the world; but often they are not well
trained. Some dogs will bring the duck to shore and
then drop it, leaving the boatman to go out and bring

it to the blind; others, after bringing them ashore, will bite their birds badly, or will carry them into the marsh and leave them there. I have heard of a dog that got tired and refused to go for his birds; but, being forced to go out, swam back to the marsh with the bird, carried it into the cane, and after being gone a long time returned to the blind with his paws and nose quite muddy. A search in the marsh by the boatman revealed the fact that he had carried the duck a little way in from the shore, and had then dug a hole and buried it so completely that only one wing and the legs showed above the earth he had heaped on it.

These dogs, like any others, require careful handling by a judicious trainer, and in addition, as they are great, strong animals, they require a great amount of work. A properly trained dog, however, is an indispensable adjunct to the point shooter, and will save him a great number of birds in a season.

The birds which pass over or stop on the marsh are its most obvious inhabitants; but there are many others which the casual visitor scarcely ever sees. Of these the largest are the half-wild horses, cattle and hogs turned out to winter by their owners. They feed among the tall cane, and only now and then come to the water's edge to drink or to eat the succulent water plants that drift against the shore.

With these animals the struggle for existence must be a severe one; for, to one accustomed to the pastures of the North or West it would seem that there is little or nothing to eat on the marsh. Of course, vegetation is not lacking; but there can be little nutriment in the hard cane or its harsh leaves, or in the coarse, round marsh grass which grows only in infrequent patches. The drifting grass, which consists of the rejected portions of the water plants pulled up by the wildfowl in their search for its roots, is scanty in quantity, and can hardly be very nourishing food. The hogs do better than horses or cattle, for they unearth the roots of the cane and the flags, and must procure not a little animal food.

The horses are confined to the outer beach, and visit the adjacent marsh only to feed. They are little animals, not unlike the well-known Chincoteague· beach ponies, and are all branded. They are a tough and hardy race, qualified through inheritance and experi-ence well to fight the battle of life. The cattle are small, wild and scrawny.

Occasionally when you are sailing through these waters you will see, as you pass a watchman's house, a fresh skin tacked up to dry, and the long, ringed tail hanging down from it at once proclaims its species. Coons are abundant here, and it is not strange that they are so. In summer the nesting birds and in winter the crippled ducks furnish them feathered food, while at all seasons the waters abound in fish. We are most of us accustomed to think of coons as passing a good part of their time in trees, but the coons of the marsh must by this time, I should think, have lost the art of tree climbing; since, except for an occasional straggling pillentary bush, there is here nothing larger to climb than a stalk of cane. Rarely seen by the gunner, the coon lives an easy, lazy life here. Now and then he puts his foot in a marshman's trap, and less often a gunner's dog, hunting for a wounded duck, may suddenly fall upon him, and the sound of the fight will empty the blind, and bring boatman and gunner crashing through the cane to learn the cause of the disturbance. It is in such ways as these that the coon is sometimes killed.

Next in order after the coon comes the mink—artful, ferocious, daring. Like the coon, he fishes and hunts, but he has ten times the coon's energy. Not satisfied with the wild game of the marsh, he prowls about the blind and may steal a duck, if one is carelessly left at a little distance. He fights the muskrat, and sometimes kills and eats him, and then he goes fishing every day. The mink is rarely killed except by the trapper.

The muskrat is everywhere, and if you have occasion to walk across the marsh you will now and then plunge thigh deep into one of the holes that it has dug. Sometimes as you sit in your blind you will see it swimming toward your decoys, or crossing some lead not far away. It does no special harm except by its burrowing, which breaks away the marsh, destroys ditches that may have been cut, and makes pitfalls for the careless to fall into.

In the winter, when I see the marsh, its reptiles are safely hidden away in their warm sleeping places. So it is that the snakes, if any there be, and the tortoises are not seen. But in summer, I am told, there are snakes and snappers and terrapin; of these last there are not many.

All through the winter, however—except when, as sometimes occurs, a freeze has locked the waters of the sound—there are fish a-plenty. Of course the most important and valuable are chub, which I take to be the large-mouthed black bass; but there are many other smaller sorts which may or may not be good to eat. The common blue crab abounds here in summer, and everywhere on the marsh its shells may be seen—the relics of feasts had by the coons.

In the spring and the late summer these marshes are the resting places of thousands on thousands of beach birds and rails. Here may be found great flocks of waders of all descriptions, from the tiniest sandpiper up to the great sickle-bill curlew. These sandpipers and rails wade busily about over the mud flats where the ducks have been swimming or probe them for food. Then gulls of many sorts winnow their slow way over the broad channels, and companies of sea swallows hunt the schools of tiny fish that swim in the shallows.

At whatever season of the year you take it, the life of the marsh is abundant, and is worth observation and study.

We are told that it is the dying swan that sings the sweetest song. Those that we see about the marsh are musical enough, but so few of them are killed that I cannot believe that the ordinary note which they utter is the one which immediately precedes death. Yet it is a soft, sweet call, high pitched, pleasing and hard to imitate. Koo, koo, kookoo, koo, is the way it goes, the flock calling to their leader, and the leader answering them again.

In ancient song and in story the swan holds a firm place, nor is his eminence confined to any land. To Lohengrin in his search for the Holy Grail, and to the Blackfoot Indian seeking out the home of the Sun, swans come as supernatural helpers.

Its size, the purity of its plumage, and its soft, sweet notes make the swan always a striking object, and it is not strange that this bird should have impressed itself on the imagination of all peoples, and that this impression should find voice in the folk stories of races which have attained the highest civilization and culture, as well as of tribes that are still savages. As the mind of man is everywhere the same, so we see that swans are used by the ancient gods as messengers and beasts of burden, and in the same way and with a like object they draw the boat of a Lohengrin and carry across the ocean an American Scarface.

The swans move slowly through the sky, with wing-beats that seem heavy and labored, but which carry them forward at a high rate of speed. If that flock were near enough for you to kill one of those birds and you did so, you would find that in falling his impetus would carry him a long way forward before he struck the earth or the water.

Swans are killed usually only when by chance they fly over the blind low enough to be reached with a shot-gun. Few gunners have swan decoys, though I have seen, on the sloops of one or two professionals, a great pile of these; for the swan will decoy readily, coming either to swan decoys or to the call alone. I remember once tying out at a point in a bay from which we put out great flocks of swans and geese, and an hour or two later a single swan was seen flying toward the bay. My boatman called to it, while I tried to change the duck cartridges which were in the gun for those loaded with buckshot, which were lying ready for just such an emergency. Alas for the chance! The day was rainy, the chambers of my gun a little foul from smoke, and the cartridges had swollen. It took me a long time to get out the ones that were in and a long time to insert the others in the chamber. While I was wretchedly working at this I was reduced to the last pitch of nervousness by the boatman, who punctuated his calls to the swan by remarks such as these: "Here he comes!" "He's heading right for us!" "Be ready now, he's almost near enough!" "Now he's right over the decoys; get up and kill him!" "Oh, shoot, shoot!" "There he goes!" "He's gone!" There was a pause, during which I managed to shove first one and then the other cartridge into the gun; but before I had closed it the boatman whispered excitedly: "Here he comes back again, right over the decoys!" Closing the gun, I stood up and killed the great bird just beyond my furthest decoys.

"Oh!" cried the boatman, as he ran to the skiff to get the bird, "that's wuth a dollar—a dollar, sir."

Sometimes swans do curious things. Once watching

a wedge of seven birds that flew over, 200 or 300 yards distant, and that were slowly lowering themselves toward the waters of the sound, I saw one bird help himself along by means of another. The last swan on one arm of the V seemed higher than the others, which were close in front of him, and with a quick stroke or two he overtook the bird immediately before him, caught his tail feathers in his bill, and, bending his neck, pulled his own breast close to the tail of the other bird, whose progress seemed absolutely stopped. Then the last bird let go the tail and they all went on. It looked as if the last bird had used the other to pull himself down to its level, being himself too impatient to wait for the slower descent of flight. The occurrence seemed to me to be a remarkable one, and called up to my mind the old story of little birds crossing the Mediterranean on the backs of owls, geese and cranes, and the story, related years ago in *Forest and Stream* by Dr. J. C. Merrill, of the "Crane's Back" of the Crow Indians.

All day long the gray clouds have hung low over the waters, and occasionally the sad heavens have dropped down their rains, which the winds have thrown spitefully against us. Now, however, just at the close of the day, the broad orb of the sun looks out at us from the western sky just as it is falling below the horizon. Slowly it sinks until only a thin red line is visible above the low, distant forest which bounds the view to the west. I take a last, long look about me to see if perhaps a duck will come before the sun has actually set; but, seeing no bird, I break down my gun and say to John, "Take up."

As he crashes through the cane to get the skiff, I unload both guns and put them in their covers, close ammunition box, and begin to carry the things down to the edge of the marsh. John is already among the decoys, taking up first the live ducks—which he puts in their coop—and then the wooden ones, which he stacks neatly in their places. Then, when he pushes the boat to the marsh, I pass him the things from the shore, handing him last of all the ducks, which he packs away on and abaft the decoys, counting them as he lays them down: "Twenty-seven, twenty-eight, twenty-nine, thirty, and the hairy crown's thirty-one. A pretty good day's work, sir!"

I put on my heavy coat and step in the skiff, and while I light my pipe, John pushes the boat through the shallow water, and presently steps the mast and sets the sail, and with a merry ripple the little boat bears us homeward.

"Well, John, it's my last day, and it has been a good one. I am sorry to go."

"I wish you could stay longer, sir; but anyhow you've had some good shooting, and you certainly have done right well—better'n I thought you could that first day."

And so I have.

SEA SHOOTING ON THE ATLANTIC.

Along the coasts of Maine, Massachusetts, Rhode Island and Connecticut great hordes of wildfowl gather each winter, driven from the North by the ice which blocks their feeding grounds. For the most part these birds are sea-ducks of different sorts, and feeding, as they do, largely on the shell-fish which they bring up from the bottom, they are not highly esteemed as food. Nevertheless, the dwellers along the seashore eat them and think them good, although in taste and appearance they are very different from the birds that live chiefly on the fresh water, whose food is largely vegetable.

These birds are chiefly the three scoters—the black scoter, the white-winged scoter and the skunk-head— old-squaw, or long-tailed duck, eider ducks, in varying numbers, with a few whistlers or golden-eyes, and occasionally a few harlequins. When not feeding, these birds commonly rest well out to sea, but in the morning and at the approach of evening they usually fly into the bays, where the water is more shallow, to feed on the clams and winkles, which they procure by diving.

The large beds of ducks break up at dawn, and the birds fly by little companies, continuing to move about until ten or eleven o'clock, when they settle down and do not fly again until evening. At many points along this coast, ducking in line is practiced, a form of sport not known elsewhere, we believe. In this, besides his gun and ammunition, the gunner requires a flat-bottomed skiff, twelve or thirteen feet long, decked over, with a combing about the cockpit, which is large enough to hold one, or at most, two persons, and an anchor rope, long enough to enable the boat to ride freely, and with the anchor at one end and at the other a buoy, with an eye fastened into it, and a light painter ten or twelve feet long, which has a snap at the free extremity. Beside this, fastened to the snap is a light line, a little longer than the painter and the distance from the bow where the painter is fastened to the cockpit. This line is made fast to the boat, just within the cockpit, and runs to the snap on the painter, to which also it is made fast. Thus, when the anchor is out and the painter snapped to the eye in the buoy, this last can be brought alongside by pulling on the light line. The painter can then be unsnapped, the boat freed and the buoy left floating on the water. This not only saves the trouble of lifting the anchor at frequent intervals, but the buoy left in place holds the gunner's position in the line, which nobody will attempt to occupy.

Ducking in line is a communal form of sport. The gunners of a locality agree all to go out on a certain day, and unless fifteen or twenty boats go, it is useless to make the start. The boats range themselves in a line off shore, from some headland or point which separates two bays in which the ducks commonly feed. The first boat is placed two or three hundred yards from the shore, the next one a hundred yards outside of that, the next still further out, until the twenty boats, extending out from the point, make a cordon of gun-

ners, extending out to sea nearly a mile from the point.
Usually lots are drawn for position, those nearest the
shore not being so desirable as those farther out. An
effort is made to be on the ground before daylight, as
the shooting begins with the earliest dawn. Often,
therefore, the gunners are obliged to rise at two or
three o'clock in the morning, to make their way to the
shore, get into their boats and perhaps pull a distance
of three or four miles before reaching the ground. At
other times all of them will congregate in some barn
near the starting point and sleep there, and the start
will be made by all together.

Warm, pleasant weather is desirable for this sport,
although it is true that the birds fly best and afford the
easiest shooting when the wind blows hard and the
weather is rough and boisterous. But it is often no
joke to pull one of these little flat-bottomed skiffs three
or four miles through the darkness against a head wind
and through a rough sea, and even after the gunner is
anchored, if the wind blows hard, the work is wet and
uncomfortable, and the reports of the guns are punctuated by the angry slapping of the skiffs upon the water,
as they rise and fall with the sea. Even if the water is
calm it may be bitterly cold, and ice may be making
along the edges of the bay, so that after the gunner has
reached his stand, and thrown over his anchor, and the
labor of rowing is at an end, he soon chills, slaps his
arms vigorously and dances jigs on the ice in the bottom of his boat. After one has reached his position
and thrown over his anchor, it is interesting to listen to

the movements of the other boats: the regular sound of
the oars, the heavy plunge of the anchor as it is tossed
out, the impatient exclamation of some neighbor who
has suffered misadventure, the loud laughter of another
who is conversing with a companion.

As the first light appears in the east the whistling of
wings begins to be heard; perhaps the plaintive cry of a
loon comes floating through the twilight, or the distant
calling of a black duck, feeding in the marsh. Presently, from near the shore, a gun is heard, followed by
the high-pitched laugh of a loon, which, in the darkness,
has flown close up to the boats, and being shot at, flies
down along the line, looking for an opening. As his
shadowy form is discerned in the dusk of the morning,
each gunner hurls after him an ounce of lead, but, un-
touched, he passes on, and finally is lost in the gray
mists of the distance. At the report of the guns, far
out over the water is heard the faint whistling of many
wings, and with them comes the melodious honking of
gangs of geese, passing high overhead. The sky
grows brighter and brighter, more gunshots are heard,
and presently the sun rises.

Now, as one looks seaward, great bunches of birds
can be seen rising from the water, and these breaking
up into small flocks, fly in all directions. Perhaps the
first to approach the line will be a bunch of great coots,
some of them white-winged, others dead black and still
others gray. They fly swiftly and steadily, and come
nearer and nearer, until they have almost reached the
line of boats, and then, noticing them—seemingly for

the first time—they try to check themselves; but it is too late to turn, and with swift and steady flight, at wonderful speed, they fly on, passing between two of the boats, and twenty or thirty feet above the water. In each boat a man springs to his knees, follows the swift course of the birds for an instant with his gun, there are four reports, and three of the birds turn heels over head, falling to the water, while two more slant downward, striking the surface with heavy splashes, one near and one much further off. The two gunners draw their buoys to the side of the boats, unsnap the painters, and, shipping their oars, row off to recover the dead, and when this is done, return to their place in the line. Many of the birds, as they strike the water, dive at once, and coming up a long way off, repeat their diving, swimming so fast and so far that they are not pursued. Others which dive are not seen to come up at all; these are believed to go to the bottom, and there to cling to the weeds until dead. Others, still, perhaps too hard hit even to dive, skulk off, with the body completely submerged, and nothing but the bill exposed above the water. If there is a little ripple, or still more if there is a sea on, it is hardly visible.

The first shooting of the season is almost entirely at coots (*Oidemia*), which are the earliest of the sea ducks to arrive off the coast. Somewhat later, as the weather grows colder, the old-squaws, or long-tailed ducks, make their appearance, and their coming adds interest to the sport. They fly with great swiftness, and very irregularly, and their long tails and dodging flight remind one of the movements of the passenger pigeon, while their continued and peculiar cry, *owl-owl-owly,* is a pleasing sound as it ripples musically across the water.

As the morning proceeds and the birds fly across different parts of the line, there is continued interest and excitement. Men are looking in all directions for birds, and such cries as, "All solid to the east'rd," "To the south'rd," "All down," and other warning cries, are constantly passed from boat to boat, as the birds are seen coming from the different directions.

Often a bunch of birds will come quite close to the line, and then, alarmed by some movement, will whirl off and away, only to return and try to cross at some other point. Sometimes they may separate, and endeavor to pass in two or three small bunches, and then the shooting is like that of a skirmish line, as every one within reach, and some who are beyond it, shoot at the birds. The interest is kept up all through the morning, and many birds fall. Most of them, probably, will be coots or old-squaws, but there may be a few broad-bills, perhaps a black duck or two, some whistlers and loons, and perhaps a crow, shot wantonly by some man who knew no better. So the sport proceeds, and the hours glide by, until, when the village spire sends its music quivering across the bay, telling the hour of eleven, anchor is weighed, and all the boats start for the shore.

In the dead of winter, when the cold is bitter, and the shores are piled with ice, so that the boats can hardly be launched, ducking in line is not practiced, but when spring comes, and the milder days of March and April are at hand, it is often resumed. At this time, however, the birds are mated, or are seeking mates, and many of them are shot over decoys. Old-squaws and coots, alike, come up to decoys well at this season, and seem to pay little regard to the boat which is anchored out on the feeding ground, of course in perfectly plain sight.

The gunner rows out to the place where he has observed the birds to be feeding, and throwing out his decoys, anchors his boat not more than twenty-five yards from them, and then, getting down in the bottom, remains there out of sight. Perhaps the birds imagine the boat, which is usually painted white, to be one of the pieces of the ice that was so lately floating around in the bay; but, at all events, they come up readily to decoys, and often afford good shooting. By this time many of the old-squaws have assumed their summer plumage, and beautiful birds they are as they rest lightly on the water, and with tail held upward at an angle, and lowered head and thickened neck, pursue their mates. At this season rarely, when the weather is foggy, there will come to such a gunner an occasional opportunity for a shot at a flock of migrating geese, confused by the fog, and flying low over the water. This is regarded as great luck, for what the grizzly bear is to the big game hunter of the West, the great gray goose is·to the gunner on the New England shore.

On the Maine coast, at the mouth of some of the rivers, as, for example, near the quaint old seaport town of Kennebunkport, there is fair coot and sea-duck shooting over decoys. These are anchored between the grounds where the birds pass the night and their feeding places nearer to the shore. No attempt is made at concealing the boat, though the gunners keep themselves out of sight as well as possible. The decoys should be out by daylight, for, before the sun rises, the birds are on the move, and a long dark line to the eastward will be seen, the birds flying toward the shore. In such places as this a few eider ducks— called sea ducks on this coast—are likely to be killed, and rarely among them will be found a king eider. Now and then a little bunch of harlequin may fly within gun-shot, and perhaps one or two of them will be knocked down, but unless they are quite dead they are not likely to be recovered, for they are most expert at diving and skulking.

In all this sea shooting the bag is likely to be a mixed one, and to contain everything, from grebe and loon up through old-squaw, coot, eider and broad-bill to black duck or goose. Those who practice it are out for shooting, and shooting they will have, no matter at what it may be.

At certain points along the rocky New England coast the bays, sounds and harbors are dotted with little islets surrounded by deep water. Often the feeding grounds of the coots, old-squaws and broad-bills are in the immediate neighborhood of such islands, and where this is the case, point shooting is not infrequently had.   The decoys are put into the water in the usual way, but often their anchor strings have to be very long to reach the bottom.   The gunners conceal themselves among the rocks on the shore.

Early in the season, when the birds are gentle, or again in spring, when they are more sociably inclined, fair shooting can occasionally be had in this way, but after it has been practiced for a little while, ducks avoid the shore and rarely come up within shooting distance. The birds commonly secured by this method are the scoter and the long-tailed duck, though occasionally broad-bills come to the decoys, and more rarely different species of fresh-water ducks.

A method of approach which can often be practiced on diving birds is worth knowing.   We have seen it used successfully on whistlers and sheldrakes, and on one or two occasions on old-squaws, which at high water happened to be feeding near the marsh.   Usually it can be practiced only where the birds are single or at least very few in number, so that occasionally all are under water at the same time.

When the bird dives, the gunner runs toward it as rapidly as possible, stopping before it comes to the surface and standing perfectly still until the bird dives again.   Usually it takes a fraction of a second—time enough for a man to halt—before the bird gets the water out of its eyes and sees clearly, and this gives the gunner the opportunity to stand quiet before he is seen by the bird.   Usually the bird does not notice the man unless he makes some motion, but will dive again. When there are a number of the fowl which are continually going down and coming up at different times and in different places in the neighborhood, it is almost hopeless to attempt this means of approach, for some one of them is quite sure to detect the gunner.

Sea shooting, as practiced along the north Atlantic coast, is everywhere much the same. The following account describes it on the New Jersey coast:

To the east the first rays of daylight were beginning to show themselves and dye the ocean a dark purple, interspersed with bars of light, that under the gentle west wind looked like beaten copper. In the distance shone the beacon of the Scotland Lightship, and further west on the Navesink hills the Highland lights were beginning to pale in the coming day. Down in the northeast a schooner could dimly be made out, standing with all sail set toward Sandy Hook. To the south the water was cold and leaden, while in-shore it was breaking into ripples, and the western horizon looked as if it had plenty of wind in store, and would shortly prove the fact to us. Around us on all sides could be made out a dozen or more boats riding at anchor, and to keen eyes each had its string of decoys aboard. While I was enjoying the picture and watching the day break, half forgetting the purpose for which I had come, I was startled by hearing C. say, "Mark southeast." This dispelled all dreaming, and turning my eyes, I made out a single bird rapidly approaching the nearest boat to the south of us. On he came, his dusky wings seeming but barely to clear the ripples, heading a little to the south of our neighbor. Then, as if seeing the decoys for the first time, he swung swiftly in toward them and prepared to pitch. A flash, a dull boom of a heavily-loaded gun, a streak of white water under him, and a cloud of smoke rising from the innocent-looking fishing-boat, seemed to have convinced him that he had made a mistake and a narrow escape, and had better change his quarters, which he did in spite of the second invitation sent after him. Straight in-shore the bird went, and in his haste and fright, miscalculating the danger distance from the in-shore boat, went down with a rush and splash before a charge of No. 2 sent at him.

"Look out, here comes one straight for you; and don't you miss the first bird for anything." "Where is he? Oh, I see him!" Yes, there he came, swift and straight as an arrow, for our stools. Stooping low, to be as much out of sight as possible, I drew back the hammers of my little gun, determined to make $3\frac{1}{2}$ drams of powder and an ounce of No. 4 do all they could to stop this visitor. In an instant he was over the furthest stool. Now steady, was the mental command to my nerves, as the gun came to shoulder, and eye ranged down the barrels showed them to be about a foot ahead. Ah! now, then! And there was instantly a transformation scene, with a bunch of feathers and a badly demoralized duck as the central figure; a splash in the water and a sigh of relief from C., whose "All right !" convinced me that the gun and myself had done our work well this time, at least.

During this little by-play of our own, the other boats had not been idle, as dull, muffled reports from all directions proved, and that they were meeting with more ·or less success the moving and anchored boats plainly showed. For an hour or so this continued. Then all of the birds seeming to have found a resting place further out at sea, where they were only occasionally disturbed by passing vessels, and, as a consequence, not giving the shooting that our neighbors seemed to think they should, a general movement for the new resting place of the ducks commenced. Our host called to us as he passed "to come out-shore," an invitation we hesitated about accepting, as the wind had increased, and the gentle ripple of the morning had given place to a decided sea, which certainly must be much larger off shore. However, after talking the matter over, we decided to follow, and getting in our decoys, commenced going out-shore. Our delay had given the other boats a long start, and before we got half way out they were among the birds, of which there seemed to be thousands. Looking over my shoulder, I could see them flying in all directions, some scooting close along the water, barely clearing the seas, others high overhead, flying in a heedless fashion from one boat to another, or hesitating a moment over a bunch of stools, and paying for their curiosity by the loss of some of their number.

For an hour or more the shooting continued, bringing us our share of birds, and at the same time a fair share of misses, some of which brought with them the plainly expressed disapproval of my companion.

The wind having increased, and the sea making shooting almost impossible, we boated our decoys and commenced our journey shoreward, which interesting point was at least two miles away in the teeth of the wind. An hour's hard work at the oars, sometimes only holding our own against the fierce flaws, which ever and anon, as if to show their power, would drive the spray clean over the boat; and again, as the force of the flaw passed, gaining a few yards, we finally reached the bar. Here, taking advantage of the first opportunity that the surf offered, we ran through it, and once more had Jersey soil under our feet.

WADING THE MARSHES.

At various points all over the land—in the marshes of the seaboard, of the Middle States, of Illinois, of the high central plateau, and of California—is practiced what is perhaps the most primitive form of duck shooting. Where such marshes are wet, and yet have a hard bottom, the gunners wade through them, startling the ducks from their moist feeding places and shooting at them as they top the reeds in their flight. The gunning is thus very much like walking up birds on a stubble, or snipe on a wet meadow, but it is extremely laborious, for often the wading is deep, and from time to time one steps into a muskrat hole, in which he may sink up to his waist, or even deeper. On the other hand, the rewards of this toil may be great, since, as it is practiced chiefly early in the season, the birds are likely to be numerous and many of them so tame and unsuspicious that sometimes they do not spring from the water until the gunner is within a few feet of them.

In work such as this a good dog is almost indispensable. Unless one has had great practice, the marking down of a bird in the grass or reeds is difficult, even if it falls close to one, while if a wounded bird scales down a long way off, it is practically impossible for the gunner to go to the place and find the game. The dog should be well broken and should follow at heel, going forward only at command and obeying the gestures of the hand. If he is so trained he will save his master many weary steps and will greatly increase the weight of the bag. In no situation is a good dog more useful than when one is wading the marsh.

While this form of shooting is practiced much more in wet countries than in dry, it is followed also with very good results at certain places in the sage deserts of the Rocky Mountains. In that country, water is likely to be scarce, and wherever there is a lake with an adjoining marsh, there the ducks, grebes, coots, and other water birds, gather in great numbers to breed; while added numbers stop during the migrations.

Many years ago a little party of three or four men had occasion to spend some weeks in the neighborhood of such a spot in Albany County, Wyoming, and during that time their fresh meat supply was drawn altogether from the ducks that lived by the marsh.

The breeding season was over, but the ducks were not yet preparing to make their flight southward. They had nothing to do now but all day long to dabble and rest in the marsh, and accumulate strength and fat for the long journey that must soon be made.

Every morning, or every afternoon, for a couple of hours, two of the men would start out to kill a few ducks for the next day's meals. The weather was warm, and they did not attempt to keep dry, but, clad in woolen shirts, overalls and shoes, they entered the marsh, and usually by the time they had walked its length once they had as many birds as could be used during the next day. The great black Newfoundland dog that belonged to the telegraph operator at the neighboring railroad station was a most useful helper to them, and brought many of their ducks, but at times his excitement got the better of him, and he would range the marsh far and wide, scaring up the ducks everywhere, and entirely regardless of the remarks made by the gunners, although these remarks were made in loud tones and were frequently repeated. It was amusing then to see the gunners come out of the marsh and provide themselves with clubs with which to punish Bingo, and then to see Bingo, perfectly conscious of his guilt, and quite unwilling to endure the punishment, sit down on the prairie a hundred yards off and utterly refuse to come any nearer. Often it was the next day before he would venture within arm's length of either of the gunners.

In this marsh were found many sorts of ducks. Mallards were perhaps the most numerous, and next after these came the red-breasted teal. Pintails, shovellers, redheads and greenwings were common, and later in the season geese were often killed. The gadwall was not a common bird.

On certain marshes in New York State, and no doubt elsewhere, when the water is high, marsh shooting similar to this is practiced with a boat, which is shoved through the grass and the weeds precisely as the skiff of the rail-shooter is shoved through the corngrass or wild rice. In bygone years we have seen good bags of ducks made in just this way, the gunner standing in the bow while the shover moves the boat forward quietly through the rustling grass.

This work of wading the marshes is better practiced only in mild weather, since it is practically impossible to keep dry while doing it.

BATTERY SHOOTING.

The battery is usually set out—"rigged" is the common term—in shoal water, from three to six feet in most places, although sometimes in the South they are put out in much deeper water. When this is done, however, the wind may make trouble for the gunner, for a battery cannot live in anything like a sea. In places like Great South Bay, however, where there may be two or three feet of grass on the bottom, and then two feet of water over that, a battery can live in what is commonly known as a two-reef breeze. This is a famous place for battery shooting, and here the decoys are commonly set on the water somewhat in the shape of a pear.

The battery lies near the larger end of this pear, and to the right-hand side looking toward its smaller end. As a result of this mode of rigging—the gunner's head being to windward and the stand of decoys being widest where he is, and tapering off to a point to leeward— the birds, as they come up, will swing to where the decoys are thickest on the water; that is, to the left of the gunner, and will thus always give him an opportunity to shoot to the left. Most men shoot from the right shoulder, and, of course, this arrangement gives them the best possible chance. A man who shoots from the left shoulder will naturally have his battery on the left-hand side of the pear, so that the birds would come up to the right, to give him a better opportunity at them.

Usually in the Great South Bay they use about 125 decoys to a single battery, and perhaps 150 or more to a double battery. Of these, twenty-five or more are brant decoys, and these are distributed close about the battery, so that their larger bodies may in a measure conceal it from the flying birds. There is a single row of the brant decoys all about the battery, perhaps seven

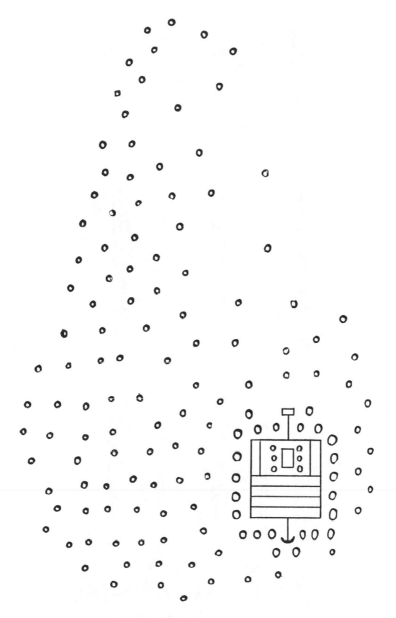

THE BATTERY RIGGED.

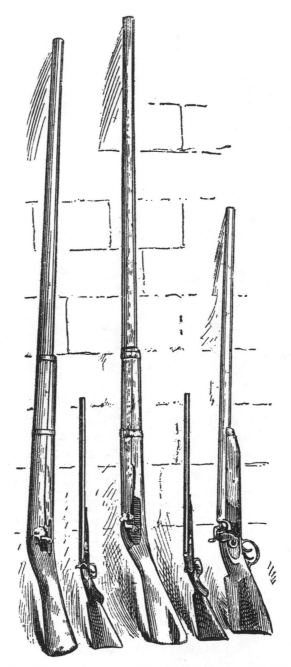

SWIVEL GUNS FROM SPESUTIA ISLAND.

or eight on either side, and four or five at either end. The decoys tail down, as the phrase is, to the point of the pear, fifty or sixty yards to leeward, where there are only a few, just enough to attract the birds.

In sinking the battery, a number of cast-iron duck decoys, canvas-backs or redheads, weighing twenty-five pounds each, are placed on the deck or platform. For a double battery, side weights, weighing about fifty-six pounds, are hung by loops on the arms running out from the side of the battery.

The gunner lies on his back in the box, with his gun at his right side, the stock near his hand and the muzzle resting on the footboard of the box. Most battery men use guns with 32-inch barrels, so that they will be long enough to rest on the footboard. A gun with 30-inch barrels is likely to slip down into the box, and so to be less easily managed. A good many accidents have occurred by men using guns that were too short, which slipped down into the battery, and, exploding, have shot off their feet.

After his battery is in position, and his decoys are tied out, the gunner takes his place in the box, lying flat on his back, with his head raised by his pillow, or headboard, high enough so that his eyes are just above the edges of the box. This position enables him to watch almost one-half the horizon, looking out over his decoys and seeing plainly about 120 degrees of the circle. As his head lies to windward, the ducks will, presumably, swing over the tail decoys and come up from the leeward to alight. As soon as he sees them he grasps the gun, which is lying by his side, and at the moment when they set their wings to alight, or when they are over the tail decoys, he rises to a sitting posture and shoots. The battery man's gun does not command a very wide range; he can shoot to the right only so far as he can twist his body, and, in his cramped position, this, obviously, is not very far; but if the birds are immediately before him, and if they swing to his left, his chance is good. Of course, he has little or no opportunity to shoot at birds coming down the wind, which will be over him before he sees them. If they are disposed to decoy, they will swing and come back to the stools; but if, on the other hand, they are going on, he will fail to have the shot which, if in a blind, he might have had at birds coming from that direction.

Although the novice in battery shooting is able to cover with his gun little more than one-third the circle of the horizon, a practiced battery shooter has a much wider range for his gun. This he obtains by what is called in Chesapeake Bay "throwing out." This means that after a man has raised himself to a sitting position, if the bird has got off too far on either hand to be easily reached by the gun, he throws his legs out of the box and onto the platform, or deck, of the battery, so that he faces the side of the battery, looking to the right or to the left, and is thus able, without difficulty, to shoot at birds on either hand. This can be done only by one who is at home in the box; but it greatly increases the effectiveness of his shooting.

After the gunner has taken his position in his box,

with gun, ammunition, and such other articles as he needs, the sloop in which he and his battery were transported to the ground leaves him, and either takes up a position well to the leeward, and so far away that by no possibility can it interfere with the flight of the birds, or else—and this is the more common practice—sails about over the waters, directing its course to any body of resting birds that it may see, disturbs them, and causes them to take wing, in the hope that in their flight they may pass near the decoys about the battery, and go to them. It is the part of the tender, also, if the shooting is lively, to cruise, at frequent intervals, half a mile or a mile to leeward of the gunner, to pick up the birds that may be killed. The tender must also keep a sharp lookout at the battery, so as to obey any signals that may be made by the battery-man, and, if called, to get to him as speedily as possible. Usually some set of signals are arranged, which may save time and effort.

Commonly, if two men go out to use a single battery, they toss up for choice as to who shall first occupy it, the first hour after dawn being usually the best for shooting.

Let us imagine the battery-man safely in his box, and deserted by his tender. The dim light is beginning to show in the east, and the first sounds of coming day are to be heard. The distant honking of geese breaks the stillness, followed, perhaps, by the wild, laughing cry of the loon, or the mellow call of a bunch of old-squaws. The faintly musical whistle of the wings of passing birds is heard, and, as the light grows, dark streaks, looking like clouds, are seen against the yellowing sky, showing where the flocks of birds have begun their flight. Suddenly, low over the water, and nearly at the tail of the decoys, the gunner sees a dark, swiftly moving mass, which presently resolves itself into a flock of a dozen broadbills, which swing over and bunch up to his left, preparing to alight. Just as they come together, he sits up in his box, aims well forward, and a little below the leading ducks, and, at the report, three of them fall to the water, while his second barrel accounts for two more which crossed, as the flock turned to fly away.

The shot was a fortunate one, for all the birds lie still upon the water, and at once begin to drift to leeward, under the light breeze. Hardly has the gunner reloaded, and sunk again to a recumbent posture, when he sees, again, to leeward, the swiftly moving wings of a single duck, which comes up over the decoys, and, with erected head feathers, glances this way and that, as if uncertain where to alight, among so many friends. Again the gun rings out, and another bird tosses lightly, breast upward, on the water. Blackheads and broadbills and tufted ducks are likely to come, through the morning, in small bunches or by twos and threes, and to give good shooting.

Beside the birds that come into the stools, many bunches will be seen flying high in air—trading birds they are called—which pass over without seeming to notice the counterfeits upon the water; yet, sometimes, these birds, often canvas-backs or redheads, may be called down by an imitation of their note; and, lowering their flight, by erratic plunges, will swing about two or three times, and, at last, come over the gunner, near enough to be shot at. On the whole, however, here, as in most other shooting, it is the birds which come singly, or in very small groups, which afford the greatest sport. A large flock of birds, shot into, are thoroughly alarmed, and fly a long way before again coming to the water.

While the gunner is having his sport in the box, his tender is working about, not far off, usually keeping a close watch on the battery with his glasses, and also on the surface of the water, prepared to recover any dead birds that he may see. Usually a net is carried for this purpose, by which the floating birds are lifted on board, as well as a gun, to be used in killing cripples.

Should the weather give signs of being bad, or the wind breeze up unduly, the tender draws nearer and nearer the battery, for, if a heavy sea springs up, the gunner will need prompt assistance.

Although the modern battery, with its canvas wings, keeps down the sea far better than the old-fashioned box, with wings formed of boards, still a battery will not live in much of a sea-way, and, as soon as water begins to come into the box, the gunner is, at least, very uncomfortable, if not in danger of sinking with his craft. It is not always easy for the men on board the tender to judge just how the battery-man is getting on, and, as the breeze increases, and the sea lifts, he is anxiously watched for any signal. Should it be necessary to take up, the sloop is anchored close at hand, the battery-man, and his possessions, transferred to the sloop, and then the men take up the decoys, bring the battery alongside, and, rolling up the head fender, take it on the sloop's deck.

During each season, of course, there will be many days when the water is so rough that a battery cannot live in it, and, on such days, which are usually the best for gunning, the battery-man must stay on board his sloop. There will be other days, perhaps, when the sound is frozen, and it is impossible to tie out in a battery. On the whole, therefore, the number of birds secured in this manner is not so great as might be supposed; but, as stated elsewhere, it is a destructive means of shooting, because, usually, the battery is tied out on the feeding grounds, and because, commonly, the sloop, or sail boat, is constantly moving about, driving the birds from their resting places, in the hope that they may go to the stools near the battery. Many years ago, in Chesapeake Bay, it is recorded, a gunner, shooting from a battery, with two guns, killed, in one day, over 500 ducks; and there is a more recent record of one man who killed 300 birds in a day.

Battery shooting is very attractive sport, and, under favorable circumstances, yields large bags.

SHOOTING FROM A HOUSE-BOAT.

To be practiced successfully, house-boat shooting requires special conditions, and these conditions exist on but few waters. The following account, from the graceful pen of Mr. Wilmot Townsend, tells how this form of sport is enjoyed on Lake Champlain:

What is a house-boat blind? Simply a flat-bottomed boat with a house thereon, covering three-quarters of its length and hidden entirely in cedar boughs, top, sides and all around. And so artfully is the cedar arranged that the resemblance to a green islet (save for its somewhat regular outlines) is complete.

With tight roof and sides, the interior of this little house is a veritable snuggery furnished with bunks, table, camp stools, gun rack, shelves for provisions and cartridges, and last but not least, a kerosene stove, which, when kept properly cleaned and trimmed, will give you a smoking hot dinner at short notice.

And after a day spent in the open air, when the lungs are filled to cracking with the pure breeze that filters down through the groves of pine and hemlock covering the hills, and comes all pungent with balsamic odors, to dance about the clear waters of Champlain, "a smoking hot dinner," sauced with the ravenous appetite of a wolf, is not to be despised.

The house, occupying three-quarters of the boat's length, leaves the bow clear, and here you have ample room to stand and with a good field glass may sweep the lake in search of fowl.

A portion of this space is occupied by a roomy and comfortable coop for the live decoys, the cedar being carried up in front and at the sides to about shoulder high, so that the fowl when lured within the "dead line," which is the space covered by an ordinarily strong shooting gun, say about 40 yards, are in plain sight when you stand erect.

A flock of ducks approach. Their every movement may be watched through sundry little peepholes among the twigs as you crouch low with ready gun.

A moment, and they are within shot. You see the bright eyes, the hovering wings, and rising, rouse the echoes with both barrels.

'Tis done! What is done? Why, you have either brought sundry ducks to bag or scared them "inside out," in which case you will form some idea of what a scared duck can do in the way of speed as he buzzes off, quacking in terror the while.

Ducking from a house-boat is the very acme of comfort in this ofttimes arduous pursuit. Blow high, blow low, you have your cozy cabin, and pleasant it is to sit within, puffing a quiet pipe and listening to the pouring rain while the storm rages.

At the first sign of clearing weather, one is literally "on deck" for business.

Fifteen miles from Burlington, Vt., over a good road, winding amid ever-changing scenery, you reach Sand Bar Bridges, a roadway connecting the mainland with Grand Island.

South and west extend the flats, it being possible to walk in some directions here quite a mile from shore without bringing the water above knee-deep.

On these flats the blind was moored, and therein

it was my fortunate privilege to spend a few days in September.

To the north and west lay Grand Island, distant about three miles. Above its rounding hills and flanking the lake shore, far as the eye could reach to the south, loomed the silent Adirondacks, grand and sphinx-like in repose. The play of light and shadow gave a wondrous depth of tone to the scene. Even the wandering clouds seem to linger with a soft caress about the mountain tops, reaching out with long, filmy streamers from summit to summit, leaving each slowly, regretfully, as though parting with an old friend.

The use of live decoys was a feature of duck shooting that was unfamiliar to me, and I looked forward with impatience to the day when Elmer was to initiate me. The decoys were sturdy specimens of black duck, nearly pure wild blood, and certainly their markings were exactly similar to those of their wild brethren. If it were not for a certain sluggishness of movement, due possibly to their having spent the summer in the barn-yard among the plebeian ducks and chickens, it would be almost impossible to distinguish them from the wary thoroughbreds that frequent the lake.

The manner of working with them is as follows: A small platform, or log, is placed some 20 yards from the blind in front, its top just flush with the surface of the water.

A decoy is tethered by a string to a peg firmly thrust into the hard sand of the flats, about 6 feet distant, the string being just long enough to allow of the decoy reaching the platform, where it will stand and preen its feathers, quacking meanwhile with energy at every passing bird, or in more subdued tones holding converse with its companions in the coop on the blind.

The live decoy occupies the apex of a triangle, the sides being strung with the ordinary wooden decoys in greater or less numbers as inclination may suggest, although the squawking of this feathered siren makes a large display unnecessary.

When a flock of ducks appear, her calls seldom fail to attract their attention, and as she stands upon the little platform she shows up in such fine form that they generally turn to investigate.

And now Elmer will take a decoy from the coop, crouching low as he grasps it firmly with both hands. A quick toss sends it high in air above the blind, where with noisy expostulation it presently sails down with outspread wings and joins its tethered mate. This manœuvre rarely fails to decide the action of the wild birds. They either at once set their wings and swiftly scale in to the decoys, or, circling a few times, alight, and after consulting together, swim up within range of the leaden death that is lurking within the cedars of the blind.

Should they act as though suspicious, the judicious tossing of a few more decoys will settle it, and it is curious to see the air of fearlessness which now pervades the flock as they swim rapidly up.

It often happens that several bunches of ducks will swim in from different directions at the same time, and then it is a pleasure to see the careful way in which the decoys are handled.

No tossing now. Instead, a decoy is quietly pushed through between the cedars on the opposite side of the blind, and quacking loudly with a sense of freedom, it hurries to its chums, who are already disporting themselves about the little platform of this tethered occupant. With bated breath we peep through the boughs at the approaching fowl. Not a sound is made by us as they come in; a look is all that is required. It says: "Are you ready?" A wink answers "Yes," and rising, we cut loose.

Not waiting to see what execution has been done, each grasps a spare gun, and again we stop a couple as they cross in wild affright, "doin' stunts," says Elmer.

With the clearing away of the fog of burned powder, we see eleven ducks scattered here and there waiting to be gathered, and wading out we attend to them.

But what of the live decoys? During all this excitement they have been huddled in a compact bunch near the little platform and are now unconcernedly swimming about among the dead and dying.

I go to the blind, raise the sliding door of the coop, and Elmer walking behind them, our duck assistants swim to the gangway and waddle up into the coop in a matter-of-fact manner that is laughable.

Fully plumed for flight, not hampered in any way, the idea that they are free to go never seems to enter their silly heads. Once in a while they will leave for parts unknown, but this seldom occurs.

In the use of live decoys it is found of great advantage in accustoming them to their duties, to have a few well-trained, older birds, whose example is quickly followed by the younger members of the flock.

It is very necessary to take pains at the outset in the arrangement of the little board or gangway which leads up from the water to the coop in the blind. The incline must be easy, so that at the first attempt on the part of the decoys to enter they will find no difficulty in comfortably ascending. If too steep an incline, they are likely to slip and flutter clumsily in the effort to regain footing, and ever after will hesitate to make the attempt, swimming and dodging about the blind until finally driven in.

This, of course, is very annoying and seriously interferes with the results of a day's sport. With proper attention to these details, however, there appears to be little trouble afterward, and certainly to one who finds something of interest in the accessories of duck shooting, and whose entire enjoyment of a shooting trip is not confined to the mere killing of game, the working with live decoys is extremely interesting.

In selecting a decoy to tether out as a caller, a female should always be taken, as she has the well-known loquacity of her sex in general, and proves, as with human beings, a greater attraction than the male. The drakes are rarely tethered, being reserved for tossing into the air.

In calm weather, when the fowl are not moving about, the door of the coop may be raised, and the whole flock will go out and disport themselves, romping and playing tag as it were, having a big time generally for an hour or so, returning of their own volition when ready. In giving them liberty, as above, always see to it that one of their number is tethered, as they are then less likely to stray. With regular feeding and plenty of exercise, a decoy will keep in excellent condition the season through. There is amusement in watching their many antics. For instance, one habit they have is to pitch into the decoy that has just been released from its tether, the instant it is returned to the coop, and the scramble that regularly takes place on these occasions is ludicrous, each one trying to thump the luckless individual and all squawking and tumbling about the coop in wild confusion.

Why they should wish to vent such spite is beyond my comprehension, but such is the case, and at each change of decoys the scene is repeated with never-failing regularity. When fowl are moving, the sport from such a blind is fine, as they come right up until one can see their eyes twinkle.

ICE HOLE SHOOTING.

It is well understood that there are a number of species of ducks which do not migrate so long as there is open water in which they can feed. On many streams in the Rocky Mountains, where there is rough and turbulent water caused by rapids, or where warm springs breaking out under the bank, or from the bottom, keep the water open through the winter, great numbers of wildfowl remain from autumn until spring, although the temperature often falls to twenty or thirty degrees below zero, or even to the point where mercury freezes.

In many places in the Middle West, the mallards seem loath to move southward, and do not go until all the marshes and streams are frozen, so that feeding is no longer possible for them. There are sloughs and rivers where the current or the springs from the bottom keep open what are called air-holes, long after the frost has sealed up the waters in general, and to such open places the late-staying ducks continue to resort in considerable numbers after their more tender fellows have taken their departure to warmer climes. So long as such open water is accessible it will continue to give food to the ducks, but gradually the area of the air-holes becomes more and more contracted, until at last the ice wholly covers them, and then the birds are obliged to move onward.

The gunner who is fortunate enough to find one of these air-holes is quite sure to have good shooting for a short time, and if there are several of them in the neighborhood, so that the birds can pass from one to another, he will have many opportunities at single birds and small bunches, from which he should get a good bag during the day.

It is, of course, well understood by every experienced gunner that if, on approaching a place such as this, many ducks are found, he should drive them away without shooting at them, in order that a little later they may return in small companies and give him many shots, whereas, if he fired at the main flock when he first discovered them, they would be seriously frightened, and would disappear not to return for a long time.

An account of shooting of this sort, written some years ago, for *Forest and Stream,* by a correspondent signing himself G. L. R., is given here:

Late in the fall, or very early in the spring, very excellent shooting may be had at times in ice holes. These holes are found in running water, or at what are generally known as air-holes. When the weather has been cold, and all the prairie ponds are frozen, driving the ducks from open land to timber, they naturally seek for water wherever it may be found. They fly through the timber and over the trees in constant search for open water—places where experience had heretofore taught them that water and feed could be found in plenty. Their flight is slow, their search thorough, and they are not unrewarded, for they find a spot where water may be had.

When they find a place like this, they alight in great numbers. The quantity lighting in the hole depends on the number of them coming. This hole, like an omnibus, always has room for one more. After the hole is filled they become generous, and wishing to make room for fresh arrivals, they crawl out and sit on the ice, quacking vigorously, or, with craws distended with corn, fruits of the last overland trip, sit on the ice preening themselves and sleeping the time away. Their loud calls vibrate and course through the still woods, carrying welcome music to the alert ears of the hunter.

He marks the direction, and stealthily proceeds to locate them. Then some noisy duck, having partaken too freely of corn, and feeling the effects of its fermentation, raises her voice so loudly that he marks the spot where they are located. He shows his open palm to his dog, and thus conveys to him warning for great caution. The dog understands this signal and crouches close to the earth. Those two friends stand silently behind a projecting tree, the gunner debating in his mind whether to step boldly out and rout the birds or attempt by crawling to get a sitting shot. He decides on the former, and when he steps out in open sight is seen, and, with a grand roar that fills the woods with its volume, the birds arise in fright, and in pairs and flocks, both great and small, fly away. The dog looks askance at his master, questioning the propriety of routing such an immense flock without firing a shot, but a reassuring pat on the head and he silently acquiesces in the judgment of his master.

The ducks are loath to leave a place like this, and soon begin to return—they will not keep out. Coolly the hunter knocks them right and left; the dog is in an ecstasy of delight. Constant exercise has caused his blood to rush through his veins. He comes and goes in and out of the water, his brown coat glistening with ice, forming brilliant beads in the sunlight; then he marks the course of a wing-tipped drake as it tries hard to follow the flock and falls one or two hundred yards from the shooter. Away he goes over ridges, brushpiles and frozen sloughs, and soon returns, the drake in his strong jaws, its good wing beating against his nose, and delivers it to his master.

When a man finds a place like this, he has found a mine which is inexhaustible for that day. If he intends staying in the neighborhood, he should hunt some other place similar to this, hunt them on alternate days, and his shooting will be good each day. It is advisable to scatter corn in the hole and around the edges on the ice, but plenty in the hole if the water is shallow. The birds will soon discover this, and come often; and, if the hunter is a good shot, will tarry long. As fast as killed, set up the dead ducks for decoys; keep on until you have a good-sized flock. No fear of having too many—the more the better.

In building a blind, advantage must be taken of locality. If in timber, secrete yourself well, with a good open place to shoot through. Better have an indifferent blind with a good place to shoot through than one where you find you cannot shoot without interference of limbs. Should you find the shooting must be had in an exposed pond or river, where a shore blind cannot be made, your ingenuity will be taxed to hide yourself, and you must depend as much on quietness and patience as on a blind. Should the ice be strong enough to bear you, build a wall ten or twelve inches high of ice or snow to conceal you. A little hay, a rubber blanket spread over it, cover yourself with a white cloth, wait patiently; it's a splendid place for contemplation, especially if the thermometer registers down about zero. You can drive away the coldness by thinking about Turkish baths, strawberries and cream, and the church sociables you enjoyed last summer.

One writer, speaking of ice hole shooting, says a good way to build a blind is: "Take a barrel, chop a hole through the ice so the barrel will slip through, nail pieces of scantling on the sides of the barrel, fill the barrel with water until it sinks down far enough, then bail the water out, first cutting narrow edges through the ice, push the scantlings down, give them a half twist, and they will hold the barrel where wanted. Put in hay and push snow against the sides and top of the barrel to hide it, and the blind is complete." No doubt this would work, but it would hardly pay to go to so much trouble. The only good way is to shoot from the shore, as first mentioned; any other manner has drawbacks that will more than offset the pleasure derived.

Never take any chances in trying to get duck shooting around ice. Better not get a shot than attempt to get to some place where there is a flight, and then take chances of breaking in. If you haven't a boat or a good dog, and know you cannot get the dead birds without retrieving them yourself over ice that might be weak; turn your back to that hole and walk away; you have no right to take any such chance, and no wise man will do it. Death by drowning is said to be an easy death. If, then, you prefer death in this way, choose summertime; the water will feel decidedly more pleasant and flowers are much cheaper.

WINTER DUCK SHOOTING ON LAKE ONTARIO.

That duck shooting is hard work and entails much exposure and suffering and danger, is a saying so familiar that it has passed almost into a proverb. Not infrequently we hear of men having been drowned or frozen to death while duck shooting late in the season, and cases of actual suffering are common. A form of sport in which there is much exposure and sometimes not a little danger is practiced at different points on the Great Lakes in winter, and the methods pursued are well described by Mr. Olin B. Coit, of Oswego, N. Y., in the following article contributed by him to *Forest and Stream* in the year 1895. He says:

Methods of hunting the same kind of game differ with the location and the season. There is no mode of ducking that is so novel or attended with greater discomfort and danger than winter shooting on Lake Ontario. The ducks that make their homes in these icy waters are whistlers, broadbills, coots, sheldrakes and old-wives. The three latter kinds are fish ducks and on the coast are strong and inferior in flavor, for they there live on fish and sea food. But the lake usually furnishes each autumn several cargoes of barley and wheat that are wrecked and scattered along its shores. Thither the ducks congregate, and after many weeks' feeding on the water-soaked grain their flesh becomes fat and fine-flavored.

They feed with ease in water that is twelve to fifteen feet deep, diving to the bottom and remaining under water an incredible time. It is often amusing to shoot at one or two ducks swimming about, and the next instant to see the water broken in all directions by the birds popping up from underneath, where they have been breakfasting. Now is the time for alertness, for if the gunners are busy enough they may slaughter many before they have made a change of elements.

Ice forms in the shoal water many yards from the shore. Anchor ice and frozen spray are piled upon this in wild confusion, until it looks like the surface of a glacier, with hillocks and crevasses. Frequently spout holes are formed, out of which the water, forced upward by the waves dashing underneath, leaps for many feet into the air, and freezing as it falls, forms a cone like those in the crater of a volcano.

The outer edge of this ice reef is formed into a line of ice cliffs and battlements containing caves of wondrous beauty and little coves and fjords like a miniature Norway coast line.

The hunters are clad in garments of white duck, white caps covering the hair, and white masks. Even white covers are used for the guns. These are arranged to be easily slipped off when the time of action arrives. An excavation is made on the edge of the ice, in which the hunters are to conceal themselves. The decoys are anchored at a convenient distance, and the boat, drawn into a little cove of the ice, is covered with a white cloth. One does not have to wait long for a shot, as the ducks fly in great numbers. The cold is often intense, and the frozen spray stiffens the clothing and covers everything with an icy armor. A wind break of blocks of ice is often an absolute necessity. But, despite cold and discomfort, it is sport, and everything goes.

Large numbers of ducks are shot in this way, but not all the slain are retrieved, for the launching of a boat in the wintry seas is a dangerous operation and a capsize is something to be carefully avoided.

SHOOTING IN THE ICE.

On many of our northern streams, when the ice breaks up in the spring, and even during a thaw in winter, ducks are frequently found searching for feeding grounds that have not already been exhausted. In such places, fairly good gunning can be had by men who are willing to work hard, and to endure discomforts of cold and wet. Mild, still weather is desirable for work of this kind; while usually, of course, the worse the weather the better for ducking. The boat used for this is either a low, flat-decked ducking boat, or something in the nature of a Barnegat sneak-boat, which, though a little larger and more conspicuous, has the great advantage of being much more roomy. The boat should be painted white, to resemble the ice, and it is common for the gunners to wear white canvas coats and white caps. Ducks are looked for in the likely places among the floating ice, and along feeding grounds close to the shore, if any such are bare.

When birds are discovered, the oars are shipped, and the boat is sculled or paddled very slowly and cautiously up to the ducks. If the work is properly done the birds will not lift their heads to look at the boat. In this work frequent advantage may be taken of the floating cakes of ice, which will cover the approach of the boat, and even if there is no such cover as this, a good sculler may often get within easy gunshot. When this is done, the gunner usually takes one shot at the birds on the water, and another as they rise; and possibly, if he has a spare gun, and the birds are confused, as they often are, he may even get two more barrels in. Then follows the work of shooting over the cripples, which should be done at once, as it is very easy to lose birds under such conditions. The ducks most commonly captured in this way are black ducks, whistlers, pintails, and sometimes redheads.

This sport necessitates much hard work, but the reward of a few birds fully compensates the gunner for his efforts.

Much more destructive than this prowling about in the rivers for small bunches of ducks, is that practiced during the spring migration at the mouths of some of the larger rivers, notably the Delaware. In this, large guns are used, and the sport is practiced chiefly by market· gunners, who ship their game to Philadelphia daily.

Concerning this method of killing ducks, the late C. S. Wescott, of Philadelphia, wrote many years ago:

I knew of but two or three amateurs that regularly indulged in this sport, and had always looked on it as a murderous method of wildfowling. The tales of my enthusiastic friends, however, led me to make trial of it, and I engaged the services of one of the most noted professional paddlers who followed the river. This was in the month of March.

Owing to the great amount of ice that had formed that year on the tributaries of the Delaware and the upper river during the winter, and the sudden breaking up, I believed that we should have good shooting, for already the fowl had been reported from below as having arrived. The continued drifting of huge masses and fields of ice at each ebb and flow of the tide, and the extensive bodies of ice collected on the flats of the New Jersey and Delaware shores from Marcus Hook to Bombay Hook, made ice shooting more dangerous that spring than it had been for many years.

The skiffs used for this description of duck shooting are light, double-end, fifteen-foot, clinker-built boats, such as rail are shot from, but are somewhat strengthened by being sheathed with copper where the surfaces are presented to the floating ice, and are also provided with narrow runners on the bottom; for often it may become necessary to haul the skiff up onto the ice, and to use it as a sledge over the great ice fields that frequently surround the shooter. From stem to stern everything is painted white, and a netting is hung along the bows for four or five feet down the gunwales on both sides, in which to place pieces of ice to form a blind for the shooter as he is being paddled on a flock of ducks. The occupants of the skiff thus hidden, and clad in white and with white cap covers, can hardly be distinguished from the drifting ice. A reliable compass is always carried, for the frequent fogs that hang over the river often obscure the shores. A strong field glass is also needed.

Thus fitted out, John Brown and I launched our skiff on the ice at a point on the river near Marcus Hook, for we could not find open water higher up. For guns, we had a single-barrel four-gauge piece, from which at each discharge were shot three or four ounces of No. 4 or 5 shot; a ten-pound ten-gauge gun, and a seven and a half pound twelve-bore, for shooting over "cripples."

I confess that I felt some fear of the hummocks of ice that at once threatened us, as soon as we had pushed our boat over the grounded ice and reached the open water, but the coolness and business-like demeanor of my paddler reassured me, and I placed myself at the oars under his direction, while he faced me in the stern with a helping paddle.

Difficulties soon began to present themselves, as the tide ebbed stronger. Immense fields and blocks of ice came tearing and grinding up against the grounded masses on the flats, and, completely shutting up the channel, bore down on us, threatening to crush our frail craft in the general rush and onward drift. Fending off the dangerous pieces with our hooks, we finally hauled the skiff up on a huge cake and felt comparatively safe as we floated down the river toward Pennsville, N. J., looking for open water where we might use our oars.

All prospect for shooting for the day was now over, as the mush ice at this point kept the ducks away, and it became apparent that the great body of fowl were to be found lower down the river, whither in the morning we must direct our course. On our ice island we floated down the stream until within sight of Pennsville pier, extending into the river, against which the ice was jamming, and where there was every probability that we would be crushed, unless we sought safety on the stationary ice, which still remained on the shoal borders of the stream. An opportunity for reaching this ice soon presented itself, and hooking to it, we pulled the boat safely up, and parted with our friendly cake, which went on to its destruction. We were now a full mile from a hotel, which we could only reach by sledging the skiff, and it was four o'clock before we were on *terra firma*.

At Pennsville Hotel we found three other duck-shooters, with their men, who had been driven in, as we had, by the thick ice.

Next morning a heavy fog hung over the river, adding some danger to the shooting, as the shore could not be distinguished seventy-five yards from the skiff. Brown and myself were the only two that started out, and we first took careful bearings by compass.

A mile below Pennsville, the ducks could be heard talking, as they drifted on the ice as it floated down stream, and directing our course by the sound, I was soon paddled up within range of a good-sized flock as I lay in the bottom of the boat waiting the signal to fire the big gun.

I dislike to recall the effect of that shot, or to remember the number of ducks slaughtered. It is enough to say that I killed and crippled many, and was obliged to "over shoot" numerous wounded ones. The huge gun had boxed me soundly, but I now think I deserved to have been kicked into the water. During the day we found sprigtails and mallards in abundance, and I was taken cleverly to them by my skillful paddler. Perhaps then I thought that I was having great sport, and truly I was killing many birds, but I have never since been satisfied with the skiff-load of ducks we took to shore, and after this trip never repeated my ice-shooting experience.

SAILING.

Sailing down on wildfowl can, of course, only be practiced on large bodies of water, and in many States is forbidden by law, as it should be in all.

As most fowl are obliged to rise from the water

against the wind, it is possible sometimes to sail down on them before the wind, and to get so close to them before they take wing that when they rise a shot is offered. Most birds will not permit so near an approach as this, and those chiefly killed in this way are the salt-water scoters and old-squaws. At the same time, we have seen geese and swans sailed up to, and occasionally killed. But this is quite unusual.

The practice is a very evil one, since it amounts to chasing the birds about continually, and after a certain amount of this pursuit, they become exceedingly wild, and are likely to desert the waters where this is practiced. To my mind, there is no sport in this, and it deserves mention only as one method by which ducks are killed. In certain waters of New York, and some other States, birds are approached somewhat in this way by steam or naphtha launches, and some shooting is had; but this method of killing ducks is open to the same objections as sailing, and ought not to be practiced or to be permitted. Any method of shooting ducks which gives them the impression that they are being chased about is open to objection and should not be practiced. The results can never justify the injury certain to be done to the shooting.

STUBBLE SHOOTING.

In portions of the Northwest, such as North Dakota and Manitoba, and in fact in many wheat-growing countries, ducks are shot in the stubble fields. In the spring of the year, mallards, pintails, widgeons and teal very commonly resort to the wheat fields to feed. Indeed, the mallards and the pintails make regular morning and evening flights, just as the geese do, and, like the geese, can be depended on to come.

In the autumn, however, the shooting in the stubble fields depends largely on the season. If the fall has been very wet, the mallards resort to the wheat fields by thousands, but other ducks seldom put in an appearance. If the fields contain pools of water, the birds will come in regularly in the morning and in the evening. On the other hand, if the fields are dry, the birds are likely to feed chiefly at night, coming into the fields just at dusk, remaining during the night, and returning in the early morning to the sloughs, where they spend the day. If very much shot at in the stubbles, they will give up feeding during the day and resort to the fields at night only. Of course, now and then a bird may come in the afternoon, but nine-tenths of them come in at night.

In shooting ducks in the stubble the same methods are used as in shooting geese, but the ducks decoy much more easily than geese.

Blinds are of course required, and the best blind is a pit such as geese are shot from. In the spring of the year, however, when the ground is frozen to a considerable depth, and a great deal of labor is required to make a pit, other blinds are often prepared. Thus low places in the field will have the stalks of pig weeds still standing, and from these a good natural blind can be made. In other places grain will have lodged, and, if the stalks can be straightened up, this makes an excellent blind. Or, again, if one has patience to do it, a straw pile may be made in a part of the field where the birds are feeding, and a blind be made in that, and if not used for a few days, until the birds become accustomed to the straw, capital shooting may be had from it.

The pit is the best blind. It can be made to look so natural that the birds come in without the slightest suspicion, and it is very much more roomy and comfortable than any other blind. A man lying flat on his back in a shallow furrow has really only a limited range for his gun, and whether one is on his back, his knees or his face, it is hard to get up and put the gun on the birds in time.

Mr. Ned Cavileer describes a pit which he uses. It is only about twelve inches deep, long enough to lie down in, and is lined with boards to keep the dirt from falling in. The boards are carefully fitted and are held in place by hooks and staples, or sometimes three of the boards may be hinged together, so as to close up and be convenient for carrying. There are two boards, one each for the head and foot, and two for the sides.

On the stubbles, mallards seem ready to decoy to almost anything. Goose decoys are better than ducks, because they are larger and can be seen at a great distance. Mallards will come readily to snow-goose decoys. The pintail also readily comes to goose decoys, and no others are needed.

CALIFORNIA MARSH SHOOTING.

Within a comparatively short distance from San Francisco are great marshes bordering the bay, and there are others at the junction of the Sacramento and the San Joaquin rivers with Suisun Bay. These are of great extent, that known as the Suisun Marsh being about twenty miles long by ten wide, and a great resort for snipe and wild fowl. This marsh was long ago taken up and is under lease to shooting clubs, who hold all the land.

The two principal forms of shooting practiced here are pond shooting, over decoys from a blind, and a form of floating practiced by sculling a boat along the narrow sloughs and leads which thread the marsh in every direction.

The ponds on which the shooting takes place vary in size from small mallard holes and mud puddles to considerable pools covering several acres. The different ponds are connected by artificial ditches with the neighboring sloughs, and sometimes the ponds are connected in the same way. It is stated that in such ponds grows the vallisneria, which is so favorite a food with all our ducks.

To such ponds resort swans, geese, and ducks of many kinds. The shooting in such places does not especially differ from such shooting elsewhere. The gunner builds a blind of reeds and grass, and either sits in the marsh, or, if that is too soft, he may sit in his boat. Great numbers of fowl are killed annually, for here the shooting lasts for five months or more. It is a wintering ground where the fowl come to stay, and being so extensive, it is possible to change the gunning grounds frequently, and so to keep the shooting good.

In the narrow leads which intersect the marsh, sculling is done in a boat of peculiar construction, which has been evolved by the gunners on these marshes, and is built only by them. They are speedy vessels which can be propelled very swiftly by a long, flexible sculling oar, and their advance is absolutely noiseless, so that the skillful sculler can approach very close to the fowl. As the boats are built for use by a single man only, the gunner sculls and shoots as well.

Besides the fowl shooting to be had here, there are many patches of snipe marsh, over which, in the dull hours of the day, the gunner can tramp with not a little benefit to his bag.

Some notion of the abundance and variety of wild-fowl found in the California marshes may be had from an account which is printed here substantially as it appeared in *Forest and Stream* in the year 1882. It treats of the abundance of birds in the marshes near the head of Suisun Bay, the extreme northern end of San Francisco Bay.

Phantom Pond, though within fifty miles of the city of San Francisco, had, up to that time, been shot on by very few men. A great many persons knew of the existence of the pond, but as it was small, and was situated on an island some fifteen miles long by from one to five miles wide, it was exceedingly difficult to find it in this marsh unless one knew just where to go. The writer of the account had made three previous efforts to find the place, and was only now, at his fourth attempt, successful. The journey to the marsh was made in a yacht, and the island was reached after various adventures. The writer, using the pseudonym "Duck Call," goes on to say:

About two o'clock Friday afternoon we came to anchor, and then we landed with three boats—one for the pond, if we should find it, one for the slough which was on the island, and one to ply between the yacht and the shore. Our first move was to haul two boats over a narrow strip of land to the island slough, which feat we were not long in accomplishing, and were soon rowing along the slough with our boats loaded with decoys, ammunition, etc.

My instructions were to row south along this slough about half a mile, and then to land and strike out directly east, and I would find the pond. Now, the next question, how to judge a half-mile on this narrow, winding slough, which had a generally southerly direction. We kept on rowing until we came to an almost impassable obstacle in the shape of an immense pile of drift tule, wood, etc., which completely blocked the slough from bank to bank, so we decided that we had rowed a mile; at least, we did not intend to carry over or around the mass of drift and stuff before us. So, landing on the east bank, we tied both boats, and after walking out of the very high rushes which bordered the slough, we shoved an oar into the ground and tied a handkerchief to it to mark the place where we had left the boats. This was a very necessary operation, as we would otherwise never find our boats again on account of the similarity of the rushes. Separating about fifty yards apart, we started to look for what I was inclined to think was a phantom pond. We walked and we walked; the sun was hot; the ground was mushy and the tules high; but no signs of a pond. Soon after we had left the boats we had come to another slough, and had followed it to the right. After walking along the bank about two miles, I should judge, and meeting other sloughs, we retraced our steps, tired and disgusted, and we had lain down to rest just at the point where we had first struck the slough we had been following.

We had hardly been lying there more than a minute or two when one of us noticed two swans flying toward us—nothing very extraordinary, as we had seen a great number of swans and plenty of ducks and geese flying around us all day. But these two swans passed us about three hundred yards to the right, and then set their wings and soon after lit about five hundred yards away. We had seen a great many birds alighting in this same spot, but there always seemed to be a slough separating us from the place, and our instructions were not to cross any slough after rowing on the first one. We jumped to our feet and both seemed struck with the same idea, at the same instant, and, sure enough, we had not walked more than two hundred yards when we commenced to hear the peculiar, noise which a large flock of wildfowl make while feeding in a pond—that is, a continued splash from their unceasing diving. Our excitement was such that we both hurried along, and soon a beautiful pond stretched out before us, just completely covered with wildfowl of every description. Instead of crawling up cautiously, as we should have done, we advanced in too much of a hurry, and let go our four barrels at the nearest of the immense flock. And then for a moment what a noise, a rush, splash, and whirr of wings. I never saw its like in my life, and hardly ever expect to see it again.

We had disturbed a wildfowls' sanctum. It was a sight to make a sportsman—well, I was going to say crazy, as we were so excited we hardly knew which way to start. The ducks, after their first fright, commenced to come back, and some even wheeled after flying not more than fifty or a hundred yards, and we shot and shot till most of our cartridges had gone, as we had left all but a few with our traps and decoys, with the boats. We then stood up and took a survey of our situation. We found the pond to be nearly circular, and 150 yards in diameter, and the slough which we had been following ran into the pond, so if we had followed it to the left instead of to the right we would have soon come to the pond.

Our flag and boats were in a direct line about 350 or 400 yards from us, so taking off our coats, and leaving our guns at the pond, we started for the boats to drag the pond boat, full of decoys, to the pond. We were not long in doing this, as we were in a hurry to get back to the pond, and as the sun was approaching the western horizon we were all fixed in our separate blinds, with the decoys out, and shooting as fast as we could wish.

It being a moonlight night, we stayed at the pond until about half-past seven, and then started back to the yacht, having first hauled the pond boat out of sight in the tule. Then, after getting our game together, we looked at it, and then at each other, and then came the question, how were we ever to get that load of game to the yacht. Among the pile were five immense Canadian geese, about three of which are all one man wishes to carry. We also had about one dozen white geese, a swan, and ducks, I was going to say innumerable. Well, we compromised. We first drew all the birds, which considerably lightened the load, and then each took a sack, which the decoys had been in, and filled them with the best ducks; the rest, with all our traps, except our guns and empty cartridge bags, we stowed in the boat and covered with rushes for the next day. We each then shouldered his sack and started for our white flag, which we soon reached, and then, after a short row, arrived at the narrow strip of land which separated us from the yacht. We were soon aboard, and after supper, to which we did ample justice, we lost no time getting to bed, so as to be up and off long before daylight.

It seemed to me that I had hardly been asleep more

than ten minutes when the whirr of the alarm clock
told us that it was time to turn out. We had to
go home during the next night, so we decided to make
one long hunt from early dawn to late at night. Just
before sitting down to breakfast I went on deck, and
found it very cold. A heavy, thick fog had settled
down on everything, dampening all but our spirits.
After breakfast we took every cartridge we could get
hold of, and started for the grounds, with instructions
to one of the men to join us about four in the afternoon
and help us out with some of the game. The boat was
found in the slough as we had left it the night before,
and after rowing along till we came to our landing, we
tied our boat and started for the pond. The fog was
so thick that we could get no bearings, and having no
compass, the first thing we knew we were lost. We
walked first north, and then south, and then east, and
found no pond. There was nothing but high rushes
and mudholes and sloughs. We tried to retrace our
steps, but got more bewildered than before, and at
about eleven o'clock we sat down and waited for the
fog to lift. At twelve o'clock the fog rolled away, and
we found that we had been completely turned around
and evidently been wandering in a circle, as we found
ourselves within two hundred yards of our flag. We
immediately struck out for the pond, which we soon
reached, very tired from carrying so many cartridges,
but nevertheless full of spirits and ready for the rest of
the day's hunt. We scared quite a goodly lot of ducks
off the pond on our appearance, and were soon en-

sconced in our blinds, banging away at a great rate, as the ducks and geese came in very lively.

We shot all the afternoon, and then, it being moon-light, though very cloudy, we shot till late at night, nearly ten o'clock. The Canada geese did not come in till late, but when they did come, they came with a vengeance. You could jump up and nearly hit them with a gun. Our man joined us about dusk and started to help us out with our game. We stopped shooting as soon as our cartridges gave out and then proceeded to get things together. We gathered in the decoys, had the game drawn and packed in the pond boat with the rest of the traps, which filled the boat to more than over-flowing. And I wondered, when I looked at that load, how we were going to get it to the yacht. Two of us took hold of the rope at the bow and the other shoved, and by dint of pulling and shoving we finally, after nearly two hours' work, got the loaded boat to the slough, where we transferred some of the birds to the other boat, and, after launching it, were, after another hour's work, aboard our yacht, with everything stowed away. We were not long in getting asleep, and the or-ders were that we were to be aroused about three A. M., as soon as the tide changed, and get under way.

The next thing I knew I suddenly awoke with the sun streaming in the cabin skylight, and on looking out the porthole above my berth I was very much surprised to see the pile of a wharf obstructing my view. In fact the two men had brought the yacht down during the night, and we two hunters, being so tired, had slept through the whole voyage, they having made the run down in about six hours. It was eight o'clock in the morning when I awoke, and we had just landed. So we proceeded immediately to clean up and get ready for the train, which passed in the afternoon. We made presents of game to all those we knew at this town, and packed the rest in sacks for our city home, where, upon our arrival, we gave to all our own friends around. And we had geese, duck and swan cooked in every style for the next week.

I will try and remember a few figures. I know we got nineteen Canada honkers, tremendous fellows; about two dozen white geese, a dozen ordinary gray geese, one swan, and I will not state how many ducks, as I suppose I might shock my Eastern friends, who have, I suspect, already put me down a black mark for shooting at night.

I have visited the "Phantom Pond" several times since, but never had such a hunt and such hard work at the same time. But the work only made the hunt more agreeable, and the game more acceptable when I got it.

CHESAPEAKE BAY DUCK SHOOTING.

The Chesapeake Bay has long been famous as a resort for duck shooters. It is told that in New England, the employer to whom an apprentice was indentured agreed as a part of the contract that the apprentice should not be obliged to eat salmon more than twice a week, and in the same way, that in early days along the shores of the Chesapeake, the slave-owners who hired out their slaves to work for others stipulated in their contracts that these slaves should not be obliged to eat canvas-back ducks more than twice a week. Copies of such contracts are declared to be still in existence in some of the Maryland counties.

This great body of water, more than 200 miles long, and from four to forty miles in width, with its innumerable bays, sounds, broad waters and sluggish rivers, has unquestionably sheltered more wildfowl than any other body of water in the country, and has been the greatest ducking ground that America has known. To write a history of Chesapeake Bay duck shooting would require a volume by itself, and here only the briefest reference can be made to a few of the more celebrated localities.

For many years Baltimore was the centre of the duck-shooting territory, but with the growth and expansion of that city its fame as a duck-shooting centre has been forgotten, and of late years the little town of Havre de Grace has become perhaps the best known of the gunning localities, chiefly because it is the point from which most battery gunners start. The Chesapeake Bay is historic ground for the wildfowl, and although its glories as a duck-shooting locality have in a large measure departed, and the gunning has become a memory rather than a reality, it is worth while, nevertheless, to speak briefly of some matters connected with

this shooting and of some of its most famous ducking
shores. Of these, there were four which perhaps had a
fame greater than any of the others near Baltimore.
These were Carroll's Island, Spesutia Island, Maxwell's
Point and Benjies. On all these shores decoy shooting
from blinds was practiced, and in the olden times with
great success. Even at present not a few ducks are
occasionally killed here. Spesutia Island is owned by
a club of New York men, and still affords excellent
blackhead and redhead shooting, although comparatively few canvas-backs are killed. At Maxwell's Point,
Carroll's Island and Benjies, there is still often good
shooting, and when the wind is right the flight from
Standing Cove to Benjies across the landward side of
Carroll's Island is often very good.

In old times in the waters near the head of the Chesapeake Bay many thousands of ducks were regularly
killed each season. Almost every foot of available land
bordering on the waters where the ducks feed was
either in possession of some sportsman, who used it for
his own shooting, or was owned by a ducking club.
Thousands of dollars have been spent on many of the
shores, and the club houses are as comfortable as money
can make them. Many of them, however, no longer
afford much shooting. The ducks are becoming more
scarce yearly. There is still, however, a supply that at
times and in certain places makes the sport good, and
it is enjoyed by thousands of Baltimoreans every
season.

Many who cannot get shores to their liking on the

rivers at the head go lower down the bay for their shooting. There has been much complaint among the gunners that the feeding grounds in the rivers—especially those in the upper parts of the streams—are often covered with mud brought down by floods, and that the ducks can be found only at the mouths of the rivers or on the bay. The fact seems to be that in the early autumn the ducks are usually found at the mouths of the rivers and in the wider waters, but in the spring, after the breaking up of the ice, the ducks work up the streams, and commonly bed in the streams just before they go off to the North. It may well enough be imagined that they have used up most of the grass and food from the open waters during autumn and winter, and that as soon as the streams are accessible they work up them in search of food. In the rivers emptying into the upper part of the bay the ducks are continually harassed, for on both shores are skirmish lines of gunners trying to kill them. On all these streams long blinds are built out from every point running into the river, so that, to escape being shot at, a bird would be obliged to follow the windings of the channel.

The Carroll's Island Club occupies what was in old times perhaps the most celebrated ducking ground on Chesapeake Bay. Carroll's Island is bounded by the Chesapeake Bay, and the Seneca, Saltpeter and Gunpowder rivers. It is fourteen miles from Baltimore, and has an area of about twelve hundred acres. Up to about 1820 it had been owned for about one hundred years by the Carroll family, but in 1822 it was leased by the widow of the late Commodore Spence, of the United States Navy. This lease, which was perpetual, was later, by order of court, transferred to James Moir, a Scotchman, for annual rent of less than seven hundred dollars. The lease was afterward purchased by Colonel William Slater, and was held by him and by his widow and her estate until about 1880, when the present club took hold of it.

There were shooting and a club at Carroll's Island as long ago as 1830. This continued under Colonel Slater, and in 1856 the Carroll's Island Company was incorporated, with Wm. Slater, C. Beatty Graf, Wm. P. Lightner, Robert Purveance, Jr., Geo. Hugh Graf, Wm. F. Giles and Geo. G. Brewer as incorporators.

The membership of the present club is made up of men from New York, Philadelphia and Baltimore.

When the new club took possession of Carroll's Island it rebuilt the club house, which is large and comfortable. The ammunition house is at a distance from the club house; it is lighted by a reflector from outside, and the usual precautions against fire and lights which are employed in all modern clubs have long been in practice there.

In old times this was the heart of the best shooting in Chesapeake Bay. All the shooting was done from the shore, much of it from blinds along the marsh, and over decoys; yet often for a time there was no decoy shooting, and all ducks' secured were killed from the bar which runs out into the Gunpowder River from the island. The blinds from which the shooting was done were boxes sunk in the marsh, each furnished with a pump for the removal of any water which leaked into the box, and provided with seats, and with shelves in front, on which to rest ammunition.

The shooting on the bar was at ducks flying from the bay to the Gunpowder River, and originally was done from blinds in the rushes on the bar. Later, boxes were sunk in the bar, from which the men did their shooting. These boxes were about fifty yards apart. Often when the ducks flew well there was great shooting here, which in its character was precisely like the pass shooting, elsewhere described. The birds came overhead, at greater or less height, according to the weather, and were shot as they flew over. As is elsewhere stated, the shooting at these overhead birds, which began with comparatively small guns, came at last to be done with very heavy No. 4 gauge weapons, in which enormous charges of No. 2 and No. 3 shot were used. Sometimes it happened that a little bunch of birds, flying up and down the stream, as they rose and bunched up to cross the bar, would be struck just right by one of these enormous loads of shot, and half of them would be killed, and the remainder, hard hit, would come to the water several hundred yards off, and there very likely be lost.

That was the uncomfortable feature of this bar shooting at Carroll's Island and at Benjies. While a certain proportion of birds hit, fell at once either on the bar or so near it that they could be recovered by the dogs without trouble, very many others came down to the water a long way off, and if it were rough, or if there were a fog, could not be retrieved.

Old members of the club will remember an incident which took place many years ago, during a thick fog, when two or three birds were knocked down in the water, and the dogs, notwithstanding the calls of their owners, rushed in to retrieve them. They were soon lost sight of in the fog, and swam about after the ducks among the ice, which was running. Soon their cries showed the men on shore that the dogs were lost, and two of the boatmen started out in a light boat to recover them. In a few moments they were out of sight, and very soon their shouts and calls told that they, too, had lost all sense of direction and knew not which way to row. The feelings of the men standing on the shore, listening to the whinings of the dogs and the calls of the lost men, can be imagined better than described. The men were subsequently picked up and brought to shore by an old lighthouse keeper, who heard their cries, and starting out with a compass, found them and brought them both in; but the men standing on the beach heard the dogs' cries become fainter and fainter, until at last they ceased, for the dogs were drowned.

Of course, as all clubs do, the Carroll's Island Club was constantly trying to improve its shooting, and at one time it built out into Hawk Cove a bridgeway, running out seventy-five yards to a box built over the water. It was hoped that this box would be so near the flyway of the ducks that they would come at once to the decoys set out near it, but for several years after it was built no ducks at all came into the cove, which formerly had been a great resort for them, and the construction was regarded as an absolute failure.

The birds were little disturbed about Carroll's Island except by the shooting on the shore. Batteries were not allowed there, and in autumn and winter no boats. In the spring, however, about the middle of March, and from that to the first of April, the fishermen were permitted to draw their nets. When Mrs. Slater owned the island and rented the shooting, there was much annoyance to the gunners from these fishermen, but when the club purchased the land this was stopped. Nevertheless, the fishing rights, rented for the spring only, brought the club an income of $300 a year.

In the old days on the bar, disputes—very entertaining to all except the disputants—sometimes occurred as to the ownership of ducks at which more than one man had shot. As the boxes were not very far apart, it might often happen that a duck flying between two of them would be shot at by two persons, and if it fell, each man would promptly claim it as his duck, and the debates about the ownership were often very earnest. After a while it came to be more or less of a proverb that at Carroll's Island no one could be a successful duck-shooter unless he were also a good claimer. Stories are told of venerable men, occupying high positions in the business or professional world, who almost came to blows over birds that had been killed, and who deliberately sat down side by side and laboriously plucked the fowl in dispute in order to determine—according to the club rule—on which side it had been shot.

Occasionally, when ducks were discovered bedded close to the shore, toling was practiced. It could be done only at such times. It is thus described to me by my friend, Mr. Wm. Trotter:

"The darky came up and told us that he had found quite a bed of birds sitting near the shore, and that he thought we could get a tole on them. Two of us went with him, and after getting as near the shore as we could, crept up on our hands and knees until we were close to it. We could see a bed of two or three hundred ducks, blackheads, redheads and widgeons, feeding about a hundred yards off the shore. The darky had with him a little white poodle dog, that followed close at his heels, and as we came along we had filled the pockets of our shooting-coats with small sticks. After we had crept up close to the shore, the darky threw a stick off to one side, on the beach, and the dog raced after it, and took it up in his mouth and shook it and played with it for a moment or two, and then stood still and looked back toward us, and the darky threw another stick up the beach, and the dog raced up along to it, and played with that for a little while, when his owner threw a third stick. This was kept up for some little time, the dog running backward and forward along the beach. The blackheads almost at once noticed the dog, and began to swim toward shore to see what it was. The redheads also seemed interested, and kept with the blackheads, and the remaining ducks followed, not apparently because they cared for the dog, but in order to keep with the bunch. They came up quite close to the shore, and when they were near enough we fired three barrels into them on the water, and three more as they rose, and knocked down a lot of them. We loaded as fast as we could, and the darky ran and jumped into a boat, and pushing off, we began to shoot over the cripples, and gathered from those six shots just forty-seven birds. That is the biggest tole I ever saw made. It was common enough to get ten or twelve, or even sometimes twenty or twenty-five birds in a tole, but any larger number was unusual."

The blackheads and redheads are regarded as the most inquisitive of all the ducks. It is doubted whether widgeons could be toled at all; yet on the Connecticut shore I have heard of old-squaws responding to this lure.

While toling used to be practiced quite extensively from these shores, it has not been in favor for many years, and naturally so, since it is so very destructive. Even those who for any reason may have occasionally taken part in it say that they will not repeat it, and that a duck or two killed on the wing, either flying by or coming up to decoys, give more satisfaction to the man making the shot than a dozen or twenty shot at a tole.

For many years prior to 1883, night shooting with big guns was practiced in the neighborhood of Havre de Grace and Baltimore by a gang of poachers, against whom the processes of the law were invoked in vain. These men went out at night in skiffs, in the bow of which were mounted these great guns, and slaughtered the ducks by thousands on their roosting beds.

These guns, which were commonly known as "night guns," are huge single-barrel shotguns, patterned after an ordinary shotgun, but weighing sometimes 150 pounds, with a bore considerably over an inch in diameter. Such a gun was mounted on a pivot in the bow of a small skiff, to be paddled through the water, or which might be mounted on runners and pushed over the ice. The stock of the gun was braced against a block in the boat, and the recoil of the discharge often sent the boat back a long way through the water. The gun was usually painted the same color as the boat, some dull, inconspicuous tint. For many years there have been laws prohibiting the killing of ducks by this means, and many efforts had been made to convict the persons who were known to practice this illegal gunning. For this reason, each gun was so mounted in its boat that it could be easily detached from its fittings, and each had a long string attached to it, running to a buoy, so that in case of an alarm the arm could be pitched overboard, and the owner paddle away, to return for his property at a later day.

The number of birds killed by the discharge of one of these guns was, of course, very great. The common load was from a quarter to a third of a pound of powder and one and a half to two pounds of shot. The gunner paddled up quietly to the raft of sleeping canvas-backs, adjusted his gun to suit himself and discharged it, sometimes gathering from 75 to 100 ducks as the result.

For years the efforts of the members of the gunning clubs around the Susquehanna, Gunpowder, Bush and Back rivers, to put an end to this illegal shooting, were fruitless. The men practicing this gunning were politically influential, and it was impossible to secure evidence against them which would satisfy the magistrate who had charge of the case. However, in the winter of 1881-82, more stringent laws were passed, and one provision allowed persons charged with this offence to be taken before a magistrate either in Harford or Baltimore County, the latter county being one in which they were without the political influence which they had in Harford.

The matter was put in charge of Mr. John E. Semmes, of Baltimore. He engaged skillful detectives, and after considerable work a force of officers in charge of Mr. Semmes raided Spesutia Island, which was then the headquarters of the gang. The poachers, however, were found armed and entrenched, and threatened to fight for their liberty. At last, however, they were persuaded to surrender, and after being arrested were informed that they would be tried in Baltimore. When they learned this the poachers were much alarmed, and Mr. Semmes proposed a compromise, offering to allow them to be taken before a Harford County magistrate if they would give up their big guns. The men begged and implored and wept and swore over parting with their guns, but at last they agreed to do so. Six of the big guns were captured, and were subsequently broken up in a junk-shop. One of them was a particularly beautiful weapon, weighing 160 pounds, with a bore of $1\frac{5}{8}$ inches, and a lock of the finest and most delicate construction. Some of these guns are shown on another page.

Prior to 1880, Havre de Grace was the headquarters of the sink-boat or battery shooters of Chesapeake Bay, and it is still the point from which most of them start out. At that time there were licensed, at a fee of $20 each, about forty professional battery outfits. These consisted each of a small sailing craft from 25 to 50 feet long, a small flat-bottomed rowboat or skiff, a sink-box or battery, and from 300 to 500 decoys. To work these outfits, three men are required. At that time, shooting was allowed only on three days in the week after the first of November—Mondays, Wednesdays and Fridays. The batteries were not allowed to go upon the shooting ground before three o'clock in the morning. No shooting could be done until one hour before sunrise, and it must cease one-half hour after sunset. Sinkboxes were not allowed to be out within one-half mile of the shore.

There was great competition for the best positions, and it was the practice of many of these craft to anchor near the line within one-half mile of the shore, and immediately after three o'clock to proceed to the ground and to put out their decoys as soon as they could see to do so. This operation takes a full hour, and by the time the outfit was in position it was late enough to begin to shoot. Of course, the earlier hours of the day are by far the best.

The terms charged by gunners in those days for complete outfit services of the men and meals were usually from $35 to $40 per day.

Beside the ordinary battery or sink-boat shooting, practiced here with a great number of decoys, ordinary batteaux or gunning skiffs are used. These are called sneak-boats. They are painted white, and have a curtain or shield of canvas running from bow to midships. The decoys are thrown out and the boat moves off to a sufficient distance, so that it does not alarm the birds flying about. They are thus likely to alight among the decoys, and when they do so, the sneak-boat is slowly and carefully sculled forward until close to the decoys. The gunner then rises to his knees, and shooting over the canvas curtain, kills his ducks. Usually in such a sneak-boat two double-barreled guns are used.

In the old times on the eastern shore of Chesapeake Bay, the Sassafras River probably marked the beginning of the shooting, while Chester River, in almost its entire length, Kent Island Narrows, Eastern Bay and Miles River, Poplar Island, the large body of water included in the Choptank River and its tributaries, the Little Choptank, Tar Bay, Hooper Straits, Fishing Bay, Holland Strait, all of the large body of water included in Tangier and Pocomoke Sound, and so on down the bay, were all teeming with wildfowl and afforded fine shooting. On the western side of the bay it was the same from the localities named above, near Baltimore clear to the James River. In Eastern and in Hogg Bay one might see in old times redheads—especially in February and March—rafted in bodies miles in extent, probably not less than 50,000 ducks in one body.

The same thing might be seen about Poplar Island Narrows and in the Choptank River. We are told that at Lou's Point it was no uncommon thing on favorable days to have an ox-cart sent to the point to haul* up the ducks of the shooters that congregated there.

In modern times—that is to say, within the last thirty years—the redhead and the large blackhead have been the most numerous of the "good" ducks in the lower waters of the bay, though widgeons, locally known as bald pates or bald crowns, were also numerous. Those three species, with the canvas-backs, were known to duck shooters as good ducks, while all other fowl of the diving sort are known as trash ducks. In former years the canvas-backs were seen in large bodies in these waters, but they do not find here the wild celery in great profusion, since the brackish and salt water of these localities is not suited to its growth.

The last good season had in the waters of Talbot County was in February and March of 1890, at which time the waters of Eastern Bay and Miles River were visited by vast flocks of redheads and bald pates. Since that time there has been no feed in those waters, and they have not been resorted to by the ducks. This feed, which is locally known as duck grass, seems to have disappeared from many bays, inlets and streams where it was formerly abundant, and no satisfactory reason for its absence has been given.

Beside the vast quantities of ducks found here in old times, many of the localities mentioned were noted for their numbers of swans and geese. Swan Point at the mouth of Chester River, Kent Point, Parson's Island in Eastern Bay, Black Walnut Point at the mouth of Choptank River, Hills Point, Tar Bay, were favorite localities. The latter is now, at the proper season, one of the best resorts left for geese. These fowl are still to be found in many localities in good numbers, since, from the character of their feeding grounds, they are less disturbed and less shot at than are the ducks. As they frequent the wide, open bodies of water through the day and come in to the shores to feed only at night or in very stormy weather, there are not many places where they can be shot over decoys. Some were killed out of sneak-boats and from booby blinds, but where they are undisturbed by night shooting with a light—which is, of course, unlawful—they are still to be seen in goodly numbers.

This is not the case with swans, which, for some reason—possibly for the want of proper food—are becoming much more scarce than formerly. They decoy readily, and good shooting is to be had at them out of a battery with swan decoys. Mr. J. G. Morris, of Easton, Md., tells of shooting them in this way, using No. 4 or even No. 6 shot and shooting at the head only.

The same gentleman writes interestingly concerning a method of killing swans and geese, which, while far removed from sport, is worth repeating. A certain gunner having discovered that swans were feeding near an old wreck off the mouth of the Chester River, lashed his gun to the timbers of the wreck in such a way as to command the shoal. When a number of swans had collected there, he pulled a string which was tied to the triggers of his gun and led to the shore. The discharge raked the feeding ground. Mr. Morris expresses his belief in this story, as he has often known of geese being killed in a similar manner. When it was ascertained where the fowl came ashore to feed at night in narrow bays, stakes were driven at the edge of the water and a duck gun lashed to them in such a position that it would rake the feeding ground. The gun was discharged from a string leading from the trigger to the blind. No matter how dark the night, the individual in the blind could usually hear the geese feeding in the proper place for a shot.

Beside this more or less open water shooting, many of the tributaries of the Chesapeake are resorted to by large numbers of marsh fowl—black ducks, mallards, teals, sprig-tail and all the marsh ducks—and fair shooting at these birds is still to be had at these places.

In addition to the failure of the feed which—in the belief of many persons—has caused the wildfowl to desert many places in Chesapeake Bay, where they were once abundant, another cause is the increase of the oyster trade, which involves the constant presence on waters formerly frequented by the game, of vessels and craft of all kinds. Besides the disturbance caused by the passage to and fro of such craft, and their working on the feeding ground, all of these boats carry guns or rifles and use them continually. This is against the law, but the game laws are little or not at all enforced on many parts of the bay.

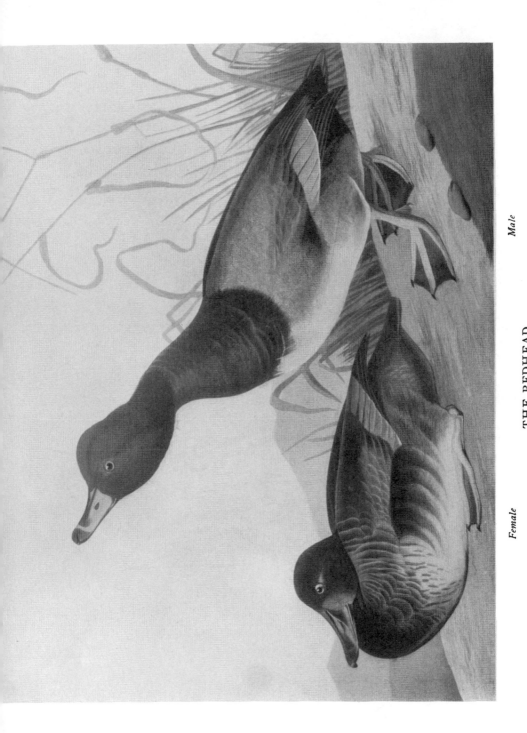

Female

Male

THE REDHEAD.
Reduced from Audubon's Plate.

PART III.

THE ART OF DUCK SHOOTING.

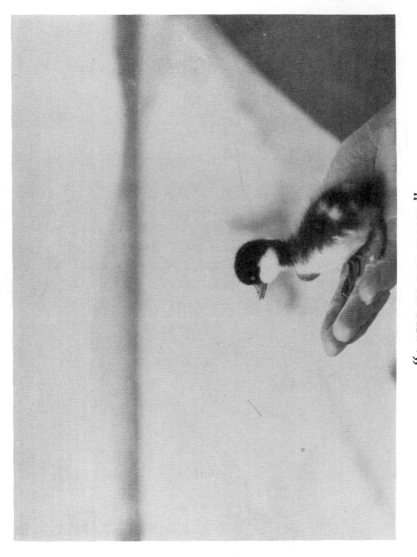

"A BIRD IN THE HAND."

Newly Hatched Golden-eye. Photographed by Wm. Brewster. (See p. 176.)

THE ART OF DUCK SHOOTING.

GUNS AND LOADING.

Wildfowl are in a measure protected against the gunner, not only by their difficulty of access, and by their wariness, but also by a coat of armor—their thick feathers—which is not easily penetrated. Few things are more important to success; therefore, than the gun which a man uses, and the loads which he puts in that gun. About these matters every individual has his own opinion, and as there are many men who gun, so there are many minds about guns and ammunition.

Practically, the 12-gauge gun shoots as strongly and as closely as a larger arm, yet its load is usually smaller, though the circle of its pattern is quite as effective. A friend, who is a remarkable shot on upland game, uses a little five-pound 12-gauge gun, from which he shoots two and a half or three drams of powder and a small charge of shot. With this arm he kills upland game at surprising distances, and on the coast of California has used it with success in duck, and even in goose, shooting. Not very long ago, during a trip to the North Carolina coast, where excellent shooting was had at canvas-backs and other ducks, he used this arm, although advised to take a heavier gun, and to shoot

larger charges.   However, after shooting for a day
and a half, he acknowledged his gun's inefficiency under these conditions, and thereafter used a heavier one.

Each individual has his personal preferences as to
size and weight of gun and the way in which it should
be loaded, and these preferences will depend largely on
the man's experience, the kind of shooting he has been
accustomed to, and that which he purposes to do at any
particular time.   For sea shooting, the choice of most
men will be a heavy gun, weighing perhaps ten pounds,
and of ten gauge, and heavily choked as to its left barrel.   The charge to be used will vary with the arm and
the gunner, for we all know that each gun has its own
idiosyncrasies, and that no hard and fast rule for loading can be laid down.   The gunner should target his
weapon with different charges, at different distances,
from forty to seventy yards, and should experiment
until he has found the combination of powder, shot and
wads to give him the most even pattern at these various
distances.

Many men always carry two guns in the blind, one
of them with the right barrel a cylinder, so-called, and
the left slightly choked, and the other with the right
barrel moderately choked, and the left full choked.
With such a combination one is prepared for almost
any contingency that may arise and can cover a wide
range.

Most men shoot heavier charges of shot than can be
efficiently used, and thereby gain nothing in numbers
killed, but add somewhat to their own discomfort.   In

a certain ten-pound gun, I shoot at fowl one ounce of shot and four drams of powder. This charge of shot will be regarded as small by many gunners, but with it this gun does better work than with any other charge.

The tendency among gunners also is to use too large shot. Number 4 is quite large enough for ducks, certainly for canvas-backs and redheads; while for mallards, pintails, and smaller ducks, No. 6, or early in the season No. 8, is quite large enough. One may kill many geese at long range with fours, although the more common practice is to shoot B shot at them. For swans, BB is large enough, though for long shots at birds far above one, T or O may be used. It is always worth while when going duck shooting to carry a few B cartridges, and eight or ten shells, loaded with the larger shot, for swans. They do not take up very much room, and are sometimes very useful.

While with perhaps a majority of gunners the nitro powders at once came into favor, there was another considerable class, more conservative, which long declined to use them. As time passed, however, the manufacturers overcame very many of the difficulties which at first gave trouble with the product, and, at the present day, the number of men who decline to use it, because they do not regard it as being as effective as black powder, is small. Although the nitro powders are a great advance on the old-fashioned black explosives, they are not yet all of them perfect. As they are chemical and not mechanical compounds, they are subject to certain changes, depending on the conditions by which they are surrounded, and which affect them to a greater or less extent. Thus, some of the powders, if kept in a very dry place, may lose an undue amount of moisture; or, if kept in a very damp place, may gain moisture. It is a good rule, therefore, always to use freshly-loaded cartridges, for after shells have been loaded for a year or two they cannot always be relied on to act evenly. Nine out of ten may seem to be as effective as if fresh, but the tenth may burn so slowly as merely to throw the shot out of the barrel. At the same time, no one who has become accustomed to shooting nitro powders is likely to go back to the jarring, punishing, black powders. There is also abundant testimony that many brands of nitro powder, if properly protected from heat and dampness, retain their efficiency for years.

By using the nitro powders we get rid of the old nuisances of smoke, dirt and recoil, and all appreciate the advantage of this. Is it certain, however, that the adaptation of the nitro powders to small arms gives us any actual advantage beside those of greater comfort?

It is believed by some gunners that the old views about where to hold to hit a cross-flying or overhead bird, must undergo more or less modification since the introduction of nitro powders. Such persons contend that these nitro powders are so much quicker and stronger than black powder that the shot reaches the bird in much less time than when propelled by that, and that, therefore, it is no longer necessary to hold so far ahead as formerly on crossing birds. Good brush shots

who once thought it necessary to allow considerable leeway on crossing shots at quail and partridges,
declare that with the nitro powders it is not necessary
to hold ahead at all, but that the shot strikes the bird if
the gun is held directly on it. It is believed by them
that the increase in the muzzle velocity of shot propelled by nitro powder is about 50 per cent. over that of
black powder. In other words, that a charge of shot
from a nitro powder cartridge will go forty-five yards
while a charge from the black powder cartridge will go
thirty yards. If this is the case, the difference in the
holding will be obvious.

Does the suggested difference in the velocity of the
flight of shot actually exist? Is it true that the nitro
powders send the shot to its mark more quickly than
the old-fashioned black powder, with its smoke, its tremendous report, its cloud of sulphurous smoke and its
jarring recoil? Not only are there many bird shooters
who believe this to be true, but men who shoot at artificial targets from the trap, and others who have had
great practice in refereeing such contests, declare that
the shot goes faster and hits harder when sent by nitro
powders than by black powder. It would seem that experiments must have been carried on by the various
manufacturers of nitro powders which would demon-
strate the truth or falsity of such beliefs.

It is certain that shooters who use the smokeless
powders instantly see the effect of the shot, while with
black powder there is a perceptible interval of waiting while the smoke clears away before the shooter

knows what the result of the discharge of his gun has been, and it is probable that this difference in the time of learning what the shooter has done may in part account for the widespread belief alluded to.

The muzzle velocities of certain powders, with certain loads, have been given in various tests. With the Dupont powder, the velocities in Mr. Armin Tenner's tests are given as slightly under 1,000 feet, the loads running from two and a half to three drams; while a load of three drams, the equivalent of thirty-seven grains, with one and an eighth ounce of shot, gives an average of 1,040 feet. The new Robin Hood smokeless powder claims a velocity of 1,100 feet, with three and a quarter drams, bulk measure, and one and an eighth or one and a quarter ounces of shot.

On the other hand, Curtis and Harvey's Sporting powder is said, as stated below, to give a muzzle velocity of 1,344 feet with a load of four and a half drams of powder and one and a half ounce of No. 4 shot. The pattern with this charge is reported as good.

From the experiments carried on at the works of the Union Metallic Cartridge Company, at Bridgeport, we have the following table, showing how many grains of each one of seven of the best known nitro powders are equivalent to drams of black powder, of which, however, the quality is not specified. In this table the new Robin Hood powder is not included, as perhaps it should not be. Mr. N. P. Leach calls it a new departure, as it is neither a nitro nor a picric powder. It is, he says, "a bulk powder, with high velocity, and gives very little chamber pressure and recoil when fired. In loading it, a black powder bulk measure should be used." This is the table:

COMPARATIVE MEASURES OF NITRO POWDERS.

Black Powder.	*E. C. No. 2.*	*E. C. No. 1 Schultze.*	*Hazard Dupont Oriental Alarm.*	*L. & R.*	*Shot Gun Rifleite.*	*Nobel's Sporting Ballistite.*	*Walsrode.*
2 drams equal to.......	24	28	25	25	24	16	..
2¼ drams equal to.......	27	31½	28	29	27	18	..
2½ drams equal to.......	30	35	31	33	30	20	22
2¾ drams equal to.......	33	38½	34	37	33	22	27
3 drams equal to.......	36	42	37	40	36	24	29
3¼ drams equal to.......	39	45½	40	42	39	26	31
3½ drams equal to.......	42	49	43	45	42	28	35
3¾ drams equal to.......	..	52½	46	48	45	30	38
4 drams equal to.......	..	56	49	50	48	32	..
4¼ drams equal to.......	..	59½	52	..	..	..	..
4½ drams equal to.......	..	63	55	..	..	..	..

The maximum load of Walsrode for a ten-gauge gun is given by the manufacturers as forty grains, which is nearly the equivalent of four and a quarter drams of black powder. For an eight-gauge the maximum charge is fifty-eight grains.

Of the new Robin Hood powder, we are told that three and a quarter drams, bulk measure, well wadded, with one and an eighth to one and a quarter ounce of shot, gives a good pattern. An increased amount of powder, when but one and a quarter ounce of shot is used, gives but a slight increase of velocity, while it destroys the pattern.

If one fires a charge of shot over the water, he sees that the pellets which compose that charge travel at varying velocities and for different distances, and reach the water in a string fifteen or twenty feet in length; and in the same way, when one fires at a target, he finds that the charge of shot spreads out more or less irregularly over a circle whose diameter may be three, four, five or more feet, according to the distance of the target from the gun's muzzle.   The pellets are most thickly clustered about the centre of the target and are greatly scattered near its edges.

Theoretically, the pellets of shot in a cartridge should leave the muzzle of the barrel in the same order which they occupied in the cartridge, each individual pellet then taking its own course.   Those on which the greatest force is exerted, and which for any reason are least retarded, go the straightest and with most velocity, and reach the target first.   Those which are held back by any cause, or which, by crushing, have been deprived of their spherical form, lose much of their velocity, and soon drop out of the direct line of flight.   No gun-barrel, as bored to-day, is a true cylinder, but toward the muzzle all are drawn down so that they are sections of cones; the pellets of shot therefore are violently jammed together just before they leave the barrel, and more or less of them are upset— that is, crushed, so that they lose their sphericity.   Such pellets become at once ineffective. Shot manufacturers have endeavored to compensate for this by hardening the shot, so that it is less easily smashed than the old soft shot, and have succeeded so well that chilled shot is now almost universally used by men who are especially anxious to do effective shooting.

It is thus evident that at ordinary shooting distances only a portion of the pellets in any charge is effective. What this portion is depends on the gun and the load which is used in it. It has been stated that in a true cylinder barrel the killing portion of the load is less than 50 per cent., the remainder of the pellets dropping to the ground, or flying off at an angle, or losing their velocity very rapidly; but in modern guns the proportion is much greater, some guns sending 70 per cent. of the shot to the target at 40 yards.

It has been determined by experiment that about 5 per cent. of the pellets of the charge simultaneously reach a target at forty yards distance from the gun. Very close after this 5 per cent. follows from 25 to 30 per cent. of the charge, and then the remainder of the effective pellets. In his "Breech-loader and How to Use It," Mr. Greener states that in a cylinder-bore gun shooting forty-two grains of nitro powder and one and an eighth ounce of No. 6 shot, the leading pellets reached the target at forty yards in .138 of a second from the time at which they leave the muzzle, while the last pellet to reach the target arrives in .187 of a second after the discharge. In other words, the difference in time is about .05 of a second.

If, as is often stated—but, we believe, without any better foundation than the merest estimate—a wild duck flies at the rate of a mile a minute, the bird during this .05 of a second would pass over a space of about four and a half feet, and, therefore, if struck by the leading pellet, the last part of the charge would miss him entirely. On the other hand, it must be remembered that there is no appreciable interval between the arrival at the target of these pellets; they continue to come, and the .05 of a second merely represents the interval between the very first and the very last pellet to arrive.

In the same work Mr. Greener gives also tables of the velocities of shot with different loads of powder, as determined by Mr. R. W. S. Griffith. The tests were made with a twelve-bore gun, with powder charges of Schultze powder running from two and a half to four drams, and with charges of shot from one to one and a quarter ounce, the sizes of shot being Nos. 1, 5, 6 and 10. The highest velocity with four drams of powder and one and a quarter ounce of No. 1 shot, at five yards, was 1,106 feet, and at sixty, 863 feet. The reader desiring to study this table is referred to the volume in question. Much interesting information is given in standard works on guns and shooting, such as "The Breech Loader," "The Gun and Its Developments," and "The Modern Sportsman's Gun and Rifle."

HOW TO HOLD.

When a charge of shot is fired at a bird, it proceeds through the air somewhat in the shape of an elongated ellipse. From this ellipsoid, which may be twenty feet in length and three or four feet in diameter at its widest part, pellets of shot are continually dropping. The space covered by this shot and the shape taken by it, while, of course, never quite the same for any two gun barrels, is at all events a large one, and it would seem that no bird at which it was discharged could get away, if the gun were held reasonably straight. But we all know that they do get away.

One of the most difficult things in the world is to learn how to hold on your ducks and when to draw the trigger. A great deal has been written on this subject, but to very little purpose. We are told that you should shoot one, two, three, or ten feet ahead of your bird, but when the bird is darting by like the wind, at an unknown distance, how is any man to estimate a distance ahead of him in feet? It may be doubted if it can be done. If birds are coming gently to decoys, or are flying toward the gunner, head on, the gun should be aimed slightly in front of the bird, and then moved ahead just at the moment of pulling the trigger, in order that the bird may fly into the charge and be struck by the centre of it; but a crossing bird, perhaps going with the wind, or flying overhead in calm weather, proceeds at such a rate that no elaborate calculation of feet or inches can be made. The best the beginner can do is to hold well ahead of the bird, trying to gauge his shooting by the effect, holding further and further ahead, until at last he manages to kill. He must learn the lesson of experience, and must strive to profit by each shot, whether he hits or whether he misses.

It will often happen that the gunner will see feathers fly from the hinder part of the crossing duck at which he has shot, and from this he knows that he is shooting too far behind. Sometimes he will aim at a duck, and missing it, will kill one flying several feet behind it.

Yet such a chance may mislead him, for, as shown on an earlier page, he may possibly have hit the first bird with the first pellets of the charge and killed the second with the last pellets. Yet if I were going to give advice to a young duck shooter as to how to hold on his birds, it would consist of these three rules:

1. Hold ahead.
2. Hold further ahead, and
3. Hold still further ahead.

It will be found that the most experienced shooters, whether at ducks or at the trap, are never afraid of holding too far ahead. What they fear is that they will shoot behind their birds. Judgment must be used, of course. One does not shoot at a gentle incoming bird as he does at one sweeping by in full flight. He must be observant and must try to learn just what the effect of each shot is. Much may be inferred from those shots fired at birds flying low over the water, where the relation of the shot on the water to the passing bird can be clearly observed. He should try to see and to remember all that he does, and many of his shots will convey to him a lesson. He should remember all these lessons, and try to profit by them.

If the gunner has with him a companion who has been trained to watch the course of shot, he may request him to watch it and tell him why his charge misses. For be it known that the trap shooters, men who spend much of their time shooting at targets and gauging the flight of shot, declare that it is quite possible to see the charge of shot flying from the muzzle of the gun toward a target, and to determine just where this charge goes with relation to the target. This acuteness of vision is said not to be peculiar to a few men, but to be common to many trap shooters. The observer stands behind and a little to one side of the shooter, and looking at the target, sees the puff of smoke come from the muzzle of the gun. This rushes out about ten feet, and from it darts forward what looks like a long shadow composed of many lengthwise strips; the course of this flying shadow—which is in fact the charge of shot—can be followed to and beyond the target, and we are told that it is the common practice for a trap shooter, when he finds himself missing his targets or his birds, to ask a friend to stand near him and tell him where his shot is going with relation to the target, whether before, behind it, or over or under.

It is rather startling to be told that a charge of shot can be seen by the unaided eye as it flies from the muzzle of the discharged gun; but since we all know that the charge of shot fired from a gun has been photographed, it appears reasonable enough that the trained human eye, under favorable conditions, should be able to detect the passage of a charge of shot through the air. At all events, the matter appears to be one of common knowledge among trap shooters.

Skill in shooting is not born in any one. Just like reading and writing, it must be learned, and, like reading and writing, the more practice one has, the more easily and the better it is done. Many a professional gunner, who is a wonderful shot, would find it labor of the hardest kind to sit down and write a four-page letter; and many a business or professional man, who goes gunning perhaps once in two or three years, finds that killing the fowl that give him shots is something that he cannot accomplish. Many men have noticed that sometimes at the end of a season they can shoot very well; and then, if for two or three years they do not go shooting, they find that they cannot hit anything, and have to begin at the beginning and learn it all over again. They have perhaps forgotten how to hold on their birds, and, beside, their muscles, through disuse, refuse at first to act with the brain as they formerly did. This reflex action, so called, can only be regained by practice.

WHEN TO SHOOT.

No one can learn how to shoot by reading about it in books. The only way that the art can be acquired is by practice. A few hints and suggestions, however, may make this practice more profitable. A common error of beginners—indeed, it is not confined to them—is to shoot at the birds too late. The gunner should shoot at crossing birds before they are up even with him. As a rule, if birds are coming from the leeward, let him rise to shoot as soon as they get over the tail of his decoys, and let him pull the trigger before they get opposite the blind. In the same way, at overhead birds, he should shoot before they are actually above him. If he waits until the moment when they are nearest to him he is almost certain to shoot behind them. While it is true that a man must keep down close and out of sight as much as possible, and while it is also true that certain birds, as black ducks, mallards, teal and widgeon, will flare and begin to climb as soon as they see him, it is better that they should do this than that they should get beyond him before he shoots. If he is obliged to twist around and shoot at them as they are going away, especially if they are birds that have flown over him, he is very likely to shoot behind them.

Experiments made years ago by Major W. McClintock, R. A., and recorded in the *Journal of the Royal United Service Institution,* have been quoted as throwing some light on the question as to how the gunner should hold on his birds. It is said that a charge of four and a half drams best C. & H. powder gives to No. 4 shot a muzzle velocity of 1,344 feet. Inferior powder would, of course, give less. The time of flight for a velocity of 1,300 feet is for 30 yards .093; for 40 yards, .1342; for 50 yards, .1797; for 60 yards, .2311, and so on. This will be about the velocity usu-

ally obtained from a ten-bore gun with four and a half
drams of good powder and one and a half ounce of No.
4 shot.   A bird flying at the rate of a mile a minute
across the line of fire at 30 yards distance would pass
over about 8½ feet while the shot passes through the 30
yards.   At 40 yards the bird would cover about 12 feet;
at 50 yards, about 16 feet, and at 60 yards, not far from
22 feet.

We thus have the basis of a very pretty theory, but,
unfortunately, we do not know the velocity at which
birds fly, and we can only guess the distance at which
they are from us, and can only estimate what 10, 15 or
20 feet ahead is, as we see the bird shooting by us
through the air.   As a matter of fact, we believe there
is no known rule for holding ahead which will do any
one any good.   The only way in which the gunner can
learn how to do this is to practice shooting, and in that
way we should certainly all be glad to learn how to hold.

FLIGHT OF DUCKS.

In connection with duck shooting and the question
as to how to aim at these birds when flying, a vast number of guesses and estimates have been made concerning
the speed with which birds fly.   It is commonly stated
that ducks fly at the rate of a mile a minute, or ninety,
or even one hundred and twenty miles an hour, but we
do not know that any satisfactory observations have

been made to test the birds' flight. The older naturalists, recording the capture of passenger pigeons in New
York with undigested rice in their crops, believed to
have been obtained in the rice fields of Georgia, made
estimates as to the time required to cover the distance
and the consequent speed of the bird in flight. The
process of digestion in all birds is rapid, but it is not
known that this process goes on during the time of
flight or when the bird is actively exerting itself.

Not very long ago an interesting observation on the
flight of the pintail duck was reported by Mr. George
Bird, of New York, whose interest in all matters pertaining to shooting and whose wide experience are
sufficiently well known.

The observation, while it does not give the speed at
which the particular species reported on flies, does show
that it easily flies at a speed of over sixty miles an hour.

In March, 1899, Mr. Bird was traveling through the
Southwest on a special train over the M., K. & T. R. R.
From a slough in the prairie at the side of the track
several pintail ducks sprang into the air and flew along
parallel with the train. Mr. Bird watched them for a
moment or two, and then, seeing that they were flying
at about the same rate as the train, it occurred to him
to look at the speed gauge, which he had been consulting but a moment before. The train was running at
the rate of fifty-two miles per hour, and the birds were
swinging along beside it and not more than forty yards
distant.

A moment or two later they seemed disposed to leave

the train, and swung out over the prairie to a distance of perhaps 1,000 yards from the train, and then, turning again toward the track, swung in and resumed their old position. After a few moments, however, they seemed again to become uneasy, and began to increase their speed, still keeping parallel with the train, but drawing slowly ahead, reminding the observer as he looked at them somewhat of the way in which the faster of two steamboats of nearly equal speed draws away from the slower. This continued until the ducks reached a point where the smoke of the engine was met with, when they suddenly flared up into the air, greatly increased their speed, and in a very few moments were quite out of sight ahead of the train.

The opportunity was one which might never occur again, and the observation one of very considerable interest. The pintail duck is not a very swift flyer if we compare it with such birds as the butterball, broadbill, redhead or canvas-back. At the same time, it is probably as swift a bird as the mallard or black duck, and perhaps somewhat swifter.

Gunners believe that the broadbill, blackhead, canvas-back and redhead are among the swiftest of all our ducks, but it is quite certain that almost all of them fly rapidly enough to at times puzzle any except the most experienced gunners.

ETIQUETTE OF THE BLIND.

Since it often happens that two gunners may shoot out of the same box or the same blind, it is evident that to avoid wasting shots, and to get the most satisfaction out of the shooting, certain rules governing the conduct of each man must be observed. These unwritten laws will be taught most men by their own good feeling and proper instincts; but, on the other hand, it often happens that a very young man in the blind, carried away by excitement and enthusiasm, may do things which in cooler blood he would not think of doing, and which may prove very annoying to his companion.

The laws governing such shooting are well understood by all men of experience, but since each one of us must have made a beginning in shooting, it will perhaps be easier for the inexperienced if some of these laws are here noted.

These unwritten rules are based on the principle that where two men shoot together they are not rivals, each striving to outdo the other, but are partners, working for the common good, which in this case means the success of the day. It is therefore important that no shots should be wasted and that each one should do all in his power to bring to bag the birds which come within shot. Besides this, of course, there are the general laws of good manners, which govern in such a case just as they should in other relations of life.

It is therefore to be understood that the two men should never interfere with each other; they should never fire at the same bird at the same time, and if several come together, the gunners should understand without words which bird belongs to each.

If a single duck comes up that man should shoot at

it from whose side it comes, and he should have the opportunity to use both barrels before his companion
shoots. If the ducks come constantly from one side,
as often they will come from the leeward, turns should
be taken on the single birds. If they come from the leeward, the man to leeward should kill first, but if this is
followed by another single, he should sit back in the
blind and let the windward man kill the duck. Of
course, in case of a miss with both barrels, the man who
has not shot is at liberty to do what he can toward killing the bird. If two or three, or more, birds come up
to the decoys, from any quarter, the man who is to leeward should shoot the bird or birds on his side, and the
man to windward those on his.

Sometimes three birds will come up, let us say, from
the leeward; the leading bird would naturally be taken
by the windward man, while the man to leeward would
take the second one, and the third would be anybody's
bird. A natural exclamation from the leeward man
would be, under such circumstances, "You take the
one in the lead!" but before the birds get up to the point
where they would be shot at, the bird which was leading may have dropped back to second place. In such a
case there is a possibility of a misunderstanding, for,
if the windward man imagined that his companion
referred to the individual duck that was in the lead,
and which is now in second place, both men may shoot
at this duck. Of course, no such blunder should ever
occur. When one speaks of the leading duck he does
not mean the particular duck that is leading at that

moment, but the duck which is ahead when the shots are fired. We have more than once seen a blunder of this kind take place, by which one or more shots were lost.

Under no circumstances will a thoughtful man, with proper instincts, shoot at a bird that properly belongs to his companion. Under no circumstances whatever will he shoot across his companion's face; and if your gunning companion be guilty of such a breach as this, he should never again have an opportunity to shoot in the blind with you.

It is not customary for men who are not well acquainted with each other to shoot in the same blind, but if, by any misfortune, a gunner should find himself in a blind with a man who evidently is so selfish that he wants to kill all the birds, no matter from which direction they may come, he should leave the blind on the very first opportunity, and decline to return to it, or ever again to shoot with this person. Characteristics such as this, which would never be seen under the ordinary conditions of life, sometimes manifest themselves in the blind, and I know of one or two men, who have high reputations as sportsmen and high standing in the community, with whom, under no circumstances, would I share a blind or a box.

Most men, however, do not intentionally impose on their companions, and many, who under stress of excitement will do things which are not fair, and which they should not do, may be checked by a quiet word, and taught by a little precept and a good deal of example to act in the blind as men of good breeding should act everywhere.

There are few things which contribute more to a man's contentment that to have with him in the blind a cheerful, good-natured, generous companion. There is nothing which so greatly detracts from the pleasure of shooting as to shoot with one who does not show a reasonable amount of self-control, and who wants all the shots, or claims all the birds. And so, unless you have as a sharer of your blind some one whom you thoroughly know, and have confidence in, it is far better for you to shoot alone.

CHESAPEAKE BAY DOG.

Every man who guns much for wildfowl ought to have a good water dog. For retrieving of this sort— except in regions where duck shooting is a regularly practiced sport—setters are very commonly used. They, however, have not sufficient strength or stamina for the work, and if constantly used are sure to break down and become valueless in a short time. The same objection applies, but in somewhat greater degree, to the different varieties of spaniels. The work of retrieving in water, mud and ice is exceedingly hard and exhausting, and an animal of great strength and endurance is required for it. Such hardy qualities we find in the Chesapeake Bay dog.

For nearly one hundred years there have been bred about the head of Chesapeake Bay, and in later years in many other localities, a strain of large reddish-yellow dogs, under this name, which are notable for their fondness for the water, and for their strength and endurance. Notwithstanding all the explanations given for the origin of the breed, the well-bred Chesapeake Bay dog shows his ancestry on the surface. He is a Newfoundland dog, and nothing more. Not the Newfoundland of the modern dog shows, which, by crossing with the St. Bernard, has become an entirely different creature, very large, long-backed, heavy-headed and long-coated; but the New-

foundland dog of old times, before there were dog
shows and before this breed had been greatly modified.

The history of this breed is partly traditional and
partly authentic. It is said that about the year 1805
there arrived at Baltimore a ship called the "Canton,"
which at sea had met with an English brig bound from
Newfoundland to England, in a sinking condition. On
this brig were found two puppies, a dog, which was
brown in color, and a bitch, black. These pups were
rescued and became the property of a Mr. Law. The
dog was named Sailor, and his mate, Canton. The
dog passed into the hands of Governor Lloyd, of Maryland, and the bitch became the property of Dr. Stewart,
of Sparrows Point. Their progeny became the Chesapeake Bay dogs.

The dog of the present day is almost always a faded
brown or dark yellow in color, though it is quite usual
to see puppies with some white markings, or even black
and white. It may fairly be assumed that the black
and black-and-white puppies, which are occasionally
produced, being esteemed a bad color for the work the
dogs are expected to do, have been gotten rid of and the
brown or yellow dogs bred from, so that the present
color is due to selection. There are two types of coat,
one short, thick and straight, or slightly wavy, and
the other much longer and tightly curled.

Not a few efforts have been made to improve the
Chesapeake Bay dog by crossing it with other breeds;
the setter, the water spaniel and the English retriever
having been used for this purpose. All of these efforts

have been fruitless. The real Chesapeake Bay dog, so far as I can learn, is better than any crossed animal, and strength, stamina and level-headedness are lost by any cross of which I have heard.

The best color for the Chesapeake Bay dog is that commonly known as sedge color, which is not greatly different from the color of the long hair on the hump of the buffalo, and but little darker than that of the dead cane or grass where the dogs are used, so that it never attracts attention. But any of the faded browns which are common to this race are useful enough.

This dog has an excellent nose, and a duck which has been brought down in the marsh is not likely to get away from it unless it creeps into some hole so deep that the dog cannot reach it or dig it out.

Like every other dog, the Chesapeake requires an education, though this need not be nearly so elaborate as that given to setter or pointer. He must be taught to obey, to remain in the blind until ordered to fetch, and to bring the birds to the hand. Some years ago a correspondent of *Forest and Stream*, signing himself "Cayuga," wrote of this dog substantially as follows:

"The Chesapeake, while still in the period of early puppyhood, takes naturally—or shall we say instinctively?—to retrieving ducks, but some special training must be given him to cause perfect retrieving to your hand. Then, again, this breed seems to require instruction in retrieving other feathered game, such as plover, snipe and rail. It is not a bad thing to give him good yard instruction, teaching him to down, or charge, to whoa, to hide, hold up, and to sneak, or crawl through cover, and, of course, to bring and carry for you. He will learn even quicker than your silky-haired setter, and when you have taught him everything you can think of, and he becomes an accomplished dog, * * * then you will pat that faded-looking coat and swear he is a darling; and when you watch him lying hidden in the wild rice or beside you in the blind, the tip of his brown nose just visible as he keeps a sharp lookout for ducks, sometimes directing your attention to a stray incomer you have not seen, you will say he is the best companion you ever had; but when you see him—at the command—dash through icy-cold water, clambering over and diving under driftwood and cakes of ice after a winged duck, and when after a chase of a mile he gets her, and breasting the billows and current back, places her in your hands so tenderly that not a feather is torn, gives himself a shake, but not close enough to wet you, ready for another plunge, then you will know him for the hero he is. Again, let off both barrels into a flock of fliers and tell him to 'fetch 'em in.' Mark his sagacity. He passes the dead ones and those sorely wounded and goes straight for some cripple that is trying desperately to get away, and she has got to leave the water to escape him. If she dives, down he goes after her. So, one by one, he brings them in, the dead ones nearest at hand last. Oftentimes, in the haste and excitement of retrieving a half dozen or more ducks, he may neglect to place the dead ones in your hand, but, bringing them to shore, leaves them and plunges in again. This may be reason or an inherited quality, but if he is a thoroughbred, properly handled, he will bring the wounded to you, and after the batch has been secured, he will fetch up the pile deposited on the shore."

In the chapter on Point Shooting I have said something about the way in which these dogs work. There are among the old-time gunners witnesses enough to pile up volumes of testimony, showing that for courage, endurance and determination the Chesapeake Bay dogs stand in the front rank of all our breeds. I may quote one or two examples of this. The first, from a writer on Chesapeake Bay waters in *Forest and Stream* signing himself J. C. S., is as follows:

"We began shooting as soon as it was light and had varying success, as neither of us was a crack shot, but with the help of George and the dog we managed to gather twenty-one ducks in a couple of hours. The wind now blew a gale and the river was fearfully rough. Just then we heard a swan trumpeting. It was coming up the river, but beyond the reach of shot. Seizing the .32 rifle, I opened on him, and at the fourth or fifth shot had the good luck to tumble him down with a broken wing. Now came the difficulty. George absolutely refused to go after it, but said the river was too rough, and it was. By this time the dog, Taylor, was almost beside himself, whining and almost crazy to go. Bob loosed him; he ran to the point, and jumped in, and swam in the direction that the swan had disappeared. We stood almost breathless and watched him out of sight. Twenty minutes passed, and no Taylor. Half an hour went by, and no signs of the dog. I felt sorry we let the dog go, and we did not fire a gun after the dog left. Bob looked down his nose and said he guessed he'd seen the last of old Taylor. We packed up and got ready to go home, when George sang out: 'Ki! yi! Bress de Lawd! Heah's Taylah!' And, sure enough, here came the good old dog, nearly fagged out, staggering along the shore, dragging that big swan. He had been gone a little over three-quarters of an hour."*

Another example of the readiness with which these dogs adapt themselves to circumstances is given by Mr. J. G. Smith, of Algona, Iowa, who says: "We had had a fine morning's shoot near a large slough, where there were quite a good many ducks and geese. About nine o'clock we thought the flight was over, so we gathered up our birds and started for the wagon. The country around us was all burnt over. We got out of the slough and onto the high ground, and were walking slowly along, when we saw a large Canada goose making for the slough. We sat down on the burnt ground and I called. The goose answered and turned directly toward us. I called again, and the goose came on, until he got within fifty yards of us. I told my friend to shoot, as he would come no nearer. He shot, and the goose fell almost to the ground. When within about four feet of the ground he seemed to recover, and I told the bitch to go. Away she went after him. They went over a ridge about one-half mile

*For other examples of the work of these dogs see p. 611.

from us. I ran quickly to the top of the ridge, and when I got there I found my bitch coming out of a large slough with the goose in her mouth. It weighed fifteen pounds."

The excellent nose which these dogs invariably have makes it quite certain that they will retrieve all birds that come to the ground. Besides this, they are commonly very careful in the way in which they handle the game, and it is very unusual to find one that will mark the bird with his teeth. This, however, is of course largely a matter of training. They are excellent house dogs, and are usually kind to children and friendly with people whom they know, while at the same time they are excellent watch dogs, always to be depended on as guardians of the home.

DECOYS.

WOODEN.

Although there are conditions under which decoys are not needed for wildfowl shooting, yet usually these are essential to success. The man who proposes to gun regularly must have decoys.

The commonest forms of these are merely wooden blocks trimmed, or whittled, to the shape of a bird's body, to which is attached a separate piece of wood representing the neck and head. Such decoys are painted to imitate the color of the bird's plumage, are weighted below with a strip of lead or iron, to keep them right side up, and to a staple driven into the part of the block representing the bird's lower breast is tied a line running to the weight or anchor that rests on the bottom and holds the decoy in position. From these primitive decoys, which the professional gunners along the shore often make for themselves, and which, in fact, seem often as attractive to the ducks as much more expensive ones, there have developed decoys flat beneath, and with a wooden keel an inch or two deep; shod with metal; decoys of cork, also usually flat beneath; others made of two blocks of cedar, hollowed out and pinned together by wooden nails, and finally, decoys made of canvas, which can be inflated, and from which the air is expelled when they are not in use, so that the decoys can be packed in very small compass.

Sometimes the decoys have glass eyes put in them, and often they are very artistically painted. Quite commonly, however, they are painted with a bright and glossy paint, which glistens and shines in the sun's rays, so that birds approaching them from certain directions instantly recognize that they are not ducks, and decline to come to them. The collapsible decoys had, at one time, quite a vogue. They are open to the objection that they are perishable, and that when holes are made in them, whether by wear or by shot carelessly fired at them, they are useless. Moreover, they are, of course, very light, and in rough or windy weather dance and roll on the water. Under certain conditions, however, they are very effective.

Most practical men seem to prefer the old-fashioned wooden decoys; and, undoubtedly, a stand of good wooden decoys, with two or three or more live decoys toward the head and tail of the stand, forms a combination more efficient than anything else.

The gunner who finds himself without decoys at a place where the birds are coming well, can often supply the lack by using the birds that he kills. If the water is shallow, canes, stiff weed stalks, or willow shoots, sharpened and passed through the neck of a dead duck up to its head, with the other end stuck in the mud, will make of the dead bird a very good decoy. Some gunners always go prepared to make the most of the birds which they kill, in this way. They carry in the boat a number of steel wires about an eighth of an inch in diameter, and two feet long, and as the birds are killed these wires are set in the mud and run up through the duck's neck just far enough to allow the duck to rest as though sitting on the water.

Sometimes at the edge of a pool, or little bay, where ducks have been feeding, a dozen sods or lumps of dirt; of the right size, scattered on the margin and in the shoal water, may attract the birds and bring them down within shot. At certain points in North Carolina we have seen these clods prove very successful decoys.

As has been said, the value of a stand of ordinary wooden decoys is many times increased if there are added to them a couple of live decoys. These, when properly trained, are usually on the watch for birds in the air, and will quack vociferously at black birds, buzzards, herons, or wild geese. If they are not trained, good work for at least a part of the day may be had by separating them, tethering the drake at the head of the decoys and the duck at the foot. They will talk to each other at frequent intervals, and when they see other ducks in the air, both will call. If the weather is mild and still, artificial decoys which have no motion loom up tremendously over the smooth water, and black ducks, widgeon and some other species will not come anywhere near them; but a single live decoy, moving about in the water, calling now and then, and dabbling or splashing, will bring in a bunch of birds at once. They seem to lose all suspicion and pin their faith to the tethered bird. In the same way, in some parts of the country, throwing up the cap is practiced in order to attract birds at a distance, and for the same purpose diving and flapping decoys have been invented. The device of having a string running through an eye on some of the decoys and then passing to the blind, so that when the gunner pulls the string the birds bob up and down, acts somewhat on the same principle.

Live decoys are commonly carried to the marsh in coops, sometimes large enough to hold only one or two birds, and at others a greater number. For one who is gunning frequently, a crate made of heavy wire, but with a wooden floor, is more convenient than the rougher soap box with slats nailed over it that is often used.

In many waters, as has already been stated, it is desirable to provide the live decoys with a stool to rest on. This consists of a long leg—sharp pointed, to be thrust down into the mud—supporting on the upper end a table six or eight inches in diameter, to which the duck may resort after it is tired of being in the water, and on which it can stand, cleanse its feathers and dry off. While a duck, if it is free, can rest on the water for a long time without inconvenience, one that is tethered is likely soon to get wet and chilled, and may become sick.

To the leg of the stool below the table is fastened a leather strap or line running up to two branches, each of which ends in a running noose. After the table has been firmly set in the mud, so that its upper surface is an inch under water, the two running nooses are slipped about the duck's legs snugly, but not so tight as to impede circulation. If these nooses are made of canvas it will be found that they slip much less freely than if of leather, and that the duck, no matter how much it may move around, will seldom or never get free.

Another method of securing live decoys is practiced on northern marshes. It is thus described by Mr. Frank D. Many, who says: "On each duck's leg I sew a small band of light canvas that has a small ring attached to it. Then I have a heavy piece of fish line with a small snap on one end of it. Then about one foot from the snap I put a small brass swivel. This keeps the line from getting tangled. Then at the end of the line, which is about 8 feet long, I fasten a pound weight. I take the duck out of the crate, snap the line to the ring on its leg, throw the weight into the water and the duck after it. The water being any-where from 6 inches to 2 feet deep, this gives the duck a circle about 16 feet in diameter to play around in, and by throwing a couple of handfuls of corn once in a while it keeps them moving and makes a perfect de-coy."

LIVE DECOYS.

At certain points in the East where ducks and geese are scarce, and success in shooting not easily had, very special attention has been paid to the question of live decoys. Not only are birds used in connection with the ordinary wooden decoys, being tethered in the ordinary fashion either in shoal water or on the shore, but beside this, birds are so trained that they may be turned loose to wander among the decoys at will, or may even be thrown from the blind up into the air to fly short distances, and then to alight among the decoys. As already stated, at Silver Lake, in Massachusetts, the various clubs possess hundreds of live goose decoys, of which a large proportion are so well trained that they are thrown into the air. Some account of the methods pursued there is given in the chapter on goose shooting.

At one club they tie out about 70 geese on the beach. These birds are always on the watch, and their calling is likely to attract any wild birds that come within sight. If the wild geese do not come readily to the decoys, the pens in which the geese are kept are opened by pulling a line, and the necessary number of birds for the work in hand are set free and used as fliers. This method of decoying the wild birds is extremely successful. It is the practice to allow the wild birds to swim in near to the decoys, and then to fire one barrel at them on the water and the other as they rise. When there are four or five men in the stand, the result of this is likely to be the destruction of the whole flock, unless it is a large one.

Mr. Townsend's account of houseboat shooting on Lake Champlain shows how black ducks are used as live decoys, as does also an article published in *Forest and Stream,* by Mr. J. O. Phillips, on duck shooting in Massachusetts:

There is a certain charm about shooting in a thickly settled region which one does not get anywhere else. The game is scarce and hard to circumvent, and when a pair or two of shy old black ducks are successfully brought to bag, the satisfaction is often greater than the killing of ten times the number in a more favorable locality.

The season is late October. For two days a northwester has been doing its best to remove the few remaining leaves, until at last the wind has died away and the evening is calm and wonderfully clear. It is likely to be the coldest night of the season, and we go to bed in the best of spirits, almost certain of a shot in the morning.

It is just beginning to lighten a little as we close the farmhouse door behind us and emerge into the breathless stillness of the early morning. The watch-dog ambles up, then wags his tail, turns about and disappears in the gloom of the yard. How hard the ground feels, and what a noise each leaf makes under our feet as we walk briskly toward the lake.

Long streaks of pink and gray appear in the east, but look closer and note that little speck against the sky as it glides downward across a bright band of orange light and drops lower and lower until it vanishes toward the lake. Ducks, twelve or fifteen at least, and we set our teeth and walk harder.

Down toward the woods the path leads. Nothing has been heard save the distant crowing of sleepy cocks, but now a new sound greets us, the cheerful quacking of my faithful decoy ducks.

We hasten into the pines and over a noiseless carpet of dry needles. How dark it is. A rustle in the brush and a faint streak, which show we have waked a rabbit, and a belated flock of robins make the air hum as they spring from a birch·tree above our heads.

Cautiously we creep out on to the point, sheltered on both sides by walls of brush. Ahead of us are the stand and coops, and as we come in sight, a watchful old drake sees us and sends out a ringing call. Instantly a chorus of duck music from out on the water fills the whole air, and we walk boldly ahead, past the coops and into the stand, knowing that no wild birds can hear us through all that racket.

Remove your hat and peer between the branches. Out there on the dark water float the bunches of wooden ducks, while in the shallow water along the beach the live decoys swim and quack. Count them all carefully. To the left there is a flock of fourteen, where there should be but nine, and even as you look, five silent shapes detach themselves from the rest and glide out in front without a ripple, and as if moved by some mysterious power.

Caution is now the word. Against the paling lean three grim sentinels; one an·8-gauge, one a 10 and one a Winchester pump. But do not reach so nervously for your gun. It is always ready loaded, and moreover there is plenty of time, for the game is still two gunshots distant.

Suddenly, with hardly a moment's warning, the wild birds rise in the air with one accord, and vanish against the dark background of the pines on the opposite shore. We feel almost ready to cry. "What frightened them?" you ask. Nothing; it is only a way these shy black fellows have, and we could have done no better.

And now we have time to note the surroundings, the great looming shapes of the distant ice houses, the tall chimneys of the pumping stations, all losing much of their artificial ugliness in the gloom of early sunrise. Behind us runs a high oak bluff, the tree-trunks just beginning to catch the rosy eastern glow. A few teams are heard rumbling over frozen roads, and across the lake we mark a night-watchman trudging homeward, his lantern still lighted and swinging by his side. Slowly and solemnly comes the sound of the Wenham bell. Six times the message is sent out over the still water, and so loud it sounds that you can scarcely believe the church is a mile away.

All this time I am sweeping the lake with the glass, and at last I make out three little specks. They look as if they were drawing toward us. Yes, they are coming, as fast as they can swim. But they are small ducks, and a morning like this we should certainly get a better shot.

Ah, I thought so. There is the bunch we saw drop in earlier. They haven't noticed us yet, but we will see what we can do.

Softly, one after another of the flyers is lifted from the coop, and sent sailing out over the line of ducks, which reply in a deafening chorus. Some of them waddle back to the expected corn, and are again scaled.

The small ducks, buffleheads they are, have approached to within 15 yards of the beach, and are resting in a little knot, their heads tucked under their feathers. It would be easy to kill all three with one barrel, but we must wait.

The big bunch have made up their minds, and slowly, ever so slowly, they begin to push toward us. You would scarcely believe they were moving, but every time you look they are a bit closer. Unless the unforeseen occurs, as it sometimes does, we are pretty certain of a fine shot.

They have reached a bunch of block decoys and stop, puzzled for a moment. Quickly hand me that little drake. See! he has done the work, and watch how eagerly they follow him, as he swims toward the beach.

Take the 10-gauge, and be very careful you do not show yourself. I will count three, and we must shoot together at exactly the same moment. Let them get as near as we want them; about 25 yards will be the most effective range for the open barrels of our big guns. I see you would pull now if I were not here to stop you, but above all things don't get excited or we are sure to make a mess of things.

One, two—hold! They have spread again, and we must wait for a better chance. One, two, three—we pull well together, and a deafening roar, a great splashing of ducks, and a chorus of squawks from frightened decoys, is the result. Lucky is the man who can single out his bird and kill with the left barrel. I missed clean, and am too busy shooting at cripples with the pump gun to see what you are about.

The fusillade is over, and we count eight dead ducks. Two only have flown away, besides the three buffle-heads, while one is swimming some 200 yards out.

Slaughter, mere butchery, I hear some one say. But come with me and watch them, possibly four mornings, your eyes glued to sky and water, with nothing but a meager ruddy duck to reward your patience. Then, when the longed-for moment arrives, you will grasp your trusty 8-gauge with as much pride as a quail shooter his light 16.

We have collected in all nine plump black ducks, fresh from their summer home, and with few exceptions as finely flavored as any bird that swims.

You will scarcely believe that we have been in the stand two hours. Game was in sight nearly all the time, and now that the excitement is over we remember that we are hungry, and shouldering our game, tramp proudly back to breakfast.

BREEDING WILDFOWL.

It is only within a very few years that breeding wild geese and ducks has been seriously attempted. At present, however, a number of persons are very much interested in this pursuit, and there seems good reason to believe that after a few years more of experiment, a number of species of our wildfowl will be so far domesticated that they can be depended on to breed in confinement. At present mallards and black ducks are practically the only live decoy ducks that are to be had, but at various points in the country a few Canada geese are being bred.

The oldest and most successful Zoological Garden in the United States is that at Philadelphia, which has long been under the able superintendence of my friend, Mr. Arthur Erwin Brown. The Zoological Society has been remarkably successful in caring for the animals exhibited. An inquiry of Mr. Brown concerning the breeding of wildfowl there, has drawn from him the following note:

"We have exhibited in our garden, 57 of the 196 species of swans, geese and ducks recognized by the British Museum catalogue, but I confess that we have not been successful in breeding them. A public garden is not the best place in the world in which to breed birds, for their nesting habits are usually shy, and there are too many people around during the long incubating period. Still, we ought to have done better, and I do not fully understand why we have not; except that our ponds are a good deal exposed to visitors.

"We have bred and raised many Egyptian geese, mallard ducks, redheaded ducks and summer ducks. The mute swan, the Canada goose, the Chinese goose and others have nested but failed to hatch. Those that we have bred, were in a large lake with cover on the island, and the young have simply been let alone, with the result that all grew up except a few that fell victims to rats. I have no doubt at all that many water fowl which do not breed in a Zoological Garden, would do so in the seclusion of private ponds."

At a club in Currituck Sound, where there is a stand of from twenty to twenty-five wild geese, two or three of the birds lay and hatch each year. The number raised, however, is comparatively small, for the eggs are few, and the danger to the goslings after they are hatched, from minks, coons, and other wild animals, very great. At other points goose breeding is more successful, and no doubt a considerable number of the birds are reared in captivity each year.

As time goes on, the captive wildfowl will no doubt adapt themselves to their surroundings so far as to breed in confinement. The late Major Fred Mather was at one time the owner of a very considerable flock of wildfowl of various sorts. He met the usual difficulties and discouragements, but was successful in raising many wood ducks, and bred other species. An account of his flock, written a year or two before his death, was published in *Forest and Stream*, and is, in part, as follows:

Discarding all the old-squaws, sea coots, whistlers, and other birds which cannot be confined to a diet of grain, vegetable and such animal food as our tame ducks get, there are ten American ducks well worthy of domestication and of keeping pure, by one who loves to have such things about him. Few know how beautiful a living wood duck or teal is, or how one gets to love them and have them about. What if a green-winged teal, the smallest of all ducks, is no larger than a pigeon; the question is not one of meat as it was with primitive man, when he domesticated the mallard. I have spent more dollars than I could well afford on this fancy, and if wealthy would prefer it as a "fad" to any other. A few surplus birds were sold, but not enough to pay for many wild birds which came dead, when the only thing left for me was the express charges. Then there was food, loss by minks and other vermin; but I never faltered.

When you get a wild bird never clip a wing, unless as a preliminary to pinioning shortly after. When you cut the stiff quills of the primaries, they will split in time and become like "hang nails" on a human hand; they split up into the flesh and become sore, do not shed, and sometimes cause blood poisoning. If they shed and new feathers grow, the bird must be caught and clipped twice a year, with a chance of its escape.

A bird once pinioned needs no more attention, and is prevented from flying while it lives. Only one wing must be pinioned, so that an attempt to fly turns it over on the ground. Lay the bird on its back, wrap a towel about one wing and the body, leaving the other free. Have your assistant, who holds the bird, press his thumb on the main artery where he feels the pulse, at the point marked P in the illustration. Pluck the fine feathers between the joint A and the line C, and

also four of the secondary feathers whose quills come
in the line of the proposed cut, B.   Never unjoint the
wing at A; it leaves a large knuckle which will continually get bruised and sore.   No surgeon would am-
putate a leg or an arm at a joint.

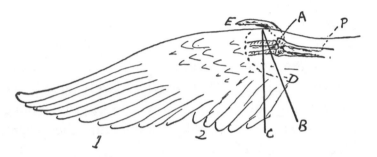

Having bared the part of feathers, make a cut on
the line B, from close to the junction of the little
thumb E, to the wing.   If you cut on the line C, there
will be several secondary feathers left, and birds so
pinioned can often fly over a fence and for some distance.   There is merely a skin over the two bones on
the line B, and but a trifling cut need be made.   Then,
with a stout knife, cut the bones, taking care not to cut
the skin back of them.   Turn up the ends of the bones;
skin back to the dotted line D, thus leaving a flap to
turn over the amputation.   Stitch this flap over the
wound with three or four stitches of sewing silk, no
cotton; bend down the little thumb with the silk so
that the scar will be protected, and let the bird go.

Properly performed, there should be no loss of blood,
to speak of, and the wound will heal in three days.
I once pinioned twelve ducks inside an hour, and if

they had been handed me without delay, I could have easily made the number fifteen. Care must be taken that no bone protrudes or the wound will never heal. I have brought pinioned birds with protruding bones, where some thoughtless fellow had merely chopped the wing off with a hatchet. Such birds are always poor, and will never breed. Of course, I amputated the wing above the joint A, and made a clean job and a healthy bird.

With young birds, at six or eight weeks old, or as soon as the pinfeathers start, all that is necessary is a pair of sharp scissors to clip the line B, leaving the thumb.

Ankylosis is a Greek term often used in pathology for a stiff joint. Our joints must be used or they protest, as we see when we have been "cramped up" in a car or coach all day. Keep an elbow or knee in a fixed position for three months, more or less, and it is no longer a joint, the disease known as ankylosis has set in, and there you are.

When a bird is pinioned, the mutilation is plainly shown when it stretches its wings for exercise of its joints, but when the wings are closed, only a careful observer would note that the primaries of only one wing reached above the back. I would not now pinion a bird larger than a mallard; because the bones are large, the birds are heavy, and there is a better way to do it, so that when at rest the birds are perfect, and only when they stretch their wings is there any evidence that they are not symmetrical.

This plan is best for geese, pelicans, sandhill cranes, swans and other large birds. The tools are fine soft copper wire and an awl of proper size.

Have an attendant or two to hold the bird, which must be blindfolded. Draw the wing back at the joint marked A in the cut; drill holes in several of the primaries and secondaries, marked 1 and 2; put the wires through in several places, binding the feathers together so as to keep the joint from moving; fasten the wires and the job is done.

The joint will become ankylosed before the next month, the feathers will be shed, but that wing can never be extended for flight, yet the bird is perfect. We occasionally meet men with stiffened joints, caused by improper treatment, but there is no suffering after the first few days of so confining a joint, Nature cares for that, and while this treatment is best for large birds, I am not sure but it would be best for smaller ones.

Of the cinnamon teal I know nothing, but have owned and bred both the blue-wing and the green-wing. If there is a wild duck that inherits less fear of man than these two teal I don't know it. Of the two, perhaps the slightly larger blue-wing is quicker to make friends with man, but here is a story of the green-wing.

At the New York fish-hatching station at Cold Spring Harbor, Long Island, I had a fair collection of my pets. There was a long, no-account pond made by throwing up a highway, and in this the tide rose and fell. A picket fence on one side and poultry netting on the other, held a few ducks, some green-wing teal among them. Every day, and several times a day, I took them watercress, duckweed, lettuce, cabbage, or other delicacies, in addition to their grain and animal food, and always talked to the birds as they fed. Talking is a most important thing in the domestication of wildfowl, as it is in the training of domestic animals. The talk was always the same: "Hello, little birds; I never did see such pretty little birds; come up here and get some good things." There was no thought that the words would be understood, but there was finally a distinct connection between them and the feeding, so that when the corduroy working coat was left off, and a morning trip to the city in frock coat and "nail-keg" hat was in order, the flock would follow me when I was outside the picket fence, if I saluted them with: "Hello, little birds," etc.

May came, and the flock was short one female green-wing. With an anathema on all minks and weasels, there was work to be done in the hatchery, and the little teal was forgotten, until one morning she appeared on the pond with four fluffy little balls of down, about as big as a piece of soap after a hard day's washing. They could swim well, and had implicit confidence in their mother, who evidently thought them young teal, but they could have taken refuge in a 10-bore gun with room to spare. I called the men from the hatchery, and we netted the family out. Mr. Teal was off conviving with friends, and paid no attention

to the raid on his family; but Mrs. Teal, when captured, looked up at me and remarked: "Quack, quack,"
and was answered in the same language. This was
satisfactory, and when she was put in a special pool
with her young, she seemed to realize that man was
not only her friend, but the friend of all that she held
most dear, and, mother-like, would give her life for.

As the blue-wing teal is the easiest to approach of
all wild ducks, so their young are naturally tame. I
would much like a chance to try the effect of keeping
the young of both these teal without pinioning, as has
been done with mallards.

I have bred more of the wood duck than any other
species. When I began the work they were the only
wild ducks that I could get in quantity. They were
netted in great numbers in Michigan for market, and
as I would pay several times the market price, I bought
large numbers, and helped stock zoological gardens in
Europe. In the late '60's and early '70's not one bird in
ten would lay eggs for me, but I raised a few. Then,
when I left Honeoye Falls, N. Y., in 1876, the flock
had to be disposed of. From that time until 1883 I
had no country home, where my pet fancy could be resumed. Then these birds were scarce, the once prolific
Michigan lake where Northern-bred birds stopped to
feed on their way South in early fall no longer paid
the netters, but I got a few.

I doubt if this bird can ever be domesticated. I
learned how to breed them with certainty, but after
being bred for ten generations in confinement, they

would escape, if possible, and never return. They distrust man after he once catches them to pinion them, when a few weeks old. They have been so tame as to run to meet me with a dish of bread and milk, or other food, and climb into it and feed greedily until once taken in hand. Then they became suspicious. No bird likes to be taken in hand. The stiff quills must hurt when pressed into the flesh. Pigeon men handle their birds by a grip on the wings close to the body; ducks should be so handled. Domestic hens may be handled by the legs. The man who takes a duck by the legs will have a crippled bird that must be killed, for their legs are weak, and all attempts to heal a broken leg by splints or plaster bandages, by me, have been failures, but then it is recorded that I am not a surgeon.

On a later trial of breeding these birds, there was a train of thought something like this: In nature every female breeds; with me it has been only one in ten; the climate is right, for they breed here; the trouble must be in the food. In western New York I have fed corn, wheat, rye and oats, with such vegetation as lettuce, purslane, "pusley," young cabbage, watercress and duckweed, all of which they were very fond of, yet they laid their eggs sparingly. Evidently something was lacking, and then the fact that they had been seen to pick insects from overhanging leaves, eat frog spawn and gobble up polly-wogs and snails as well as small frogs, suggested that what was needed to round out their natural diet was animal food. The new ration having been issued in the next February, there was rejoicing in April and May, when every pair of wood ducks began nesting.

All the wildfowl of my acquaintance nest on the ground, with the following exceptions: some "tree ducks" of Central and South America, wood ducks, Chinese mandarins and the pretty little "hooded merganser," also called "little saw bill." If the other mergansers, or "sheldrakes," nest in trees, I do not know, but suspect them of it.

The ducks which nest on the ground may be left to their own devices, if you give them a chance for seclusion, but for those which nest in hollow trees we must provide natural conditions. Take a box 12 inches high by 7 inches square inside, tight on all sides, but with a round 4-inch hole in the middle of one side, set it on a post 2 feet above ground, with a slanting board leading to the hole, in which fine straw and leaves are placed, and the bird will do the rest. The male wood duck and mandarin will stand guard at the entrance for a while, but tire of it before the four weeks are up, and abandons the job. Some males injure the young, and it is best to remove the drakes before hatching. I have had two broods in a season by removing the first nesting eggs, but otherwise one brood is the rule. The male moults in June, and will not take any part in a second brood; he then resembles the female, and does not get his bright plumage again until August. Young drakes show red on the bill at two months old.

Hens are useless for hatching the small, tender ducks, and the little woodie is very tender. The young ducks come to her for shelter, and she kicks them to death by scratching for them. I have lost several broods in this way. Then I got the "call ducks," those dwarf, or bantam, mallards bred in Holland for calling wildfowl—cute little ducks, the female being persistently noisy if separated from her mate—but the "calls" were not broody when I wanted them to be, or I did not have enough of them.

The first year a wood duck has four to six eggs, the next year eight to twelve. The greatest number that I ever got from one was seventeen.

Some writers claim that the mother takes them in her bill and others say that she carries them on her back. I had a string of pens back of my house—a pair in each, for they are better to be separated—and usually I found the mother and her brood on the water in the morning; but on two occasions I saw them leave the nest. The mother went first to the pool and called: she had brooded them for twenty-four hours, or more, and they were strong. Then one after another the little things climbed out of the box and tumbled to the ground, or to the water.

They had to climb 4 to 6 inches of plain board, but they did it. I have seen them climb a 10-inch base board and go through a 1-inch poultry netting when alarmed. They weigh nothing worth mentioning, and they have claws as sharp as cambric needles. They have pricked my hands until they bled when pinioning them at eight weeks old. I can easily believe that they can climb up a hollow tree and drop 20 feet into the grass without injury. What need of such sharp claws and climbing ability if not for leaving the nest?

I once had a wood duck that climbed 3 feet of poultry netting by aid of wings, and then sat on the selvage wires, which were less than $\frac{1}{4}$ inch in diameter, and this shows how small a thing their feet can grasp. She went outside into a swamp every day, and tried to coax her mate out, but he wouldn't, or couldn't, and she gave it up and nested in the box provided for her. Usually there was a 3-inch strip on top of the netting to prevent this.

I have spoken of the mandarin duck. It is a Chinese bird that in everything but color is a wood duck. The prevailing hue with them is old gold. The male has two "fans" on its wings, broad-webbed single feathers, which it can erect, swan fashion. Tastes differ in comparing the mandarin with our native bird; the colors are not so bright, but there is the softness of hue which we admire in Oriental rugs.

The redhead is bred in Europe, where it is known as "pochard," but the canvas-back they have not. I had many inquiries for this bird from over the water, and went to Havre de Grace, Md., to try to get cripples or netted birds, but got only promises. The gunners there get $3, and over, a pair for them, and I offered $15, and would take ten pairs, but got none.

The widgeon, both American and European, I have had, but never bred from them; the minks would not permit it. The pintail I bred once, but lost the brood.

If I ever try to breed our beautiful wildfowl again, the pools will be made mink-proof by a brick or stone foundation 2 feet under ground, and 1 foot above it. The fence on this, with inviting openings for a mink to enter and remain in a trap until he has an interview with me.

Mr. Wilton Lockwood, of Boston, Mass., is an enthusiastic devotee of wildfowl breeding and has had great success, but I am unfamiliar with the details of his work.

BLINDS, BATTERIES AND BOATS.

HOW BLINDS ARE MADE.

In duck shooting a blind is anything that conceals the gunner from the birds. It may be a pit, or a sunken barrel, or a fringe of leaves or bushes, or a pile of ice cakes, or a stone wall; but whatever it is, it must be something to which the birds are so far accustomed that they will not notice it as markedly different from the rest of the landscape and so be suspicious of it.

Of late years various artificial blinds have been devised. One is a screen made of burlap, behind which the gunner hides. Burlap is of precisely the proper color for a blind in autumn or spring, but an obvious objection to putting up a more or less tight screen of this sort is that when the wind blows, as one always hopes it will when he is duck shooting, the blind is likely to be carried away, or at least to be flattened to the ground.

Another artificial blind is a coat and hood made of grass. This turns the gunner into what looks like a Robinson Crusoe, but we can imagine that under some conditions it may be a useful disguise.

Along the South Atlantic coast, the commoner forms

of blinds are made from the reeds or bushes of the marsh along which point shooting is done. On the great lakes and rivers of the North, blocks of ice or heaps of snow are used for winter shooting; and for fall shooting, hiding places composed of flat stones laid up into a wall, and built so early in the season that when the ducks arrive in their migrations, they see the blinds and become accustomed to them as natural features of the landscape. In the West, weeds, cornstalks, straw and other material commonly found in the fields may be used in the construction of blinds.

The bough houses in the Chesapeake Bay are built early, and being unoccupied until the shooting season begins, have no terrors for the ducks, which have become accustomed to them. These bough houses are commonly built over the water—often at quite a long distance from the shore—by driving down four stout poles until they are solidly fast in the mud or soil, connecting these poles by strips of scantling or two-inch stuff, placing a flooring of plank on this frame, and then, at the height of three and a half or four feet above the flooring, tacking a railing to the corner posts. Over the four sides of this structure, boughs of evergreens—cedar or pine—are tacked so as to conceal the fresh lumber and the persons within the blind. On the fourth side, which usually faces toward the shore, a door or passageway is left for ingress and egress. Often the water in the neighborhood is baited. Such bough houses are provided with chairs, shelves for ammunition and other conveniences.

The bush blinds of the eastern shore of Virginia, of Back Bay, Currituck Sound, and the other sounds to the southward, which are to-day such favorite resorts for fowl, are much simpler. As a rule, the waters are very shoal, and the bush blinds consist of nothing more than a number of stiff pine branches, with the foliage still attached, shoved down into the water close to the sides of the gunner's skiff. After he has tied out his decoys, he poles his skiff into the open end of this cluster of surrounding bushes, and, crouching down, is perfectly concealed from the birds, except when they are immediately above him. As the bush blinds are often built on the feeding grounds, they are likely to interfere greatly with the comfort of the fowl, which perhaps pass from one bush blind to another, constantly shot at as they sweep over the decoys, and if they find all their feeding grounds occupied, may fly a long way, and for some time afterward shun the places where they have been so fusilladed.

As the goose shooter in the West digs his pit in the stubble, so the goose shooter in the East occupies his goose box, which may be wholly above land or water or may consist of a cask or box deeply sunk in the edge of the marsh or in the mud flat. In either case the gunner is wholly out of sight until he rises to shoot, and the birds have no warning whatever. In character, these devices thus are approaches to the battery or sink-box and the sneak boat, which are floating engines sunk so nearly to the water level that they cannot be seen until the birds are immediately over them.

THE BATTERY.

The battery is a watertight box, just long, wide and deep enough to contain a man lying down, set in the middle of a solid platform which floats it. From one end and the two sides of the platform, wings—loosely hinged to the sides so that they may rise and fall with the waves—run out over the water. Usually all about the margin of the box are narrow screens of sheet lead which, when turned up, oppose four or six inches of height to any wave that by chance may break over the wings and deck, and so keep the water out of the box in which the gunner is reclining. The deck and its wings should be as near the level of the water as possible, and to this end the box must be ballasted; more weight, of course, being required for a light man than for a heavy one. On the platform commonly rest a number of decoy ducks, cast from iron, to sink it to its proper level. At the head end of the box, there is often what is called a head-board, a little pillow of wood to raise the gunner's head, so that his eyes are just above the level of the box.

The battery is commonly anchored on the feeding ground, head to the wind, and the decoys are put out about it and strung away to leeward, though most of them are on the side of the box toward which the gunner shoots. (See diagram facing page 434.) The fowl coming up to the decoys are expected to fly over those to leeward, and to the left, and the gunner, as they come, rises to a sitting position and shoots.

Sometimes double batteries—to be used by two men —are employed.

Boxes are sometimes made about four feet square at the water's level, and four feet deep, the sides sloping inward toward the bottom, so that there the box is only about eighteen inches square. There is a small platform, and there are small wings, a seat, and a shelf. There is abundant room to get down out of sight if the birds are coming.

A better notion of the battery and its constructions will be had by referring to the plans and specifications given herewith. The gunner's comfort depends largely on the box, and it should, therefore, be constructed of the best material—that is to say, of white pine or white cedar—and be absolutely tight. The ends of the box may be of the same material as the sides, but should be thicker. Sometimes the ends are made of white oak, one and a half inch thick. Running across the platform at the head and the foot of the box, are two oak timbers firmly bolted to either end of it. These should be six inches longer than the platform is wide, and should project three inches on either side, thus offering some support to the side wings, and not leaving the hinges to bear all the strain. The platform should be well fitted and tight, and battens may be nailed across the boards at either end of the platform, and one on either side of the box, running out to the edge of the platform, and firmly braced to the box by angle irons.

In old times the wings were made of boards hinged

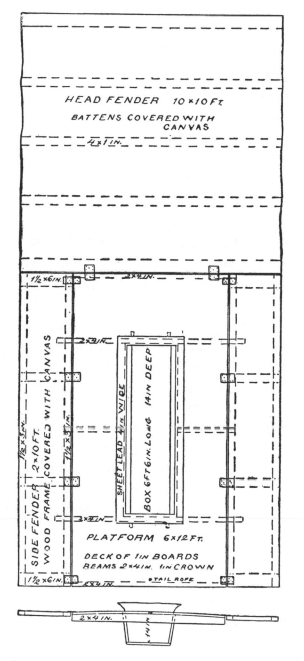

HEAD FENDER 10×10 FT.
BATTENS COVERED WITH CANVAS
4×1 IN.

1½×6 IN.   2×4 IN.

2×3 IN.

SIDE FENDER 2×10 FT.
WOOD FRAME COVERED WITH CANVAS
1½×3 IN.

7½×3 IN.

SHEET LEAD 4 IN. WIDE
BOX 6 FT. 6 IN. LONG   14 IN. DEEP

2×3 IN.

PLATFORM 6×12 FT.
DECK OF 1 IN. BOARDS
BEAMS 2×4 IN. 1 IN. CROWN

1½×6 IN.   2×4 IN.   TAIL ROPE

2×4 IN.   14 IN.

PLAN OF SINGLE BATTERY—TOP AND END VIEWS.

together, but they did not keep down the sea, were
noisy, and had other objections.   The modern battery
differs from that of old times chiefly in its head wing,
or head fender, as it is often called.   This is a piece of
canvas nearly square, stained gray, and as wide as the
platform and the two side wings, which is tacked to
four or five strips of wood which keep it floating
on the water, the strips lying under the canvas.   The
color of the canvas should be made, as nearly as possible, that of the water in which the battery is to
be used.   To the middle of the last strip—that is
to say, the one furthest from the battery—an anchor rope is tied, to which the anchor is fastened.
When the battery is rigged, this anchor is thrown
overboard and the head fender is unrolled to its full
length.   This is commonly done by using a light
boat-hook ten feet long.   The point of the boat-hook
is inserted in the hole through which the anchor rope
is fastened, and the head fender is thus forced away
from the battery until it lies flat upon the water;
then by using the boat-hook as a pole and shoving
on the bottom, the battery is pushed to leeward until the anchor rope is taut.   The battery will usually
then swing so that the head fender is directly to windward of the battery.   But sometimes—for example,
when the tide is running at right angles to the wind,
and the wind is light—it may be necessary to use the
boat-hook to overcome the force of the tide, and to
anchor the battery in its proper position.

From the foot of the platform or deck, another rope

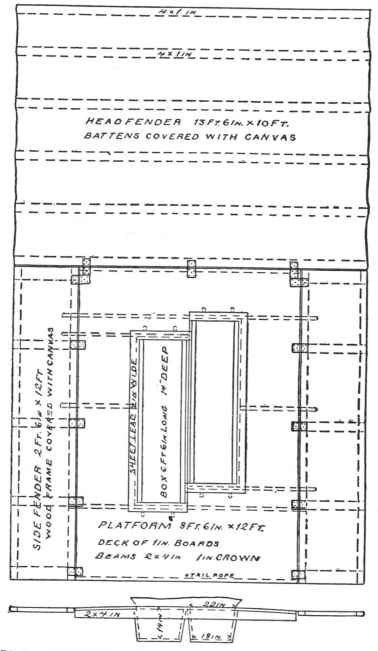

PLAN OF DOUBLE BATTERY—TOP AND END VIEWS.

runs out, and to this a stone is attached for a foot anchor.   This is thrown overboard after the head anchor
rope is taut, and this holds the battery head and foot.
The foot anchor is within reach of the gunner occupying the box, and the stone is used because it can
easily be hauled up, while often an anchor could not be
lifted.   In case of a change of wind, this arrangement
enables the gunner to trip the foot anchor and let the
battery swing with the wind.   He can then throw out
his foot anchor again, and still have his battery properly adjusted to the wind.

If, however, there should be a decided change in the
direction of the wind, both battery anchors must be
lifted, and the battery towed around to a new position
and the decoys rearranged to suit the change.

When the battery is on board the sloop, the head
fender is rolled up and rests on the battery's deck,
being secured by a stop at each end.

A boat-hook is a necessary implement with a battery.
It should be light but strong, and it is a good plan to
mark the staff, from the point of the hook up the pole,
with a scale in feet and half feet, so that it can be used
as a sounding rod to ascertain the proper depth of
water to rig in on the flat.   This depth rarely exceeds
six feet, the average being perhaps four and a half
feet.   The boat-hook is kept in the stool boat, but it is
a great convenience to have in the box a rod just short
enough to lie in the box, and armed with a hook at
one end.   Such a rod is very convenient in hauling up
the tail stone, or pulling in the side fenders, or regulat-

ing the decoys near the battery. It is especially necessary when the tail stone has been pulled out on account of some slight shift of wind, and the decoys must be reset alongside of the battery.

Most single batteries are equipped with eight iron duck · decoys, each weighing about twenty-three or twenty-five pounds. The weight of the gunner, of course, regulates the number of these to be used, and the weather conditions may also have a bearing on this, since, sometimes by removing a few of the iron decoys, a battery may be used in quite rough water, although the ducks will not come up as well if the battery stands high.

Double batteries require an increased number of the iron duck decoys, or sometimes the number is lessened, and side weights, weighing usually fifty-six pounds—and by batterymen called 56's—are hung on the timbers of the battery platform under the side fenders. These are cut away on the end, so as to be somewhat notched, and the weight is hung by a looped rope. A hook, something like a cotton-hook, is used to lift these weights off and on.

Since the gunner reclines in the box, it is evident that any water which may enter it will cause him discomfort; it is therefore the practice to have a bottom-board of some light stuff, about the length of the box, but less wide by one quarter of an inch on either side, so that the water which enters may flow down under it. This board is raised above the box by very thin cross strips tacked to it, and at its lower end it is cut in two, so that a piece, perhaps a foot long, may be raised to bail out water if it should become necessary. On the top of the bottom-board, perhaps ten inches from the head of the box, a narrow strip is tacked, which holds the edge of the slanting head-board, which lifts the gunner's head so that he can see over the top of the box.

Most batteries of to-day have in them a head-board —just referred to—that is to say, a slanting board running from the end of the box down to the bottom, at a gentle angle, which serves as a pillow to lift the batteryman's head high enough so that his eyes are above the edge of the box. Upon this head-board may be placed a rubber pillow, but most men use an old coat or something of the sort to rest the head on.

The method of setting out decoys in battery shooting has been described and illustrated already.

SPECIFICATIONS FOR DOUBLE AND SINGLE BATTERIES.

BOXES—Inside length, 6 ft. 3 in. to 6 ft. 6 in.; inside width, at top 22 in., at bottom 18 in.; depth, 14 in.; sides, 1 in. thick; ends, 1 1-4 in. thick; bottom, 1 in. thick and laid crosswise. Boxes pinned to platform by locust-wood pins, two to head and two to foot of each box.

PLATFORMS—Beams, 2 in. thick and 4 in. deep at centre, with 1 in. crown to upper side; deck, 1 in. thick.

HEAD FENDERS—Battens, 1 in. thick and 4 in. wide, with canvas tacked on top.

SIDE FENDERS—Frame of 1 1-2 in. strips from 3 to 6 in. wide, as per plans, with canvas tacked on top.

FENDERS joined to platform by hinges of leather or canvas.

SHEET LEAD 6 in. wide to be tacked around edges of boxes, to be bent as required when seas wash over the platform.

SKIFFS AND SNEAK BOATS.

It is hardly necessary to say much about gunning skiffs, for there are almost as many sorts of these as there are places where gunning is practiced. Usually the gunners of each locality have developed for themselves the form of a boat best suited to their needs, and as a rule the wandering sportsman may have confidence in the boat of the locality.

On the New England coast, the commonest gunning skiff is flat-bottomed, partly decked over, but with a roomy cockpit protected by combings. A much larger vessel of the same type is used on the southern broadwaters. These skiffs are good and serviceable boats, both speedy and stiff. Sometimes, on the New England coast, one will see one of the little flat sculling boats shaped like a pumpkin seed, flat in the water, and just about long enough for a man to lie in. In the South, open, flat-bottomed skiffs drawing very little water are used, or sometimes dug-outs. One of the most useful boats for general purposes, and one which has a wide popularity North and South, is the Barnegat sneak box. It can be sailed, or rowed or poled, and may also be used somewhat like a battery, being sunk almost to the water's level by taking sand or water-bags aboard, and concealed by spreading sand or dead grass on the flat deck.

On some waters gunners carry rubber bags in their boats, and when they reach the ground, fill the bags with water, and placing them on either side of the centreboard trunk, sink the sneak boat until its deck is awash.

The following description of one of these boats is taken from *Forest and Stream:*

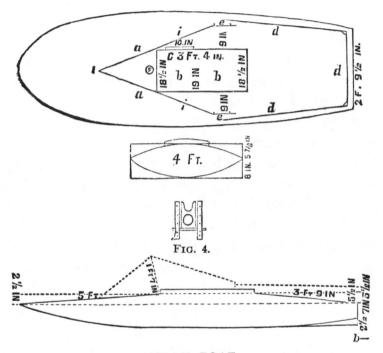

FIG. 4.

SNEAK BOAT.

a, a—apron. *i, i, i* shows where it is nailed to deck. *b, b*—Cockpit. *c*—Trunk. *d, d, d*—Stool rack. *e, e*—Rowlocks. Fig. 4 shows rowlocks.

Length, 12 feet; width amidships, 4 feet; width of stern, 2 feet 9½ inches; depth of stern, 7 inches. Sprung timbers, all of one pattern, 9-16 x 13-16 inch; distance apart, 8 inches; deck timbers, natural bend, 1 x 7-9 inch.

Cockpit, inside measurement, length, 3 feet 4 inches; width at bow and stern, $18\frac{1}{2}$ inches; amidships, 19 inches. Combing, height of inside at bow and stern, $2\frac{3}{4}$ inches; amidships, 2 inches. From bottom of combing to top of ceiling, 13 inches. Trunk on port side, set slanting to take a 15-inch board trunk placed alongside and abaft of forward corner of combing. Boards of boats, white cedar, $\frac{5}{8}$ inch; deck, narrow strips, tongued and grooved. Rowlocks, height, 6 inches, from combing, 9 inches; middle of to stern, 4 feet 7 inches, made to fold down inboard and to fasten up with a hook. Stool racks run from rowlocks to stern, notched at ends into fastenings of rowlocks, also notched at corners and hooked together, rest against a cleat on deck outside, and are hooked to the deck inside. In a heavy sea the apron is used. It is held up by a stick from peak to combing. Thus rigged, the boat has the reputation of being able to live as long as oars can be pulled. The apron is tacked to the deck about two-thirds its length. The wings are fastened to the top and bottom of the rowlocks. Mast hole, $2\frac{5}{8}$ inches; 2 inches from combing. Drop of sides from top to deck, $5\frac{7}{8}$ inches; dead-rise, 8 inches. Over cockpit a hatch is placed. Everything connected with the boat is placed inside, gunners often leaving their guns, etc., locking the hatch fast. The boats sail well and, covered with sedge, are used to shoot from. With the hatch on, a person can be protected from rain; and with blankets, can be accommodated with a night's lodging.

A variety of boats and canoes used on the lakes and

waterways of Illinois, Indiana, Wisconsin and Michigan are described and figured below, substantially from an article which appeared in *Forest and Stream* in the year 1890.

There are a number of boats which may claim the old Indian birch in their ancestry. Some of the duck shooters of Canada use a "Rice Lake canoe," which is near about a white man's canoe, without the teeteriness and skittishness of the birch, though a lighter goer

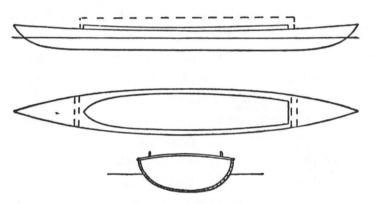

NEE-PE-NAUK BOAT.

among the rushes. Something like a birch is the idea of the Nee-pe-nauk boat, used by the Chicago club men on the Northern Fox River.

This is a smooth-skinned boat, and the skin is made by screwing one longitudinal piece directly upon another, the boat being formed upon a mold. There are no ribs in the boat, and no braces except under the deck, fore and aft of the cockpit. The deck is light, and the cockpit ample for paddling, which is the method of pro-

pulsion. About the cockpit is a folding canvas combing, which can be raised in case of a sea. The boat
sits low in the water. It is stiff, easy-going and suitable for its purpose, which includes a long journey
daily to and from the club house, partly in open water.

The birch canoe folded and closed at the ends and
provided with cockpit and combing, a sort of kayak
model indeed, may have been in the mind of Mr. Alex.
T. Loyd, of the Grand Calumet Heights, of Chicago,
when he devised the racy lines of what we may call the
Loyd boat.

LOYD BOAT.

This is a slender and graceful craft, about 18 feet in
length. It is provided with out-riggers and is very
speedy under oars, being really a better river runner
than marsh boat. Under sail it is very fast and stiff,
being provided with a keel which is detachable at will.
At night the captain of the boat usually employs the
keel as the ridge pole of his boat tent, simply reversing
the position of the rods which fasten it in position.
The owner of this boat has two or three airtight cases
stowed fore and aft under the decking, and these would
float the boat strongly if it were overturned, which,
however, it has not yet been. This boat was born of a

necessity which implied long daily journeys over open water, which was often rough, and it has often been out when the whole fleet of marsh boats were storm-bound.

The birch canoe is a creature of the past. The dug-out is the aboriginal boat of the South. A queer little craft is the St. Francis River (Missouri) dug-out, and this is the type, too, of the boats used on the great New Madrid duck marsh and in much of Arkansas.

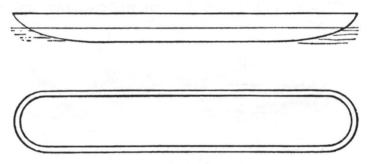

SASSAFRAS DUG-OUT.

This boat is made of sassafras, and its size depends much upon the size of the tree handy to the builder. The boat is only 10 feet long and about 10 inches deep, and as wide as the tree was. It is perfectly flat on top, the ends being simply spoon-shaped. It has no seats. For leakiness and tipsiness it is hard to beat.

A very highly finished and graceful dug-out is the little Mexican pirogue, which parts the waters before the paddle of the hunter of the far Southwest. Our illustration is taken from a little boat made by some Latin hand near Vera Cruz, Mexico. This pretty little dug-cut—for such a thing is possible—was used by Mr. George T. Farmer, of Chicago, as a marsh and river boat in duck shooting.   It is 12 feet long and 14 inches

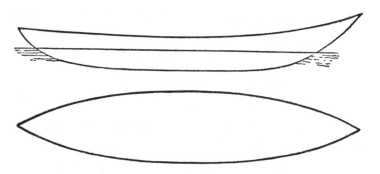

MEXICAN CYPRESS PIROGUE.

deep.   The thin edge is strengthened by a light strip for a rail.   This is an easy sort of boat to fall out of. Up on Wolf River, in Wisconsin, they have a hunt-

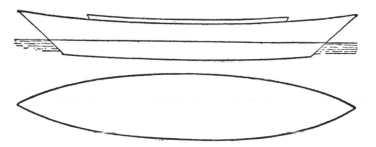

WOLF RIVER CANOE.

ing and trapping canoe, for paddling or pushing, which is an odd-looking but serviceable boat.   It is 16 feet long and about 20 inches deep.   It is decked about

3½ feet fore and aft of the cockpit, which is protected by a combing.

This boat is clinker-built, but it has only three strips

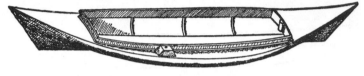

BOB STANLEY, FOX LAKE, ILL.

on each side, the bottom being of one or two boards. It answers well the requirements of its locality.

On the open waters of Fox Lake, a boat is needed which can on occasion stand a good deal of sea and pos-

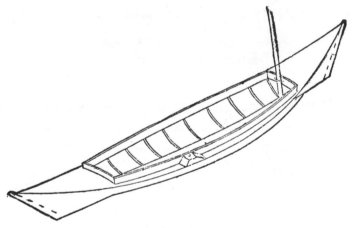

BOB STANLEY.

sibly some ice, and a good deal of wind. Mr. Bob Stanley, an old-timer on that lake, had this in mind, doubtless, when he constructed the wonderful and ponderous inland ship, with which he sometimes plows

the main while in quest of a pot shot at the wily canvas-back of that country. It is greatly to the credit of
this boat that it can carry sail.

In the Illinois River country, and among the sturdy
duck hunters who shoot early and late each year there,
and therefore meet high waters and often fields or
floes of tough, keen ice, we will find another type of
boat evolved from such environment. This is the Illi-

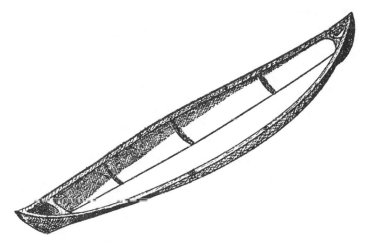

SENACHWINE IRON SKIFF.

nois River or Lake Senachwine sheet-iron skiff, which
all shooters of that region pronounce a boat well
adapted to their purposes. This boat is well shown in
the cut. It is about 16 feet long, stiff and beamy, and
weighs from 75 or 100 pounds to 150. It is sometimes
made with airtight compartments, but the natives scorn
this model, which is too heavy. The iron skiff must
be kept free from a breaking sea. It is valuable when

it comes to an ice field, and is about as good a sled as it is a boat.

The Hennepin duck boat, which is used in much the same waters as the above, is rather more of a fair-weather boat, but is a very good marsh boat for punting, being built with a long and roomy cockpit. It can also be put under oars. This is a local boat, and is built by Mr. James Cunningham, the keeper of the Hennepin Club.

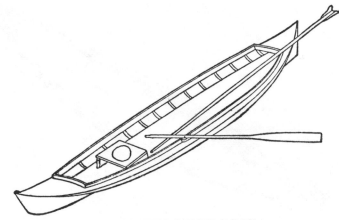

HENNEPIN DUCK BOAT.

A very popular and very good marsh boat is that commonly known among duck shooters as the "Monitor" model, or more commonly still, as the "Green Bay boat." This is a light, shallow craft, intended for no form of propulsion but the push-paddle or punting-pole. It is 15 feet in length, 34 inches in width, and only 7 inches deep. Its cockpit runs long fore and aft to give the pusher room. Its total weight is 75 or 80 pounds. This, or Mr. Douglas' worthy and not very dissimilar "Waukegan boat," is the boat most used on the Kankakee marshes of Indiana. It is good for a long journey up the shallow streams and bayous, and in the covered marsh its well-fashioned bow parts the

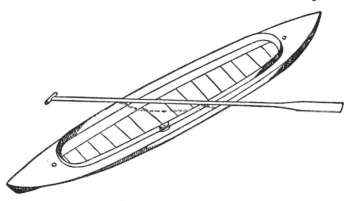

MONITOR MARSH BOAT.

rushes and rides down the drift about as well as any boat could do. The Green Bay is no deep-water boat, and is not calculated for sail or sea.

There is a pretty little red cedar boat made at De

DE PERE RED CEDAR BOAT.

Pere, Wis., which is also the place where the Green Bay boat is made. This latter boat weighs only 64 pounds, is 15 feet long, 32 inches beam, and 9 inches deep. The cockpit in this boat is not so long, but the craft is a very tidy one.

The Mississippi scull boat is a solid and sturdy craft. It is of the "pumpkin-seed" type and similar to a like boat used on the Atlantic coast.

The boat sits low and has often more deck than shown in this cut.   On this deck may be piled the sedge, brush or ice which is used as a blind.

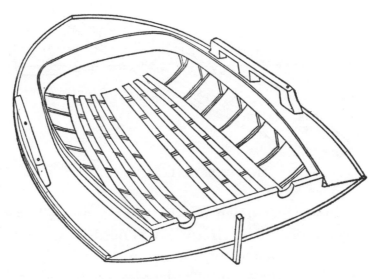

MISSISSIPPI SCULL BOAT.

Somewhat similar in character is the Koshkonong (Wis.) flatboat, but every sink boat and sneak boat shooter will at once catch the idea.   Twelve feet long and 8 feet across its wide "wings," this vehicle lies awash with most of its bulk beneath the surface. The shooter lies in the box, below the level of the water. This is a light cover or open-water boat, and is usually towed to the shooting point.

The "Koshonong Monitor" is a businesslike duck boat. Its deep canvas covering can be raised or lowered at will, and forms a protection alike against sea or wind. It is not a bad rowing boat and slips easily though the rushes and weeds. The rowlocks are shipped in two upright sections of gaspipe, which offer no

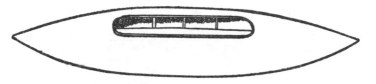

KOSHKONONG FLATBOAT.

entanglements to grass or reeds, and permit easy unshipping of the oars. The deck of this boat is sometimes made of canvas, though wood or tin may be used. The boat, with its load on board, sits low in the water and attracts little attention. There are two or three

KOSHKONONG MONITOR.

varieties of this boat made about Lake Koshkonong, but all conform practically to the type shown. They are heavy boats, usually sheathed with tin. They are suitable for use on a shallow inland lake.

The Tolleston Club, whose grounds lie on the marshy Little Calumet, below Chicago, has a light, little, three

or four board boat, on rather a simple, home-made
model.   It has no ribs or knees, and only one thwart,
with a seat in the stern for a paddler, the latter seat
coming pretty well up flush with the gunwale.   This
boat paddles easily on the river and punts well on the
marsh.   It is a good deal like just a plain boat, but it
is a very well-made, cheap boat.

The shooters at Grand Calumet Heights Club, on
Lake Michigan, sometimes use an odd craft in shooting

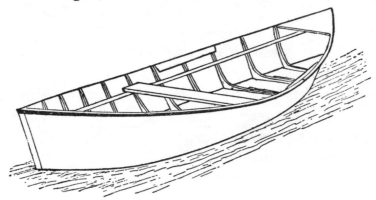

TOLLESTON BOAT.

ducks on the open lake.   On a low-lying platform,
something like the Koshkonong flatboat, they build a
deep cockpit, or roofless cabin, whose walls are about
3 feet high.   About the sides of this they arrange
brush or material for a blind, and anchor the boat out
in deep water, the decoys being arranged by means of
another boat.   This craft is called the "Merganser"
boat.   It will take a heavy sea, but is unwieldy and
unmanageable.

Over on the Canada line they have two or three distinct types of boat. The Point Mouille boat is a double-ender, decked, made of three boards, sides and bottom, built light and shallow, and a bird of a boat on the marsh. The open-water shooting of the St. Clair Flats is done from a very light and shallow sneak, much like a condensed and etherealized Koshkonong flatboat. This boat is intended to lie fairly awash in the water, and the shooter lies in it on his back. They call this a "lying-out boat."

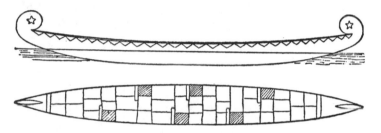

NORTH CANOE.

The North canoe closely resembles the ordinary birch bark, but is said to be even more easily propelled. It is used on some of the northern waters in duck shooting as well as in fishing and travelling. Although requiring a certain amount of practice in its use, it is easily handled and a useful boat.

The boats made for the use of the duck shooter are many. They are constructed of cedar, canvas, metal, and other material, and all have their good points and may be used to advantage in certain localities. Over a country as wide as the United States it is impossible to recommend any one type of boat for all waters.

OTHER CRAFT.

As a rule, on inland waters, the purpose of the gunner's boat is merely to transport him and his paraphernalia from place to place. Along the seacoast, the case is somewhat different, since it may often be necessary to travel considerable distances in the vessel, when speed and staunchness are of most importance.

Whatever type of boat the gunner uses, he must not forget that it must be made as inconspicuous as possible, and, therefore, he will see that it is painted as nearly as may be the color of its surroundings. For the broad and shallow bays of the South, it should be the color of the mud flats; in other localities, the color of dead grass. For winter shooting, white; and so on through the range of the natural colors.

The gunner who visits a special locality year after year, will be likely to provide himself with as good a boat as possible for the particular shooting that he is to engage in, and will fit it with everything necessary to his comfort. Just what these different things are, he will know better than any one else.

ICE WORK.

In many parts of the country, where duck shooting is carried on over wide waters, which from time to time are frozen, and over which it is therefore more

or less difficult to get about, a light freeze is not very
troublesome. The gunner, standing in the stern of
the skiff, throws the boat's nose out of the water, and
pushes her up on the ice, which before long breaks
under her weight, and he then pushes her forward
again. All very thin ice can be shoved through, but it
is necessary where much work is done in the ice to have
the boat sheathed with light copper from her nose, on
both sides, to beyond the swell. If this is not done,
the ice will cut the sides and leave them ragged with
splinters, which makes the boat hard to row or sail.
Sometimes, however, the ice may become so thick that
the boat can neither be shoved through nor over it,
and when the bow is pushed up onto the ice, it hangs
there, or, at most, merely bends down the ice without
breaking through. On the other hand, over warm
springs, and in places where the current moves a little,
the ice may be so thin that it will not support a man's
weight. It is sometimes recommended that iron shoes
be fastened to the bottom of the boat, that it may be
shoved over the ice by the gunner, who walks behind
holding to the stern. In case he comes to an air-hole,
or a weak spot, he can then draw himself aboard the
skiff. This does not appear to be a profitable way of
arranging for ice work. The ordinary gunning skiff,
with its wide beam, made to hold a great stand of decoys, two or three men, and possibly some goose coops
in forward, is too large to be used on the ice.

Much better than this is to have a very small and
light skiff for ice work, and fitted to the bottom of the

skiff, but removable at pleasure, a sled, with runners on each side, on which the skiff can be set. Then, by means of a light, long pole, shod with a small boat-hook, the gunner can rapidly shove himself over the ice in all directions; can visit air-holes, and can have the comfort of being on board his boat the whole time. Short uprights on the sides of the sled may fit against two narrow cleats tacked on either side of the skiff; or slight protuberances on the runners of the sled may fit into slight hollows in the bottom of the skiff, the weight of the boat and its load always keeping the skiff firm on the sled. Or, on the same light skiff, may be tacked shoes running nearly the whole length of the bottom on either side and provided with runners of half-round steel.

With an arrangement of this kind, we have known men to cross ten or twelve miles of dangerous broad-waters with little exertion, and with absolutely no danger, where days of the hardest kind of work would not have brought a gunning skiff across, and where the men would have been obliged constantly to leave the boat, and expose themselves at least to the danger of getting wet, if not of drowning.

While these narrow and light skiffs will not carry a great load, they are large enough to hold a couple of men, their guns and ammunition, and a few decoys. They should be used only in ice work, however, as they are so frail and cranky that they would not live in rough waters. On some of the southern broad-waters, in Maryland, Virginia and North and South Carolina, freezes occur every year, which are often hard enough to make ice in which a common gunning skiff cannot be used; and this often puts an end to the gunning of many men who are not prepared for ice work, and at the very time when the fowl are likely to be most abundant, and most easily obtained by those prepared to go out for them.

THE DECREASE OF WILDFOWL

The constant decrease of the number of our wildfowl is a subject of frequent complaint by gunners
whose memory goes back twenty-five or thirty years.
They compare the scarcity of to-day with the abundance
of old times, and continually inquire why it is that the
birds are growing yearly less and less in number.

Various explanations of the change are given. The
blame is laid on the market-shooter, on the supposed
destruction of birds and eggs on the northern breeding
grounds, and on supposed changes in the lines of flight
by the migratory birds, but most gunners are unwilling
to accept the logic of events and to acknowledge that
the principal cause of the lessened number of the fowl
lies with the gunners themselves, and is an inevitable
accompaniment of civilization, not to be changed except by radical measures. Many of these men, no
doubt, merely repeat what they have heard other people
say, but there are others who advance these remote
causes through pure selfishness, realizing that if they
admit the enormous destruction by gunners they must
logically advocate the abridgment of the shooting season, which means the abolition of spring shooting.

One of the most grotesquely fantastic explanations
of the scarcity of wildfowl was put forth several years
ago in the newspapers, and was soon afterward fathered
by a society bearing the impressive name, National

Game, Fish and Bird Protective Association. This
story told of an enormous destruction of wildfowl
eggs in the Northwest for commercial purposes; millions, shiploads and trainloads of such eggs, it was
gravely related, being annually gathered in Alaska and
British America, and shipped thence to points in the
East, where they were manufactured into egg albumen
cake. The story took with the newspapers, and those
who had fathered it were eager to be interviewed and to
tell what they said they knew about it. They even induced a Senator—the Hon. John H. Mitchell, of Oregon
—to make a speech in the Senate on Alaskan egg destruction, and to ask for an appropriation of $5,000 for
the purpose of sending some one to Alaska to find out
more about it. Incidentally, another Senator, the Hon.
H. Cabot Lodge, of Massachusetts, introduced and
pushed through Congress a bill forbidding the importation of the eggs of wild birds, with the result that now
if any man wants to import from England the eggs of
pheasants, partridges, black game or capercailzie for
hatching out birds to stock his land, he finds that the
law forbids him to do so.

In 1895, *Forest and Stream* set on foot an investigation to learn what truth there was in the story; what
was the basis, if any, for the alarming statistics quoted;
whether an abuse that required checking actually existed. The climax was reached when the president of
the Protective Association already named gave out to
a Chicago newspaper a quotation from the report of a
certain Mr. Storey, who at that time was the local

secretary of the association for Oregon. Among other things, Mr. Storey said: "Another work that has been pushed by your secretary for this State, and in which I am now prepared to ask your hearty coöperation, is the protection from egg-hunters of our wildfowl breeding grounds in Alaska. A careful investigation shows that millions of eggs are gathered and shipped from these grounds annually, and countless numbers of partly matured eggs destroyed. I have furnished our United States Senator, the Hon. Jno. H. Mitchell, with the proper information relating to the above facts, and if the State secretaries of this association will bring the matter before their several Senators at Washington, asking them to coöperate with Senator Mitchell, I am sure the effect will be for the best."

It was obvious that if anything approaching the quantity of eggs mentioned were shipped each season from railroad points on the North Pacific coast, some one would know about it. There would be a great coastwise traffic in these eggs; trains of merchandise are not loaded up at night and shipped off secretly to unknown consignees, nor are shiploads of eggs received from foreign countries without entry at the Custom House. A man does not start from the shores of the Arctic seas with an egg in his pocket, come down a thousand miles or so to the border line, smuggle the egg across, and then go back for another. Yet a careful inquiry among the persons who professed to know most about this subject, and who were most eager to be quoted on it, elicited no information whatever.

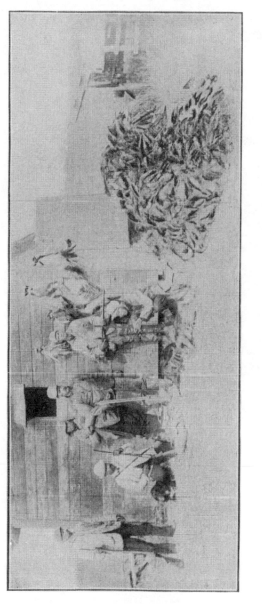

INDIANS GATHERING DUCK EGGS IN ALASKA.

"Countless numbers of partly matured eggs destroyed."

A PRAIRIE SHOOTING WAGON.

Devised by the Messrs. Merrill.

Mr. Storey was asked for facts bearing on the matter, but never responded. No one could be found who had knowledge of any such trade. Nothing definite was written about the matter, and no particle of evidence was ever brought forward to show that such trade existed. No names were given of those who gathered the eggs or shipped them, nor of the consignees to whom they went, nor of the vessels by which they arrived, nor of the people who received the eggs and manufactured them. There was never a word of detail, not a scintilla of evidence—just a series of generalities about millions and carloads of duck eggs, set in a glittering frame painted over with pictures of the far-stretching tundra and the on-moving clouds of ducks, geese, swans and auks.

In the *Forest and Stream's* investigation, inquiry was made first of the transportation lines; second, at the custom houses, and third, of those persons concerned with the manufacture of commercial albumen, where these carloads and shiploads of millions of eggs were supposed to be consumed.

It was found that the transcontinental railway lines, by which of necessity the wildfowl eggs must have reached the East, had never transported any. Inquiry at the different custom ports showed that wildfowl eggs had never been imported through any of the custom houses along our northern or northwestern border; and, finally, the largest manufacturers of albumen in this country stated that practically all the albumen product used in this country was obtained in Russia,

Germany and France, where hens' eggs are very cheap. Albumen is used chiefly for food purposes, most of it in the making of cakes and candies, and one pound, worth from 48 to 50 cents, represents a product of 150 eggs, or about 4 cents a dozen.   At the time when this story was going the rounds, photography was extremely popular, and almost every one carried a camera. The men who occupied themselves in retailing the story about Alaska duck eggs declared that the most of the albumen from these eggs was used in the manufacture of sensitized paper.   Yet a little inquiry showed that at that time comparatively little albumen was used in photography, since gelatine and other materials had even then almost entirely taken its place.

This, then, was the conclusion of the whole matter: Those who professed to have information on the subject were unable to substantiate the stories which they told; the transportation companies have carried no such eggs; none have ever been received at the ports of entry; the albumen trade knows nothing whatever about them, and, in view of the total lack of evidence to support the story, there is no doubt that it is a pure invention.

The situation is very well summed up by Mr. Wm. W. Castle, of Boston, Mass., who, in a letter in *Forest and Stream*, said: "My opinion is that more eggs are destroyed in the Mississippi Valley by the spring shooters—a thousand, or even ten thousand, to one—than it would be possible to destroy in any collection that could be carried out, even if eggs were worth $1 à dozen, at the breeding grounds. Wildfowl, while gregarious in migration, are by no means so in breeding. * * * I have seen miles of country (barren) in the Northwest that to a superficial observer might seem to be a vast breeding ground, but would really hold but few birds in comparison to its apparent capabilities, and even those which were to be seen flying about were by no means all breeders.

"With sea fowl it might be different, but my experience on the Pacific has been that, with few exceptions, there are no .such breeding grounds accessible to any one commercially disposed as there have been on the Gulf of St. Lawrence and Labrador coast. I thought at the time that the matter of commercial egg destruction was opened up, that it was simply a weak invention of those who are butchering spring birds to throw dust and endeavor to blind people as to the real cause of decrease, viz., spring shooting."

Another correspondent of *Forest and Stream,* writing from St. Louis, Mo., made some statements with regard to the destruction of birds in the swamps of Missouri and Arkansas which are worth quoting. He said: "I have read with much interest your article pertaining to the gathering of wild duck eggs for commercial purposes. The theory, whenever mentioned, never fails to produce audible smiles. * * * The secret of decimated ranks lies more with those fortunate enough to get where ducks are, and with the market-shooter in particular, who is on the ground all the time. No; wild ducks are not all dead yet, not if we may judge from the vast multitudes to be seen in the swamps of the sunk land of Missouri and Arkansas.

"In October of '94 a party of four from this city, and four from Cincinnati, shot over one thousand ducks in one week, and, from the hordes still seen, it did not look as if any were missing. To the average amateur, the piles of ducks would have looked like three times the quantity, as nine-tenths of them were choice mallards.

"Nor were these all the ducks shot in this quiet and celebrated spot that week. Five market-hunters were in there all the time, and in this particular week averaged from 80 to 140 ducks per day each.

"A netter was also at work, who made a shipment of twenty barrels of mallards at one time. Again, to the average amateur, or even to the semi-professional, this may sound fishy. If the receipts of the steamboat which brought the ducks to this market will be proof, they can be produced. The netter made no more shipments, for the natives forced him out of the country with Winchesters. * * *"

CAUSES.

Two prime causes exist for the diminution of wild-fowl. These are over-shooting, and the settling up of the country.

The abuses under the head of over-shooting which ought to be corrected are :

(*a*) Shooting seasons far too long; in some States lasting from September to May, or for eight months of the year. The ducks are shot from the time they arrive from the North in the fall until they leave for the North in the spring.

(*b*) Methods that are too destructive, as batteries, night shooting, bush blinds, sailing.

(*c*) Big bags by sportsmen who shoot for recreation.

(*d*) Shooting for market. Certain men devote all their time while the fowl are with us to shooting them for sale to game dealers. Often they kill by methods that are illegal.

In consequence of the diminution of the number of our birds, other causes which were formerly trivial have assumed a greater relative importance. Two of these are the destruction of eggs and fowl, young and old, on their breeding ground, by natives, and poisoning by lead taken in with the food. The last, though odd and unexpected, is not sufficiently destructive to require serious consideration.

Up to the year 1860, gunning was practiced by comparatively few individuals in this country, and they were not enough to make any considerable impression on the hordes of wildfowl that had always thronged our lakes, streams and bays. During the five years of the Civil War, all Southern ducking-grounds, and most of those in the North, had almost complete rest, and the number of fowl killed was inconsiderable. They had time during these years of almost no shooting to re-establish themselves, and to fill the gap in their ranks that had been made in earlier years. Witnesses who visited southern ducking-grounds in 1865 tell of the countless number of fowl then found there, and of their tameness. They say, too, that then there were no gunners, and that the only birds killed were a few shot by the residents for their own consumption.

At this time the West was practically unknown, and, of course, unsettled. Beyond the Missouri River there were no white inhabitants. Over the vast extent of territory between the Mississippi and the Rocky Mountains the fowl bred undisturbed, and in their migrations passed to and fro over a territory where they were not molested. If there was an occasional army post in that wild region, its presence there had no effect on the ducks and geese, for the shotgun was unknown, and the man who desired sport or food took his rifle and hunted four-footed game.

But gradually a change came. Settlements increased along the lines of travel; railroads were built into new territory; ranchers began to take up land in regions away from the railway, and each newcomer made the country less possible for the wild creatures that had hitherto inhabited it or passed through it. Concurrently with all this, came the greatly increased interest in shooting, by which the number of the gunners was many times multiplied. As their numbers increased, they soon shot out the old places to which the fowl had always resorted, and were forced to search out new localities of game plenty. Let us see with what result.

In 1880, travelers over the Union Pacific Railroad learned that during the migration geese resorted in vast flocks to the Platte River, and gunners began to go in great numbers to Nebraska for the goose-shooting. They brought back marvelous tales of the abundance of the fowl, and soon the gunners gathered on the sand bars of the Platte in such numbers as, after a time, to almost line the river. In 1884, Mr. Burr Polk, a contributor to *Forest and Stream*, wrote: "The gunners have so increased in the last three years that the weary goose, coming down from the North, or in from the fields, to rest and slake its thirst, can hardly find a place out of the range of some one's gun. Blinds line the bars in the stream for one hundred miles so thickly as to preclude all chance of a fair bag. A flock of geese coming into the river can rarely strike it at any point without a volley being fired at it, and as the terror-stricken fowl move on up stream, hunting a place of safety, their progress can be marked by the booming of the guns as they pass the gauntlet of blinds along their course.

"We first tried the river at Newark, but after slight scores, and having our blinds robbed one night of nearly all of our decoys and game, we pulled up and drove twenty miles down the river along the bank in quest of some unoccupied spot. But none was to be found. Hunters were quartered at farm-houses or camping in tents on both sides of the river at short intervals. As we went down we met parties going up, in the hope that had actuated us. The result of all this is to break up the habit of the geese of loitering on the Platte in their flight southward, and to hurry them on their journey where they can at least rest one day in peace. The chances are that, if this wholesale hunting of them is continued for another year or two, they will seek other lines in their migrations, and that we will never again see geese on the Platte in great numbers. At the station, where we took the train coming home, we met a couple of gentlemen who had been in the habit of going out on the Platte annually after geese. This year they had occupied blinds just above us. They told us that one day neither of them got a shot."

In 1885, the same correspondent told a similar story. He said that the geese had not come as usual to the Platte River, nor had they appeared much about the lakes and ponds, nor in the corn fields of the farmers, as had been their habit in former years; nor, indeed, had many been seen in flight going southward over this region. He then adds, naively:

"No one seems to be able to account for this sudden diminution of wild geese along the Platte. It never occurred to me that it would happen during my lifetime. There are various theories regarding it. One is, that they have taken a different line in their migration southward; another, that, as the country has settled up further northward, and grain has been grown there, they stop along the lakes in that region, and remain because they are not disturbed; another, that they did come down here, but as every farmer had a gun, to pop away at them in the fields where they went to feed, and the bars in the river were covered with gunners, they hurried southward to seek peace and rest; and still another, that, through the despoiling of their eggs in their nesting-grounds, and the spring and fall killing of the fowl by the myriads of hunters, their ranks had become so˙depleted they could no longer make the big display of former years. I do not know, I am sure.

"Pretty much the same may be said with reference to ducks. Indeed, the falling off in their case has been greater than that of the geese. I have not heard of a creditable bag, even by the most successful hunters. If they have come this way in any considerable numbers, they have done it so slyly and quietly that none of us has been aware of their presence. We people of this part of Nebraska have begun to realize that, like our more eastern friends, if we want to do much successful work among the ducks, we will have to seek other regions for the sport. How quickly do the settlement of a country, and the modern gun, cause the game to disappear!"

The writer of these paragraphs had evidently forgotten in 1885 that one year earlier he had himself given ample reasons for the disappearance of the geese, and, in fact, had predicted that disappearance. Indeed, it was only ten years before the date of his earlier letter that the buffalo along the Platte had been destroyed in precisely the same manner that the geese were. Half a dozen years earlier than 1874, people had talked constantly of the millions of buffalo, of the impossibility of ever exterminating them, and of how they would continue to roam the plains for many, many years; but, as a matter of fact, it took only three or four years to destroy these millions in this region. Of course, after a time, migratory wildfowl learn to avoid regions where they are continually persecuted, and, no doubt, this has been the case with the geese and the ducks which formerly spent weeks along the Platte River, remaining until driven South by the freezing up of the waters.

By this time the fowl had become so scarce in many parts of the Middle West that gunners almost gave up looking for them, and turned their thoughts to more distant regions, the newly-settled wheat lands of North Dakota, for example; where, had it not been for the wisdom of that State in limiting the number of birds to be killed by one man in a day, the story of the Platte River might have been told over again.

This is one example of the effect on fowl shooting of the settling up of the country, and the bringing distant localities within the reach of the gunner. Another and still more potent cause of decrease, is the advance of the settlements, which makes it impossible for the birds to build their nests and hatch their young where they did formerly.

The story of many Atlantic coast shooting grounds that were formerly famous is similar to that of the Platte River. Yet, on these shooting grounds, the destruction has not been so complete, since the far greater extent of water makes it impossible for gunners to occupy the feeding grounds of the birds, as they did along the Platte. Nevertheless, the use of batteries, or sink-boats, on the feeding grounds, the employment of big guns at night, and night shooting generally, with or without lights, have had a tendency to break up the birds on Chesapeake Bay and on the Susquehanna Flats, and to drive them to other grounds.

SPRING SHOOTING.

Sportsmen, generally, are agreed that most of our upland game should be protected during the early months of the year, when they are preparing to mate and to build their nests. It is commonly averred by the advocates of spring shooting, that, as the wildfowl and the snipe are migratory birds, which do not nest with us, there is no reason why they should not be shot in the spring, during their passage from South to North. Such reasoning is based on false premises.

The assumption that the migratory wildfowl do not breed with us is false. They do not now breed commonly, because they are not allowed to do so, and those which might remain with us and rear their young within our borders, are destroyed before they have an opportunity to prepare their nests and lay their eggs. In years gone by, however, the English snipe, and many species of our waterfowl, commonly bred in all the northern tier of States, and did so in great numbers. Even to-day, in States where spring shooting is forbidden, they breed to a limited extent, and would do so generally if they were free from disturbance by man. Certain species do so to-day in New England and New York, and require only protection in spring to do so on a much larger scale.

As it is, they are shot over almost the whole United States, and part of Canada, at a time when they are preparing to nest, when they are not fit for food, and when their destruction has a more immediate bearing than at any other time on the supply of fowl for the coming winter.

Spring shooting ought to be forbidden by public sentiment and law alike, on the ground that it is too destructive to our waterfowl. It ought to be forbidden for the same reason that catching trout out of brooks and rivers with seines is forbidden—because it destroys so many of the fowl that the general supply suffers too great depletion.

One of the chief arguments used by those who advocate spring shooting, and especially by persons living in the Mississippi Valley, is, that if the spring shooting is abolished they will get no duck shooting through the year. These persons claim that in their locality there is no fall duck shooting; that the flyway of the birds on their southern migration does not touch them. In spring, however, they say that the birds come to them in good numbers, but that the flight is short, although while it lasts the shooting is excellent. Such an argument is purely selfish, and might, with equal force, be advanced in favor of netting trout, night shooting, or any other improvident practice.

If the claims of such men are founded on fact, their case is certainly a hard one, but, manifestly, laws limiting the shooting of fowl should not be applied to any one section, but should be general.

Within the recollection of men who are not yet old, more than one species of bird and mammal have become extinct in America, while over large sections of the country many species have been practically exterminated. If gunners generally could be induced to take a broad view of these matters, and to consider the general good, rather than their own selfish advantage, the cause of game protection would be greatly helped, and the gunners themselves, after a few years, would be greatly benefited. It is to be hoped that before long most of the States will have followed the worthy example set them by a small number of those in the Northwest, and will enact laws leading to the better protection of our fowl.

Years ago, the suggestion that spring shooting should be abolished was commonly laughed at, but slowly a belief in the necessity of limiting the shooting has grown, until now there are a few States which prohibit spring shooting altogether, and a few others which prohibit it in a more or less half-hearted way. In Vermont the season for shooting wild ducks ends January 1st, and in New Hampshire, February 1st. Of course, long before these dates, all the ducks and geese have gone South, not to return until the ice breaks up in the spring. In Minnesota, the season for wildfowl closes January 1st, and in Idaho, March 1st, in both cases, of course, before the birds have begun to return from the South.   It is seen that, therefore, in two of our newest States, the game protective idea is far more advanced than in most of the older States.

In Michigan the open season closes for the most of the State, May 1st, but for the Upper Peninsula, January 15th.   In Wisconsin the wildfowl season closes January 1st, except as to geese, for which it is open to May 1st; and the same dates apply in North Dakota. Newfoundland and Ontario have the duck season close in the middle of winter, December 15th and January 12th, but the season is open for geese until May 1st.

Most of the other States have the shooting season for wildfowl close during April or May, although in California, North Carolina, British Columbia, and Nova Scotia the close time begins in March.

The experiment of having certain days during each week when shooting is not permitted has been tried in some Southern States, with great advantage to the gunning and to the birds; and even the market-gunners, who at first were bitterly opposed to any such law, now acknowledge that it has worked for their benefit, and that on the shooting days they get better gunning than they used to when each day of the week was open to them.   It is especially noticeable that the gunning on Monday—after the birds have had two days of rest —is usually better than on any other day of the week.

CONTRACTION OF FEEDING GROUNDS.

Certain natural conditions have, at various times within the past few years, tended to injure the shooting of the Chesapeake Bay region. On a number of occasions great floods have swept down alluvium and drift stuff from the rivers, covering large portions of the feeding grounds, and thus destroyed the food. At other times, unusual cold has frozen the waters over the shallower flats, quite to the bottom, killing or tearing up by the roots the grass on which the fowl feed. Of course, such wholesale destruction of the food prevents the fowl from visiting the grounds until the grass has re-established itself once more, and this is a very slow process.

It is reported, also, and probably with truth, that many of the flats which formerly were excellent feeding grounds for the canvas-back and other fowl, are constantly filling up, and becoming too shoal for certain kinds of duck food to grow. This, if true, must in time very greatly reduce the area of the feeding grounds, and the result of this will be not to concentrate the birds on the diminished area, but to drive them to other localities.

In the Chesapeake Bay, as also in certain bays on Long Island, there has been in the past great complaint that ducks were caught in nets set over their feeding grounds. The nets are placed close to the bottom, ostensibly to catch fish, and the ducks, diving, become entangled in their meshes, and drown. Laws exist in certain States forbidding the setting of nets for the purpose of catching ducks, but as no method has as yet been discovered for exposing what goes on in a man's brain, it has never been possible to prove that any individual set his nets for the purpose of catching ducks, and no convictions under this law have ever been had. Of late years there has been little or no complaint of this practice.

SIZE OF BAGS.

The man who shoots merely as a matter of recreation usually has great—and sometimes just—complaint to make of the market-shooter. Many men declare that if there were no shooting for the market, game would be as plenty as ever. The average gunner looks with disfavor on the man who turns the fruits of his shooting into money, and attributes the diminished number of our fowl very largely to the slaughter which he causes.

As a matter of fact, it is hard to see where the market-shooter is any more to blame for the destruction of birds than is he who shoots merely for recreation. The market-shooter, to be sure, is a professional, in the sense that he turns his skill in a branch of sport into money. But in this there is nothing necessarily disgraceful, and we have known more than one market-shooter who, to our mind, was a far truer sportsman than many of that class who contemn him. The harm wrought by the market gunner is due to the fact that he works at gunning day after day through the shooting season, and so, individually, kills a vast number of birds. The ravages of the market hunter will cease when laws shall be put in force properly regulating the sale of game.

Within the past few years the question of the size of catch of fish or bags of game has been taken hold of by the legislature of various States, and laws have been passed limiting the quantity of fish, birds or mammals that one person can kill in one day. Some States have gone further than this, and have placed a limit not only on what shall be taken in a day, but also in a season. Such legislation has the support of public opinion, and so, enforced by the game wardens, it cannot fail to do great good. Neither the market-shooter nor the non-professional gunner has sufficient self-control to stop shooting when he has killed a fair bag of birds. Instead of this, he will continue to shoot as long as the fowl fly, and in this respect the two classes are equally blameworthy. Every man remembers the many days which were almost blanks, and those other days on which but few birds were killed; it is but human— when the occasional good days come—that the gunner should wish to make the most of his opportunities, and should try to average up the bad days. Bags of sixty, eighty, and sometimes even a hundred birds are not uncommon. Yet, under the conditions which exist in

America to-day, no man ought to wish to kill birds in such a wholesale way.

In the years between 1870 and 1875 it was not uncommon for fifteen thousand ducks to be killed in a single day on the Chesapeake Bay. At the present day one-fifth of this number would be a very large score.

It is greatly to be desired that all States may enact laws something like those of North Dakota, where the number of birds that may be killed in a day is limited to twenty-five. If such a law could be put into operation, and the shooting season could be shortened, so that it would last for three or four months, instead of eight, the effect on our wildfowl would soon be seen.

NATURAL ENEMIES.

In the old times, when wildfowl were so enormously abundant over most of the country, it seemed as if their numbers could never be greatly reduced. At that period, those interested in the subject imagined that the only important dangers to which the birds were exposed were such wholesale methods of destruction as over-shooting and netting. Now, however, since the birds have grown fewer, since hundreds use the shotgun where ten did formerly, when the western and a part of the northern breeding grounds have been turned into farms and summer resorts, and when, notwithstanding all this, the shooting continues over eight months of the year, it is necessary to consider certain minor causes of destruction which formerly were not worth thinking of.

The fable that wildfowl eggs were gathered for commercial purposes undoubtedly had its origin in the fact that Indians collect the eggs for food. From time immemorial the Indians and Eskimos who dwell in the country where the ducks breed have collected for food quantities of their eggs, and during the moulting season great numbers of young and of adult birds. They do so still; but, as the population of the North is very sparse, they cannot destroy any considerable numbers. Beside this, it may be said that in many places the Indians and the Eskimos are disappearing more rapidly than the ducks. These savage peoples are to be counted as the natural enemies to the wildfowl, and the destruction which they cause is, perhaps, no greater than that caused by other natural enemies—the wild animals and the rapacious birds which feed on the fowl or their eggs when they can. In comparison with the other causes already enumerated, the destruction caused by the natives is absolutely inconsiderable. The true reason for the decrease of the birds is the spread of civilization over the continent, which means their destruction by civilized man; and every attempt to cover up this truth and to lay blame elsewhere is a real injury to the cause of game protection.

LEAD POÏSONING.

Another quite unexpected danger to wildfowl, which was discovered only in 1894, having been then announced in *Forest and Stream*, is the self-poisoning of ducks, by means of lead taken into the stomach in the form of shot.

In Texas, at Galveston, at Stephenson Lake, and on Lake Surprise, twenty-five miles northeast of Galveston, as well as at points in Currituck Sound, on the North Carolina coast, there are frequently found ducks, geese and swans, dead, or sick and unable to fly. On examination they prove to be unmarked by shot, and often appear externally in good condition. An investigation, however, shows that the gizzard contains, with the sand and gravel always to be found there, particles of lead—shot or its remains—picked up by the bird in feeding. The condition of some of these particles shows that they have recently been taken into the gizzard, for they have lost nothing in size or surface. Others have evidently been subjected for some time to the grinding process, and have lost much of their weight. It is said that in Texas sometimes such gizzards contain, beside particles of lead, old percussion caps.

The matter was first brought to my personal attention during the winter of 1893-4, and shortly after I wrote about it, substantially as follows:

During a recent visit to Currituck Sound, I heard much of a disease to which wildfowl there are subject, and which is locally known as "croup." This sickness seems to be common to ducks, geese and swans, and I saw a number of the affected birds. The local gunners believe it to be a disease of the respiratory organs; and, on capturing a sick bird, rub its throat, under the impression that something is choking the fowl. Of course, the sick ones are not under observation during the early stages of the disease, but only after they become so weak as to be easily captured; the symptoms are a rattling in the throat, as if there were difficulty in breathing, and an occasional dribbling of a few drops of yellowish fluid from the bill, which is held open much of the time. In the geese, the voice is changed, being less resonant than in health. A "croupy" goose, captured near the point of Narrows Island, January 14th, seemed in good condition, sleek and quite strong. It swam vigorously, but did not attempt to fly, and when caught, struggled with a good deal of force. As it was being put in the boat, its head and neck hanging down, it disgorged two or three tablespoonfuls of a yellowish fluid, and died. A swan caught on Brant Island, a day or two earlier, was brought in alive and put in the goose pen, where it lived for a short time, but was found dead one morning. At times this bird seemed to feel pretty well, dabbling in the water and dressing its plumage, but much of the time it stood or sat with its bill open, breathing hard, and with the yellowish fluid dropping from its beak.

A dissection of the two birds mentioned revealed
the disease from which the fowl suffers and its cause.

All the organs were found in a healthy condition
until the gizzard was reached.   In the case of the goose,
the crop and upper gizzard were filled with fresh
grass, on which the processes of digestion had not begun.   The posterior part of the gizzard contained perhaps two ounces of fine sand, mingled with coarser
gravel.   Distributed through this sand was a small
quantity—perhaps one-quarter of an ounce—of particles of lead, evidently shot.   Some of these particles
were large and round, others were flattened, others
still were no larger than No. 10 or No. 12 shot, and
were not round, but oval or bean-shaped.   The surfaces of all were dull, and, on close examination, were
seen to be finely pitted by attrition against the harder
sand and gravel which grinds up the bird's food.   The
gristly lining of the gizzard of this goose was greenish
in color, and in character entirely different from the
same membrane in a healthy bird.   Its inner membrane
was soft and decayed, or corroded, easily to be pulled
to pieces or rubbed off with the finger, and in some
places had degenerated into a soft, jelly-like mass of
yellowish color.   The thicker tough lining of the gizzard was also corroded and could be picked away in
small pieces, while in a healthy bird it would have
stripped away in a single piece from the white membrane upon which it lies.   This white membrane
showed here and there pinkish or purplish spots, indi-
cating inflammation.   The right lobe of the liver was

discolored, having a dark, unhealthy look. The small intestine showed evidence of intense inflammation through its length, and the rectum was also inflamed.

The swan was examined a few days later than the goose, and several days after its death. Its gizzard contained perhaps twenty or thirty grains of corn, which were softened, but not at all digested, or even abraded. The gizzard contained no sand, but it did contain a quantity of yellowish, jelly-like matter, which appeared to be the broken down walls of the gizzard lining. At the posterior part of the gizzard were a dozen particles of lead, two of them evidently No. 4 shot, and the others small ground-up fragments of shot which had lost shape and size. The tough lining membrane of the gizzard was black in color, had lost all character, and could be picked off piece by piece like rotten wood or burned leather. The subjacent white membrane showed the pink and purple spots of inflammation noted in the same membrane of the goose. The small intestine was highly inflamed throughout its whole tract. The liver was absolutely black and very soft.

From these examinations I conclude that the birds dissected died from chronic lead poisoning, the cause of which was sufficiently obvious.

Each season great quantities of shot are fired on the waters of this sound, and much of it falls on the feeding grounds of the wildfowl. In feeding, the geese, ducks and swans—whether by accident or design—take into the stomach with sand and gravel and food, more

or less of this shot.   When the shot has passed into the
gizzard it is subjected to the same grinding process as
the grass, grain or other food, and, being softer than
the sand, it is ground into minute particles.   These fine
particles, acted on by the acids of the digestive organs,
yield a soluble lead salt, which, being absorbed into the
general system, causes death.*

In a subsequent note to *Forest and Stream,* signed by
A Member of the Narrows Island Club, additional
facts bearing on the subject were printed, as follows:

"At Narrows Island the goose pen stands on the border of a channel known as the Little Narrows, which,
in times of severe cold weather, is always open, and
during a freeze-up is a great flyway for ducks.   Gunners shooting about this channel at such times have for
many years scattered shot over the marsh, the water
and the mud.

"Until a year or two since, the goose pen stood partly
on the marsh and partly over the muddy shore, and en-
closed no high land.   The live decoy geese and ducks,
being unable to supply themselves with sand or gravel,
were industrious in searching through the mud for the
hard particles necessary to the proper digestion of their
food, and until recently we were constantly troubled
by having our decoy geese and ducks sick with the
'croup.'   However, after the death of Capt. Ryder, our
former superintendent, we moved and enlarged the
goose pen, so that it now takes in a piece of high
ground, where there is some sand, with plenty of bro-

*The London *Field* (1902) gives instances of similar lead poisoning, in England, of pheasants and partridges.

ken oyster shells. We also give the geese the best corn we can buy, and every once in a while feed them with grass. As the birds can now readily obtain sand and fragments of oyster shells, they supply their wants with these substances, and are thus much less likely to take in any considerable quantity of the shot which may still remain within the limits of the pen. It is, of course, evident that to keep these captive birds in a state of health they should be surrounded as nearly as possible by natural conditions."

It would appear that the ducks, in their feeding through the borders of the marsh and in the mud in which they dabble, often come upon the particles of shot so thickly scattered over the shooting ground and take them into the alimentary canal, whence they pass down into the gizzard. Until they reach the mill in which the wildfowl grinds his food, these pellets do the bird no harm, but when reduced to powder and acted on by acids they become a violent poison.

SELF-DENIAL NEEDED.

It must be obvious to any one who will take an unprejudiced view of the subject that the settling up of a large portion of the North American continent has deprived our wildfowl of much of their ancient breeding ground. It must also be evident that the great and constantly increasing number of gunners scattered over the country where the wildfowl spend nearly two-thirds of the year, and shooting during all this time, must destroy more of these fowl than, under the most favorable circumstances, can be bred in the far North, where they are comparatively little disturbed during their sojourn there during the breeding season.

We must look at fowl-shooting just as we do at every other form of field sport. As game and fish become more scarce, limitations must be placed on their capture, and those methods of destruction which are most sweeping in their results must be forbidden by law or by public sentiment. Game laws are enacted for the general good—for the good of people to-day, and in the future—and they ought to be framed to subserve the greatest good to the greatest number, and to preserve for the use of all our people as great a number as possible of our beautiful wild creatures. Although the seining of trout affords a most successful means of taking fish, it is made illegal by statute, because it destroys on such a wholesale scale that a few men might soon capture all the fish in a stream, and there would be none left for others.

Thus, if we are to continue to have any duck shooting, limitations of one sort or another must be put on this sport, just as such limitations are put on the shooting of other birds and animals, and the taking of fish. Gunners must consent to practice self-control. Fewer birds must be killed each season.

These limitations should act in two directions, viz., in shortening the time during which fowl may be shot, and in doing away with those methods of shooting which are most destructive. The time for shooting can be shortened only by cutting off several months from the present season, and it would undoubtedly be for the advantage of all gunners if all the States were to pass laws forbidding the shooting of ducks from February 1st to September 1st. Such a change would give five months of gunning to people living in the South, but only three months to those who live in the North, an apparent hardship, but one that must be borne.

BATTERIES AND BUSH BLINDS.

In order to lessen the destruction of fowl, those methods of gunning which are most destructive should be done away with. One of these destructive modes of gunning is battery shooting. This should be given up, not in order to benefit or to injure any man, or any class of men, but solely in order that fewer birds may be killed. Up to a certain point, wildfowl are able to protect themselves from shore shooters. They can, if they please, sit out in the broad waters, and away from the shore, but they cannot protect themselves from batteries placed on their feeding grounds, nor from sail boats which follow them from place to place. The birds must eat, and when they wish to do so they are sure to go to their feeding grounds, and to the decoys anchored there, and so expose themselves to the gunner. In many localities where batteries are used it is a common practice for the tender, after the morning flight is over, to visit in his sail boat all the rafts of fowl in the vicinity, and "stir them up," in the hope that some of them may go to the decoys near the box.

Battery shooting is still practiced in our southern coast waters. The batteries are located on the feeding grounds, and are rigged out with large stands of decoys. There is nothing whatever to arouse the suspicion of the oncoming ducks, which go directly to the decoys, and then are shot at, apparently from the surface of the water. It is true that after a time birds learn to know the batteries, and after they have been shot at a few times they often scatter, leaving the ground where the batteries are anchored, and disperse in small bunches to other localities where batteries are not anchored.

The bush blinds, so often referred to, are commonly used by gunners on the Chesapeake Bay and its tributary waters, as well as on shoal waters further to the southward. They are described in another place. Usually they are set up on shoals, in the broad water, and on feeding grounds near the shore, in the line of the ducks' flight, and, being built before the birds come on in the autumn, do not for some time become objects of suspicion to the fowl. When surrounded by a good stand of decoys, they are very deadly, and if set up, as they often are, during a freeze, in air holes, wonderfully good shooting may be had from them.

They are very destructive to fowl, and the different

States should forbid their use, for the reason that they interfere with the feeding of the fowl, and tend to render them suspicious even of the waters over which they fly.

NIGHT SHOOTING.

Fifteen or twenty years ago night shooting, often with "big guns," was commonly practiced on many of the best ducking grounds in the Chesapeake Bay. The gunner, usually with a reflecting headlight in the bow of the skiff, paddled quietly up to the great rafts of fowl resting on the water, and shot into them with huge guns, ten or twelve feet long, and carrying a pound or more of shot. The use of such guns was forbidden by law, but it was exceedingly difficult to procure evidence against the men who used them. The public sentiment of the community was on the side of the law-breakers, and people generally were willing to give them warning of the approach of law officers. In 1883, some of the ducking clubs on the Chesapeake Bay made special efforts to put an end to this shooting, and several of the big guns were captured and their owners were arrested. The local gunning population discovered at last that the members of the clubs were in earnest, and a treaty was entered into by which the law-breakers agreed, if they were not prosecuted, to give up their big guns and the practice of night shooting. Since then there has been comparatively little law-breaking in this particular respect.

WHAT SHALL BE DONE?

Over, at least, one-fourth, and probably a greater area of the country, the inhabitants now have duck shooting in neither spring nor fall. If they desire to have a day or two in the blind or in the battery, it is necessary for them to travel some hundreds of miles, and to spend considerable sums of money, on the chance that they may get gunning. This state of things will continue, and as population increases, and as the fowl become fewer, the number of men who must go without shooting will increase. It is one of the conditions under which we live, and there is no escaping it.

It is difficult to suggest how a general and effective change in the shooting laws of all the States and Provinces of the continent can be brought about. A few States, from time to time, have passed laws prohibiting spring shooting, but these laws have not always received the support of public sentiment, and have in some cases been repealed. To accomplish much good, such laws should exist in all the States.

The time is coming, however, and it cannot be long delayed, when gunners will be obliged to make a choice between having no shooting at all, or giving up some portion of the season that is now open. The operation of the game preserve system, which within a few years has become so extensive, is doing something to protect the birds, yet, in the nature of things, it cannot affect them much. Each year the ducks become less and less. Occasionally there are periods when, as in the autumn of 1899, some special cause—as a great drought prevailing over much of the country—concentrates the ducks where water can be had, and makes for those regions an apparent abundance; but it is quite certain that the greater numbers found there mean an absolute dearth somewhere else. Something radical must be done. Fewer fowl must be killed in order that more breeders may be left, and the stock of birds thus increased.

If for five years gunning were stopped all over the country February 1st, the shooting at the end of that time would be so much better than it has been at any time for the last fifteen years that gunners throughout the land would be practically unanimous to have such a law made permanent for all time.

The action, first advocated years ago by *Forest and Stream,* and since then made law in a number of States, that the sale of game should be forbidden, is a long step in the right direction. This would put an end to shooting for the market, and would thus cut off one serious cause of the destruction of fowl. If such a law should meet with general favor, if the shooting after the 1st of January or 1st of February should be forbidden, if the bags should be limited to twenty-five or thirty birds a day, new conditions would soon greet the gunner, and birds might once again be seen on their old feeding grounds, in something like their old-time plenty.

I repeat, then, that to bring back the ducks in their old-time abundance the gunners must agree to

Stop spring shooting;
Limit the size of bags for a day and a season;
Stop the sale of game.

FURTHER NOTE ON THE CHESAPEAKE BAY DOG.

By a mischance, which I greatly regret, certain interesting examples of intelligence in this breed of dog were omitted from this chapter in the first edition. The first of these deals with a dog owned by Mr. J. G. Morris, of Easton, Md.

Mr. Morris was shooting from a floating blind not far from the land, and his dog on the shore was gathering the birds as they fell, taking them there and putting them in a pile. Mr. Morris' blind was just off a fence, which ran down into the water between two fields. The dog had made his pile of ducks close to this fence, and near the water's edge. In the same field with the dog and the ducks were confined some young cattle, and the path which they used in going to the water passed close to the fence against which the dog had collected the ducks, by which he lay.

As the day passed, the young cattle, following this path, attempted to go down to water, but when they approached the dog, he got up and drove them away. This was repeated several times, for the cattle persisted in coming down to the water by their usual path, and the dog would not permit them to approach his pile of ducks. At last the situation became so annoying to the dog that he rose to his feet, took a duck in his mouth, jumped over the fence into the adjoining field, and leaving the duck there, jumped back and got another one, and continued this until he had transferred all the ducks to the other side of the fence, when he again lay down by them. The next time the cattle attempted to go down the path to water, the dog paid no attention to them, but permitted them to pass him and drink.

To my mind, this was a clear case of the reasoning out by the dog of a special remedy for a set of conditions that were entirely new to him, and so the facts are well worth putting on record.

A second example took place on a marsh in Currituck Sound, where my friend, Mr. C. R. Purdy, was shooting. Harrison, the watchman for the marsh, had a dog named Grover, that he had reared from a puppy, and kept with him on the island. He was a useful animal to Harrison, for he brought him an income of perhaps $75 to $100 a season from the sale of the cripples which he recovered. Harrison was accustomed to shove around the marsh morning and evening, letting the dog run along the shore while he pushed his light skiff close to the land. Whenever the dog crossed the trail of a cripple that had gone into the marsh, he would follow it, bring the bird out and deliver it to Harrison. In this way each week a considerable number of birds were recovered, which otherwise would have gone to feed the minks and the coons.

On the particular occasion referred to the birds were

flying very well. Flock after flock of widgeon came up to the decoys in the narrow pond, where Mr. Purdy was tied out, and a number of birds were being killed. The flocks came so frequently that it was impossible to recover the wounded birds, which fell in the marsh, but the gunner, his boatman and Harrison watched them, and counted five that went down at different distances before the flight lulled. When the birds stopped flying, the dog, without a word from any one, started off across the pond and into the marsh, and making five trips, brought back to the blind five widgeons, which he had marked down and recovered. Then he lay down by his pile of ducks.

To any one familiar with the work of these dogs, the accurate marking down of the birds will not appear remarkable. But that he should have made five trips and brought five birds—all that there were—and then should have stopped, does seem odd. Those who witnessed the performance believe that he counted the birds, and knew when he had brought them all, but perhaps it is not necessary to assume this.

What seems possible enough is that the dog, having marked down these birds, may have carried in his mind the different directions in which they went, and have remembered them all. For a man, this would be a difficult task, but it must be remembered that the dog had all his life been accustomed to doing just this thing, and the recalling of the several spots in which the birds fell may have been natural enough.

Again, it is conceivable that the dog may have gone

into the marsh to the leeward of the birds and on his first journey may have passed so far beyond the furthest duck that he was sure that there were no more. Then it would be simple for him to bring first the duck that was furthest away, then the next furthest, and so on to the last. It is a common practice for old and wise dogs to bring from the water the most distant birds first.

'Another incident of like character has recently been related to me by Mr. Morris, whom I quote so frequently in connection with this breed, and who, through many years' experience in gunning on Chesapeake Bay waters and of breeding these dogs, is probably the first authority on them in the world to-day. He said:

"I was shooting off a point of marsh over decoys, the wind blowing hard off shore, and my skiff covered with reeds and sedge made the blind. Under these circumstances it was my dog's habit to bring his ducks to the boat and make a pile, curling himself up alongside it.

"A flock of mallards came in, out of which I was lucky enough to kill two drakes—very large ones. My dog, Marengo, went first for the one which fell furthest off, and in coming back met the other drifting out. He tried his best to get both ducks in his mouth, but finding that impossible, he held the second duck under his jaw in some way, with the aid of the first, which was in his mouth. In this manner he succeeded in bringing both some distance, but the sea then washed the second duck from its position. He went through the same performance again, apparently getting the second duck under his jaw as before, and pushing it forward as he swam.

"When he had brought both ducks as far as the decoys, the second again washed out from under his jaw. Here he hesitated and looked toward the shore, and finding it not far off, he abandoned the second duck, took the one he had in his mouth to the bank, dropped it there, went back to the drifting duck, got it and brought it to the pile in the boat. He then jumped out of the boat, got the duck he had left in the edge of the marsh, took it to the pile in the boat, and before curling himself down gave me a most intelligent glance, which said as plainly as language could, 'Master, don't you think that was well thought out?'

"I fully agreed with him."

The whole matter of the intelligence shown by these dogs in their work in the water and the marsh is very interesting.

The gunner who for the first time witnesses the work of the Chesapeake Bay dog is likely to be astonished by sometimes seeing the animal plunge into the water, and, swimming to the place where a wounded bird has fallen, take up the scent and follow on the water the trail of the "sneaking" duck, which has passed along over the water swimming toward the marsh.

We usually assume that water washes away scent, and believe that deer and other animals take to the water to throw the dogs off their trail. This is undoubtedly true, and yet, as I say, it is a common thing to see a crippled bird fall in the water and swim away toward the marsh and to see a dog going after it, turn when he reaches the place where it fell, or the path where it passed, and follow the watery trail to the marsh, and then up on to the bank.

In some cases it is possible that the dog may smell blood which has flowed from the bird's wound and left its odor on the water, but I do not think that such an explanation will account for the dog's actions in a majority of cases.

I am inclined to believe that particles of grease detach themselves constantly from the well oiled plumage of the ducks and geese and float upon the water, and that it is the odor of these particles which the dog smells and follows.   It is often to be observed that to the leeward of a duck which has fallen in the water, or of a live decoy, there is an area of water smoother than the surrounding water—a sort of "slick"—which is probably caused by the oil which comes from the bird's plumage.   This hypothesis would seem to account for the power of the Chesapeake Bay dog to follow the trail of a swimming duck over reasonably quiet waters.

INDEX.

Africa, 88, 104.
Aix sponsa, 139-142.
Alabama, 336.
Alaska, 35, 40, 41, 49, 54, 63, 64, 71, 73, 109, 114, 124, 133, 135, 149, 161, 166, 168, 174, 179, 182, 186, 191, 196, 198, 206, 210, 212, 227, 231.
Albemarle Sound, 150, 172.
Aleutian Islands, 64, 116, 182, 198.
America, Arctic, 52, 83, 136, 186, 210, 212, 218, 402.
America, British, 114, 166, 168, 174, 182, 320, 577.
America, Central, 78, 111, 119, 124, 148, 165, 168, 542.
America, North, 22, 23, 26, 40, 41, 60, 72, 85, 91, 104, 107, 116, 119, 130, 132, 135, 146, 148, 161, 165, 166, 168, 171, 174, 182, 186, 193, 211, 218, 221, 224, 231, 235.
America, South, 78, 130, 221, 224, 542.
Anas, 19.
Anas americana, 110-115.
Anas boschas, 87-92.
Anas carolinensis, 118-121.
Anas crecca, 116, 117.
Anas discors, 122-125.
Anas fulvigula, 95, 96.
Anas fulvigula maculosa, 97, 98, 99.
Anas obscura, 93, 94.
Anas penelope, 107-109.
Anas strepera, 103-106.
Anatidæ, 19, 22, 225.
Anatinæ, 23, 85.
Anderson River, 218, 232.
Anser, 41, 53.
Anser albifrons, 53.
Anseres, 19.
Anserinæ, 39, 75.

Anticosti, 104.
Autonnierre, 124.
Apium, 158.
Archæopteryx, 19.
Arctic Ocean, 54, 60, 63, 71, 90, 119, 135, 206, 210, 353, 578.
Arkansas, 562, 581, 582.
Arkansas River, 260.
Asia, 88, 104, 117, 165, 182, 190, 196, 210.
Assemblyman, 215.
Atlantic Coast, 35, 40, 44, 47, 54, 60, 63, 67, 70, 71, 89, 90, 105, 106, 112, 148, 161, 190, 193, 201, 203, 212, 214, 221, 235, 264, 273, 282, 294, 296, 332, 402, 546, 568, 588.
Audubon, J. J., 25, 36, 44, 63, 125, 212, 228, 236, 237.
Aythya affinis, 167-169.
Aythya collaris, 170-172.
Aythya marila nearctica, 164-166.
Aythya vallisneria, 147-159.

Back Bay, 548.
Back River, 483.
Bald-crown, 115, 486.
Bald-face, 115.
Bald-head, 115.
Bald-pate, 110, 111, 219, 486.
Baltimore, 473, 474, 481, 483.
Barnston, G., 44.
Barren Lands, 54, 214.
Bass River, 298.
Batteries, 549-556, 605, 606.
Bellot's Straits, 70.
Bendire, Capt. C., 52, 149.
Benjies, 474, 477.
Bering Sea, 64, 71, 72, 73, 191, 206, 210, 215.

617

Bering Straits, 210.
Bermuda, 105, 218.
Bill, 19, 20.
Bird, G., 509.
Bittern, 360, 365, 400.
Blackbird, 348, 387, 399, 524.
Black-head, 138, 163, 165, 183, 236, 398, 438, 474, 480, 481, 486.
Black-head, Creek, 168.
Black-head, Little, 165, 167-169, 171.
Black-head, Ring-billed, 171.
Black-head, Ring-necked, 171.
Black-jack, 376.
Black Walnut Point, 487.
Blinds, 546-548.
Blossom-bill, 219.
Blossom-head, 219.
Blue-bill, 165, 355, 362, 363, 364, 365.
Blue-bill, Little, 168.
Blue-bill, Marsh, 168, 171.
Blue-bill, Mud, 168.
Blue-bill, River, 168.
Boardman, G. A., 101, 112, 175, 182, 227, 235.
Boats, 557-575.
Booby, 222.
Brandywine Creek, 158.
Brant, 39, 40, 45, 54, 64, 65, 67-71, 279-316, 360, 362, 365, 368, 373, 374, 376.
Brant, Bald, 45.
Brant, Black, 40, 67, 69.
Brant, Blue, 45.
Brant, Goose, 63.
Brant, Harlequin, 54.
Brant, Pied, 54.
Brant, Prairie, 54, 254.
Brant, Salt-water, 55.
Brant, Sea, 215.
Brant, White, 278, 402.
Brant Island, 599.
Branta, 40.
Branta bernicla, 67, 68.
Branta canadensis, 56-64.
Branta canadensis hutchinsii, 56, 58.
Branta canadensis minima, 56, 59.
Branta canadensis occidentalis, 56, 58, 59.
Branta leucopsis, 65, 66.
Branta nigricans, 67, 69.

Brass-eye, 177.
Breeding-grounds, 27-31.
Brewer, Dr. T. M., 28, 63, 90, 136.
Brewster, W., 176.
Bristle-tail, 222.
British Columbia, 64, 105, 592.
Broad-bill, 24, 163, 164-166, 167, 168, 330, 423, 425, 426, 438, 453, 510.
Broad-bill, Bastard, 171.
Broad-bill, Fresh-water, 168
Broad-bill, Hard-headed, 222.
Broad-bill, Little, 168.
Broad-bill, Mud, 168.
Broad-bill, Red-headed, 163.
Broad-bill, River, 168.
Broad-bill, Sleepy, 222.
Broady, 133.
Brown, A. E., 533.
Bull-head, 177.
Burlington, 442.
Bush River, 483.
Butter-ball, 81, 153, 182, 183, 184, 376, 510.
Butter-box, 184.
Butter-duck, 184.

Calais, Me., 101, 112, 162, 172, 175, 179, 182, 228.
California, 35, 41, 42, 47, 52, 54, 63, 64, 72, 78, 79, 89, 105, 109, 114, 127, 148, 161, 165, 172, 186, 190, 212, 215, 221, 278, 335, 340, 430, 464, 465, 493, 592.
Camptolaimus labradorius, 192-194.
Canada, 31, 90, 91, 98, 177, 570, 590.
Canard Français, 91.
Cape Cod, 295, 297, 300, 315.
Cape Malabar, 298.
Carroll's Island, 332, 474-479.
Cary, W. A., 315.
Cascade Mountains, 149.
Castle, W. W., 580.
Cavileer, N., 463.
Celery, Wild, 157, 158, 318, 486.
Champlain, Lake, 224, 441, 527.
Charitonetta albeola, 175, 181-184.
Chase Pass, 320, 321.
Chatham, 296, 299, 302.
Chen, 41, 53.

Chen cærulescens, 43-45.
Chen hyperborea, 46, 47.
Chen hyperborea nivalis, 48-50.
Chenalopex, 75.
Chesapeake Bay, 35, 98, 112, 149, 158, 162, 212, 218, 244, 274, 280, 436, 440, 472-489, 515, 519, 547, 589, 593, 596, 606, 607.
Chester River, 485, 487, 488.
Chile, 130.
China, 141, 231.
Choptank River, 485, 486, 487.
Clangula hyemalis, 185-188.
Cob-head, 177.
Cock-robin, 237.
Coit, O. B., 453.
Cold Spring Harbor, 538.
Colorado, 105, 120.
Columbia River, 127.
Commander Islands, 73, 182.
Connecticut, 99, 120, 136, 418, 481.
Cook's Inlet, 64.
Coot, 201, 212, 214, 215, 218, 219, 296, 330, 331, 421, 422, 423, 424, 425, 431, 453, 534.
Coot, Bell-tongue, 215.
Coot, Booby, 222.
Coot, Brant, 215.
Coot, Brown, 219.
Coot, Bull, 215.
Coot, Butter-boat-billed, 219.
Coot, Gray, 219.
Coot, Hollow-billed, 218.
Coot, Patch-polled, 219.
Coot, Pied-winged, 215.
Coot, Quill-tail, 222.
Coot, Sleepy, 222.
Coot, Spectacle, 219.
Coot, Spectacled-bill, 219.
Coot, Uncle Sam, 215.
Coot, White-winged, 214, 421.
Coppermine River, 206.
Core Sound, 150, 172.
Coues, Dr. E., 127.
Cow-frog, 133.
Crane, 347, 348.
Crane, Sandhill, 38, 362, 365, 377, 538.
Cuba, 49, 54, 119, 135, 174.
Cub-head, 177.

Cunningham, J., 566.
Curlew, Sickle-bill, 413.
Currituck Sound, 35, 40, 49, 54, 61, 65, 150, 151, 157, 172, 236, 244, 246, 378, 380, 383, 402, 403, 534, 548, 598, 599.
Cutbank Creek, 52.
Cygninæ, 22, 33-38.
Cygnus, 33.
Cygnus buccinator, 36-38.
Cygnus columbianus, 34, 35.
Cygnus cygnus, 35.

Dafila acuta, 82, 134-138.
Dakota, 133, 135, 148, 161, 168, 212, 253, 255.
Dakota, North, 165, 251, 318, 321, 327, 461, 588, 592, 596.
Dakota, South, 251.
Dall, Dr. W. H., 35, 73, 124, 149, 166, 210.
Dapper, 184.
Darlington, Dr., 158.
Dawson, 320.
Dead Buffalo Lake, 318.
Decoys, 61, 70, 89, 101, 162, 244, 252, 253, 254, 257, 260-263, 268-273, 279, 300, 301, 303, 304, 372, 373, 377, 384-387, 391, 435, 436, 434-436, 441, 443-447, 463, 469, 484, 485, 522-532, 549, 555.
Delaware, 49, 457.
Delaware Bay, 278.
Delaware River, 40, 203, 218, 457.
Dendrocygna, 23, 75.
Dendrocygna autumnalis, 76-78.
Dendrocygna fulva, 79, 80.
Denmark, 196.
Derbyshire, 191.
Die-dipper, 184.
Dipper, 183, 184, 330.
Dipper, Little, 177.
Dipper, Scotch, 184.
Distribution, 26.
Diver, 184, 360.
Diver, Dip-tail, 222.
Diver, Saw-bill, 237.
Dogs, 406-410, 431, 515-521, 611.

Domestication, 52, 59, 61, 62, 66, 70, 77, 100, 117, 142, 372, 532-545.
Dopper, 184.
Douglas, Mr., 567.
Dovekie, 402.
Drake, Sea, 201.
Drake, Welsh, 106.
Drake, Wild, 91.
Duck, Big Fowl, 165.
Duck, Black, 24, 25, 52, 91, 93, 94, 98, 99, 100, 101, 102, 132, 136, 232, 292, 296, 312, 330, 331, 355, 378, 387, 390, 392, 398, 403, 421, 423, 425, 443, 456, 488, 507, 510, 524, 527, 532, 533.
Duck, Black-bellied Tree, 76-78, 80.
Duck, Blaten, 106.
Duck, Brewer's, 25.
Duck, Brown Tree, 79.
Duck, Buffalo-headed, 184.
Duck, Buffle-head, 175, 181-184, 330, 531.
Duck, Butler, 133.
Duck, Call, 543.
Duck, Canvas-back, 24, 112, 137, 144, 147-159, 160, 161, 162, 169, 236, 319, 320, 332, 355, 376, 379, 382, 391, 392, 398, 438, 473, 474, 482, 486, 493, 495, 510, 544.
Duck, Channel, 215.
Duck, Conjuring, 177, 184.
Duck, Corn-field, 77.
Duck, Creek, 106.
Duck, Deaf, 222.
Duck, Domestic, 87, 88, 91.
Duck, Dusky, 93, 98, 101.
Duck, English, 91.
Duck, Fiddler, 77.
Duck, Florida, 96, 97, 102.
Duck, Florida Dusky, 95, 96, 101, 102.
Duck, Fool, 222.
Duck, French, 91.
Duck, Fulvous-bellied Tree, 79, 80.
Duck, German, 106.
Duck, Gray, 91, 106.
Duck, Harlequin, 81, 189-191, 418, 425.
Duck, Heavy-tailed, 222.

Duck, Isles of Shoals, 201.
Duck, Labrador, 192-194.
Duck, Little Brown, 184.
Duck, Long-legged, 77.
Duck, Long-tailed, 81, 185-188, 418, 422, 426.
Duck, Mandarin, 21, 141, 542, 544.
Duck, Masked, 223, 224.
Duck, Mottled, 97, 98, 99, 102.
Duck, Mountain, 191.
Duck, Muscovy, 25, 91.
Duck, Old-squaw, 82, 185-188, 215, 219, 330, 418, 422, 423, 424, 425, 426, 437, 453, 461, 481, 534.
Duck, Pacific Eider, 84.
Duck, Painted, 191.
Duck, Pied, 193.
Duck, Pied Gray, 138.
Duck, Raft, 165.
Duck, Red-headed Raft, 163.
Duck, Ring-necked, 170-172.
Duck, Rock, 191.
Duck, Ruddy, 153, 177, 220-222, 224, 532.
Duck, Rufous-crested, 145, 146.
Duck, Sand-shoal, 193.
Duck, Scaup, 83, 165.
Duck, Scotch, 184.
Duck, Sea, 201, 218; 305.
Duck, Shoal, 201.
Duck, Skunk, 193.
Duck, Sleepy, 222.
Duck, Smoking, 115.
Duck, Spirit, 177, 184.
Duck, Steller's, 195, 196.
Duck, Stock, 91.
Duck, Summer, 533.
Duck, Surf, 218.
Duck, Tufted, 171, 376, 438.
Duck, Washington Canvas-back, 163.
Duck, Wheat, 115.
Duck, Wild, 91.
Duck, Wood, 25, 139-142, 175, 176, 235, 356, 357, 363, 365, 366, 367, 535, 540-544.
Duck, Yellow-bellied Fiddler, 80.
Duckinmallard, 91.
Ducks, Diving, 143-224, 486.

Ducks, Fish, 23, 225-237.
Ducks, Fresh-water, 24, 25, 81, 85, 98, 112, 136, 137, 144, 169, 426, 431.
Ducks, Non-diving, 85-142.
Ducks, Sea, 23, 24, 81, 143, 144, 214, 225, 232, 418, 425.
Ducks, Shoal-water, 23, 143.
Ducks, Tree, 23, 75-80, 542.

Eagle, White-headed, 398.
Eastern Bay, 485, 486, 487.
Economic value, 26, 27, 31.
Eel-grass, 158, 296.
Eggs, Exportation of, 577-579.
Eggs, Importation of, 577.
Egret, Snowy, 360, 365.
Eider, 27, 28, 29, 30, 81, 84, 187, 305, 331, 418, 425.
Eider, American, 202-204.
Eider, Common, 200, 201, 202, 203.
Eider, King, 208-210, 425.
Eider, Pacific, 205-207.
Eider, Spectacled, 197-199.
Elliot, D. G., 64, 112, 144, 179, 183, 232, 237, 246.
Elliot, H. W., 73.
Enemies, 596, 597.
England, 66, 106, 577.
Enleonetta stelleri, 195, 196.
Erie, Lake, 179, 210.
Erismatura rubida, 220-222.
Eskimo, 44, 61, 74, 198, 250, 597.
Europe, 65, 66, 70, 88, 104, 109, 111, 165, 174, 179, 186, 190, 191, 201, 227, 231, 235, 544.

Falkland Islands, 130.
Fargo, 329.
Farmer, G. T., 563.
Fielden, Capt., 69.
Fisherman, 233.
Fisherman's Lake, 278.
Fishing Bay, 485.
Flight, 508-510.
Floating, 464.
Florida, 35, 101, 102, 109, 124, 127, 168, 186, 236.

Food of Ducks, 23, 24, 80, 85, 98, 99, 100, 112, 124, 125, 143, 148, 157, 165, 169, 176, 188, 204, 206, 210, 214, 225, 229, 353, 371, 418, 454, 462, 464, 486, 534, 539, 541, 593.
Food of Geese, 41, 48, 50, 55, 70, 251, 283, 297, 372.
Food of Swans, 245.
"Forest and Stream," 150-157, 175, 176, 228, 251, 255-259, 264-267, 268-273, 274-278, 295-315, 317-330, 336-340, 341-351, 355-365, 416, 449-453, 453-455, 465-472, 517-520, 528-532, 534-545, 558, 560, 577, 579, 580, 581, 585, 598, 602, 609.
Fort Brown, 78.
Fort Missoula, 52.
Fort Tejon, 78.
Fort Yukon, 149.
Franklin Bay, 71.
Fraser River, 37.
Fuca, Straits of, 71.
Fuligulinæ, 20, 23, 143.
Fulix affinis, 137.
Fundy, Bay of, 203, 210.

Gadwall, 25, 83, 103-106, 433.
Galveston, 598.
Gavia imber, 308.
Goose, 19, 21, 22, 39-74, 250-278, 331, 332, 360, 363, 365, 366, 367, 368, 369, 370, 376, 404, 405, 406, 421, 424, 425, 433, 437, 461, 462, 463, 464, 467, 487, 488, 495, 524, 527, 534, 538, 585, 586, 599.
Georgia, 509.
Georgia, Gulf of, 215.
Giraud, J. P., 106, 193.
Glaucionetta clangula americana, 173-177.
Glaucionetta islandica, 178-180.
Golden-eye, 173-177, 178, 180, 418.
Golden-eye, Barrow's, 175, 178-180, 231.
Golofin Sound, 71.
Goosander, 225, 227, 229, 231, 404.
Goose, Bald-headed, 45.
Goose, Barnacle, 40, 65, 66.
Goose, Blue, 40, 43-45, 49, 254, 374.

Goose, Brant, 67.

Goose, Cackling, 56, 59, 64.

Goose, Canada, 22, 40, 41, 56-64, 68, 254, 258, 296, 374, 377, 402, 469, 471, 472, 520, 533.

Goose, Chinese, 533.

Goose, Egyptian, 533.

Goose, Emperor, 72-74.

Goose, Eskimo, 63.

Goose, Great Gray, 40, 41, 353, 362, 402, 424, 472.

Goose, Greater Snow, 48-50, 51.

Goose, Hutchins's, 56, 57, 58, 59, 63, 254.

Goose, Laughing, 54, 374.

Goose, Lesser Snow, 46, 47.

Goose, Marsh, 63.

Goose, Mud, 63.

Goose, Prairie, 63.

Goose, Ross's, 40, 49, 50, 51, 52, 67.

Goose, Snow, 40, 52, 55, 254, 374, 377, 402.

Goose, Tundrina, 64.

Goose, Western, 56, 58, 59.

Goose, White, 469, 472.

Goose, White-cheeked, 56, 57, 58, 59, 64.

Goose, White-fronted, 41, 53-55, 254, 374, 377.

Goose, White-headed, 45, 74.

Gotdhaab, 70.

Grand Island, 442, 443.

Grand Lake Stream, 228.

Greaser, 222.

Great Britain, 66, 117, 196.

Great-head, 177.

Great Lakes, 143, 203, 210, 214, 218, 453.

Great Slave Lake, 124, 136, 149.

Great South Bay, 162, 166, 273, 280, 282, 283, 294, 434.

Grebe, 431.

Greece, 88.

Green River, 374.

Greenhead, 91.

Greenland, 22, 27, 35, 54, 65, 70, 135, 210, 216, 231, 402.

Grouse, 326.

Gulf States, 124.

Gull, Bonaparte's, 232.

Gunpowder River, 476, 477, 483.

Guns, 493-495.

Hairy-crown, 237, 403, 404.

Hairy-head, 237.

Hapgood, W., 295.

Hard-head, 222.

Hardtack, 222.

Havre de Grace, 158, 473, 481, 484, 544.

"Hen, Guinea," 74.

Hennepin Club, 566.

Heron, 352, 360, 365, 400, 401, 524.

Hickory-head, 222.

Hills Point, 487.

Histrionicus histrionicus, 189-191.

Hogg Bay, 486.

Holding, 502-506.

Holland, 543.

Holland Strait, 485.

Hooper Straits, 485.

Horse-head, 219.

Hough, E., 317, 341.

Hudson River, 351.

Hudson's Bay, 37, 44, 47, 49, 65, 90, 161, 186.

Hudson's Bay Co., 31.

Hybrids, 25, 91, 109, 402.

Ice work, 572-575.

Iceland, 27, 28, 179, 186, 190, 191, 201, 231.

Idaho, 135, 591.

Illinois, 89, 105, 109, 210, 335, 371, 374, 430, 560.

Illinois River, 210, 356, 565.

India, 88.

Indiana, 89, 236, 335, 374, 560, 567.

Indians, 37, 44, 49, 61, 129, 130, 161, 250, 354, 416, 597.

Iowa, 99, 120, 520.

Ireland, 66, 117.

Iron-head, 177.

James Bay, 44.

James River, 485.

Japan, 135, 231.

Jutland, 30.

Plaster-bill, 219.

Platte River, 254, 255, 256, 260, 585-589.

Plover, 360, 400.

Plumage, 20, 21, 81-84.

Poacher, 115.

Pochard, European, 163, 544.

Pocomoke Sound, 485.

Point Barrow, 83, 198.

Polk, B., 585.

Poplar Island, 485, 486.

Powder, Nitro, 495-499.

Pribilof Islands, 73.

Prince Edward's Island, 297.

Prince William Sound, 191.

Printannierre, 124.

Providence Club, 295, 316.

Purdy, C. R., 283, 285.

Pyramid Lake, 105.

Rail, Carolina, 399.

Redhead, 24, 25, 109, 112, 148, 160-163, 171, 319, 320, 332, 343, 355, 379, 433, 438, 456, 474, 480, 481, 486, 495, 510, 533, 544.

Redhead, Creek, 171.

Rhode Island, 418.

Ridgway, R., 4, 59, 83, 105, 161, 190, 218.

Rio Verde, 127.

Roanoke River, 274, 276.

Robin-dipper, 184.

Rock River, 374.

Rocky Mountains, 47, 49, 89, 111, 127, 161, 168, 174, 179, 190, 191, 431, 447, 584.

Ross, J., 63, 149.

Rupert House, 65.

Russia, 117, 196.

Sa-sar-ka, 74.

Sacramento, 161, 278.

Sacramento River, 464.

Sacramento Valley, 278.

Sailing, 460, 461.

St. Lawrence, Gulf of, 104, 581.

St. Lawrence Island, 196.

St. Lawrence River, 179.

St. Mary's Lake, 50.

St. Michael's Island, 71.

St. Paul, 321.

San Diego, 71.

San Francisco, 464, 465.

San Francisco Bay, 465.

San Joaquin River, 464.

Sandpiper, 413.

Sassafras River, 485.

Sawbill, 233, 404.

Sawbill, Big, 233.

Sawbill, Little, 237, 542.

Scaup, Ring-necked, 171.

Scotchman, 184.

Scoter, 187, 201, 330, 426, 461.

Scoter, American, 211, 212.

Scoter, American Velvet, 213-215.

Scoter, Black, 418.

Scoter, Surf, 212, 217-219.

Scoter, Velvet, 216.

Scoter, White-winged, 212, 418.

Semmes, J. E., 483.

Sennett, G. B., 97, 102.

Sharp-tail, 138.

Sheep Island Point, 153.

Sheldrake, 28, 30, 228, 230-233, 290, 314, 426, 453, 542.

Sheldrake, European, 30, 75.

Sheldrake, Pied, 233.

Sheldrake, Swamp, 237.

Shelduck, 233.

Shepard, C. W., 28, 179, 191, 231.

Shinnecock Bay, 273.

Shooting, Bar, 294-316, 330, 331.

Shooting, Battery, 433-440, 484, 485.

Shooting, Brant, 279-316.

Shooting, Brant, from a battery, 279-294.

Shooting, California Marsh, 463-472.

Shooting, Cornfield, 371-377.

Shooting, Duck, 317-489.

Shooting, Duck, in Chesapeake Bay, 472-489.

Shooting, Duck, in the overflow, 333-335.

Shooting, Duck, in the wild rice fields, 351-371.

Shooting from a house-boat, 440-447.

Shooting, Goose, 250-278.

Shooting, Goose, driving, 274-278.

Shooting, Goose, on the sand-bars, 254-260.

Shooting, Goose, on the stubbles, 251-253.
Shooting, Goose, with live decoys, 260-274.
Shooting, Ice Hole, 447-453.
Shooting in the Ice, 455-460.
Shooting, Night, 481-483, 607.
Shooting, Pass, 317-332.
Shooting, Point, 377-417, 426.
Shooting, Pond, 464.
Shooting, River, 335-351.
Shooting, Sea, 418-430.
Shooting, Spring, 589-592.
Shooting, Stubble, 461-463.
Shooting, Swan, 244-249.
Shooting, Winter Duck, 453-455.
Shot, 500-502.
Shot-pouch, 222.
Shovel-bill, 133.
Shoveller, 19, 91, 131-133, 433.
Shoveller, Blue-winged, 133.
Shoveller, Red-breasted, 133.
Shuffler, Ring-billed, 171.
Siberia, 66, 73, 206.
Sierra Nevada Mountains, 105, 190, 191.
Silver Lake, 268, 527.
Sitka, 179.
Skunk-head, 217-219, 418.
Sleepy Brother, 222.
Sleepy-head, 222.
Smew, 237.
Smith, J. G., 520.
Smithsonian Institution, 210.
Snipe, 137, 360, 365, 400.
Snuff-taker, 219.
Somateria dresseri, 202-204.
Somateria mollissima, 305, 313.
Somateria mollissima borealis, 200, 201.
Somateria spectabilis, 208-210.
Somateria v-nigra, 205-207.
South Carolina, 70, 112, 149, 162, 236, 274, 574.
Southern States, 89, 100, 112, 141, 335, 592.
Spain, 88.
Species, Number of, 26, 85.
Speckled Belly, 54, 106.

Speculum, 21.
Spesutia Island, 474, 483.
Spike-bill, 237.
Spike-tail, 138.
Spindle-tail, 138.
Spine-tail, 222.
Spitzbergen, 66, 70, 186.
Split-tail, 138.
Spoon-bill, 132, 324, 363.
Sprig-tail, 113, 138, 362, 363, 366, 389, 460, 488.
Squealer, 191.
Stanley, B., 564.
Steel-head, 222.
Stejneger, Dr. L., 27, 30, 182.
Stephenson Lake, 598.
Stewart's Island, 71.
Stick-tail, 222.
Stiff-tail, 222.
Stone, N. C., 54.
Stone, W., 82-84.
Stub and Twist, 222.
Suisun Bay, 464, 465.
Suisun Marsh, 464.
Surprise, Lake, 598.
Susquehanna Flats, 149, 589.
Susquehanna River, 483.
Swaddle-bill, 133.
Swan, Australian Black, 22.
Swan, Common, 22, 34, 35.
Swan, Mute, 533.
Swan, Trumpeter, 22, 34, 36-38.
Swan, Whooping, 35.
Swans, 21, 22, 33-38, 39, 244-249, 363, 413, 414-416, 461, 464, 467, 469, 472, 487, 488, 495, 519, 538.
Sweden, 196.
Sylt, Island of, 28, 30.

Tadorna, 30.
Tangier Sound, 485.
Tar Bay, 485, 487.
Tarsus, 39.
Teal, 25, 132, 325, 340, 355, 356, 363, 365, 368, 375, 376, 462, 488, 507; 535.
Teal, Blue-winged, 83, 120, 122-125, 358, 362, 363, 364, 538, 540.
Teal, Cinnamon, 83, 123, 126-130, 538.
Teal, European, 116, 117.

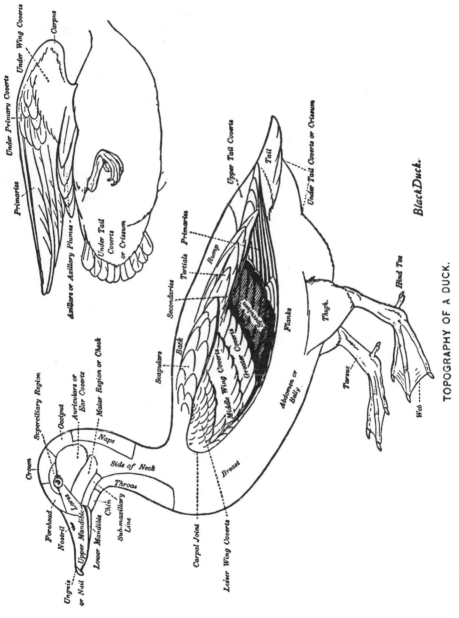

Primaries

Under Primary Coverts

Under Wing Coverts

Carpus

Axillars or Axillary Plumes

Under Tail Coverts or Crissum

Upper Tail Coverts

Tail

Under Tail Coverts or Crissum

BlackDuck.

Tertials

Primaries

Secondaries

Rump

Back

Scapulars

Middle Wing Coverts

Greater Coverts

Flanks

Thigh.

Abdomen or Belly

Tarsus

Hind Toe

Web

Superciliary Region

Occiput

Auriculars or Ear Coverts

Malar Region or Cheek

Crown

Nape

Side of Neck

Throat

Forehead

Nostril

Lores

Upper Mandible

Lower Mandible

Chin

Sub-maxillary Line

Ungais or Nail

Carpal Joint

Lesser Wing Coverts

Breast

TOPOGRAPHY OF A DUCK.

Teal, Green-winged, 107, 116, 117, 118-121, 123, 125, 133, 135, 363, 433, 535, 538, 539.
Teal, Red-breasted, 130, 433.
Teal, Scotch, 184.
Teal, Spoon-billed, 133.
Teal, Summer, 123.
Texas, 47, 49, 63, 77, 79, 80, 102, 133, 163, 224, 320, 598.
Toling, 480, 481.
Tolleston Club, 569.
Tough-head, 222.
Townsend, W., 441, 527.
Trotter, W., 480.
Truckee River, 105.
Trumbull, G., 63, 91, 104, 115, 133, 138, 168, 184, 191, 201, 215, 219, 222.
Two Medicine Lodge Creek, 52.

Unguirostres, 20.
United States, 22, 23, 30, 31, 35, 37, 56, 72, 75, 89, 101, 105, 111, 112, 120, 127, 135, 141, 148, 149, 161, 168, 171, 174, 250, 251, 533, 571, 590.
Utah, 99.

Vallisneria spiralis, 158, 464.
Van Dyke, T. S., 355.
Vermont, 591.
Virginia, 70, 109, 136, 149, 162, 165, 274, 280, 548, 574.

Wading the Marshes, 430-433.
Walker, Dr., 70.
Wamp, 201.
Washington, 35, 253.
Water-pheasant, 237.
Waterton, C., 83.
Wavy, Blue, 49.
Wavy, Large, 49.
Wavy, Small, 49.

Wescott, C. S., 457.
West Indies, 75, 168, 224.
Whistler, 153, 173-177, 178, 179, 232, 330, 376, 418, 423, 426, 453, 456, 534.
Whistler, Brass-eyed, 177.
Whistle-wing, 177.
White-belly, 115.
White-scop, 219.
White-wing, Great May, 215.
White-wing, May, 215.
Widgeon, American, 24, 25, 83, 105, 106, 108, 109, 110-115, 132, 137, 148, 355, 363, 365, 390, 462, 480, 481, 486, 507, 524, 544.
Widgeon California, 115.
Widgeon, English, 25, 403.
Widgeon, European, 107-109, 544.
Widgeon, Gray, 106, 138.
Widgeon, Green-headed, 115.
Widgeon, Sand, 106.
Widgeon, Sea, 138.
Widgeon, Southern, 115.
Widgeon, Spoon-billed, 133.
Winnipeg, 99.
Wisconsin, 90, 120, 161, 172, 182, 210, 224, 560, 563, 567, 568, 592.
Wool-head, 184.
Wren, Marsh, 352, 399.
Wyoming, 25, 37, 91, 120, 127, 133, 135, 143, 161, 212, 432.

Xantus, Mr. 78.

Yarrow, Dr. H. C., 99.
Yellow-legs, 360, 400.
Yellowstone Lake, 37, 143, 212.
Yellowstone Park, 22.
York Factory, 99.
Yukon River, 35, 49, 124, 136, 137, 179, 182.

Zostera marina, 296.

Teal, Green-winged, 107, 116, 117, 118-121, 123, 125, 133, 135, 363, 433, 535, 538, 539.
Teal, Red-breasted, 130, 433.
Teal, Scotch, 184.
Teal, Spoon-billed, 133.
Teal, Summer, 123.
Texas, 47, 49, 63, 77, 79, 80, 102, 133, 163, 224, 320, 598.
Toling, 480, 481.
Tolleston Club, 569.
Tough-head, 222.
Townsend, W., 441, 527.
Trotter, W., 480.
Truckee River, 105.
Trumbull, G., 63, 91, 104, 115, 133, 138, 168, 184, 191, 201, 215, 219, 222.
Two Medicine Lodge Creek, 52.

Unguirostres, 20.
United States, 22, 23, 30, 31, 35, 37, 56, 72, 75, 89, 101, 105, 111, 112, 120, 127, 135, 141, 148, 149, 161, 168, 171, 174, 250, 251, 533, 571, 590.
Utah, 99.

Vallisneria spiralis, 158, 464.
Van Dyke, T. S., 355.
Vermont, 591.
Virginia, 70, 109, 136, 149, 163, 165, 274, 280, 548, 574.

Wading the Marshes, 430-433.
Walker, Dr., 70.
Wamp, 201.
Washington, 35, 253.
Water-pheasant, 237.
Waterton, C., 83.
Wavy, Blue, 49.
Wavy, Large, 49.
Wavy, Small, 49.

Wescott, C. S., 457.
West Indies, 75, 168, 224.
Whistler, 153, 173-177, 178, 179, 232, 330, 376, 418, 423, 426, 453, 456, 534.
Whistler, Brass-eyed, 177.
Whistle-wing, 177.
White-belly, 115.
White-scop, 219.
White-wing, Great May, 215.
White-wing, May, 215.
Widgeon, American, 24, 25, 83, 105, 106, 108, 109, 110-115, 132, 137, 148, 355, 363, 365, 390, 462, 480, 481, 486, 507, 524, 544.
Widgeon California, 115.
Widgeon, English, 25, 403.
Widgeon, European, 107-109, 544.
Widgeon, Gray, 106, 138.
Widgeon, Green-headed, 115.
Widgeon, Sand, 106.
Widgeon, Sea, 138.
Widgeon, Southern, 115.
Widgeon, Spoon-billed, 133.
Winnipeg, 99.
Wisconsin, 90, 120, 161, 172, 182, 210, 224, 560, 563, 567, 568, 592.
Wool-head, 184.
Wren, Marsh, 352, 399.
Wyoming, 25, 37, 91, 120, 127, 133, 135, 143, 161, 212, 432.

Xantus, Mr. 78.

Yarrow, Dr. H. C., 99.
Yellow-legs, 360, 400.
Yellowstone Lake, 37, 143, 212.
Yellowstone Park, 22.
York Factory, 99.
Yukon River, 35, 49, 124, 136, 137, 179, 182.

Zostera marina, 296.

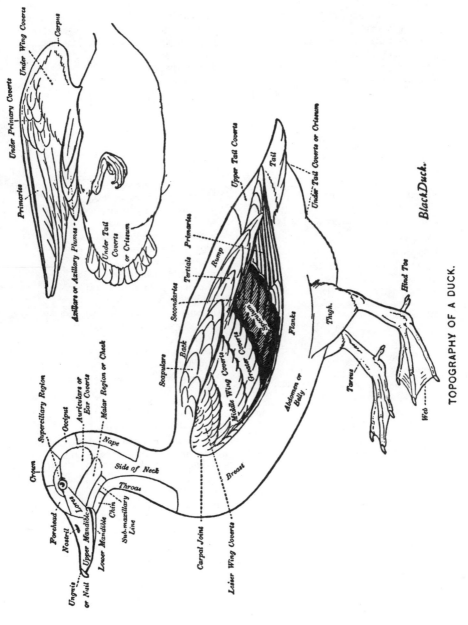

TOPOGRAPHY OF A DUCK.

BlackDuck.

BY PERMISSION OF MR. CHARLES B. CORY.

Kamschatka, 135.
Kansas, 102.
Kendrick Lake, 175.
Kennebunkport, 425.
Kennicott, R., 136.
Kent Island Narrows, 485.
Kent Point, 487.
Kentucky, 236.
Kipp, J., 52.
Koshkonong, Lake, 569.
Krider, J., 228.
Kuskokwim River, 198.

Labrador, 30, 44, 201, 203, 212, 214, 218, 581.
Labyrinth, 20.
Lady, 191.
Lamellæ, 19, 225.
Lamellirostral Swimmers, 19.
Lapland, 117.
Larus philadelphia, 232.
Lead-poisoning, 598-603.
Light-wood knot, 222.
Linden, C., 210.
Little Choptank River, 485.
Loading, 495-502.
Lockwood, W., 545.
Long Island, 27, 40, 47, 65, 105, 110, 132, 136, 149, 162, 273, 538, 593.
Long Island Sound, 160, 166, 188, 201, 209.
Long-neck, 138.
Loon, 308, 399, 421, 423, 437.
Lophodytes cucullatus, 234-237.
Lord, 191.
Lores, 39.
Lou's Point, 486.
Louisiana, 77, 79, 80, 102, 133, 237.
Loyd, A. T., 561.

Macfarlane, R., 49, 63, 71, 218, 231.
McIlhenny, E. A., 83.
Mackenzie River, 37, 54, 135.
Maine, 44, 101, 136, 174, 190, 219, 231, 235, 418, 425.
Mallard, 25, 52, 67, 81, 83, 87-92, 98, 100, 114, 124, 131, 132, 135, 136, 137, 138, 153, 259, 333, 336, 337, 338, 340, 342, 343, 345, 355, 356, 357, 358, 362,

363, 364, 365, 366, 367, 368, 369, 373, 376, 388, 390, 403, 433, 448, 460, 462, 463, 488, 495, 507, 510, 533, 535, 537, 540, 582.
Mallard, Gray, 91.
Manchester Club, 295, 316.
Manitoba, 99, 251, 354, 461.
Many, F. D., 526.
Marcus Hook, 457, 458.
Marionette, 184.
Market, Gunning for the, 31, 32, 221, 222, 457, 582, 592, 594, 595.
Maryland, 109, 133, 260, 473, 574.
Massachusetts, 70, 99, 136, 174, 179, 221, 224, 260, 267, 280, 296, 418, 527, 528.
Maxwell's Point, 474.
Mediterranean Sea, 186.
Merganser, 19, 23, 81, 175, 177, 225-237, 542.
Merganser, American, 226-229.
Merganser, Hooded, 153, 175, 176, 225, 234-237, 403, 542.
Merganser, Red-breasted, 84, 230-233, 404.
Merganser americanus, 226-229.
Merganser serrator, 230-233.
Merginæ, 23, 225-237.
Mergus, 30.
Mergus albellus, 237.
Merrill, Dr. J. C., 52, 78, 416.
Merry-wing, 177.
Mesquin, 133.
Mexico, 78, 79, 88, 105, 111, 124, 162, 182, 224, 320, 562.
Mexico, Gulf of, 44, 60, 119, 135.
Michigan, 90, 161, 540, 560, 592.
Michigan, Lake, 179, 210, 540, 570.
Migration, 25, 26.
Miles River, 485, 486.
Milford, Conn., 99.
Milk River, 52.
Minneapolis, 321.
Minnesota, 41, 90, 99, 105, 148, 161, 168, 172, 335, 354, 591.
Mississippi River, 37, 44, 45, 46, 54, 56, 67, 105, 114, 124, 127, 212, 333, 568, 580, 584, 590.
Missouri, 581, 582.

Missouri River, 22, 61, 351, 584.
Molt, 37, 59, 60, 74, 81-84, 109, 206.
Montagu, G., 82.
Montana, 47, 50, 52, 120, 133, 135, 148, 161, 166, 168, 191.
Monomoy, 296, 298, 312.
Monomoy Branting Club, 295, 301-316.
Morris, J. G., 487, 488.
Mud-hen, 360.
Mud-shoveller, 133.
Muscle-bill, 219.
Myers, E. J., 264.

Nantucket, 299.
Nanset, 312.
Narrows Island, 599, 602.
Narrows Island Club, 61.
National Game, Fish and Bird Protective Association, 576, 577.
Naumann, J. F., 30.
Nebraska, 37, 99, 235, 251, 253, 255, 585, 587.
Nelson, E. W., 137, 198, 210.
Netta rufina, 145, 146.
Nevada, 79, 105, 161.
New Brunswick, 98.
New England, 26, 27, 40, 60, 70, 89, 98, 99, 100, 105, 112, 119, 124, 132, 136, 149, 162, 165, 167, 168, 172, 177, 186, 187, 188, 201, 209, 212, 214, 215, 218, 219, 232, 236, 260, 295, 331, 332, 472, 557, 590.
New Hampshire, 101, 591.
New Jersey, 165, 193, 210, 457.
New Orleans, 237.
New York, 89, 101, 109, 116, 146, 165, 193, 224, 330, 402, 433, 509, 538, 540, 590.
Newberry, Dr., 149.
Newfoundland, 592.
Noddy, 222.
Nomonyx dominicus, 223, 224.
North Carolina, 25, 49, 65, 70, 98, 101, 109, 112, 133, 136, 149, 162, 165, 274, 378, 379, 381, 402, 493, 524, 574, 592, 598.
North Park, 120.
Norton Sound, 37, 64, 71, 74, 212.

Nova Scotia, 65, 98, 592.
Nova Zembla, 186.
Norway, 27, 28, 201.

Ogdensburgh, 179.
Ohio, 236, 335.
Oidemia, 422.
Oidemia americana, 211, 212.
Oidemia deglandi, 213-215.
Oidemia fusca, 216.
Oidemia perspicillata, 217-219.
Oie bleu, 45.
Olor, 33.
Ontario, 592.
Ontario, Lake, 453.
Oregon, 35, 52, 149.
Over-shooting, 582-589.

Pacific Coast, 35, 44, 47, 52, 60, 63, 64, 67, 71, 72, 105, 161, 182, 206, 212, 214, 215, 235, 578.
Paddy, 222.
Pamlico Sound, 150.
Parson's Island, 487.
Patagonia, 130.
Patch-head, 219.
Pelican, 538.
Pennsville, N. J., 459, 460.
Pennsylvania, 109.
Pewaukee Lake, 182.
Phantom Pond, 465, 472.
Pheasant, 136.
Pheasant, Sea, 138.
Pheasant, Water, 138.
Philacte, 41.
Philacte canagica, 72.
Philadelphia, Academy of Natural Sciences of, 81.
Philadelphia Zoölogical Garden, 533.
Phillips, J. O., 528.
Picket-tail, 138.
Picot, L. J., 274.
Pictured-bill, 219.
Pierson, Messrs., 191.
Pigeon, Passenger, 509.
Pintail, 25, 82, 83, 91, 106, 113, 134-138, 222, 331, 403, 433, 456, 462, 463, 495, 509, 510, 545.
Pishaug, 219.